Explaining Imagination

Peter Langland-Hassan is Professor of Philosophy at the University of Cincinnati. He was a postdoctoral researcher in the Philosophy-Neuroscience-Psychology program at Washington University in St. Louis, and holds a PhD in philosophy from the CUNY Graduate Center, and a BA in philosophy from Columbia University. His published work spans the philosophy of mind, the philosophy of cognitive science, and empirical psychology. He was a co-editor and contributor to *Inner Speech: New Voices* (OUP, 2018).

Explaining Imagination

PETER LANGLAND-HASSAN

OXFORD
UNIVERSITY PRESS

Great Clarendon Street, Oxford, OX2 6DP,
United Kingdom

Oxford University Press is a department of the University of Oxford.
It furthers the University's objective of excellence in research, scholarship, and education by publishing worldwide. Oxford is a registered trade mark of Oxford University Press in the UK and in certain other countries

First published 2020
First published in paperback 2023

Published in the United States of America by Oxford University Press
198 Madison Avenue, New York, NY 10016, United States of America

British Library Cataloguing in Publication Data
Data available

Library of Congress Cataloging in Publication Data
Data available

ISBN 978–0–19–881506–8 (Hbk.)
ISBN 978–0–19–890438–0 (Pbk.)

To Antoinette

Contents

Acknowledgments

When you work on something for a decade or so, the debts start to mount. Recognizing my own limitations in imagining the past, I'll confine these acknowledgments to the last five years, when the book mainly took shape.

Jonathan Weinberg was kind enough to read early drafts of several chapters, written in 2015 when I was a Taft Center Fellow. His comments during a subsequent visit led to some important reorganization of material—and to a recognition that I would need to fully confront the issues surrounding fiction consumption. Around that time, I met with Amy Kind and Shannon Spaulding at the Southern Society for Philosophy and Psychology to pitch my general program; their reactions helped me to see where I would need to focus energies. Among other helpful recommendations, they suggested a certain egg-shaped diagram (see Figure 3.1, pg. 62) for mapping the relationship of attitude imagining to imagistic imagining. A plan was hatched.

I'm especially grateful to Amy Kind who, soon after—and with the help of Eric Peterson—started the *Junkyard of the Mind* blog, devoted to the scholarly study of imagination. In a series of posts, I was able to audition a few arguments that are now more fully developed in Chapters 9, 10, and 11. I'm indebted to the many who commented on those posts and, in the process, helped me to clarify and sharpen my arguments—including (but not limited to) Shannon Spaulding, Neil Van Leeuwen, Shen-yi Liao, Alon Chasid, Luke Roelofs, Gregory Currie, and Eric Peterson.

Christopher Gauker was an enormous help to me on several fronts, helping to guide me through the literature on conditionals and providing detailed comments on several chapters, including, especially, those on mental imagery and conditionals. Neil Van Leeuwen and Shen-yi Liao also each commented on at least half of the manuscript and raised important challenges that helped me to solidify and clarify the kind of explanatory paradigm I wanted to pursue. Bence Nanay helped me to see some holes in my discussion of mental imagery, and inspired me to reorganize that material in important ways. Others who generously gave me written reactions to (sometimes multiple) chapters include: Kathleen Stock, Margot Strohminger, Tom Polger, Alon Chasid, Maxwell Gatyas, and my entire graduate seminar class from Fall 2018, who read through an early draft of the complete manuscript. I also had helpful conversations about the book's material with Heidi Maibom, Margot Strohminger, Richard Samuels, Declan Smithies, Jenefer Robinson, Dorit Bar-On, and Tony Chemero. Finally, I'm grateful to two anonymous reviewers for Oxford University Press for their comments and criticisms—especially to the aptly-named "Reader Y," who provided both penetrating and amusing blow-by-blow reactions to the arguments across all twelve chapters.

I feel lucky to have Peter Momtchiloff as an editor at Oxford and don't wish to imagine an OUP without him. I also thank the University of Cincinnati for awarding me a TOME grant that has allowed for the open access publication of this book in digital format, and the Taft Research Center at the University of Cincinnati, for supporting the early development of the book during my tenure as a Taft Center Fellow in 2014–2015. *Philosophical Studies*, *Philosophy and Phenomenological Research*, and *The Pacific Philosophical Quarterly* have my gratitude as well, for allowing me permission to reprint here portions of articles previously published in those venues. While none of the chapters in this book reproduce those previous works wholesale, there are paragraphs here and there that appear with only minor modifications.

Finally, and most importantly, I thank my wife, Antoinette, who has supported me from dream to dream and year to year, keeping me company in exotic, undreamt locales—including the Midwestern United States—so that I could do work that I love. I thank also my parents (all four of them) for affording me the priviledge of a life examined, and reexamined. And, lastly, to my sons, Avery and Jude: I couldn't imagine you if I tried.

PLH

Cincinnati, OH
May 2020

Preface

If you can't make one, you don't know how it works.

So said Fred Dretske in "A recipe for thought," and so I'm inclined to believe. He offered the slogan both as "something like an engineer's ideal, a designer's vision, of what it takes to understand how something works," and as an axiom at the heart of philosophical naturalism—one that applies as much to the mind as to anything else (Dretske, 2002).

Knowing how to make something, in Dretske's sense, entails knowing how to write a recipe for it. Such a recipe can't include, as an ingredient, the very thing it is a recipe for. "One cannot have a recipe for a cake that lists a cake, not even a small cake, as an ingredient," Dretske explains. "Recipes of this sort will not help one understand what a cake is." Likewise for intelligence: "if you want to know what intelligence is, you need a recipe for creating it out of parts you already understand" (Dretske, 2002).

The same points apply to imagination. We won't understand what imagination is—won't be able to *explain* imagination—until we can write a recipe for making it out of parts we already understand. What you have in your hands (or, perhaps, hard drive) is a compendium of such recipes.

What ingredients appear in the recipes? On my telling, they are other familiar mental states like beliefs, desires, judgments, decisions, and intentions. In different combinations and contexts, they constitute cases of imagining.

Granted, it might seem that we don't understand these ingredients themselves all that well. It's certainly true, in one sense, that we don't know how to write full recipes for *any* mental faculty, state, or process. There are no artificial minds widely agreed to be the equivalents of our own—no recipes for creating such. On the other hand, we aren't entirely clueless in that endeavor. There are longstanding research programs in philosophy and cognitive science for modeling human memory, perception, reasoning, and language in artificial systems. In tasks of limited scope, many of these systems have abilities far exceeding our own. We say that IBM's Watson knows the answers to Jeopardy questions, that Google Photos recognizes faces, that DeepMind's AlphaGo plans and executes creative strategies for winning at Go and chess. The question of whether we use the mental idiom literally in such cases grows more delicate each year.

We can at least call the products of these research programs *proto*-recipes for things like belief, memory, perception, inference, and the like. Their development is made possible by the fact that we know, at least roughly, what we need to make a system *do* so that it might qualify as doing something *like* remembering, something *like* perceiving, something *like* reasoning, or something *like* understanding a question. Imagination presents a contrast. It's far less clear, at least on the face of it, what we need to make a system *do* so that it might qualify as imagining. That's why we can make progress on explaining imagination by breaking it into parts like beliefs, desires, judgments, and decisions, whose functions are better understood, and for which we already have proto-recipes.

Contemporary philosophers have implicitly granted as much in their theoretical accounts of imagination—accounts in which imagination is alternately described as "belief-like" (Currie & Ravenscroft, 2002; Nichols, 2004a; Weinberg & Meskin, 2006b) or "perception-like" (Currie & Ravenscroft, 2002; Goldman, 2006a). There's no point in emphasizing the likenesses of one thing to another, after all, if our understanding of each is equally opaque. The problem is that imagination nevertheless remains an unreduced phenomenon in each of these accounts—a mental state *similar to*, yet *entirely distinct from*, states like belief, perception, desire, and so on. The cake recipes still list cake as an ingredient.

Some may worry that the reductive approach I will recommend is dismissive, deflationary, or even *eliminative* of imagination proper. But that is a misunderstanding. My aim is to explain imagination, not to question its importance, or to make it disappear. Think how a master baker—the author of award-winning cookbooks—would feel if you told her she had written cakes out of existence! The real message is this: there can be no understanding of the human mind without an understanding of imagination. And, because we already have the beginnings of an idea of how to make something with beliefs, desires, perceptions, memories, and so on, then—if the recipes offered herein succeed—we already have an inkling of how to make something with an imagination as well. This seems like good news to me.

I'll conclude this preface with a brief user's guide. Admittedly, this isn't a short book; but neither does it ask that each chapter be read in sequence. All *approved* itineraries begin with Chapter 1, which serves as a précis for the book as a whole. It sets out the terms of the debate, responds to the most obvious objections, and provides thumbnail examples of reductive explanations developed more fully in subsequent chapters. Thereafter, chapters can be consumed *à la carte*. This isn't to say that they are unrelated; to the contrary, they build on each other and pursue the same goal in much the same way. The point is that you should feel free to dive in where you like—to let your interests guide you—after having read Chapter 1.

Chapter 2 is a meditation on the nature of the ingredients used in later chapters: just what *are* beliefs, desires, intentions, and other folk psychological states? Are they mental representations? Dispositions? Neurobiological states? I discuss the ambient options and explain how the position one adopts influences the project of explaining imagination. Chapters 3 and 4 turn to mental imagery, investigating its nature and relationship to imagination generally. I develop a framework in which mental-image-involving states can be seen as beliefs, desires, judgments, decisions, and the like. Thereafter, the book focuses on four key contexts where imagination is commonly held to play an explanatory role: *conditional reasoning* (Chapters 5 and 6), *pretense* (Chapters 7 and 8), *fiction consumption* (Chapters 9, 10, and 11), and *creativity* (Chapter 12). Reductive "recipes" are sought for the imaginings at work in each context.

Like any philosopher, my deepest, most irrational desire is that each claim in this book—no matter how heterodox—will be believed by all. But I'll be satisfied if the general *strategy* defended here gains traction—the strategy of breaking imagination into smaller, more recognizable parts. I dream of a world where the question is not whether a reductive approach to imagination is possible, but which reductive approach is *best*. In this fantasy, the kinds of non-reductive theories criticized here still have a seat at the table. Sure, I think they're untenable in their current iterations. But they may have a redemption story of their own.

It seems to me that the conversation is just beginning.

1
Explaining Imagination

1.1 Introduction

Suppose you awoke one day having lost your imagination.

Some things would be easier. There would be no wavering on what clothes to wear. You wouldn't be able to imagine the different possibilities. The creativity of your work might suffer, however. And you would do well to avoid films and novels with absurd or devastating plot lines. Unable to imagine the events described, you'd have no choice but to corral them, somehow, into your view of the real.

Games of pretense would come to an end, confounding your partners in charades. How can you pretend that you're a bodybuilder, if you can't imagine being one? Worse, your empathy would diminish, as you could no longer imagine what it's like to be someone else—no longer stand in anyone's shoes but your own.

Yet few could rival your honesty. When you can't imagine things being different than they are, you won't conceive of a lie, much less tell one. This would affect your personal relationships in interesting ways. Even so, you'd have an enviable peace of mind. What's there to worry about, when you can't imagine the future?

This is all to say that I don't really imagine it would be *you* who woke up, having lost your imagination. Imagination is too central to who and what we are to remain ourselves without it. There are animals—crickets, crocodiles, crayfish—that, arguably, cannot imagine. But that's not us. If we lost our imagination, we wouldn't be around to miss it.

The centrality of imagination to who and what we are hints at this book's main thesis: when we imagine, we don't make use of a distinct faculty of mind or collection of *sui generis* mental states, quarantined from our actual beliefs, desires, and intentions. "The imagination" is not something that, like sight, or knowledge of a second language, could be carved off the mind while leaving our self-defining commitments and inclinations intact. Instead, when we imagine, we make use of our most basic psychological states in complex bits of reasoning, planning, and contemplation. Indeed, imagining is nothing over and above the use of such states—beliefs, desires, and intentions central among them. To see how this can be so is to arrive at an explanation of imagination in simpler, more general terms.

Explaining Imagination. Peter Langland-Hassan, Oxford University Press (2020). © Peter Langland-Hassan.
DOI: 10.1093/oso/9780198815068.001.0001

1.2 What It Is to Imagine

Despite its importance to who and what we are, imagination remains an elusive explanatory target—"one of the last uncharted terrains of the mind" (Byrne, 2005, p. xi). Even in broad outlines, it just isn't clear *what* imagination is supposed to be. Describing our plight without it, I relied on an intuitive notion of imagination as means for thinking about the world being ways it is not—for considering fictions, possibilities, and fantasies. And I relied on the fact that, for each of the abilities I imagined us losing—be it for hypothetical reasoning, pretense, empathy, or the enjoyment of fictions—there are philosophers and psychologists who have held imagination to be its cognitive engine.[1]

However, characterizing imagination by appeal to the diverse capacities it enables invites the charge that we've lumped together a heterogeneous collection of quite distinct mental states and processes (Kind, 2013). Why think that what counts as imagining in the context of enjoying a fiction, or considering someone else's perspective, is the same mental phenomenon as imagining during a daydream, or during hypothetical reasoning? Indeed there are longstanding concerns that imagination is an ill-defined notion (Moran, 1994, p. 106; Strawson, 1970, p. 31). Stevenson (2003) counts no fewer than twelve distinct conceptions of imagination at work in philosophy. And P. F. Strawson finds the different uses of "imagine" to compose a "diverse and scattered family," where "even this image of a family seems too definite" (1970, p. 31).

A natural reaction is to draw distinctions. The current landscape is littered with them: propositional imagination is contrasted to sensory imagination (Stock, 2017), recreative imagining is distinguished from creative imagining (Currie & Ravenscroft, 2002), sympathetic imagining from perceptual imagining (Nagel, 1974), enactive imagining from suppositional imagining (Goldman, 2006a), constructive imagining from both attitudinal and imagistic imagining (Van Leeuwen, 2013), imagining "from the inside" from imagining "from the outside" (Peacocke, 1985; Shoemaker, 1968), imagining *proper* from supposing and conceiving (Balcerak Jackson, 2016; Chalmers, 2002), and so on. Yet, somehow, the

[1] With respect to imagination's role in pretense, see, e.g., Nichols & Stich (2000) and Carruthers (2006); for conditional reasoning, see, e.g., Williamson (2007, 2016) and Currie & Ravenscroft (2002); for the appreciation of fiction, see, e.g., Walton (1990), Currie (1990), and Stock (2017); for third-person mindreading, see, e.g., Goldman (2006a, 2006b) and Nichols & Stich (2003). For the claim that remembering is imagining, see Michaelian (2016a, 2016b). There is controversy surrounding some of these putative roles, of course. Matravers (2014), for instance, questions whether we need to appeal to imagination in explaining our responses to fiction; Debus (2014) and Robins (2020) reject the claim that episodic remembering is imagining; and, in earlier work (Langland-Hassan, 2012), I have argued that pretense can be explained without invoking imagination. These controversies will be discussed in due course.

fog surrounding imagination remains equally thick within each of its slices. As Amy Kind and Peter Kung comment in their introduction to a recent anthology:

> The problem is not simply that philosophers give different theoretical treatments of imagination but rather that there doesn't even seem to be consensus about what the phenomenon under discussion is. Among contemporary philosophers in particular there is a surprising reluctance to offer a substantive characterization of imagination; instead, it is understood simply as a mental activity that is *perception-like but not quite perception*, or *belief-like but not quite belief.*
>
> (Kind & Kung, 2016, p. 3, emphasis in original)

I take Kind and Kung's point to be that we are not in the usual situation where there is a clear phenomenon to be explained—e.g., temperature fluctuation, or animal reproduction—and a set of competing theories about its nature and causes. Rather, in the case of imagination, "there doesn't even seem to be consensus about what the phenomenon under discussion is," much less agreement concerning its deeper nature. In trying to characterize "the phenomenon" of imagination, comparisons are made between imagination and states like perception and belief; but it's emphasized that imagination remains quite distinct from those states. Attempts to specify the precise ways in which it is distinct—and to thereby distinguish what it is we aim to study—threaten to leave us knee-deep in theory, before we've clearly identified what the theory is supposed to be theory *of.*

Here is how I aim to move forward. I will follow a common practice in drawing a distinction between two primary senses of the word 'imagining.' Then I will give superficial characterizations of these two kinds of imagining—more superficial than is normally offered, in fact. Importantly, they will be characterizations that mesh with our practice of associating imagination with a range of distinct abilities—from pretending, to daydreaming, to counterfactual reasoning, to engaging with fictions, and being creative—while remaining neutral on questions concerning its deeper nature. In short, I aim to say clearly what the phenomenon of imagination *is*, such that it can be approached from a variety of different theoretical standpoints. A deeper account will then follow, the outlines of which are sketched by chapter's end. The first step, now, is to distinguish two ways in which a word or concept might be "heterogeneous."

1.3 Cats and Bats

There are many kinds of cat. The class of cats is heterogeneous, we might say, insofar as it contains sub-types. There are Siamese cats, Silver Tabby cats, Maine Coon cats, and more. However, the very notion or concept of a cat is not heterogeneous or equivocal. Nor is the *word* 'cat' ambiguous in its reference. It always refers to one and the same kind of thing—namely, cats (if we may overlook all the *jazz cats* out there).

The situation is different with bats. There are bats used to hit baseballs; and there are bats that hang upside down in caves. Is the class of bats therefore heterogeneous? Not exactly. It is more proper to say that we have two distinct concepts, each of which corresponds to the same string of English letters. Assuming that the meaning of a word is one of its essential properties, we also have two distinct *words* in play: there is 'bat' referring to the cave-dwelling creatures; and there is 'bat' referring to the ball-hitting implement. These distinct words have the uncommon feature of being both homonyms *and* homographs. There is a kind of heterogeneity here that is different than what we saw with 'cat.' It is a heterogeneity of concepts corresponding to one and the same string of English letters. Of course, with respect to each 'bat'-concept, there is the same kind of heterogeneity that we saw with the concept of a cat, relating to sub-types. There are both wooden and aluminum bats for hitting baseballs; and, among the cave-dwellers, there is the golden-capped fruit bat, the vampire bat, and many others besides.

'Imagine' is a lot like 'bat.' There is a heterogeneity of concepts corresponding to a single string of letters. Further, with respect to each concept, there *may be* a heterogeneous collection of states and processes that fall within its extension, as sub-types. I will briefly explain the heterogeneity of concepts now, as a means to clarifying this book's proper subject. Controversial elements of this picture will be flagged, with their proper defense occurring only later, in Chapters 3 and 4.

1.4 Imagistic Imagining and Attitude Imagining

Just as there are distinct concepts corresponding to 'bat,' there are at least two distinct concepts of philosophical interest corresponding to the term 'imagine.' I will refer to them as *imagistic imagining* and *attitude imagining*, respectively.[2] While I will define them in ways that make them my own terms of art, they align closely with other conceptions of imagination in the literature (e.g., Van Leeuwen, 2013; Kind, 2016b).[3]

[2] The one salient sense of 'imagine' I will not discuss is the one that means, roughly, "to believe falsely and without good reason," as in: "He imagines himself the Canadian Casanova." This sense corresponds to definition six for 'imagine' in the *Oxford English Dictionary*: "to form an idea or notion with regard to something not known with certainty; to believe, fancy 'take into one's head' (that). Often implying a vague notion not founded on exact observation or reasoning" (*Oxford English Dictionary*, 2009).

[3] A particularly close fit is Van Leeuwen's (2013, 2014) distinction between imagistic imagining—which closely tracks my notion of imagistic imagining—and both his and Kind's (2016b) "attitudinal imaginings," which correspond roughly to my attitude imaginings. However, my understanding of attitude imagining is importantly different from theirs, in ways I will discuss.

At a first pass, imagistic imagining (or "I-imagining") refers to the use of endogenously generated mental states that appear image-like, or to have sensory character, to the people having them. This meshes with the first sense of 'imagine' recognized by the *Oxford English Dictionary*: "to form a mental image of…to picture to oneself (something not present to the senses)" (*Oxford English Dictionary*, 2009). This sense of 'imagining' is at work in the platitude that imagining involves image or picture-like mental states. We describe ourselves as *visualizing*, or as *seeing an image in our mind's eye*, or, yes, as *imagining*, where the 'image' in 'imagine' is emphasized. Whether the mental states so described *really are* image-like is a matter of debate (Block, 1981; Kosslyn, 1994; Pearson & Kosslyn, 2015; Pylyshyn, 2002); but there is no controversy surrounding the claim that most people make occasional, or even frequent, use of mental states that seem to them to be image-like, or to have sensory character—where such states arise not from an external stimulus impinging on a sense organ but from endogenous causes of some kind.[4] Making use of such mental states is equivalent, in my terms, to using *mental imagery*. I-imagining, then, is simply the use of mental imagery in thought.[5] Conjure a mental image, no matter the reason or context, and you are imagining, in the I-imagining sense. So understood, I-imagining is not a distinctive type of mental process (at least, not obviously) but, rather, any sort of cognition or mental process at all that involves a mental image. To trigger a memory of this morning's breakfast is to engage in I-imagining, provided that the memory involves a mental image. (Whether episodic memories are imaginings in some *other* sense of 'imagine' is more controversial—see fn. 1). I will offer a few refinements to this characterization of I-imagining in Chapter 3. For now, this general definition will suit our needs.

The second sense of 'imagining'—attitude imagining (henceforth, "A-imagining")—has it that imagining is a kind of thought process that allows us to step outside of what we really believe to consider mere possibilities. It is in this sense of 'imagine' that the things we imagine are, well, *imaginary*. Here the emphasis is on the capacity of imaginings to enable rich, elaborated thought about the possible, fictive, pretended, and fantastical, without any attached stipulation that the thoughts are image or picture-like. Of course, delusions and hallucinations are also rich and elaborated ways of thinking about the possible, fictive, and unreal—as are sequences of false judgments generally. This highlights another important aspect of imagining in the attitude sense. A-imagining is a way of engaging in rich, elaborated cognition about the possible, fantastical, pretended, and so on, that is *epistemically compatible* with things not really being the way they are being thought about, and with one's not believing things to be that way. People who are imagining in the A-imagining sense are not epistemically at fault

[4] Reports of "aphantasia" are the exception (Zeman, Dewar, & Della Sala, 2016).

[5] More thorough characterizations of mental imagery and I-imagining are developed in Chapter 3.

or at risk—are not being unreasonable—when they engage in elaborated cognition about a situation that does not (and never did) obtain, or about an object they believe does not (and never did) exist.[6] A-imaginings allow us to *safely* step outside of what we really believe, without subjecting ourselves to epistemic scrutiny. The *Oxford English Dictionary* recognizes several senses of 'imagine' that mesh with this characterization. Its second entry for 'imagine' is: "to create as a mental conception, to conceive; to assume, suppose"; its third: "to conceive in the mind as a thing to be performed; to devise, plot, plan, compass"; its fourth: "to consider, ponder, meditate" (*Oxford English Dictionary*, 2009). Note that none of these definitions invoke mental images or the act of "picturing to oneself"; yet all of them allude to thought about imaginary things. On the face of it, we have two different notions.

To foreshadow: A-imagining aligns roughly with the idea, common in philosophy, that there is a propositional or cognitive *attitude* of imagining, or a *sui generis* psychological *mode* of imagining. This is why I have resorted to using the term 'attitude imagining' in naming these imaginings. I aim to be talking about the same basic phenomenon as these other theorists. However, in my usage, the notion of an "attitude" does not occur within the definition of A-imagining itself. This is important. Cognitive (and conative) attitudes are common theoretical constructs within philosophy. As we will see, in Chapter 2, what it is to bear an attitude toward a proposition is itself a matter of controversy. When we define imagination, in one of its primary senses, by appeal to an *attitude* of some kind—one with a certain force or "direction of fit" (Searle, 1983)—we have moved into explaining imagination before we have said what it is we aim to explain.[7] We should instead remain as neutral as we can in our initial characterization of imagining. The definition of A-imagining as "rich, elaborated, epistemically safe thought about the possible, fantastical, unreal, and so on," aims for that kind of neutrality. It is akin to characterizing believing as "taking to be true" or desiring some state of affairs as being impelled to its attainment. Such definitions are consistent with a wide range of more substantive views about the deeper nature of the states. Yet they have real value. Asked why we find it intuitive to say that such different activities as pretending, reading fiction, reasoning counterfactually, daydreaming, and writing a poem all involve *imagination*, we can respond that they all involve one's engaging in rich, elaborated, and epistemically safe thought about the possible, fantastical, unreal, and so on. Even in light of the diverse contexts in which imagining occurs, the class of A-imaginings retains a kind of unity.

[6] Cf. Currie & Ravenscroft: "Belief, however weakly characterized, is normative in that an agent who has contradictory beliefs... is in a less than ideal epistemic situation. It is no defect in any agent's epistemic condition that she imagines things contrary to what she believes" (2002, p. 17).

[7] This point is elaborated and substantiated in Chapter 3.

One might worry, however, that this maximally neutral definition of A-imagining is too broad—that it risks including acts like supposing and conceiving that, arguably, are not cases of *imagining* at all. For that matter, it may seem to include some ordinary acts of reasoning about possibilities that we might not want to describe as imagining. Yet this broadness is a feature of the definition and not a bug. The strategy is to begin with a maximally broad characterization and then, to ensure that imagination *proper* does not slip through our fingers, tether our investigation to imagination's instances in contexts where common sense tells us it typically occurs. Familiar platitudes tell us that people who are *pretending* are imagining, that when we *daydream* we are imagining, that when we *consider different possible plans of action*, we are imagining different situations, that when we *make up a story*, we do so by imagining, that when we *enjoy a fiction*, we are imagining the story it tells. And so on. These generalizations and platitudes are essential guides. Asked for uncontroversial cases of imagining in the "thinking of imaginary things" sense, this is where we should look. If we can then give an explanatory account of the kind of thought that occurs in each context, we can justly claim to have explained imagination, in the A-imagining sense. No harm is done if our net pulls in and forces us to explain other things as well.

1.5 The Relation of I-imagining to A-imagining

The conceptual distinction between I- and A-imagining brings with it no assumptions concerning whether, or to what degree, each notion picks out the same class of phenomena. This follows from our starting with a theoretically neutral definition of each. Some I-imaginings may also be A-imaginings, and vice versa. (Here we have a difference with bats, insofar as fruit and vampire bats are not, to my knowledge, used to hit baseballs.) For all I have said, it may be that *all* I-imaginings are also A-imaginings and that all A-imaginings are I-imaginings, just as all renates are cordates and all cordates renates, despite the distinction in the concepts relating to each. If, for instance, all uses of mental imagery are also cases of rich, elaborated, and epistemically safe thought about the possible, unreal, or fantastical, then we could say that A-imaginings include I-imaginings as a sub-set. The view I will defend, in Chapter 3, is that the concepts' extensions only partially overlap. Some, but not all, I-imaginings are also A-imaginings; and some, but not all, A-imaginings are also I-imaginings. For the time being, distinguishing A- from I-imagining allows me to clarify that my main project in this book is to explain A-imagining. But it would be wrong to conclude from this that I am not also explaining paradigmatic cases of I-imagining (or "sensory imagining," or "perceptual imagining") as well. Many I-imaginings are simply A-imaginings that involve mental imagery; so there can be no comprehensive explanation of

A-imagining that is not also, in part, an explanation of I-imagining. In particular, some have argued that there is a kind of imagining that both involves mental imagery *and* constitutes a *sui generis* mental image-involving *process*, *procedure*, or *attitude* (see, e.g., Arcangeli, 2019; Kind, 2001). This view is just as much a target for my reductive approach as is the more general claim that A-imagining involves use of *sui generis* imaginative states. These matters are sorted out in more detail in Chapter 3.

1.6 Explaining in What Sense?

There are many kinds of explanation. The sort of explanation I want to offer works by breaking a complex phenomenon into simpler, more general parts. The parts are more general in the sense that they are found both within and outside of the phenomenon they are called on to explain.

An example: the fact that H_2O composes water explains many things about water. Yet it would explain little if we had no understanding of hydrogen and oxygen *outside of* their roles in composing water. If, for instance, hydrogen and oxygen were found nowhere but in water, and if their relations to other molecules were obscure, then water's being composed of H_2O would explain little. Of course, hydrogen and oxygen have rich theoretical lives outside of their roles in constituting water. That is why they can appear in explanations of water and its properties.

This kind of explanation works by *unifying*. In a classic paper in the philosophy of science, Philp Kitcher (1981) argues that a theory's explanatory value lies in its ability to unify a diverse set of phenomena under a single set of principles or "argument patterns." It is explanatory *unification*, so achieved, that brings understanding. Scientific theories provide this kind of understanding-through-unification insofar as they uncover a certain core pattern or style of argument that can be "used in the derivation of descriptions of many, diverse, phenomena" (Kitcher, 1981, p. 514).

Newtonian mechanics and Darwinian evolutionary theory are two of Kitcher's examples. The theories provide understanding of a diverse set of facts by showing them to be instances of a single core pattern. Understanding is provided even when the theory offers few means for predicting which specific phenomenon (e.g., which specific species, in the case of Darwin's theory) we should see next. Indeed, part of Kitcher's project is to distinguish mere prediction from explanation, as there can be reliable predictive devices—e.g., barometers—that fail to explain what they predict. Explanatory argument-patterns typically apply a small set of primitive terms—such as 'force,' 'mass,' and 'acceleration,' in the case of Newtonian mechanics—to a broad set of phenomena. These unifying terms may themselves be primitive terms, in the sense that they are not unified under yet more general principles or argument patterns. Explanatory theories simply aim to "reduce, in so far as possible, the number of types of facts we must accept as brute" (1981, p. 530).

Without any suggestion that the theory developed here has the significance of Newton's or Darwin's, I want to ask how we might break imagination into smaller, more general parts. How can imagination be unified within a broader framework for understanding the nature of the mind? We don't have to endorse Kitcher's precise account of scientific explanation to see that, in answering such questions, we move toward a better understanding of imagination.

One way to provide an explanatory unification of imagination would be to show how imagining involves the use of particular neural states and processes—neural states and processes that we have some independent understanding of and that are also used in cognition outside of imagination. A theory that invoked such neurobiological states and processes might thereby unify imagination with other modes of thought. However, that is not the approach I will take here. While I think it holds promise, there is important prior work to be done. To break imagination into neural parts at this stage would be getting ahead of ourselves. It would be like trying to understand the world's biodiversity by appeal to the molecular structure of DNA, in advance of evolutionary theory. (My *argument* for this point occurs across the entire book to come.)

Another possibility would be to show how imagining can be broken into smaller *cognitive* components, where these components are understood as parts of a functionally specified cognitive architecture. Cognitive architectures—which seek to detail the actual information-processing algorithms, representational structures, and data stores exploited in human cognition—abstract away from the specifics of neural implementation to describe a computational processing architecture that could, in principle, be instantiated in non-neural cognitive systems. This "boxological" approach to explaining imagination has proven popular in recent years (Doggett & Egan, 2007; Nichols, 2006c; Nichols & Stich, 2000; Schellenberg, 2013; Weinberg & Meskin, 2006b). I'll have much to say about it in due course; yet it offers another path I will avoid. In my view, recent attempts to analyze imagination in boxological terms—as in many of the essays in Nichols (2006c)—only obscure its nature. My skepticism with respect to those approaches doesn't stem from any general misgivings about cognitive science or the practice of understanding cognition in computational or functional terms. As elaborated in Chapter 2, my concern is rather that, in the case of imagination, the move to the level of box-and-arrow diagrams brings with it questionable assumptions about the representational format of cognitive states, and needlessly forecloses dialogue with those who don't share those assumptions.[8]

[8] To endorse boxology in its canonical form (Fodor, 1987; Nichols & Stich, 2000; Quilty-Dunn & Mandelbaum, 2018) is not equivalent to being a functionalist about mental states; boxology requires, in addition, the existence of *mental representations* that are tokened "in" the various boxes that are posited. A (mere) functionalist about mental states need not be committed to mental representations at all. These matters are discussed in Chapter 2.

What options then remain for breaking imagination into smaller parts? My approach will be to break imagination into independently understood *folk psychological* states and processes. By "folk psychological states and processes" I mean the kinds of mental states and processes that ordinary adults know and talk about. Beliefs, desires, and intentions are examples of folk psychological *states*—as are hope, gratitude, and resentment. Folk psychological *processes* include mental events like thinking, judging, deciding, remembering, and—yes—imagining. Mental states, capacities, and processes known only to those with a background in empirical psychology or neuroscience—such as working memory, semantic memory, or feed-forward neural networks—are not folk psychological kinds, however real they may be. Because folk psychological states like belief, desire, and intention play a prominent role in our discourse about the mind outside of situations having anything to do with imagination, they are the right sort of pieces with which to explain imagination.

These pieces will not themselves receive an explanation or deep analysis here. The project is instead to reduce questions about A-imagining to questions about states like beliefs, desires, intentions, decisions, judgments, and the like—mental kinds that have a life outside of imagination. One folk psychological process, imagining, will be explained in terms of a collection of others. At the same time, I won't propose any adjustments to the most superficial, platitudinous accounts one might give of these other states and processes. To believe something is to take it to be true; to desire something is to be impelled to its attainment; to intend something is to have it in mind as something to be done; and so on. Views about the *deeper nature* of these states—concerning, e.g., their representational format and realization in the brain—are relevant to only some of the specific arguments in this book. Chapter 2 is an extended meditation on the nature of folk psychological states and the question of when and why their format and neural realizations are relevant to the project of explaining imagination.

1.7 What We Do When We Imagine

The idea that imagination can be reduced to other kinds of folk psychological states is roundly rejected by most philosophers and psychologists now working on imagination. In fact, "most" is, to my knowledge, an understatement. I do not know of anyone else who proposes the sort of reduction I pursue here. In her introduction to *The Routledge Handbook of Philosophy of Imagination*, Amy Kind presents the claim that "imagination is a primitive mental state type (or group of types), irreducible to other mental state types" as one of "four basic claims about imagination that enjoy near universal agreement" (2016, p. 2). According to this consensus, if we listed a person's current set of beliefs, desires, intentions, judgments, decisions, hopes, wishes, fears, and so on, and fully described their ongoing use of those states in practical and theoretical reasoning, we will have left open whether they are imagining. For the facts about what, if anything, a person is imagining are thought not to be entailed by any facts about these other kinds of folk psychological states one might be in.[9] This is the sense in which imagination is thought to involve an irreducible or "primitive" type of mental state—one's *sui generis imaginative states*, for lack of a better term. I will be in conversation with this view throughout the book.

My view is that A-imagining is a complex folk psychological process that can be broken down into, and explained in terms of, more basic folk psychological states and processes. I won't, however, be arguing that A-imagining is just the same thing as believing, or judging, or desiring. My argument is not that imagining that *p* is the same thing as believing that *p*—or even as *weakly* believing that *p*. It is rather that some uses of beliefs, desires, judgments, memories, and so on—*none* of which may have the precise content *p*—constitute cases of imagining that *p*. Further, whether they constitute cases of imagining that *p* will at times turn on matters extrinsic to the states themselves, such as the reason for which the judgments are made, or the social context in which they occur. By loose analogy, J. L. Austin (1975), in *How To Do Things With Words*, emphasized that some vocal utterances *constitute* acts of naming, dedicating, taking a vow, and so on, depending on the context of the utterance. Similarly, I'll argue, some uses of beliefs and desires, judgments, intentions, and decisions constitute instances of imagining, and whether they do depends in part upon the context in which they occur.[10]

To some, the kind of reductive explanation pursued here will seem to involve an "elimination" of imagination—a kind of denial that imagination *really* exists. But that misinterprets my view. Showing that a phenomenon—water, say—can be explained in more basic terms—molecular composition, say—doesn't write the phenomenon out of existence (not on my metaphysics, anyhow). People really do imagine things, and that ability brings with it the important capacities mentioned at this chapter's opening. My project is to explain *what we do when we imagine*, not to establish that there is no imagining.

Why has no one else pursued this sort of view? Mustn't it be crazy, by dint of its novelty alone? While the view is indeed novel, the approach is not as idiosyncratic as it might at first seem (and perforce not as crazy). The most common explanatory strategy in the philosophy of imagination over the last twenty years has been to characterize imagination in terms of its similarities to other folk psychological states—imagination being said to be *belief-like* (Arcangeli, 2018; Currie & Ravenscroft, 2002; Nichols, 2006a; Van Leeuwen, 2014), *desire-like*

[9] Most will allow that we can sometimes make reasonable *inferences* as to what, if anything, a person is imagining, from facts about the other mental states she is in. The point is that, on the orthodox view, facts about what a person is imagining are neither logically entailed nor metaphysically determined by facts about the other folk psychological states the person is in.

[10] Thanks to Amy Kind for suggesting the analogy to Austin.

(Currie, 2010; Doggett & Egan, 2007), or *perception-like* (Currie & Ravenscroft, 2002; Kind, 2001) in its instances. Implicit in these proposals is the thought that we can gain a better grasp on the nature of imagination by appreciating its similarities to other, less mysterious folk psychological states—and, indeed, that we have a good enough idea of what these other states are like to make it worth highlighting imagination's similarities to them. I share those guiding assumptions and thus am engaged in much the same explanatory project—albeit with more enthusiasm.

There are, nevertheless, clear reasons others have not followed me as far as I wish to go. Some of those reasons can only be explained and addressed over the course of several chapters. Yet many of what initially seem to be the most powerful objections to my approach are also the most easily defused. Doing so will be my project in the balance of this chapter, where my aim is to create some breathing-room for this book's larger thesis. I will, in the process, preview some of the central arguments to come in later chapters. This chapter is, in effect, an extended trailer for the book as a whole—some spoilers included.

1.8 Simple and Complex Attitudes

To see why a reduction of imagination to more basic folk psychological states seems so implausible to so many, it helps to contrast cases where such reductions are more obviously available. Thankfulness, regret, and suspicion are good examples. Each is a folk psychological state that can be invoked to explain or predict someone's behavior. Yet few are inclined to hold that thankfulness, regret, or suspicion are *sui generis* folk psychological states. It seems that we can explain each in more basic folk psychological terms. In that sense, we can say they are each *complex* attitudes, insofar as they can be understood as combinations, or particular types, of more *simple* attitudes (Schroeder, 2006). For example: I am thankful that my university gave me a full academic year free of teaching to work on this book. What does this thankfulness consist in? Here is a sketch: I believe that I have the full academic year free of teaching; I desire to have the year free of teaching; I believe that I could have, without injustice, not had the year free of teaching. I have feelings of relief when I recall that I have the year free of teaching. And so on. Perhaps I have not completely nailed thankfulness with this characterization. But it seems that we could get there if we really tried. Once we give a full specification of my current beliefs, desires, and intentions—and, perhaps, my dispositions to go into certain affective states—we will have captured what it is that qualifies me as being thankful to have the year free of teaching. The same goes for regret: to regret that *p*, I need to believe that *p*. I probably also need to desire that not-*p* and to believe that I could have done something to prevent it from being the case that *p*. Perhaps, too, I must experience some negative affect when I recall that *p*. If something along these lines is correct, regret is a complex psychological state with these more basic parts. Similarly for suspicion: if I believe that *p* with less than full certainty, or if I believe it is somewhat probable that *p*, it seems fair to say that I suspect that *p*. My suspecting that *p* is nothing over and above my having such beliefs. If that is right, we need not include suspicion among the *sui generis* folk psychological states.

In each of these reductions of complex to simple states, we find a characteristic asymmetry: it is possible to believe that *p* without being thankful that *p* and without regretting that *p*. But, arguably, it is not possible to be thankful that *p*, or to regret that *p*, without believing that *p*. And it is possible to believe that *p* without suspecting that *p* (as when I am certain that *p*). But it is not possible to suspect that *p* without believing that it is somewhat likely that *p*. This apparent asymmetry is essential to belief's being more basic than these other mental state kinds. It also alerts us to a possibility: perhaps being thankful (or regretting) that *p* is simply a matter of believing that *p* with a few accoutrements (including, perhaps, relevant desires). Likewise, perhaps suspecting that *p* is nothing other than believing it is somewhat likely that *p*. After all, why should believing that *p* (or that it is likely that *p*) be necessary to being in these other states, if these states were not going to decompose into simpler parts, one of which was belief itself?

Matters are different with imagination and its ilk (viz., conceiving, entertaining, supposing, assuming, considering). Not only is it possible to believe that *p* without imagining that *p*; it is *also* possible to imagine that *p* without believing that *p* (and without believing that it is somewhat likely that *p*). Or, at least, so says common sense—and so I will agree. Similarly, just as one can desire that *p* without imagining that *p*, one can also imagine that *p* without desiring that *p*. A simple reduction of imagination to the two most distinguished folk psychological states appears stopped in its tracks.

It is crucial to see, however, that such observations only stand in the way of the most simplistic, homogeneous reductions we might pursue. The fact that a person can imagine that *p* without believing that *p* only shows that not every case of imagining that *p* is a case of believing that *p*. But it is quite compatible with *some* cases of imagining that *p* consisting in one's believing that *p*. It is also compatible with *all* cases of imagining that *p* consisting in one's believing something other than *p*. The same goes for desire: not every case of imagining that *p* can be equated with one's desiring that *p*, sure. But this does not, by itself, show that none can. It is only if one assumes, at the outset, that every instance of a complex attitude must reduce to simple attitudes *in just the same way*, if it is to reduce at all, that the project of reducing imagination is defeated by platitudes such as that we can imagine that *p* without believing that *p*. Fortunately, there is no reason to limit our investigations with an assumption that any reduction of imagination must be homogeneous in this manner. After all, as we saw at the outset, a starting point for many theorists is to claim that the term 'imagining' picks out a diverse and "scattered" family of states. Even after we have distinguished two concepts of imagining—I-imagining and A-imagining—we may find that each concept picks out a heterogeneous disjunction of different, more basic kinds of folk psychological states.

Compare: within philosophy, many apply the phrase "entertaining the proposition that *p*" to any of a heterogeneous set of occurrent mental episodes during which the proposition *p* is "before the mind." On this usage, we entertain the proposition that *p* when we judge that *p*; and we also do so when merely wondering whether *p*, or when deciding that *p*. The fact that entertaining the proposition that *p* is not strictly the same thing as judging that *p* does not stand in the way of reducing entertaining that *p* (as a mental state type) to a heterogeneous class of other occurrent states.

"Fine," comes the response, "but, in the case of imagination, what on earth could this heterogeneous array of other folk psychological states *be*?" Well, I will come to that. That is what this book is about. But let's not underestimate the importance of the point just made. It is no barrier to *one* instance of imagining being identified with some more basic folk psychological state that the same *type* of state cannot be identified with *all* imaginings. Put otherwise, showing that imagination is a *sui generis* mental state kind requires more than establishing that there is some particular imagining that is not reducible to a specific combination of more basic folk psychological states. It requires showing that there is *no* collection of more basic folk psychological states with which the token imagining can be identified. And *that* is not so easily done.

I will aim to make this point more concrete, and more plausible, by applying it to specific cases below. For now, two summary conclusions to keep in mind:

1. *Don't assume content-mirroring*: In order for a token mental state of φ-ing that *p* to consist in one's being in some more basic token state, that more basic state need not also have the content *p*. For instance, we saw that suspecting that *p* is not precisely reducible to believing that *p*; but it is plausibly reducible to believing that *q*, where *q* is the proposition that *it is somewhat likely that p*.
2. *Don't assume homogeneity*: An instance of φ-ing that *p* may consist in one's being in some particular set of more basic mental states Δ, even if another instance of φ-ing that *p* does not consist in one's being in Δ. To assume otherwise is to presume a kind of homogeneity to the class φ-ing that may not exist. The case of entertaining the proposition that *p* was offered as an example of a class of mental states whose instances are heterogeneous. This possibility is especially salient when theorizing about a kind, such as imagination, which even on its face appears heterogeneous to many.

1.9 What Do I Mean by "More Basic"?

Before applying these points to specific examples, I'd like to make a last clarification. I have said that I'll reduce A-imagining to more basic folk psychological mental states and processes—and so provide an explanatory unification of imagination with those other states. Above, I briefly explained the sense in which belief is more basic than suspicion in terms of a certain asymmetry: for any situation where we might attribute a suspicion to a person, we could alternatively, and equally plausibly, attribute a certain belief; by contrast, there are many cases where we attribute a belief where we could not alternatively, and equally plausibly, attribute a suspicion. For instance, I believe that I am sitting at my computer, typing. I do not suspect—or even *strongly* suspect—that I am sitting at my computer, typing. Nor do I suspect that my name is 'Peter,' that I am a human being, or that I am thinking now; though I certainly believe those things. Thanks to this asymmetry—depicted in Fig. 1.1a—we can say that belief is more basic than suspicion.

Because, in my view, imagination reduces to a heterogeneous set of folk psychological states, the sense in which these states are more basic is not as straightforward as with suspicion and belief. It is not the case that, for any situation where we attribute to a person an imagining that *p*, we could alternatively, and equally plausibly, attribute a belief with a certain content. I will argue instead that, for any situation where we attribute an imagining to someone, we could alternatively, and equally plausibly, attribute either a belief, desire, or intention—or one of their occurrent counterparts (viz., a judgment, desire, or decision). Further, for each of belief, desire, and intention, there are many contexts where we attribute one of those states where we could not alternatively, and equally plausibly, attribute an imagining. A second diagram—Fig. 1.1b—helps to clarify the relationships I have in mind.

We can interpret each rectangle in Fig. 1.1b as containing the set of situations where we can plausibly—and, for explanatory purposes, profitably—attribute to someone a belief, desire, or intention (or one of their occurrent counterparts). Likewise for the circle, with respect to imaginings. If the diagram is correct, then belief, desire, and intention are collectively more basic than imagining. This is similar to the way in which belief, desire, and certain basic emotions are collectively more basic than regret or thankfulness, as earlier discussed. A difference, however, is that the reduction of thankfulness and regret to this more basic collection of states is relatively homogeneous: every case of being thankful that *p* is identifiable with the same kind of collection of beliefs, desires, and emotions (or so I suggested). In the case of imagination, there is not a single reductive recipe of this kind, even if, on a case-by-case basis, each imagining is identifiable with some collection of more basic states.

The most obvious way to object to this picture is to hold that there are cases of imagining that do not fully overlap with any combination of the other three

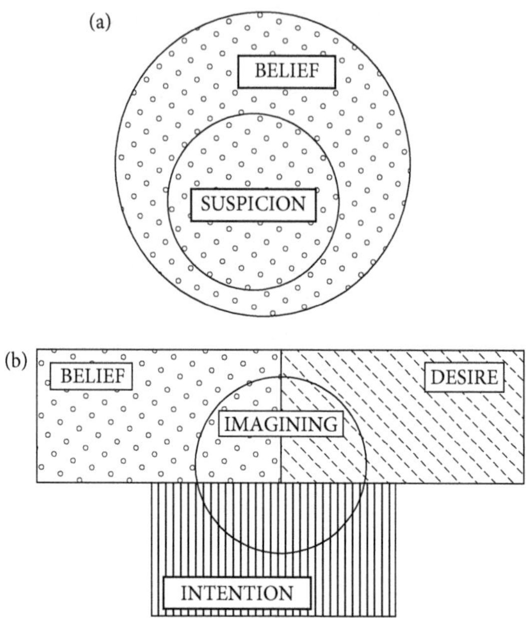

Fig. 1.1a The relationship of belief to suspicion
Fig. 1.1b The relationships among belief, desire, intention, and imagining. Note that the rectangles are intended to include both dispositional and occurrent versions of these states. Thus, the 'belief' rectangle includes judgments and the intention rectangle includes decisions.

boxes. Here I want to mention two subtler forms of objection, rooted in concerns about the notion of basicness at work in my accounts of reduction and explanation. First, some may grant that belief, desire, and intention are collectively more basic than imagining in the way I have suggested, yet deny that this shows imagining to be *reducible to*—or even explainable in terms of—those states. Second, some may object that the relations mapped in Fig. 1.1b are misleading, because the same kind of reduction I propose for imagination (in terms of three other, more basic states) is possible for one or more of the other states as well. For instance, they may propose that every context where we ascribe a desire is one where we could alternatively, and equally plausibly, ascribe a belief, intention, or imagining. If that were correct, then there would be no sense in which desire is *more* basic than imagining; the two would be on a par, with each notion or state being analyzable into three others. Because these more subtle worries cannot be adequately addressed without first distinguishing different views one might have on the ontology of folk psychological states generally, I table their discussion to Chapter 2 (sections 2.6 and 2.7).

1.10 The Delicious Mud Pie

I turn now to applying the above points to explicit arguments commonly given for viewing imagination as irreducible to other folk psychological states. These arguments appeal to broad generalizations in how imaginings differ from states like belief or desire. Echoing claims endorsed by many others (including Sinhababu (2016), Nichols (2006a), Stock (2017), and Picciuto & Carruthers (2016, pp. 316–17)), Shannon Spaulding (2015) catalogs a number of differences between imagination and belief, as a means to establishing that imagination is "not reducible to belief." While the point is tangential to her main argument in the paper, her list is a helpful compendium of common objections that need addressing by an account like mine. Noting that imagination bears important similarities to belief, Spaulding emphasizes that:

> Imagination is not *reducible* to belief. Imagination guides action differently than belief. Imagining that a mud pie is a delicious treat guides my action differently than believing it is. Imagination is subject to conscious, voluntary control, whereas belief is not. Imagination is less restrictive than belief insofar as one can imagine many false and absurd propositions that one in no way believes. Imagination-induced affect typically is less intense, less durable, and sometimes quite different than belief-induced affect. The upshot of these considerations is that imagination . . . is not reducible to belief. (Spaulding, 2015, pp. 459–60)

I will consider each point on Spaulding's list in turn. But, first, let's reflect on the structure of the argument and its aims. In order for observations of this sort to count as *evidence* for imagination's irreducibility, they cannot assume what is in question. If imagination just is a species of belief—or even if only some imaginings are beliefs—then imagination does *not* guide action differently than belief, is not related differently to the will, is not less restrictive than belief, and does not trigger affect differently (at least, not always). In short, it begs the question against the advocate for imagination's reducibility to offer such differences as *evidence* for its irreducibility. And yet, the platitudes Spaulding lists are hard to deny; indeed, I don't deny them, properly understood. So we need a way to take this putative evidence for imagination's irreducibility on board without assuming what is at issue.

Here is how: the generalizations Spaulding lists can be neutrally characterized as differences in believing that *p* and imagining that *p*, respectively. A person who imagines that *p* will behave differently than a person who believes that *p*; a person can imagine that *p* at will but cannot believe that *p* at will; a person can imagine that *p* while believing that not-*p*; the affect a person experiences in response to imagining that *p* is usually different than what she will experience in response to believing that *p*. These differences between the person who believes that *p* and the person who merely imagines that *p* can then be considered *evidence* for the claim that imagining is irreducible to belief *tout court*—without, in fact, assuming the point.

This is not particularly *good* evidence for imagination's irreducibility, however. It leaves open the possibility that many, even all, cases of imagining that *p* will reduce to beliefs of some kind or other—just not the belief that *p*. It also leaves open the possibility that all cases of imagining will be reducible to some collection or other of more basic folk psychological states, many of which are beliefs.

To see concrete possibilities of this sort, let's look at each putative difference in turn.

1.10.1 Imagination and Action

Spaulding observes that imagination "guides action differently than belief." A well-worn example, tracing to Walton (1990), is that "imagining that a mud pie is a delicious treat guides my action differently than believing it is" (Spaulding, 2015). Sinhababu also highlights this difference in action-tendencies when arguing that imagination is a distinct state of mind from belief, observing that "daydreaming about being Spider-Man typically doesn't result in actually trying to shoot webs, and imagining that one is Harry Potter while reading of his adventures doesn't usually result in trying to cast spells" (2016, p. 113). Nichols concurs that it is a "central fact about the propositional imagination" that "imagination and belief generate different action tendencies" (2006, pp. 6–7). I have noted that, for these observations to not beg the question with respect to imagination's reducibility, we need to view them as assertions about the different behavioral dispositions associated with imagining that *p* and believing that *p*, respectively. Granting those differences, the question now before us is whether the dispositions to action associated with imagining that *p* can nevertheless be ascribed through the use of *other*, more basic folk psychological terms—terms other than "believing that *p*."

Enter Uncle Joe, who *believes that* he is playing a pretense game with his nephew, where the point is to act like a mud pie is a chocolate pie. He *judges*, and thus comes to *believe*, that holding the pie to his face while saying "Mmm, tasty!" is a good way to act like the mud pie is a chocolate pie. This is, after all, how one might behave around a real chocolate pie. Given that he has these beliefs, and wants to continue playing this game, how is he disposed to act? It seems to me that he is disposed to act exactly like someone who is imagining that a mud pie is a delicious treat (and who has a desire to play the game). After all, he's not eating the mud pie; the disposition to do *that* only holds of people who *believe* the mud pie is delicious. He is stopping short of doing anything that would put him at digestive risk. He is only doing things you would do if you were, well, *imagining* that the pie is a delicious treat and wanted to play along with your nephew. This is a case where imagining that a mud pie is a chocolate pie generates the same action tendencies as an ordinary judgment—not the specific judgment that a mud pie is a chocolate pie, of course, but judgments about how to act like a mud pie is delicious. (I will take judgments to be occurrent mental processes through which one comes to have a certain dispositional belief.) So, in this case, the mere fact that imagining that *p* has different associated action-tendencies from believing that *p* gives no reason to think that imagining is generally irreducible to other, more basic mental states. For it turns out there is *another* collection of beliefs and desires that does give rise to the same dispositions to action as imagining that *p*.[11]

One response in favor of imagination's irreducibility might be that a *sui generis* imaginative state is what enables a person to generate the beliefs and judgments just mentioned. For instance, it might be thought that Uncle Joe needs to have a belief-distinct (imaginative) mental representation with the content "this is a chocolate pie," in order to see what the appropriate actions would be *if* the mud pie really were delicious. (This idea mirrors Nichols & Stich's (2003) and Currie & Ravenscroft's (2002) account of the role of imagination in pretense and hypothetical reasoning.) This is indeed a possibility for how we arrive at such judgments; it's one I reject in Chapters 5 and 6, on conditional reasoning. For the time being, note that the debate has now shifted to whether having and acquiring certain beliefs is best explained by one's having a particular sort of mental representation that is not itself a belief. Gone is the platitudinous, undeniable claim with which we began—that imagining that *p* guides action differently than believing or judging that *p*. It has been replaced with a more controversial proposal about the mental states necessary for arriving at certain other beliefs. If we accept that claim, it must be for reasons other than that we accept the platitude that imagination guides action differently than belief. The platitude on its own—rendered neutrally as the claim that imagining that *p* and believing that *p* have different associated behavioral dispositions—is little evidence for imagination's irreducibility.

Another objection may be to grant that *in this special case* the dispositions to action associated with imagining that *p* are the same as those associated with having certain beliefs, desires, or making certain judgements, while objecting that there are many other cases where no such translation will be available. Again, this might be so. But there is nothing special about the case just considered. The mud pie pretense is a standard example, handed down through the generations. More

[11] One might object that the present example is simply one where a pretense does not involve imagination and where we would normally ascribe an imagining. Granting the possibility, I am only, at this point, explaining a general strategy—one that is applied to a full variety of pretenses in Chapters 7 and 8.

importantly, the objection again shifts the argument for imagination's irreducibility from "imagination guides action differently than belief" to "there are at least some cases where the behavioral dispositions we ascribe by saying someone is imagining that *p* cannot equally well be ascribed through any other plausible collection of beliefs, desires, judgments, intentions, and so on." Once the objection is put this way, it hardly seems obvious. Its truth, or falsity, will be a delicate matter.

1.10.2 Imagination and the Will

The next reason Spaulding gives for thinking that imagination is irreducible to belief is that "imagination is subject to conscious, voluntary control, whereas belief is not." Sinhababu again agrees, noting that "it's easy to perform an intentional action of imagining something that isn't the case. It's hard or impossible to perform an intentional action of believing something that isn't the case" (2016, p. 113). Nichols is also on board: "belief is not at the whim of our intentions," he observes, "but imagination is" (2006, p. 7).

In order to view these claims as *evidence* for imagination's irreducibility, and not mere assertions of it, we should again see them as noting a difference in imagining that *p* and believing that *p*, respectively. There are cases where we say a person has freely imagined that *p* where we would not say he could have freely judged or come to believe that *p*. The truth of this platitude, however, does not offer much reason for thinking that imagination is irreducible to other folk psychological states.

After all, this special freedom of imagination is fully evident in the mud pie example. There's Uncle Joe again, holding the mud pie to his face: "Mmm," he says, "*delicious!*" He is imagining that the mud pie is a delicious treat. That is what we are inclined to say as we watch. This game involving the mud pie, and the imagining that supports it, are things he does voluntarily. No one put a gun to Uncle Joe's head. Of course, he didn't—and can't—choose to *believe* that the mud pie is a delicious treat. But that is irrelevant. For while we can't choose our beliefs, judgments, or parents, we *can* choose the topics on which we'd like to reason. And that's exactly what Uncle Joe has done. In choosing to imagine that the mud pie is a chocolate pie, he has chosen to reason on the topic of how to act like a mud pie is a chocolate pie; and he has judged that holding it to his face while saying "Mmmmm... *delicious*" is a good way to do so. He could have *instead* chosen to reason about how to act like the pie is a Frisbee, or how to act like a catfish. He was free to do so. Had he so chosen and put the reasoning to use in related games of pretense—arriving at judgments about how to make the pie Frisbee-like, or how to make himself catfish-like—we would have declared him to be imagining that the pie is a Frisbee, or that he is a catfish. Such freedom, genuine as it is, offers no reason to think that imagination is irreducible to collections of beliefs, desires, and judgments.

Again one may object that, in order to make the judgments in question (about, e.g., how to act like the mud pie is a delicious treat), Uncle Joe must (voluntarily) token a *sui generis* imaginative mental representation with the content "The mud pie is a delicious treat," or "The mud pie is a Frisbee," or "I am a catfish." And, again: *maybe* that is required. But here is another possibility: to voluntarily pretend that some *X* (e.g. a mud pie, or Uncle Joe) is a *Y* (e.g. a delicious treat, or a catfish), you simply need some beliefs about what *Y*s are generally like and a desire to make *X* saliently *Y*-like (Langland-Hassan, 2014b). Uncle Joe knows some things about catfish: they've got whiskers, they're feisty, they make barking sounds when out of water. During a pretense, he can draw on this knowledge to make himself catfish-like in various respects, without ever thinking something he disbelieves (such as: I, Uncle Joe, am a catfish). This is a possibility that must be foreclosed if the voluntary nature of imagination is to offer reason for thinking that imagining is irreducible to other folk psychological states.

Again we may hear the objection that the mud pie example is a special case and that there are very many freely chosen imaginings that will not fit this explanatory mould. Two points in response: first, in line with the possible heterogeneity of A-imagining, my claim is not that the freedom of *all* imaginings is to be explained as a freedom to engage in reasoning on a topic of one's choice; other cases, such as idle daydreams, may be explained in other ways. (More on this in a moment.) Second, with this objection the argument has again changed shape. It is no longer: "imagination is subject to conscious, voluntary control, whereas belief is not," but rather: "there are at least some cases in which we ascribe a freely chosen imagining where we could not have alternatively, and equally plausibly, ascribed any other collection of more basic folk psychological states." That is an interesting claim, but not an obvious one. We'll just have to see whether it's true, by examining—in Chapters 5 through 12—a wide variety of paradigmatic contexts where A-imagining occurs.

1.10.3 Imagining What We Disbelieve

Similar points apply to Spaulding's observation that "imagination is less restrictive than belief insofar as one can imagine many false and absurd propositions that one in no way believes." Schroeder & Matheson give cognitive-scientific dress to this platitude: "Imagining that *p* is most obviously distinguished from believing that *p*, in that imagining that *p* does not lead one to automatically store in one's memory that *p*" (2006, p. 25). (Sinhababu (2016, p. 112) and Nichols (2006a, p. 6) echo this claim, noting that we can imagine that *p* while not believing that *p*.)

However, on the account I have suggested, it remains correct to describe Uncle Joe as having imagined a false and absurd proposition—that *the mud pie is a delicious treat*—that he doesn't believe. Yet, in line with points already made, we could have alternatively ascribed the particular judgments and desires mentioned above. Thus, when asked *what it is* for him to imagine the (disbelieved) proposition that the mud pie is delicious, we can say that it amounts to his having made those judgments and having had those desires—just as we can say that someone's regretting that *p* consists in his having certain beliefs, desires, and emotional dispositions. The truth of the platitude that we can imagine what we don't believe remains compatible with an imagining's being reducible to other kinds of mental states—beliefs included.

1.10.4 Imagination and Emotion

The last consideration Spaulding gives for thinking that imagination is irreducible to belief is that "imagination-induced affect typically is less intense, less durable, and sometimes quite different than belief-induced affect." Nichols finds it "common wisdom in psychology that imagining scenarios can have significant affective consequences." While he is more impressed with the *similarity* of the emotions felt in response to imagining that *p* and believing that *p* than their differences (2006a, p. 8), Nichols agrees that emotional responses to an imagining are often quite different than they are when we believe the same content (2006b). A comparable connection between imagination and affect—where imagination has some, *but not all*, of the same relationships to affect as belief—is proposed by many others (see, e.g., Schroeder & Matheson, 2006; Meskin & Weinberg, 2003).

We can again grant the superficial, platitudinous phenomenon: when we say that someone has imagined that *p*, we don't expect them to experience the depth of emotions they would if they were to have judged that *p*. But neither are we surprised if they feel some semblance of those emotions. Admittedly, it is not obvious what emotions, if any, Uncle Joe experiences in imagining that the mud pie is a delicious treat. But consider a different example: imagining that your family is inside a burning house. Imagining this may cause unpleasant affect. This affect would be much different, however, were you to judge that your family is inside a burning house. Yet this is no reason to think that imagination is irreducible to more basic folk psychological states. Imagining that your family is inside a burning house could very well have the *same* emotional impact as some *other* related judgment—such as the judgment that your family *could* someday be caught inside a burning house and that, if they were, terrifying events would unfold. Although it is only a judgment about what *could* happen, dwelling on the possibility may be enough to raise a lump in your throat. Once again, so long as there is *some* judgment, desire, intention, or decision with the same associated dispositions to generate affect as the imagining, we can make a case for identifying the imagining with those more basic states. The mere platitude that imagining that *p* has different associated emotional dispositions than believing that *p* does little, by itself, to establish imagination's general irreducibility.

So much for the most common reasons given for thinking that imagination is irreducible to more basic folk psychological states. I want now to consider a slightly different form of objection—one grounded in introspection.

1.11 Introspection and Mental Imagery

It might seem obvious that we know, just through introspection, that the states we enter into when imagining are not occurrent judgments, desires, or intentions of the kind I have so far proposed. Just as a matter of first-person phenomenology, it might seem clear that (1) we know *when* we are imagining and that (2) we can tell that our states of imagining are not some other kind of state—judgments, beliefs, desires, intentions, or whatever. For instance, you may find that you are now imagining a ninja eating popcorn and that this episode is no belief, desire, or intention. What do I say to this?

My response is that the argument is question-begging. If you are indeed aware of an imagining that is not any other kind of state, then, sure, that imagining is not any other kind of state. The question is why we should think a person is well placed to introspectively discern that an occurrent mental episode is an imagining and nothing else. I see no reason to think people are authorities on this. After all, if it were obvious to introspection that we can discern what is an imagining and what is not, there would be no need to consider the arguments made by Spaulding, Sinhababu, Nichols, and others in favor of imagination's irreducibility. We could simply recede into the comfort of our own minds, notice that our imaginings are one thing, our beliefs, desires, and intentions another, and move on with our lives. Some readers may have done just that. But if you have taken the trouble to follow the argument this far, you probably agree that we have no such ability; arguments of a different kind will be needed to determine which mental states are basic, and which are not.

It may help to observe that in many ordinary cases of folk psychological explanation, we don't expect the attributions to tell us much about the person's conscious life. When Andrew breaks away from the televised soccer game to grab a beer from the fridge, we explain it by saying he desired a beer and believed that there is beer in the fridge (such is the classic example). But we don't thereby assume that he said to himself "there is beer in the fridge" or "a beer would be great right now," or that he consciously reflected on the question "where should

I go, if I want a beer?" before doing so. We don't expect the belief/desire attributions to have obvious phenomenological implications. The same goes for the attributions beliefs and desires relevant to explaining Uncle Joe's pretense behavior, which, on reflection, we may identify with his token A-imagining.

One place where introspection *does* seem to get a grip, however, is with respect to mental imagery—especially as I have defined it. For we certainly can tell, introspectively, whether we are currently making use of mental states that *seem to us* to be image-like in nature. A separate, empirical question—the subject of historical debate (Block, 1981; Pearson & Kosslyn, 2015; Pylyshyn, 2002; Tye, 1991)—is whether the representational format of these putative images is indeed picture-like in some important respect. Let's assume, for the moment, that the empirical question is settled: the mental imagery we are aware of through introspection does indeed occur in a pictorial, iconic, or analogue format. A common, but by no means universal, view in philosophy is that "propositional" folk psychological states like beliefs, desires, intentions, and so on, do *not* occur in an imagistic, picture-like format (see, e.g., Fodor (1975)). If that view were correct, and if it were indeed the case that mental imagery occurs in a picture-like format, then we could tell, just through introspection, that one of our current mental states was not what I have termed a "basic folk psychological state" (viz, a belief, desire, or intention) just by noticing that it involved a mental image. And, of course, in many of the paradigmatic situations where A-imagining occurs we do find ourselves making use of mental imagery. This would entail that at least some A-imaginings (i.e., those involving mental imagery) are not reducible to more basic folk psychological states.

My response is to deny the thesis that mental images never form proper parts of "propositional" folk psychological states like beliefs, desires, intentions, and so on. (Nor am I alone in rejecting this thesis (see, e.g., Kaplan, 1968; Kind, 2001; Martin, 2002; Van Leeuwen, 2013).) The mental images we introspectively discern may instead be proper parts of more basic (propositional) folk psychological states, such as judgments, desires, and decisions (Langland-Hassan, 2015). This can be true whether or not such images actually occur in an imagistic format—a point I will explain and defend in Chapters 3 and 4. For now, the shape of my response to the objection from introspective-awareness-of-imagery should be clear: given that many basic folk psychological states—including beliefs, desires, judgments, and decisions—have mental images as proper parts, introspective awareness of a mental image cannot serve as evidence that we are in some state that is irreducible to those folk psychological states.

1.12 More Case Studies as Prelude

I will conclude this bird's-eye view of the book to come with a few more case studies in reducing A-imagining to more basic folk psychological states. The aim of these examples is not to convince one of the overall account but to advertise the shape of things to come.

1.12.1 Daydreaming: Imagining that I Am Rich and Famous

Kendall Walton offers the following as a "paradigm instance of an exercise of the imagination":

> Fred finds himself, in an idle moment, alone with his thoughts. Feeling unsuccessful and unappreciated, he embarks on a daydream in which he is rich and famous. He calls up images of applauding constituents, visiting dignitaries, a huge mansion, doting women, fancy cars. But alas, reality eventually reasserts itself and Fred gets back to selling shoes. (Walton, 1990, p. 13)

The orthodox view of imagination has it that Fred makes use of a *sui generis* imaginative state in the course of this daydream. In the face of cases like these, we have to ask if there are no other, more basic kinds of folk psychological states at work in disguise. Clearly, Fred wants to take leave of his position at the shoe store. He wants to be applauded by constituents, visited by dignitaries, housed in a mansion, pursued by women, driving Lamborghinis. Fred has many unfulfilled desires flooding his mind as customers wait for him to deliver their loafers in the correct size. We *could* describe it as his imagining these things—these objects of desire. But it would be more perspicuous call it what it is: the conscious uprising of Fred's outlandish desires. Some of these desires may have mental images—of cars, of women, of adoring fans—as proper parts. But they are desires all the same.

Granted, even if some of what get called "daydreams" are simply occurrent desires, not all of them are. In some cases, we simply tell ourselves a story; in others, we confront our fears. These and other examples of daydreams are addressed in Chapter 4, on imagistic imagining, and Chapter 12, on the role of imagination in creativity.

1.12.2 Pretense—a Sketch of Chapters 7 and 8

Bananas not only dominate sales of produce. They are also ubiquitous in discussions of pretense (Friedman & Leslie, 2007; Leslie, 1987; Nichols & Stich, 2000; Richert & Lillard, 2004). A weathered example is someone holding a banana to his ear and speaking into one end, pretending that it is a telephone. When we look under the hood, what, psychologically, does this little caper require? Inspecting the banana, a man—Carl, let's say—judges it to be shaped like the receiver of an (old-fashioned) telephone. He wants to have some fun, to play a little game. So he decides to treat the banana in telephone-like ways, holding one end to his ear, talking into the other. Carl is able to do this—to temporarily make the banana telephone-like in various respects—because he knows some things about telephones. Of course, he does not *believe* that the banana is a telephone. That's why we describe him as only pretending. We might also say that he is "imagining that the banana is a telephone." But it might offer a clearer view of his mind to simply say that he believes that the banana resembles a telephone receiver, wants to play a little game, and, in order to do so, has decided to make the banana telephone-like in various respects, while believing it is not, in fact, a telephone.

True enough, this is not a template for explaining *all* pretenses. Some pretenses require us to reason hypothetically about what would be the case in some possible situation or other. Pretending that an airplane engine has landed in my backyard, for example, might require me to form some judgments about what would happen *if* an airplane engine landed in my backyard. Those if-then conditional judgments could then guide my pretense. This raises a question: does evaluating and making judgments about conditionals require *sui generis* imaginative states?

1.12.3 Conditional Reasoning—a Sketch of Chapters 5 and 6

We have many beliefs of the form: if *p* then *q*.[12] How do we arrive at these beliefs, in cases where we don't already believe that *p*? A popular proposal is that we *imagine* that *p* and, with *p* fixed in imagination, observe what else emerges as likely *in imagination* (Nichols & Stich, 2000; Currie & Ravenscroft, 2002; Williamson, 2016). If *q* is one of those things, we will then come to believe that *if p then q*. Imagining that *p* enables us to infer the likely consequences of *p* being the case, it is said, just because imagination is "belief-like" in its inferential properties (Nichols & Stich, 2000; Currie & Ravenscroft, 2002).

Here is a different approach. I judge that, if my coffee cup turns over, then the coffee will spill out. How did I arrive at this belief? I don't believe that my coffee cup is now turned over, or that the coffee has spilled out, after all. However, I have lots of relevant background beliefs about liquids and spills. In particular, I believe that, *ceteris paribus*, when a container holding a liquid is knocked over, the liquid spills out. Asked what would happen if my cup turns over, I access that belief and infer straightaway: If my coffee cup turns over, then the coffee will spill out. This is not a deductive inference, of course. Such is the case with most of our conditional judgments. They are based on past experience and our knowledge of how

[12] In this chapter, I don't distinguish between subjunctive and indicative conditionals, though that distinction is important and prominent in the full discussion of conditional reasoning in Chapters 5 and 6.

things normally go. We can make use of that knowledge to infer conditionals, without ever representing to ourselves something we disbelieve.

In some cases, it may seem there are no relevant past experiences, no relevant "way things normally go," to be used in arriving at the new conditional belief. This may seem to be the case with the airplane engine landing in my backyard. One question is whether these appearances are correct. Are there really no generalizations or past experiences on the basis of which I can infer what would happen if an airplane engine landed in my backyard? Another question is whether *sui generis* imaginings would offer any help to the inference if there are not (Langland-Hassan, 2012). The surrounding issues—concerning the truth-conditions of both indicative and subjunctive conditionals, their relation to the material conditional of formal logic, and the psychological processes by which we arrive at our beliefs in each kind of conditional—are complex. I explore them across Chapters 5 and 6, arguing that we gain no traction on the psychology conditional reasoning by invoking *sui generis* imaginings. We can better explain the key inferences at work by appeal to beliefs alone.

1.12.4 Consuming Fiction: The Barest Sketch

Imagination is often cited in philosophical discussions of fiction (Currie, 1990; Friend, 2008; Matravers, 2014; Meskin & Weinberg, 2003; Nichols, 2004a; Stock, 2017; Walton, 1990; Weinberg & Meskin, 2006b). Cindy, let us suppose, is watching the Steven Spielberg classic, *E.T.* E.T. levitates Elliot's dirt bike on their way to meet the mothership that will return E.T. to his home planet. They are silhouetted by the moon. As Cindy watches, we can say she is imagining that E.T. is going home. She doesn't really *believe* that E.T. is going home, after all. Alternatively, if we are pursuing an explanatory reduction, we could say that she is judging that, in the film *E.T.*, E.T. is going home. This is something she believes. This judgment leads her into a certain emotional state—a state of wistfulness. For she wanted it to be true, in *E.T.*, that E.T. goes home; but she *also* wanted it to be true, *in E.T.*, that E.T. and Elliot remain close friends on Earth. Her wistfulness makes sense, given her beliefs and conflicting desires. We get a clear picture of her overall cognitive situation if we identify her episode of imagining with these states.

But why does Cindy care about what is happening in a mere fiction? Why should beliefs about what is happening *in a fiction* generate any affect at all? These questions lie behind the well-known "paradox of fiction" in aesthetics (Friend, 2016; Lamarque, 1981b; Radford, 1975). I won't venture a summary reply here; Chapter 11 is devoted to the topic and develops a novel response. Other puzzles relating to fiction-consumption and imagining—including how we extract implicit truths from a fiction and how we are to define fictional truth itself—are addressed across Chapters 9, 10, and 11, with Chapter 10 generating a special challenge for any view at all that tries to find work for *sui generis* imaginings in fiction consumption.

1.13 Summary

In my experience, differences in the general platitudes surrounding imagination and belief—that we can imagine that *p* without believing that *p*, and so on—are what underlie the seeming *obviousness* of the view that imagination is irreducible to belief (or indeed to any more basic set of folk psychological states). It makes sense that this would be so. If it is indeed obvious that imagination is irreducible to other kinds of folk psychological states, its obviousness should lie on the surface. It is that superficial obviousness that I have tried to chip away at here. I hope that imagination's reducibility to other folk psychological states now seems an open, even delicate question.

In the chapters to come, my strategy for explaining imagination will be to identify contexts and abilities commonly agreed to involve imagination (in the A-imagination sense) and to show how the mental states and processes at work in those contexts can be understood as more basic folk psychological states. These abilities include conditional reasoning (Chapters 5 and 6), pretending (Chapters 7 and 8), engaging with fictions (Chapters 9, 10, and 11), and creativity (Chapter 12). In each case, my aim is to tell a *how plausibly* story where the cognition we associate with imagination is composed of other, more basic folk psychological states. At the same time, I aim to cast independent doubts on explanations of these abilities that have appealed to *sui generis* imaginative states.

By the end of Chapter 12, there is no general reductive definition of imagination offered—no identification of all A-imaginings with certain specific kinds of other states or patterns of inference. Instead, there is a collection of strategies for showing how paradigmatic contexts where imagination occurs can be understood as exclusively drawing upon a more basic collection of mental states, including beliefs, desires, and intentions. This is the right *form* of reduction, in my view, given that imagination is not a natural cognitive kind but is instead a heterogeneous collection of more basic mental states and processes that acquire the label 'imagining' on the basis of being cases of rich, elaborated, epistemically safe thought about the possible, fictional, and fantastical.

2
Folk Psychology and Its Ontology

2.1 Introduction

When we ask about imagination's relation to states like beliefs, desires, intentions, judgments, decisions, and so on, our answers will turn, in part, on what we take those other states to be—on how we view *their* ontological status. To inquire after the ontological status of such states is to ask for a deeper account of their nature than the platitudinous definitions we might find in a dictionary. Two people can agree that to believe something is to take it to be true, for instance, while disagreeing about what beliefs *are* in a deeper sense. Likewise, they may agree that to imagine is to engage in rich, epistemically blameless thought about the possible, fantastical, or fictional while disagreeing about the deeper nature of imaginings. Notoriously, there are rather different views in philosophy concerning the "deep" nature of folk psychological states. This chapter surveys some of those views with an eye toward explaining how their differences bear on the project of explaining imagination.

One goal is to show that the project of explaining imagination, as pursued here, is open to researchers who don't share assumptions about the nature of folk psychological states. For instance, many debates about imagination occur among theorists who share a background belief in the representational theory of mind (Aydede, 2015; Fodor, 1987; Nichols, 2006a). But one needn't accept that theory of mental representation and its relation to folk psychology in order to find the project of explaining imagination both approachable and important. I will argue that, whatever your take on folk psychological ontology may be, a theory that breaks imagination into states like beliefs, desires, and intentions has the potential to offer a genuine explanation of imagination. This is so even if you are an *eliminativist* about folk psychological states (Churchland, 1981), or even if you think that cognitive science has no need for the notion of *mental representation* (Chemero, 2011).

My second goal in this chapter is to defend the reductive style of explanation I pursue against a few objections. These are not objections to specific examples or contexts where I propose that imagination-talk can be replaced with talk of other kinds of states. They are instead objections to the effect that, *even if* we could replace imagination-talk with talk of other kinds of folk psychological states—in ways I previewed last chapter—this still would not constitute an explanation (or *reduction*) of imagination. This sort of objection is best addressed by distinguishing different views one might have on folk psychological ontology; that is why I take it up here, in sections 2.6 and 2.7.

Explaining Imagination. Peter Langland-Hassan, Oxford University Press (2020). © Peter Langland-Hassan.
DOI: 10.1093/oso/9780198815068.001.0001

A last goal of this chapter is to clarify how different sources of evidence bear on the question of explaining imagination. In making claims about imagination and its relationship to other mental states, we seem to pronounce on the structure and nature of a biological phenomenon: the human mind. It is not always clear how such claims could be supported by the kinds of considerations philosophers typically adduce—deriving, for instance, from introspection, the mining and refinement of commonsense platitudes, and appeals to parsimony. (We are well advised by Bechtel & Richardson (2010) to expect complexity, not parsimony, when discovering the nature of organisms.) On the other hand, it can also be hard to see how a harder-nosed empirical approach could gain better traction on the questions that concern us. Clarity on these matters comes when we recognize that the proper epistemological approach to explaining imagination will depend in part on our broader views concerning folk psychological ontology, in ways I hope to elucidate.

As this chapter is largely meta-theoretical in nature, it can be skipped without compromising one's ability to follow most of the arguments in later chapters. There will, however, be places later on where the distinctions drawn here—between "heavy-duty" and "light-duty" ontologies, for example—are essential to grasping the issues at play. Also, for any who wondered, last chapter, whether the kinds of explanations I'll pursue are *explanations* in good standing, this chapter is essential reading. So the recommended approach is to take time now to draw the distinctions we'll need later, and to confirm that we're on solid explanatory footing.

2.2 Folk Psychological Ontologies—a Brief History

One of the great innovations of twentieth-century philosophy was the idea that everyday psychological terms—words like 'belief,' 'desire,' and 'imagining'—could be seen as *theoretical* terms (Sellars, 1956). The supposed theory featuring those terms came to be called *folk psychology*. According to legend, this was the theory of the *folk*—ordinary folk you might see at the post office, or waiting in line to vote. Not that they would have told you they had a psychological theory. But, stepping back, we could view them as using one—one that enabled them to understand and predict others' behavior by attributing to them states like beliefs, desires, and intentions.

Why was Jason taking off his shoes? The folk could explain: he *desired* to pass through airport security and *believed* he must remove his shoes to do so. Why wasn't Jim? Well, he didn't *believe* it was required. Why was Julia leaping over hurdles? She *desired* to win the race and *believed* that jumping the hurdles would be faster than running through them. Why was Julia's mom so happy? She desired that Julia would win and believed that Julia was winning.

The philosophical attraction in this was that we could avoid relying upon introspection to identify and categorize mental phenomena, instead treating mental states as unobservable entities that, like electrons or quarks, are *posited* in order to explain phenomena that we can all observe together (Chihara & Fodor, 1965). Psychological notions like belief and desire could earn their keep in the same way that other theoretical entities do: by their usefulness to explanations of outwardly observable phenomena. And the best part of it was that, despite our having done no formal experiments, we already had the relevant theory in hand—"folk" psychology—just as a function of being competent speakers of a natural language that incorporates mental state terms like 'belief' and 'desire.'

It would be hard to overstate the impact this doctrine has had on how philosophy and psychology approach the study of mental states and processes. Within philosophy, in particular, there arose near universal agreement that folk psychology is a powerful and useful means for predicting and explaining human behavior. It seems we would be hard-pressed to say *why* Jason is removing his shoes if we were *not* allowed use of any folk psychological terms. Simply appealing to environmental context—saying that Jason is removing his shoes *because it is required*—doesn't explain why Jim, who is standing next to him, fails to do so. The problem is solved if we can reference their respective states of mind; and attributing different folk psychological states is a good way of doing that. Sure, there might be some other story to tell that would distinguish Jason from Jim—one involving retinal stimulation, neural firings, and the like. Be we're not yet in any position to tell it. And who's to say it would offer a *better* explanation? For power and ease of use, folk psychology is hard to beat.

And yet, despite wide agreement about the power and usefulness of folk psychology *as a practice* for predicting, explaining, and rationalizing behavior, there has never been a consensus concerning the ontology it implies. Exactly what *sort* of things (if any) are we claiming to exist when we grant that folk psychological terms offer useful means for predicting and explaining behavior? Answering requires us to clarify the distinction between folk psychological *talk*—that is, our everyday practice of attributing folk psychological states like beliefs, desires, and imaginings, to each other—and the actual states of our minds, brains, bodies, and environments that are causally responsible for our behavior. For some in contemporary philosophy—including many who work on imagination—there is little distance between the two. According to this family of theorists, to say that Jane believes that *p* is just to say that Jane has, realized in her brain, a *mental representation* of a certain sort—one with *p* as its content. This mental representation is then thought to play various causal roles in shaping her behavior—behavior on the basis of which we infer that she believes that *p*. It is thought that we can move from the truth of a folk psychological description—that Jane believes that *p*—to a specific (albeit defeasible) claim about the structure of Jane's mind—viz., that it contains a mental representation with the content *p* (Dretske, 1991; Fodor, 1987).

It is important to see why this inference, correct or not, is far from inevitable. Not all who find folk psychological *talk* explanatorily useful feel obliged to posit corresponding mental representations. A second family of theories finds it useful to attribute folk psychological states, but resists any move from there to the conclusion that the mind contains mental representations of a particular sort. Some in this family hold that cognitive science will not include folk psychological states in its account of what the mind contains, and, on those grounds, advocate eliminativism about the states (Churchland, 1981; Stich, 1983). Others take a dispositionalist view of folk psychological states, holding that to have a certain belief or desire is simply to fulfill a certain dispositional stereotype (Ryle, 1949/2009; Schwitzgebel, 2002, 2013). This approach makes no comment on the causal bases of those dispositions and, typically, views with skepticism the idea the causal bases are mental representations whose contents mirror the contents of the that-clauses featured in folk psychological talk. (The "that-clause" in the folk psychological ascription, "Jim believes that Mars is hot," is "Mars is hot"). Also in this family is Daniel Dennett, who holds that to have folk psychological states is simply to be the sort of "intentional system" whose behavior can be explained and predicted by attributing to it such states (with their associated dispositions)—again without comment on the nature of the internal features of the system that make it suitable for description in such terms (Dennett, 1989, 1991). Still others in this group defend a "minimalist" approach, holding that folk psychological states are semantically evaluable, causally efficacious internal states, while eschewing any commitments about whether this implies the existence of corresponding mental representations with a semantics that roughly matches that of the that-clauses used in ordinary folk psychological attributions (Egan, 1995; Graham & Horgan, 1988).

In short, two broad families of theory—each with influential members—agree that it is useful to ascribe beliefs, desires, imaginings, and the like to people when predicting and explaining their behavior. But they disagree on the sort of things that are being ascribed when we say of someone that she believes or desires that *p*. It will be useful to look more closely at each approach now in order to appreciate how their differences bear on the project of explaining imagination.

2.3 Heavy-Duty Ontology

The most general commitment uniting the first family of theories—what I will call *heavy-duty* views of folk psychological ontology—is that folk psychological mental state ascriptions refer to discrete mental representations tokened in individuals, where the semantics (or meaning) of these representations typically bears a close relationship to the semantics of the that-clauses we use to ascribe them. On this view, when we say that Joe believes (or desires, or intends) that *there is coffee in the mug*, the statement is made true by the fact that Joe has a mental representation realized in his brain with the content *there is coffee in the mug* (or something semantically close to that)—where this mental representation has the distinctive causal role of a belief (or desire, or intention). It is the causal interaction of such mental representations with each other that, on the heavy-duty view, serves to bring about the behaviors or dispositions that we predict and explain through folk psychological talk. So characterized, the heavy-duty view is a close cousin to the representational theory of mind (RTM) in philosophy and psychology; the two views only diverge if defenders of RTM don't insist on a close relation between the semantics of (at least many of) the mental representations used in human cognition and semantics of the that-clauses typically used in folk psychological state attributions.[1] Others have called this sort of view *intentional realism* (Pitt, 2020). That label strikes me as pejorative, however, as it wrongly implies that rejecting it makes one an anti-realist about folk psychological states (more on this later).

The most famous heavy-duty view comes from Jerry Fodor—especially Fodor (1975) and (1987, Ch. 1). For Fodor, it is just because our internal mental representations closely mirror—in both their syntactic structure and semantics—the natural language sentences we use to describe someone in folk psychological terms that our commonsense view of ourselves as rational agents stands to be vindicated. The idea that we act *for reasons*—reasons we are able to describe ourselves as having—can be seen to cohere with our being causally efficacious parts of the physical world, he argues, if the causes of our behaviors are internal representations that share semantic properties with (relevant portions of) the folk psychological sentences we apply to ourselves. One of the key thoughts inspiring Fodor and his followers is that, with the development of computers, it becomes possible to see beliefs and desires *both* as having meanings *and* as being physical states in the brain. The analogy of thinking to computing allows us to see how it is possible for a system to be set up so that the causal interactions that occur among its internal states (as a function of their intrinsic physical properties or "shape") mirror the inferential relationships we would expect to hold among symbols with certain meanings. Patterns of semantic entailment—sentence A rationally entailing sentence B—are realized in sequences of physical symbols whose causes and effects "contrive to respect" the semantic values we've assigned to them (Fodor, 1987, pp. 10–20; Aydede, 2015).

An important feature of the Fodorian version of the heavy-duty view is that mental representations have a relational structure, involving a mental sentence—one with a particular *meaning* or *content*—and an attitude taken toward that sentence. On most iterations of this view, the "mental sentences" in our heads don't

[1] Typically, defenders of RTM posit mental representations whose semantics *do* closely mirror the semantics of ordinary folk psychological state attributions. However, there is room in logical space for someone to defend a representational theory of mind without holding that the mental representations used in human cognition bear an appreciable relation to those of the sentences we use to attribute folk psychological states. This is why I have defined *heavy-duty* views so as to explicitly require a close mirroring between the semantics of mental representations and those of the that-clauses used in ordinary folk psychological state attributions.

occur in a natural, spoken language, but rather in a proprietary "language of thought," sometimes called *Mentalese* (Fodor, 1975). Not only do these representations have meanings that closely mirror the meanings of the that-clauses used in folk psychological attributions, they also are said to have a language-like syntactic structure, insofar as they are composed of discrete meaningful symbols, where the meaning of a complex representation (e.g., a belief) is a function of the meaning of its parts, together with the syntactic rules for combining them.

Whether a mental representation qualifies as a belief, desire, or some other kind of state is then said to be determined by the causal-functional role of the representation in the broader cognitive economy. Bearing the relation of belief, as opposed to desire, to a mental representation with the content *p* will be a matter of the kinds of causes and effects the state has—its "functional role." I will call the different causal-functional profiles characteristic of different kinds of folk psychological states *psychological attitudes.* So, where ordinary folk psychology speaks of *believing* that *p*, *desiring* that *q*, *wondering whether r*, and so on—these being different "attitudes" one can take toward the propositions *p*, *q*, and *r*—the heavy-duty theorist posits corresponding *psychological* attitudes that are different relations one can bear to mental representations with the contents *p*, *q*, or *r*. Unlike the notion of a (mere) propositional attitude, the notion of psychological attitude is intended to carry with it the idea that there are mental representations tokened in one's brain toward which one takes the relevant attitude, where one's taking the attitude is to be understood in terms of the representation's having a certain functional role in one's cognitive economy.

Often, theories that posit psychological attitudes follow Schiffer (1981) and Fodor (1987) in speaking of "boxes" corresponding to each attitude; these boxes are meant to summarize, within a diagram, the kinds of causes and effects distinctive of each attitude-type. So, to believe that *p* is to have a representation with the content *p* "in" one's Belief Box and to desire that *q* is to have a representation with *q* "in" one's Desire Box. The boxes are not assumed to have any geographic reality in the mind itself; boxes, *qua* boxes, exist only in the diagrams meant to map out the causal-functional relations among mental representations with different contents. The use of the box metaphor *does*, however, presume the existence of certain kinds of mental representations that reside "in" the boxes, insofar as those representations have certain causes and effects. Specifically, it assumes mental representations whose contents (or semantics) closely mirror those of the that-clauses we would use to accurately describe someone in folk psychological terms. Note that this does not require any further assumption that the representations are language-like in structure. So, while many heavy-duty views come with specific commitments about the format of the mental representations in the boxes they posit (viz., that they are language-like), the only commitment I attribute to all heavy-duty theorists is the idea that the success of our folk psychological talk is, in general, explained by the existence of mental representations with a closely matching *semantics*—where each representation has a discrete location in space and time. Further, heavy-duty theorists needn't hold that *every* instance of a successful folk psychological explanation is itself explained by the presence of semantically-matching mental representations (hence the "in general" above). They can allow that a formal cognitive scientific inventory of one's mental states will involve some "cleaning up"—or even dismissal of—ordinary folk psychological talk. They are simply committed to the final inventory including representations whose semantics have a fairly transparent relationship to the semantics of the that-clauses we use in ordinary folk psychological explanations, and to the idea that such representations account for the usefulness of folk psychological talk *most of the time*.

I have found these claims about what "boxes" presuppose to be controversial in some quarters. It has been objected to me that box-talk is simply shorthand for functionalism in general, and needn't commit one to the existence of mental representations of any sort. I think that is incorrect. Within cognitive psychology, box-and-arrow diagrams are intended to map the flow of information through the mind and brain. Typically, a diagrammatic distinction is made between boxes, which represent data stores, and hexagons, which represent mechanisms capable of operating on the data stores (see, e.g., Nichols & Stich, 2000, p. 121). The distinction between a data store, on the one hand, and a mechanism that operates on the data, on the other, is at odds with a "merely functionalist" picture, where mental states are defined in terms of their functional roles, without comment on corresponding mental representations—representations that have discrete locations in time and space. After all, for a mechanism to operate on a mental state, the state must be physically realized in some form; one's being in the state cannot simply be a matter of one's having certain dispositions (as on some of the "light-duty" functionalist views discussed below). So talk of boxes and mechanisms thus brings with it the need for mental representations that are tokened "in" the boxes, such that other mental mechanisms can transform them in various ways. I will assume as much going forward in my use of "box" terminology. (For a functionalist picture of folk psychological ontology that lacks any commitment to corresponding mental representations, see Egan (1995).)

In recent decades, many have proposed that imagination involves use of a proprietary psychological attitude as well—one with similarities to belief, but which is ultimately quite distinct (see, e.g., Carruthers, 2006, pp. 89–91; Currie & Ravenscroft, 2002, Ch. 2; Friedman & Leslie, 2007, p. 115; Gendler, 2006, pp. 183–5; Nichols & Stich, 2003; Schellenberg, 2013; Schroeder & Matheson, 2006; Spaulding, 2015; Stokes, 2014; Weinberg & Meskin, 2006b). In some cases, they go so far as to posit an "Imagination Box" (Doggett & Egan, 2007; Liao & Doggett, 2014; Nichols, 2008; Schellenberg, 2013; Weinberg & Meskin, 2006b). This view is at odds with the reductive account I will pursue.

2.4 Light-Duty Ontology

In characterizing heavy-duty views, I highlighted a distinction between what is a quasi-scientific hypothesis about the nature of our minds—viz., that they contain mental representations with specific contents and functional roles—and what is something that anyone who successfully makes use of folk psychological descriptions must grasp. The latter includes more superficial phenomena, *behavioral dispositions* central among them. The competent user of the term 'belief' understands that someone who believes that *p* and desires that not-*p* has certain characteristic dispositions to behavior, whether or not they have any views about what it is that gives the person those dispositions—just as one might know that a vase is fragile, and so disposed to break when dropped, without having any clear idea of what it is about the vase that makes it fragile.

Folk psychology aside, we routinely ascribe dispositions to people on the basis of noticing superficial features that are reliable markers for the dispositions, without any understanding of the causal bases for the dispositions. Noticing that a husband and wife are both tall and blonde, we infer that they are disposed to have tall, blonde children. We needn't have any idea of the causal bases (grounded in their genetics) for those dispositions, in order to exploit knowledge of the dispositions in making predictions about their offspring. We move from superficial features we can observe, to knowledge of associated dispositions, to predictions and explanations of specific phenomena. In the same way, what I will call the *light-duty view* holds that we are able to infer, on the basis of a person's superficial behavior (and context), dispositions they are likely to have. Our folk psychological ascriptions, made on the basis of observed behavior, serve to attribute dispositions that will further manifest in their future behavior. Thus we can predict and explain specific behaviors on the basis of their having the dispositions we ascribe with the use of folk psychological terms—even if we remain clueless about the causal bases for the dispositions. Light-duty views take these superficial phenomena to capture the essence of folk psychological states.

To get a better grasp on this, consider David Lewis's (1972) distinction between the causal-functional role of a mental state and the occupant of that role. The causal role of a mental state, Lewis held, can be extracted from the set of platitudes that competent speakers of the language accept about the state. These "roles" are dispositional in nature. Lewis characterizes them thus:

> When someone is in so-and-so combination of mental states and receives stimuli of so-and-so kind, he tends with so-and-so probability to be caused thereby to go into so-and-so mental states and produce so-and-so motor responses.
>
> (Lewis, 1972, p. 256)

The dispositions Lewis lists are both dispositions to have certain behavioral ("motor") responses and dispositions to go into other mental states. These mental states themselves *could* be understood as mental representations, in the manner of the heavy-duty view; but they can also be understood, more superficially, as *states of having certain further dispositions*, without comment on the causal bases of the dispositions. This more cautious, superficial understanding of folk psychological states is where light-duty views set up shop (see, e.g., Schwitzgebel, 2002, 2013).

Lewis himself thinks of mental states as the "occupants" of the causal-functional roles we extract from folk psychological platitudes: "When we learn what sort of states occupy those causal roles definitive of the mental states," he writes, "we will learn what the mental states are... exactly as we found out what light was when we found that electromagnetic radiation was the phenomenon that occupied a certain role" (1972, p. 256). The key difference between Lewis and heavy-duty theorists, as characterized above, is that he assumes we do not *yet* know what the mental states are. We just know that, if they exist, they will be the occupants of certain causal roles; they will be the states that cause people to have the dispositions we attribute to them when we attribute them beliefs, desires, and the like. By Lewis's lights, these occupants *might* be mental representations of certain kinds; or they might be non-representational neurobiological states; or they might—with less likelihood—be conglomerations of glue and sawdust. Our expertise with folk psychological explanation does not prejudge an answer (though our broader understanding of nature and biology might). The heavy-duty theorist, by contrast, has in mind an account of what those occupants are: mental representations, realized in the brain, with contents mirroring those of the that-clauses used in appropriate folk psychological descriptions.

So both light- and heavy-duty views will agree that if Joe *desires* to keep a dying fire lit and *believes* that adding another log will do the trick, then, all else equal,[2] he will add another log. In ascribing such a belief and desire pair to Joe, both heavy and light views agree that Joe has a number of interesting dispositions, such as to agree with others that the fire should be kept lit, to assist in searching for a log, to be pleased when the fire remains lit, and so on. The light-duty conception remains "light" in making no comment on the nature of the internal states in virtue of which Joe has those dispositions; whereas, on the heavy-duty view, when Joe believes that the fire is almost out, there is a representation realized in Joe's brain whose meaning is that the fire is almost out; this representation causally interacts with other mental representations so as to *result in* his having log-adding dispositions.

Whether folk psychological ascriptions are ever strictly speaking *true* is answered in different ways by different light-duty theorists. Eliminativists hold that the ascriptions are strictly speaking *false*, despite their frequent utility

[2] The *all else equal* clause is notoriously difficult to fill in. To start, Joe must not have a stronger countervailing desire; he must not believe there is a better, easier, way to keep the fire lit; he must believe he is allowed to add a log; and so on. These difficulties are shared by both the light- and heavy-duty views.

(Churchland, 1981). Other light-duty theorists remain agnostic concerning the truth or falsity of the ascriptions. For instance, a light-duty theorist may, like Lewis, identify folk psychological states themselves with their causal bases, *whatever they turn out to be*. (Lewis leaves open the possibility that there will be no unified realization base for the causal-functional roles and, in that case, appears ready to conclude that no such states exist (Lewis, 1972, p. 252).) Alternatively, a light-duty theorist may identify being in a folk psychological state simply with the possession of certain dispositions, and not with any putative causal bases for the dispositions (Schwitzgebel, 2002, 2013; Ryle, 1949; Sellars, 1956). For instance, on Eric Schwitzgebel's "phenomenal dispositionalist" view, being in a certain folk psychological state amounts to "having a dispositional profile that matches, to an appropriate degree and in appropriate respects, a stereotype for that attitude, typically grounded in folk psychology" (Schwitzgebel, 2013). (He includes within such dispositional profiles "phenomenal dispositions" to have certain kinds of conscious experiences (Schwitzgebel, 2002, p. 252).) Schwitzgebel contrasts his "superficial," dispositional account of the attitudes to "deep" views of the Fodorian kind. And, indeed, Schwitzgebel's distinction between "superficial" and "deep" views of folk psychological states aligns closely with my distinction between "light-duty" and "heavy-duty" views. (I'm indebted to Schwitzgebel's description of the terrain, though I don't wish to saddle him with my slightly different understanding of it.)

While each person who believes that *p* will have dispositions in common with every other person who believes that *p*—provided their *other* relevant folk psychological states are similar enough—there is, on the light-duty view, no expectation that we will find an interesting *type* of internal state shared by all and only those who believe that *p*—one that makes it the case that they have those dispositions. In individual cases, we may be able to answer the question: what is it about *S* that makes him have the dispositions associated with believing that *p*? But, broadening our search for the *more general* internal causes of the dispositions we associate with believing that *p*, we may find only a messy disjunction of different kinds of states. Light-duty theorists, including Schwitzgebel, Dennett (1991), and Egan (1995), are typically skeptical that cognitive science will discover mental representations realized in the brain with contents mirroring the meanings of the that-clauses used in folk psychological ascriptions. While they can leave the door open to such a discovery, their hunch is that folk psychological notions like *believing that p* will break into many different neuro-cognitive pieces when it comes to discovering their implementation in individual systems.

Dominic Murphy gives voice to this view in a paper on the place of folk psychology in cognitive science:

> The question whether science makes use of representational systems isn't really open to doubt any longer: many areas of psychology and neuroscience take for

> granted the existence of semantically interpretable internal states...What is open to doubt is whether representation, as used in the sciences of the mind, has the properties that philosophers have found in intentional content, as presupposed by folk psychology. (Murphy, 2017, p. 138)

Murphy goes on to articulate a light-duty view that still finds an important role for folk psychological notions in cognitive science:

> The concept of belief will do very little useful explanatory work in any mature cognitive science. But it might nevertheless be decomposable into a family of successor notions that can suggest and guide useful neuroscientific hypotheses. (p. 138)

Note that, while Murphy thinks that belief will not be a central notion in a mature cognitive science, he suspects it will play an important role as a kind of *ancestor* notion, the exploration, refinement, and revision of which will constitute crucial steps in understanding how the mind really works. For that reason, the notion retains value in the here-and-now.

Most light-duty theorists, like Murphy, will allow that there are mental representations of some sort underlying human cognition; they just doubt that the contents (or semantics) of those representations bear any appreciable relation to the contents of the that-clauses featured in folk psychological ascriptions. Nevertheless, they *need not* hold that there are any such mental representations in order to maintain that folk psychological ascriptions are true—true either because one's having certain dispositions suffices for their truth (as in Schwitzgebel's view), or because being in any kind of internal state at all that leads one to have those dispositions—no matter how disjunctive it may be across cases—suffices for their truth. At the limit, a light-duty theorist can hold that folk psychological ascriptions are for the most part true, while maintaining that a mature cognitive science will have no use for the notion of mental representation at all (Chemero, 2011).

2.5 Heavy-Duty Incredulity about Light-Duty Dispositionalism, and Principled Agnosticism

Those with heavy-duty views sometimes react to the light-duty perspective with incredulity. How, they ask, does the light-duty theorist propose to *explain* all the dispositions we cite so regularly, *other than* by positing internal representations of a heavy-duty sort (Fodor, 1987; Quilty-Dunn & Mandelbaum, 2017)? This sort of incredulity is worth discussion, as it helps to clarify what is at stake in debates about folk psychological ontology.

Light-duty theorists can push back in several ways. First, they can hold that there are, in fact, other well-developed possibilities for explaining the dispositions. For instance, a light-duty theorist may think that *connectionist networks* offer a better model for how the brain accomplishes the information-processing relevant to explaining human behavior (P. S. Churchland & Sejnowski, 1989; Van Gelder, 1990, 1998). Such networks are standardly held to involve mental representations and computations over those representations. Yet these representations don't have contents that mirror those of the sentences we use to describe someone in folk psychological terms. In a network set up to identify images of dogs, for instance, there are no representations with the content "dogs have four legs," or "dogs have hair." Instead, the networks have characteristic patterns of activation, according to the "weights" assigned to different connected nodes in the network (where the connection weights between nodes are intended to mirror the connection strengths between neurons, or sets of neurons). Whatever semantic relationships hold among different states of these networks—in virtue of which they qualify as representations at all—they do not bear any isomorphic relation to the serial reasoning steps we attribute to people from a folk psychological perspective. The light-duty theorist can take comfort in the fact that such networks underlie many of the most striking recent advances in artificial intelligence, including speech recognition (Hinton et al., 2012), face recognition (Parkhi, Vedaldi, & Zisserman, 2015), abstract problem solving—as deployed in games like chess and Go (Silver et al., 2016)—and pattern recognition more generally (Schmidhuber, 2015).

A second contemporary paradigm for explaining human cognition appeals to Bayesian models of probabilistic inference. Within such frameworks, different kinds of representations are hypothesized to underlie a person's knowledge in different domains (Tenenbaum et al., 2011). The point is to understand the transitions among those representations as obeying Bayesian principles of probabilistic inference. Within some Bayesian models of cognition, tree-structured representations are used; in others, two-dimensional spaces or grids are invoked, or representations resembling graphs (Tenenbaum et al., 2011, p. 1281). According to (the Bayesians) Tanenbaum et al., "Our best accounts of people's mental representations…resemble simpler versions of how scientists represent the same domains" (p. 1281). It is no presumption of Bayesian approaches that the representations they posit will, in general, bear transparent semantic relationships to the that-clauses of useful folk psychological talk. Again we have a flourishing research program that is not tethered to the core commitment of heavy-duty approaches. (Similar points apply to yet another popular paradigm for understanding perception and cognition: the *predictive processing theory* (Clark, 2013, 2015; Hohwy, 2013). No part of that framework assumes that the mental representations involved in such predictions correspond in any close way to our folk psychological ascriptions.)

A second avenue of response for the light-duty theorist, in the face of heavy-duty incredulity, is to grant the lack of an explanation for the dispositions we ascribe with folk psychological terms, while countering that the heavy-duty approach offers only a pseudo-explanation. Churchland & Sejnowski (1989), for instance, lampoon the heavy-duty approach to explaining human behavior by comparing it to nineteenth-century homuncular embryology, which joined the ancients in explaining the complex structure found in organisms by positing sperm which already possess the same structure in a smaller form. According to such theories, a sperm is a miniature human that, like a sponge in water, simply expands during its time in the womb (p. 161). Churchland & Sejnowski complain that Fodorian heavy-duty views explain the kind of complex linguistic behavior shown by humans—including rational inference as described via language—by appeal to mental states that have the very structure and inferential characteristics we are seeking to explain in linguistic behavior. The kinds of sentences people can say and comprehend is systematic, the Fodorian observes; so we posit a structure in the mind that is itself systematic in the very same ways. This is not unlike explaining the ten fingers and toes of adult humans by positing ten fingers and toes on a tiny human within the sperm. The heavy-duty view of human cognition is consistent with, and even "predicts," human linguistic behavior in all the ways that the homuncular theory of embryonic development predicts the growth and appearance of adult human beings. The mere fact that a *post hoc* story can be concocted that is consistent with the facts as we already knew them to be is not reason to give it special credence.

There is, of course, much more to be said on each side of the debate between heavy- and light-duty views. My aim has been to explain the nature of the debate and make room for light-duty views, without trying to settle things one way or the other. In my view, agnosticism concerning the cognitive ontology responsible for the dispositions we ascribe with folk psychological talk is reasonable at our stage of inquiry; that tilts me toward a light-duty view. But my arguments in this book won't assume either approach. My concern in the balance of this chapter is, first, to show how the project of explaining imagination differs as a function of one's being either heavy or light duty in orientation; and, second, to respond to some objections concerning the general project of explaining one folk psychological state ("imagining") in terms of a collection of others.

2.6 Explaining Imagination for Light-Duty Theorists

Supposing that one has a light-duty view of folk psychological ontology, what does it mean to explain imagination in terms of a more basic collection of folk psychological states? It means that the abilities and dispositions we attribute and predict by ascribing imaginings to a person can *alternatively* be attributed and predicted by ascribing certain collections of beliefs, judgments, intentions, desires, and so on—all while remaining agnostic about the underlying cognitive ontology corresponding to such attributions. Consider again the folk psychological state of *suspecting*. We can, on the one hand, attribute certain dispositions to a person by saying that he *suspects that he left the stove on*. Doing so will allow us to predict and explain his behavior in various ways. On the other hand, we can attribute him the very same set of dispositions by saying that he *believes that it is somewhat likely that he left the stove on*. From the perspective of a light-duty view, neither form of ascription has greater ontological *oomph*; both attribute the same set of dispositions; both latch on to the same pattern in human behavior and inference (Dennett, 1991). For the light-duty theorist, there is no ontological dispute between the two ways of speaking—no turf battle to be waged between the notions of belief and suspicion. The phrases "Jones believes it is somewhat likely that *p*" and "Jones suspects that *p*" describe the same state of affairs. (As we will see, this is not so for the heavy-duty theorist.)

The light-duty theorist can, however, maintain that the ascription involving the word 'belief' makes use of a more general *notion*, insofar as we ascribe beliefs to people at times when it would not be appropriate to ascribe them a (mere) suspicion. By contrast, any case where a suspicion is ascribed will also be one where we could have ascribed a less than certain belief. This is the asymmetry noted in section 1.9. We can posit that there is a state of Jones in virtue of which he has those dispositions, in each case. But, for the light-duty theorist, there is no more reason to call that state "the belief that it is somewhat likely that *p*," than there is to call it "the suspicion that *p*." The light-duty theorist suspects that the notions of belief and suspicion will both have fallen out of the picture by the time we have a plausible, empirically supported theory of the state.

In many cases where two folk psychological terms serve to attribute the same dispositions and enable the same predictions, their doing so is fairly obvious. We saw this with the notions of thankfulness, regret, and suspicion, in Chapter 1. Matters are more interesting in the case of imagination. For it is *not* always easy to see how ascribing an imagining could amount to ascribing the same set of dispositions that we might with some collection of other psychological states, such as beliefs and desires. If it were, no one would raise an eyebrow at this book's core thesis. The trend in philosophy has instead been to think of imagination as a *sui generis* folk psychological state—one that, *unlike* suspecting, or being thankful, or regretting—cannot be analyzed in terms of other more general folk psychological notions such as belief, judgment, intention, and desire. To say, as a light-duty theorist, that imagination cannot be reduced to other folk psychological states is just to say that, try as we might, we cannot find a satisfying translation of the platitudes and dispositions associated with imagination-ascriptions to platitudes and dispositions we attribute with sets of other more general folk psychological terms. It is to say that the phenomena—both mental and behavioral—we predict and explain with imagination-talk cannot alternatively be predicted and explained with belief, desire, intention, judgment, and decision-talk. Much of the work of later chapters is to show that there is in fact no such barrier; we can indeed capture the explanatory and predictive power of imagination-talk in terms of talk of beliefs, desires, and intentions (and their occurrent counterparts).

If a plausible analysis of imagination can be given along these lines, light-duty theorists should take interest. For even if explaining imagination in terms of more basic folk psychological states only amounts to showing how one set of platitudes and disposition-attributions can be translated into another, this still serves as a (surprising, to most) elucidation of imagination. Imagination is then no longer a *sui generis* mental phenomenon. A unification of one set of dispositions with another, broader set, is an explanatory unification, in Kitcher's (1981) sense (see Chapter 1). Note that the situation would be entirely different if we had no prior, independent understanding of belief, desire, intention, and so on. It would, for instance, be of far less interest to show how imagination-talk can be translated into talk of three newly invented states, described herein for the first time. The point is not simply that there is another conceivable set of states that could do the explanatory work that *sui generis* imaginings supposedly do. The key to the light-duty explanation lies in assimilating imagination-talk to talk of states we already believe in, understand, and ascribe in myriad conditions. *That* is how we reduce our stock of primitive notions.

Second, this kind of light-duty explanation has the advantage of being insulated from tumultuous debates in empirical psychology concerning the nature, format, and use of mental representations in human reasoning. Should it turn out that there is no such thing as the Belief Box or Desire Box—because there exist no mental representations with the kind of semantics and functional roles assumed by heavy-duty views—the light-duty explanation of imagination in terms of other folk psychological states retains its relevance.

Third, like anyone else, light-duty theorists expect attributions of beliefs, desires, decisions, judgments, and so on, to map, however noisily, on to *something* in the world, be it brain states, brain-body-environment pairings, or patterns of activation in neural networks—something that explains why a person has the dispositions we ascribe to him when we ascribe the state. What those things are, if their hunch is correct, just won't be all that similar to the sentences we use to ascribe folk psychological states. If cases of imagining can be understood in more basic light-duty terms, then the search for imagination's causal bases can be merged with the more general project of understanding the causal bases of the dispositions we associate with ascriptions of beliefs, desires, decisions, judgments, and so on. Questions about imagination are thereby reduced to questions about these other mental states. Here even the eliminativist about folk psychological states can take interest; for to eliminate the most basic folk psychological states—beliefs, desires, and so on—by discovering new and better explanatory kinds will now be to eliminate imagination as well. The eliminativist will have one fewer ontological dangler.

2.6.1 Objections to this Form of Explanation, from a Light-Duty Perspective

There are worries one may nevertheless have about this sort of explanation, pitched in light-duty terms. One objection grants that the relationship mapped in Chapter 1 (Fig. 1.1b) holds, insofar as belief, desire, and intention are collectively more basic than imagination. However, it maintains that there is a sense in which imagination remains *un*reduced on such an account, precisely because (unlike suspicion), imagination is identified with a heterogeneous disjunction of different kinds of states. Arguably, where a certain type of state is identified with a heterogeneous collection of states in different token instances, the "higher level" state remains unreduced (Fodor, 1974). This is most often said to be the case when the kind-to-be-reduced enables us to make counterfactual-supporting generalizations and predictions we could not otherwise make. In such situations, the higher level kind retains an ontological significance of its own, even if, in token instances, we can perhaps do the same explanatory work by attributing some other kind of state in its stead.

Now, as it happens, I don't think that imagining *is* something like a counterfactual-supporting psychological natural kind. I think that (A-)imagining is any episode of rich, elaborated, epistemically safe thought about the possible, unreal, or fantastical. I think that's all we mean by 'imagining' when it's used in the ordinary folk psychological sense of 'imagining' captured by entries 2, 3, and 4 for 'imagine' in the *Oxford English Dictionary* (see Chapter 1). So understood, there is no reason to expect deep unity to the causal-functional profile of imaginative episodes. An imagining that occurs during a daydream can have a quite different causal role than one with the same content that occurs in the context of hypothetical reasoning, or when enjoying a fiction. (I will return to this point below.)

But even if imagining were a homogeneous counterfactual-supporting kind and, as such, retained a kind of independent ontological status, this would not stand in the way of our *explaining* imagination in terms of other psychological states. For there can be *explanatory reductions* that are not ontological reductions. Characterizing acts of imagining in other, more basic folk psychological terms provides an understanding of imagination that we previously lacked, even if one remains committed to the existence of imagination as a natural kind. The explanatory reduction allows us see how, by giving an artificial system beliefs, desires, and intentions of the right kind, we can endow it with an ability to imagine. The value of such an explanation only increases if the disjunction of states with which imagining is characterized is not *wildly* disjunctive—if, instead, there is a smallish set of strategies for converting imagination-talk, in its paradigmatic instances, to talk of other states. That is the sort of picture I will defend by book's end.

Much the same response can be made to the objector who claims that, just as imagination-talk can be analyzed in terms of belief-, desire-, and intention-talk, so too can belief-talk be analyzed in terms of desire-, intention-, and imagination-talk. (You can take your pick of which of belief, desire, or intention gets analyzed in terms of the other two notions plus imagination. The challenge is simply that the kind of reduction proposed for imagination can be run with respect to one of the reducing states as well, with imagination serving as a primitive in *that* reduction.)[3] I don't, myself, find it at all likely that *plausible* redescriptions of this sort will be forthcoming. Which combination of desires, intentions, and imaginings will play the explanatory role of the belief that my name is 'Peter'? But let the so-motivated seek them out and convince us otherwise. If it turns out that such redescriptions are available, I would have to abandon my claim that belief, desire, and intention are collectively *more basic* than imagination. But we would still have available an explanation of imagination in other folk psychological terms. Learning that these terms are interdefinable in such ways (if they are) is to gain an important insight into the nature of the states to which they refer. And, again, appreciating the availability of such redescriptions allows us to see things—and to draw explanatory connections—that we couldn't before.

2.7 Explaining Imagination for Heavy-Duty Theorists

We've seen that when two folk psychological states have the same associated platitudes and dispositions, the light-duty view is not forced to a decision about which sort of state the person is *really* in when we ascribe one of those states. Both ascriptions point to the same place: a single set of dispositions, the causal bases of which we know not. One notion might provide explanatory leverage on the other. But, on the light-duty view, there is no deeper fact of the matter concerning which kind of state the person is in.

By contrast, the question of which attitude is ontologically *real* becomes legitimate and indeed pressing from the perspective of heavy-duty views. After all, they see psychological attitudes, taken toward concrete mental representations, as being the internal states that explain the dispositions we attribute with folk psychological talk. The heavy-duty theorist cannot lightly duplicate causes—admitting, for instance, both suspicion and belief "boxes" in the mind—in the same way light-duty theorists happily admit descriptions involving 'suspicion' and

[3] This challenge was put to me by Shen-yi Liao and Neil Van Leeuwen over lunch one day.

'belief that it is somewhat likely' as being ontologically on a par. This means that, if ascriptions of beliefs, desires, intentions (and their occurrent counterparts) really can do all the same explanatory work as ascriptions of imaginings, the heavy-duty theorist is forced to a decision on whether imagining (*qua* psychological attitude) really exists.

How will that decision be made? Consider the more neutral case of belief and suspicion: what should the heavy-duty theorist say is the *psychological attitude* that serves as the referent for ascriptions of both beliefs that it is somewhat likely that *p* and suspicions that *p*? Belief seems like the natural choice, if only because it is the more general notion. We will be able to appeal to belief in explanatory contexts including and beyond those where suspicion is an appropriate term. Why bring suspicion into our cognitive ontology, after all, if all the causal work it would do, and then some, can be done by a single psychological attitude of belief? The less than certain aspect of suspicion is accommodated through an adjustment in the content of a corresponding belief. Someone who suspects that *p*, the heavy-duty theorist can say, takes the psychological attitude of belief toward the mental sentence: it is somewhat likely that *p*. Now extend this line of thought to imagination. If the heavy-duty theorist is already committed to beliefs, desires, and intentions, and if those psychological attitudes can do all the explanatory work of imaginings *and more*, then imagination (as a psychological attitude) arrives on the chopping block.

Matters are not so straightforward, however. The nature and number of psychological attitudes is, for the heavy-duty theorist, a matter for empirical inquiry. As much as one might value parsimony in a theory (*modulo* the complexity of biological organisms), we can imagine evidence from neuropsychology that would warrant a *prima facie* less parsimonious cognitive architecture. Returning to the case of belief and suspicion, we might discover that some individuals who never show less than full certainty—political pundits, say—have a neural infarct that renders them incapable of mere suspicion. Their black-and-white views, it turns out, are a result not of careful deliberation but of dead neural tissue in Broadmann Area 10. Correlations between neural lesions at a specific site and a complete lack of suspicions might give us some reason to think that suspicion is, in fact, a distinct cognitive attitude—one that can blink out while belief chugs forward. So, while heavy-duty theorists may provisionally, on grounds of parsimony, favor views that explain both belief- and suspicion-talk in terms of a single cognitive attitude of belief, they can also leave the door open to expanding their cognitive ontologies in light of the right kind of evidence.

Imagination again presents an interesting test case, as most people haven't seen a way for cognitive attitudes like belief and desire to do the causal or explanatory work demanded by ascriptions of imaginings. If we are *already* heavy-duty theorists and cannot, from the armchair, see how more basic folk psychological terms could be used to attribute the dispositions and abilities associated with imagination, the inference to a distinct psychological attitude of imagination—with its corresponding Imagination Box—will feel inevitable. However, we can now see that, even if it *can* be shown (for example, by me, in the balance of this book) that psychological attitudes to which heavy-duty theorists are independently committed—viz., belief, desire, and intention—are able to do the explanatory work set out for the Imagination Box, there are reasons a heavy-duty theorist might still favor a cognitive architecture that contains an Imagination Box.

The case I gave as an example, involving suspicion and political pundits, was admittedly far-fetched. However, more plausible examples have been put to work in the imagination literature. People with autism spectrum disorder (ASD) have been shown to have deficits both in their ability to engage in group pretenses and in their understanding of other minds more generally—even while maintaining high cognitive capacities in some other domains. Nichols & Stich (2003) and Currie & Ravenscroft (2002) both argue that this pattern of deficits suggests a cognitive-level dissociation between imagination and belief. They propose that their theories, which posit a distinct cognitive attitude (hereafter, a "DCA") of imagination, are better placed to explain the phenomena than accounts that posit no such distinct attitude (Nichols & Stich, 2003; Currie & Ravenscroft, 2002). (Their DCA is equivalent to my notion of a "distinct psychological attitude.") This is the sort of surprising data that *could* weigh in favor of positing a DCA of imagination (or *sui generis* imaginative states), even if, in principle, imagination-talk can be replaced with belief-, desire-, and intention-talk. However, I argue in Chapter 8 that the pattern of deficits seen in ASD offers no special support for the idea that there is a distinct cognitive attitude of imagination.

A second reason a heavy-duty theorist might posit a psychological attitude of imagination, even when belief, desire, and intention can potentially do the same explanatory and predictive work, is that the theory invoking the Imagination Box is simpler or more powerful. Of course, identifying the simplest—*qua* most time- and energy-efficient—cognitive architecture is never straightforward. To know with any certainty which proposal is more parsimonious in the relevant sense requires more than counting boxes and arrows. It requires knowing a great deal about the actual implementation of our cognitive capacities, and the costs—evolutionarily, ecologically, and metabolically—of developing and using those capacities. In many cases, weighing in on such matters with confidence will require us to know far more about the neural implementation of our mental capacities than is now understood. Arguments from parsimony are nevertheless compelling when one view attributes states to people not attributed by the other *and where both views otherwise attribute all the same states* (in terms of contents *and* attitudes). I argue in later chapters that my (imaginative-state-free) proposals are more parsimonious in this robust sense in their explanations of pretense and our engagements with fiction. It's not only the case that we can do without a *sui generis* attitude of imagination; those who posit such an attitude must, in addition to that attitude, also posit all the same beliefs, desires, and intentions as I do. (The relevance of parsimony is more difficult to determine in situations where one view posits, say, an additional attitude not posited by the second, while the second view posits more complex contents for certain states than the first.)

Of equal importance to simplicity for a theory's power is its precision. Here more can be said on behalf of eliminating a psychological attitude of imagination. When deciding whether to include an Imagination Box in our ontology, we have to ask whether doing so enables less *noisy* predictive and explanatory generalizations than a corresponding architecture involving only belief, desire, and intention. In the case of belief and desire, we have fairly sturdy *ceteris paribus* theorems that allow us to predict and explain behavior, such as: if someone desires that p and believes that φ-ing will make it the case that p, then she will endeavor to φ, provided she has no stronger countervailing desires. There are exceptions to this sort of generalization—hence the *ceteris paribus*. People have seizures, trip over roots, or are simply too drunk or too tired to φ. These phenomena constitute noise in the pattern picked out by the theorem; yet all sides tend to agree that *ceteris paribus* generalizations remain genuinely explanatory, as they appear in all but the most basic sciences (Dennett, 1991; Fodor, 1987).

We can suppose that there are also theorems, or *ceteris paribus* predictive patterns, involving the term 'imagines.' Those patterns will also be subject to exceptions; they will be noisy. Should it turn out that they are *much more* noisy than patterns we can exploit when redescribing the same behavior in other folk psychological terms, then the replacing terms (i.e., those of the redescription) will have greater explanatory power—they will predict more things correctly, more of the time. Imagination will have been explained in the sense that the considerable noise within explanations involving 'imagines' will have been reduced. From a heavy-duty perspective, such reductions in noise are reasons to think that the psychological attitudes posited by the noise-reducing theory better match reality. From a light-duty perspective, less noisy explanatory patterns are epistemically preferable in allowing for more predictive success, provided they are not much more difficult to exploit (Dennett, 1991).

There is reason to think that the folk psychological theorems that invoke 'imagining' are indeed noisy and subject to exceptions, relative to those involving terms like 'belief' and 'desire.' It is common to encounter proposals about what a person who imagines that p *can* or *may* do; but it is rare to find claims about what they *will* or *must do, ceteris paribus*. For example: it has been said that a person who imagines that p and believes that if p then q will tend to imagine that q; this platitude finds its way into formal characterizations of imagination's role in hypothetical reasoning (Carruthers, 2006; Nichols & Stich, 2000; Van Leeuwen, 2014, p. 795). And yet: we may at any time imagine that p and believe that if p then q, without then imagining that q—and not because we had a seizure, tripped on a root, were distracted, or too drunk. We may fail to imagine that q simply because doing so doesn't fit our goals or interests at the time, or because it never occurred to us to be so realistic in what we were imagining. For instance, I believe that if I arrive to teach unprepared, the class session will be tedious and stressful. And yet, I just imagined that I arrived at class unprepared and had a great, lively discussion. Have I flouted a norm? Hardly. Unrealistic imagining is par for the course; it's part of what makes imagining *imagining*. To say that common sense provides *ceteris paribus* generalizations about the causal or inferential role of imaginings is an overstatement.

Kathleen Stock makes much the same point, noting that:

> There are barely any platitudes about the causal role of the imagination, implicit in ordinary language...unlike other mental entities such as belief and desire, the functional role of imagining is relatively unclear...There is little distinctive behavior associated with either imaginings with particular contents, or imaginings generally...Equally, there seem to be few predictable generalizations connecting imagining to other mental states or events. (2017, p. 4)

Note the difference between Stock's plausible claim there are no platitudes about the *causal role* of imagination, and the false claim that there are no platitudes *whatsoever* about imagination. While there are indeed plenty of platitudes about imagination—many of which were reviewed in Chapter 1—Stock's point is that such platitudes don't coalesce to paint a clear picture of the causal-functional role of an imaginative state. In support she lists several examples where an imaginative state with the content *p* has a causal role in one context quite unlike what it has in another. Her conclusion is that conceptual analysis—which limits itself to facts about a state's causal role known by any competent speaker—will be of limited use in analyzing imagination (2017, p. 5).

Here is a different conclusion we might reasonably draw: we do not, with imagination, have our hands on a single psychological kind (at least, not from a causal-functional point of view),[4] but instead a heterogeneous assortment of different, more basic folk psychological states which *do* have comparatively clean causal roles. Supposing *this* hypothesis is true, our ability to replace imagination-talk with talk of these other kinds of states will greatly improve our predictive and explanatory abilities. This point holds relevance for both heavy- and light-duty views.

[4] Imaginings do retain a *kind* of unity on my view, relative to the two senses of the word "imagine" distinguished in Chapter 1. They are all cases of rich, elaborated, epistemically safe thought about the merely possible, fantastical, and so on (in the case of A-imaginings); and they are all cases of seemingly image-like thought (in the case of I-imaginings). The presence of this kind of unity, in each case, explains why we are tempted to analyze imaginings as a class in the first place. Yet neither is a kind of unity that enables much in the way of behavioral and inferential predictions and explanations, as the characterizations do not suggest a single causal-functional role for either type of imagining.

An alternative, more common, reaction to the kind of heterogeneity Stock observes is to propose a "cleaning up" of the notion of imagination—keying one's predictive generalizations involving 'imagines' to situations where imagination operates in a (supposed) *default mode* (Williamson, 2016, p. 116),[5] or when particular *constraints are applied to it* (Kind, 2016a). That is fair game, but it increases the complexity of one's overall picture. The generalizations and predictive heuristics we employ no longer simply involve the term 'imagines' in its ordinary (not-cleaned-up) sense. So the relevant patterns and generalizations no longer fall naturally out of the platitudes competent speakers will accept about imagination. Making use of them will require explicitly articulating and empirically validating a new, more complex vocabulary for describing human inferential and behavioral dispositions. The resulting theory will no longer have folk psychology's simplicity and implicit validation-through-use on its side. By all means, if new constructs are indeed needed to explain the phenomena, we should get to work in formulating and testing them. But if we can, with equal or better predictive and explanatory success, employ an existing folk psychological vocabulary we already successfully use in other contexts . . . well then that's much better!

Finally, there remains an easily-overlooked challenge worth noting to any heavy-duty account positing a distinct cognitive attitude of imagination. As we saw earlier, the platitudes surrounding imagination do not paint a clear or univocal picture of its causal role. Yet when heavy-duty theorists turn the cognitive attitude of imagination into an explanatory *posit*, they have to give it a fairly precise causal role: it must have the role of causing whatever it is they have called on it to explain. In all likelihood, some of the messiness in the pre-reflective, folk psychological notion of imagination will have been trimmed off. What are we to do with the clippings? We can't sweep them into the trash without a second thought. Cleaning up the concept of imagination, so as to give it a respectable causal role, does not make the shorn behaviors and mental phenomena *disappear*. If, for instance, the psychological attitude of imagination does a great job in explaining highly constrained hypothetical reasoning while leaving fantastical daydreams a mystery, then the psychological attitude of imagination doesn't explain all of what we want explained by a theory of imagination. These gaps must be acknowledged when the theory is compared to others that *do* explain the full set of phenomena—perhaps by finding imagination to be a heterogeneous kind, constituted by a collection of more basic folk psychological states.

[5] "Left to itself, the imagination develops the scenario in a reality-oriented way, by default" (Williamson, 2016, p. 116).

2.8 Summary

When we think of folk psychological states in light-duty terms, we see them as sets of mental and behavioral dispositions whose causal bases we know not. Working from the philosopher's armchair, we needn't be bashful about our knowledge of folk psychological states *so conceived*. We want to be discussing imagination itself, not just the concepts surrounding imagination, after all. The light-duty view shows how this can be done, without our proposing to limn the structure of the mind in the process. If it turns out that the generalizations and patterns associated with imagination-talk are a mess, and even self-contradictory, we have good reason to seek other ways of attributing the same dispositions and capacities with better-behaved, more basic folk psychological terms. But even if we think imaginings are a well-behaved folk psychological kind, we can still arrive at an explanation of imagination by seeing how behaviors and cognitive capacities associated with imagination-talk can be alternatively described and cataloged through the use of other familiar mental state terms. Such an explanation is all the more powerful if the patterns and generalizations invoked are less noisy and have greater predictive precision than those featuring 'imagines.'

The light-duty view's conservativeness about mental ontology also facilitates a kind of explanatory pluralism. Our ability to articulate questions about imagination's relation to other states in light-duty terms allows us to pitch present debates in a relatively theory-neutral way. Cognitive boxologies can be rejected as wrongheaded by one party, for instance, while the question of imagination's relation to—and possible reducibility to—other folk psychological states remains a shared theoretical question.

The heavy-duty approach, by contrast, pronounces on the contents of certain mental representations realized in the brain—namely, those that explain our having of the dispositions ascribed by folk psychological talk—and the psychological attitudes taken toward them. And, at times, it appeals to surprising empirical results in support of doing so. Yet the heavy-duty theorist can also argue against imagination's reducibility to (or explainability in terms of) other folk psychological states in just the same way as the light-duty theorist. If it turns out that we cannot capture the behavioral patterns and dispositions associated with imagination-talk in more basic folk psychological terms, the light-duty theorist concludes that imagination is a *sui generis* folk psychological mental phenomenon; the heavy-duty theorist concurs but goes further in holding that we have defeasible evidence for the existence of a distinct psychological attitude of imagination—an "Imagination Box."

On the other hand, if the arguments in later chapters succeed, then we can indeed replace imagination-talk with talk of beliefs, desires, and intentions. This will be reason to think there is no such psychological attitude (or DCA) as the heavy-duty theorist proposes. Imagination would not thereby be *eliminated*. Rather, a particular theoretical construct that sometimes goes by the name of 'imagination'—one that only occurs with certain heavy-duty ontologies—would be eliminated. Imagination, as a folk psychological phenomenon, would persist. On a light-duty ontology, nothing at all gets eliminated if my arguments in later chapters succeed. Instead, we come to see that the notions of belief, desire, and intention can serve in explanations of what it is to imagine.

3
Imagistic Imagining Part I
Imagery, Attitude Imagining, and Recreative Imagining

3.1 Introduction

In Chapter 1 I introduced a distinction between two senses of 'imagine': imagistic imagining ("I-imagining") and attitude imagining ("A-imagining"). That distinction is a foundational piece of this book's larger framework for explaining imagination. The characterizations I've so far offered of each leave it open whether and to what degree they pick out the same set of mental states and processes. Earlier I simply stated my view on the matter: A-imagining and I-imagining share instances, yet neither's instances are a sub-set of the other's. Some, but not all, I-imaginings are also A-imaginings; and some, but not all A-imaginings are also I-imaginings. This suggests that we can't expect an explanation of one to be a full explanation of the other. Yet neither can we pursue entirely independent explanations of each; our account of one must be answerable to the constraints imposed by our account of the other.

It is not in itself a radical proposal that only *some* uses of mental imagery constitute cases of imagining in the A-imagining sense—at least, not insofar as my conception of A-imagining meshes with other conceptions of attitude imagining in the literature.[1] But it's important to see what arguments can be made in defense of the claim, as it presents a direct challenge to at least one other influential proposal for what constitutes the broadest classes of imaginings. This is the idea that there is a class of "recreative" (Currie & Ravenscroft, 2002) or "enactive" imaginings (Goldman, 2006a) whose nature it is to "recreate," "simulate," or "stand-in" for some other, non-imaginative type of mental state. Within this class, there are sometimes said to be many different imaginative "counterpart" states that serve to simulate or recreate a wide variety of non-imaginative mental states (Arcangeli, 2018). Were there such a broad class of imaginings, both A-imaginings and I-imaginings would fall within it as sub-types. The notion therefore assumes a kind of unity to A- and I-imaginings that I reject. Influential though it is, the idea that imaginings are, in the broadest sense, "recreations" or "simulations" of

[1] Cf. Nanay (2016): "Propositional imagination can, of course, also involve the exercise of mental imagery, so these two categories are not meant to be exclusive" (p. 132, fn.1). See also Van Leeuwen (2013), Kind (2001), Williamson (2016), and Gaut (2003).

Explaining Imagination. Peter Langland-Hassan, Oxford University Press (2020). © Peter Langland-Hassan.
DOI: 10.1093/oso/9780198815068.001.0001

other kinds of mental states presents an impediment to understanding and explaining imagination. Or so I will argue here—most pointedly in section 3.7.

The first matter of business, however, is to explain in more detail the distinction between A-imagining and I-imagining that I briefly introduced in Chapter 1, and to argue that the extension of each notion only partially overlaps with that of the other.

3.2 Imagistic Imaginings and the Nature of Mental Imagery

Imagistic imaginings (or "I-imaginings") are cases of thought that involve mental imagery as a proper part. Mental imagery, at a first pass, is a kind of mental state that seems, to the person having it, to involve image-like mental states, or states that have sensory character, and where such states arise not from an external stimulus impinging on a sense organ but from endogenous causes of some kind. As earlier remarked, *The Oxford English Dictionary* also links imagining to mental imagery in its first definition of 'imagine,' which is, "To form a mental image of...to picture to oneself (something not present to the senses)" (*Oxford English Dictionary*, 2009). Imagistic imagining, and the mental imagery it involves, occurs when we describe ourselves as visualizing, or as having a mental image, or as "seeing an image with the mind's eye." It also occurs within other sense modalities, when we sing a song silently to ourselves, or imagine the smell of roses. To say that someone has made use of a mental image in thought may seem to involve a substantive, "heavy-duty" (see Chapter 2) claim about the nature and format of the mental representations in the person's mind—one that goes beyond common sense and folk psychological platitudes. But it need not. It can remain an open question how we are to understand the nature of the (seemingly) picture-like (or sensory-experience-like) mental states that we pick out in this intuitive, first-personal way, and from which flow various platitudes about mental pictures and the mind's eye. While there is a long debate in philosophy and psychology—viz., the *imagery debate* (Block, 1981; Tye, 1991; Pearson & Kosslyn, 2015)—concerning the representational format of states underlying mental imagery, there is no similar debate about whether there is a phenomenon of people having mental states that seem to them to be image-like. It is the underlying nature of this phenomenon that's at issue in the imagery debate.

I-imagining, as I have characterized it, is similar but not equivalent to what some others refer to as "sensory imagining" (Kung, 2010), "perceptual imagining" (Currie & Ravenscroft, 2002), and, indeed, "imagistic imagining" (Van Leeuwen, 2013). Each of these terms is used to mark a form of thought that features mental images essentially—images keyed to some sense modality or other. Where my notion of I-imagining perhaps stands out is in explicitly including *all* (apparently) image-involving thought within its extension (though this fits with

Van Leeuwen's (2013) understanding of "imagistic imagining"). It is not always clear if others who invoke a notion of "sensory," "perceptual," or "imagistic" imagining mean to include only *some* image-involving thought within the class, or all.[2] I choose the term 'imagistic imagining' over these other terms in order to highlight the idea that, when theorizing about imagining in this sense, we are focused on the apparent imagistic format of the mental states, as opposed to any particular *use* or *functions* to which the mental states might be put, and as opposed to any different "attitudes" we might take toward states involving such imagery. It is within one's right to hold that, in addition to this "format sense" of imagistic imagining, there is a distinct "attitude sense" of imagistic imagining, where "imagistic imagining" in the attitude sense marks a distinctive kind of mental-image-involving *process* (Arcangeli, 2019). In my terms, this would be to say that there are A-imaginings that both involve mental imagery and constitute a *sui generis* mental process, mode, or attitude—one that is irreducible to collections of judgments, memories, desires, decisions, and so on. My argument—occurring over the course of this book—is that we needn't countenance such a process or attitude; all image-involving A-imaginings can be identified with a more basic collection of (image-involving) folk psychological attitudes, such as beliefs, desires, and intentions.

3.2.1 Defining 'Mental Imagery'

Despite its ambition for neutrality, my first-pass characterization of mental imagery has controversial implications we should explore. First, if it is a requirement on mental imagery that it *seems* a certain way to the person having it (namely, to be image-like, or to involve sensory character), then there can no mental imagery that a person is not conscious of—no imagery that seems no way at all to the person having it. While that may be a happy conclusion for those who view imagining as an essentially conscious phenomenon, others will—rightly, I think—object that there can be unconscious episodes of mental imagery, just as there can be unconscious perception (Nanay, 2010, 2018b). It would, in any case, be question-begging to rule out the possibility of mental imagery we are not conscious of in our very definition of the phenomenon. Second, if a thought-episode's *seeming* to be image-like, or *seeming* to have sensory character, were sufficient for

[2] Currie & Ravenscroft (2002, p. 27) are clear that all image-involving thought qualifies as perceptual imagining, in their sense, while Van Leeuwen (2013) is similarly clear that the use of mental imagery in thought is both necessary and sufficient for an I-imagining, in his sense. Amy Kind (2001), however, finds imagery to be necessary but not sufficient for imagining—and holds, further, that all relevant forms of imagining involve imagery. Others who invoke the notion perceptual or sensory imagining—including Noordhof (2002), Martin (2002), Peacocke (1985), and Byrne (2007)—leave it ambiguous whether it is to include all (apparently) image-involving thought or only some.

its really being a case of mental imagery, then any type of thought episode at all (image-like, or not) could be a case of mental imagery, provided the person having it was convinced that it was image-like, or had sensory character. We should avoid in our definition of 'mental imagery' any suggestion that we might transform a phenomenon into mental imagery simply by judging it to be image-like.

Bence Nanay (2018b) offers a definition of mental imagery that avoids these problems; he also claims that it meshes better with the way mental imagery is understood by psychologists and neuroscientists. (He has in mind researchers such as Pearson & Westbrook (2015) and Kosslyn, Behrmann, & Jeannerod (1995).) Mental imagery, on Nanay's view, is "perceptual processing that is not triggered by corresponding sensory stimulation in a given sense modality" (2018b, p. 127). This definition avoids the kind of reliance on subjective impressions that proves problematic on my account. There is no requirement that perceptual processing of a relevant sort must seem a certain way to the person having it; and there is no suggestion that people will be infallible judges of when such perceptual processing occurs. Neuroimaging, and even single-cell recordings, can provide independent evidence of when mental imagery has been triggered, provided that the relevant areas for perceptual processing have been identified. Nanay respects the intuition that, unlike perception, mental imagery is causally independent of an outside stimulus by holding that it is "not triggered by corresponding sensory stimulation." Finally, and importantly, his definition is also neutral on the question of the representational format of imagery—be it pictorial, language-like, or something else.[3] His definition simply suggests that we should understand the format of mental imagery in whatever way we understand the format of perceptual processing generally.

Why not go with Nanay's characterization, defining I-imagining as the use of mental imagery in his sense? My main concern is that it is too broad. We shouldn't assume that all perceptual processing that is not triggered by corresponding sensory stimulation in a given sense modality forms a natural kind. There may be important differences among instances of such processing that speak against lumping them together as "mental imagery." The fact that some mental imagery is under agential control, and thus suitable to serve in cases of stimulus-independent thought, while others, on Nanay's (2018a) view, occur as an ordinary aspect of perception, would be one *prima facie* reason. Further, there may be instances of mental imagery, in Nanay's sense, that have little or nothing to do with mental imagery (and I-imagining) as it is conceived by common sense—viz., as episodes

[3] Nanay highlights the importance of *retinopy*—the fact that human visual cortex is organized in ways that mirror the structure of the retina (Grill-Spector & Malach, 2004)—to understanding perceptual processing and mental imagery (Nanay, 2018b, p. 127). Whether or not retinopy warrants thinking of the format of perceptual processing as *pictorial*, *iconic*, or *analog* in nature is an interesting question that I must leave for another occasion.

of visualizing and "seeing with the mind's eye." Evidence linking *some* cases of perceptual processing not triggered by corresponding sensory stimulation to subjective reports of visualization and "seeing with the mind's eye"—as we find, e.g., in Kosslyn et al. (1999) and Slotnick, Thompson, & Kosslyn (2005)—is not strong evidence that all cases of one are cases of the other. There is, indeed, considerable empirical evidence that the neural regions supporting visual perception overlap only partially with those activated when people describe themselves as having visual imagery (see Brogaard & Gatzia (2017) for a review).

Here Nanay could respond that he and the cognitive scientists he cites are not concerned with preserving the commonsense understanding of mental imagery; they are doing science, not lexicography. So they can pursue their investigation with whichever conception seems theoretically most fruitful. That is fair enough, but there are limits. The scientific investigation of mental imagery, still in its early stages, cannot turn its back completely on the commonsense notion of "images in the mind's eye" that gave rise to it. The parent phenomenon—recorded in the *OED*—of mental states that seem image-like to the people having them, and that occur without an outside stimulus, still has partial custody. To discover mental imagery's place in the brain, one hand must be kept on this initial characterization, the other on where the science leads—else we risk changing the topic.

We these points in mind, I propose a Kripkean (Kripke, 1980) compromise between my and Nanay's account. The features highlighted in my definition of mental imagery—its seeming image-like to the people having it, and so on—can be seen as properties of mental imagery by which we *fix the reference* of the term 'mental image'; but we needn't assume they are essential properties. Compare the familiar Krikean story about water and H_2O: we start with an idea of water as the predominant clear, drinkable liquid in lakes, rivers, oceans, and so on; this understanding allows us to fix the reference of the term 'water.' Subsequent scientific investigation reveals water to have a certain chemical composition, H_2O. Chemistry then gives us good reason to think of H_2O as a natural kind. With water reconceived as a natural kind, we can see how there can be instances of water—of H_2O—that don't have the properties by which we initially fixed the reference of the term; and we can see how there can be instances of things other than water that do have those properties (Putnam, 1975).

Here is a revised definition of mental imagery that brings these thoughts together:

Mental imagery: the kind (or kinds) of mental state or process that, when people are aware of having it and reflect on its nature, is typically described as image-like, or as having sensory character, while not being caused by an outside stimulus.

This characterization still links mental imagery to the way it seems to us, introspectively, while not requiring *all* episodes of mental imagery to be introspectively apprehended. It simply holds that, when it is introspectively discerned and described, mental imagery is *typically* characterized as being image-like, or as having sensory character. These are the characteristics by which the reference of 'mental imagery' is fixed. Yet they ensure that, if there happens to be a kind of perceptual processing that is never or rarely described by people as being image-like, or as having sensory character, then it is not mental imagery. For that's not the kind of thing we were ever referring to with the term 'mental imagery.' The definition is also compatible with other kinds of endogenously-caused mental states that are not mental imagery being described as image-like, or as having sensory character, so long as they are not *typically* described that way.

The question of whether there is a kind of perceptual processing that is not triggered by corresponding sensory stimulation *and* that is never or rarely described as image-like by the people having it cannot be answered without an established scientific means for typing different kinds of perceptual processing (nor without relevant empirical investigations). Nanay may think that neuroscience already offers that means and that there simply is no kind of endogenously-produced perceptual processing that is distinct from the kind whose instances are typically described as image like, or as having sensory character, when their possessors are aware of them. I am skeptical that current science warrants that confidence (see, again, Brogaard & Gatzia (2017)), but I don't pretend to have established the point. Instead I propose to move forward with my amended "reference-fixing" definition of mental imagery, noting that it is compatible with Nanay's deeper account being correct in the end.

A last important point: thinking is not the same thing as perceiving. Thought is stimulus-independent in a way that perception is not (Beck, 2018). When I define imagistic imagining as any kind of *thought* that involves mental imagery, I am excluding from the class of imagistic imaginings any case of perception that involves mental imagery. On some views, mental imagery forms an essential ingredient to ordinary perception (Grush, 2004; Nanay, 2010, 2018a). Even if those views are correct, such perceptual experiences will not be cases of imagistic imagining, because they are not cases of stimulus-independent thought (or of "cognition"). The reasons for distinguishing imagistic imagining from these other mental-imagery-involving episodes are the same reasons we have for distinguishing thought from perception.

3.3 Attitude Imaginings—Keeping the Definition Neutral

Attitude imaginings (or "A-imaginings") are, again, cases of rich, elaborated, epistemically safe thought about the possible, pretended, unreal, and so on. A-imaginings enable us to consider what could have been or may yet be—to contemplate the fictive and fantastical. As we saw in Chapter 1, the *Oxford English*

Dictionary gives several definitions for 'imagine' that mesh well with this conception. Recall senses 2, 3, and 4, in particular:

imagine: . . .
2. To create as a mental conception, to conceive; to assume, suppose . . .
3. To conceive in the mind as a thing to be performed; to devise, plot, plan, compass . . .
4. To consider, ponder, meditate . . . (*Oxford English Dictionary*, 2009)

Both my characterization and these of the *OED* leave A-imagining's relationship to mental imagery unresolved. My notion of A-imagining is, I think, similar in spirit to what other philosophers have discussed under the heading of propositional imagination (Nichols, 2006c; Nichols & Stich, 2000), belief-like imagining (Currie & Ravenscroft, 2002), or, indeed, "attitude imagining" (Van Leeuwen, 2013, pp. 223–4) and "attitudinal imagining" (Kind, 2016b, p. 5). The important difference is that A-imagining, as the *OED* and I characterize it, is relatively theory-neutral. Many who speak of "propositional" or "belief-like" imaginings tie them—either implicitly or explicitly—to "heavy-duty" (see Chapter 2) ontological or theoretical commitments of one kind or another. Such imaginings are, for instance, held to occur "in the same code" as beliefs (Nichols, 2004a), to have the "same logical form" as beliefs (e.g., Nichols & Stich, 2003; Currie & Ravenscroft, 2002; Schroeder & Matheson, 2006; Carruthers, 2006), or to be non-imagistic in nature (Currie & Ravenscroft, 2002).[4] Others invoke the theoretical notion of a *cognitive attitude* in their most basic characterizations of the phenomenon (Van Leeuwen, 2013; Kind, 2016b). For instance, Van Leeuwen, whose "attitude imagining" term I share, holds that attitude imaginings occur when someone "takes a cognitive attitude toward [the proposition] *c* that nevertheless treats *c* as somehow fictional" (2013, p. 221). The level of ontological commitment is ambiguous in this kind of characterization. If taking a cognitive attitude toward *p* requires one to token a mental representation with the content *p*, then—as we saw in Chapter 2—such a definition of attitude imagining is not open to theorists with a light-duty folk psychological ontology.[5] On light-duty views, there are no

[4] That Nichols & Stich view propositional imaginings as not involving mental imagery can be inferred from the fact that they analyze belief and propositional imagining as involving the processing of propositionally structured representations, and "are skeptical that perceptual states can be entirely captured by representational accounts" (2003, p. 164). Mental images are likely "perceptual states" in the relevant sense and thus, for Nichols & Stich, unlikely to be "in the same code" as beliefs and propositional imaginings. However, this involves some extrapolation from their explicit remarks, as they are generally silent on the role of mental imagery in imagination.

[5] It appears that Van Leeuwen favors a heavy-duty interpretation of this characterization. He later summarizes attitude imaginings as cases where one's "cognitive system represents *c*, through taking it to be non-real"; this implies the existence of mental representations with a specific content (2013, p. 224).

mental representations whose contents mirror the contents of the that-clauses that occur in ordinary folk psychological ascriptions. And, yet, a light-duty theorist—including dispositionalists about folk psychological kinds (Dennett, 1991; Schwitzgebel, 2002, 2013)—will not deny that people imagine that *p* any more than they will deny that people believe that *p*. So we need a way of picking out the phenomenon we want to study—the phenomenon of imagining that *p*—that does not force anyone into eliminativism from the outset.

If, on the other hand, taking a cognitive attitude toward *p*—one that treats *p* as "somehow fictional"—does not, by definition, require one to token a mental representation with the content *p*, then the characterization is simply not as clear as it could be. What is it, exactly, to treat a proposition as somehow fictional? We do not need a *deep* answer at the outset. But we need to hear more. We need something along the lines of my characterization of A-imagining—something that will give us a better idea of just what processes we aim to explore, while leaving it uncontroversial that they occur at all. Kind (2016b) goes some distance toward meeting this demand, by characterizing attitudinal imaginings as having a "mind-to-world direction of fit," where the relevant world is "best understood to be a make-believe or fictional world rather than the actual world" (p. 5). The trouble here is that the characterization employs a combination of theoretical notions—"direction of fit" and "fictional world"—that are no clearer than what they are called on to explain. It requires us to understand what it is to fit, or fail to fit, a non-existent fictional world, before we can understand what it is to imagine. In cases where we imagine in response to an independently existing fiction—*Moby Dick*, say—it may seem we have a reasonably clear picture of what it would be for the imagining to "fit" what is true in that fictional world (though this question itself generates heated debate, as we will see in Chapters 9 and 10).[6] However, many paradigmatic imaginings—including daydreams, fantasies, cases of conditional reasoning, and creative cognition—lack any corresponding fictional world that the imagining can be said to faithfully, or unfaithfully, represent. For instance: I am now imagining that my office is covered in tinfoil and that unicorns live on the dark side of the moon. It is hard to grasp what it might be for these imaginings to fit, or *fail to fit*, a fictional world. In relation to which fictional world are we to assess their accuracy? Can such imaginings *be* inaccurate? How? And if there are no conceivable conditions under which they would be inaccurate, how can

[6] Relatedly, it is common to analyze truth-in-a-fiction by appeal to what the fiction (or its author) prescribes one to imagine in response to the fiction (Currie, 1990; Stock, 2017; Walton, 1990). If those accounts are correct, we cannot know what is true in a fiction until we know what we are prescribed to imagine; and, plausibly, we cannot know what we are prescribed to imagine if we don't yet know what it *is* to imagine. So, for those who define truth-in-a-fiction by appeal to prescriptions to imagine, there can be no elucidation of imagination by appeal to its fitting, or not fitting, what is the case in a fictional world. Our grasp of what is true in any fictional world—and hence of whether an imagining fits those truths—will have depended on a prior grasp of what it is to imagine.

they be defined in terms of accuracy conditions? Perhaps there are answers here.[7] But we shouldn't need those answers before we can know what we're talking about when we talk about imagining (in the attitude sense).

What we need is a characterization that our next-door neighbor can understand—one that, like the *OED*, captures what competent speakers take imagining to be when they use 'imagining' in the attitude sense. The key is to avoid technical terms like "proposition," "attitude," "possible world," and "direction of fit." For one thing, most people don't grasp those notions, despite being competent users of the term 'imagine.' For another, they are all theoretical notions within philosophy; once they are invoked, the explanation of A-imagining has already begun. As philosophers, we feel that we are moving toward an explanation of imagination precisely because imagination is being brought into the fold of other mental states whose theoretical definitions partake in the same notions. The problem is that attempted explanations-cum-characterizations of this sort foreclose *other* explanations that are worth considering. So, if possible, we should avoid such terms in the most basic characterization of what it is to imagine.

A-imagining, I have held, is rich or elaborated thought about the possible, fictive, unreal, and so on, that is, in general, epistemically safe. With the exception of "epistemically safe," this is something our neighbors can understand. (We can remove "epistemically safe" for them by saying that A-imagining is engaging in rich, elaborated thought about the possible, fictional, unreal, and so on, that does not call one's sanity, knowledge, or reasonableness into question.) I recommend this characterization as a neutral starting point for theorizing about imagining in the attitude sense. Importantly, it leaves open the role of mental imagery in such imaginings. And it makes no comment on the relation of concepts, propositions, modules, modes, possible worlds, attitudes, directions of fit, and other theoretical notions to A-imagining. Yet it remains substantive enough to give us a sense of when imagining occurs in everyday life and when it does not. Further, it leaves the existence of A-imagining uncontroversial among theorists with divergent folk psychological ontologies. No one is driven to eliminativism from the outset.

While this understanding of A-imagining may seem overly broad in what it counts as imagining, its breadth is a virtue. It allows us to see why so many different cognitive acts in so many different contexts come to be called 'imagining' in the first place; and it offers a plausible picture of why generalizations about imagining are so messy and subject to exception (see Chapter 2). There is no

[7] Alon Chasid (2017) has proposed to understand facts about fictional worlds in terms of a distinct mental state—what he calls "design-assumptions." On his view, one's design assumptions guarantee that thus and such is true in a fictional world, and then one's imaginings can be said to be fit, or fail to fit, the fictional world to the extent that they cohere with one's own design assumptions. Yet this appears to leave us with the same question we were trying to answer; for we now need an account of design assumptions and *their* "direction of fit." So it is not clear that the proposal moves us forward. Alternatively, if design assumptions can be characterized without appeal to a direction of fit, then perhaps imaginings can as well.

prima facie reason to think that all instances of epistemically safe, elaborated thought about the possible, fictional, and unreal would share enough similarities to enable law-like generalizations about imaginings *as a kind*. We should expect them to be a heterogeneous group. Finally, there is no need to worry that imagination—the *real* imagination—will slip through our fingers when we begin with a broad definition of this sort. As earlier noted, by focusing on explaining the cognition at work in paradigmatic contexts where A-imagining occurs—including pretense, conditional reasoning, and consuming and creating fictions—we can ensure that any (putative) narrower class of imaginings *proper* is not overlooked.

3.4 The Relationship between A- and I-imagining

We can now turn in earnest to consider the relation of I-imaginings to A-imaginings. Two central questions we can ask are:

1. Do all A-imaginings involve mental imagery, and so qualify as I-imaginings? And,
2. Do all cases of I-imagining amount to rich, or elaborated, epistemically safe thought about the merely possible, fantastical, and so on—and so qualify as A-imagining?

My answer to both questions will be no: there are A-imaginings that involve no mental imagery; and there is I-imagining that is not A-imagining. There is, however, overlap between the two. Fig. 3.1 maps this relation, with the left oval representing I-imagining, and the right oval representing A-imagining. To some, this map of the terrain will seem immediately right; to others, it will appear question-begging or false. It is important to carefully consider the reasons for and against mapping the terrain in this way and to ask whether there are important phenomena it obscures or fails to address.

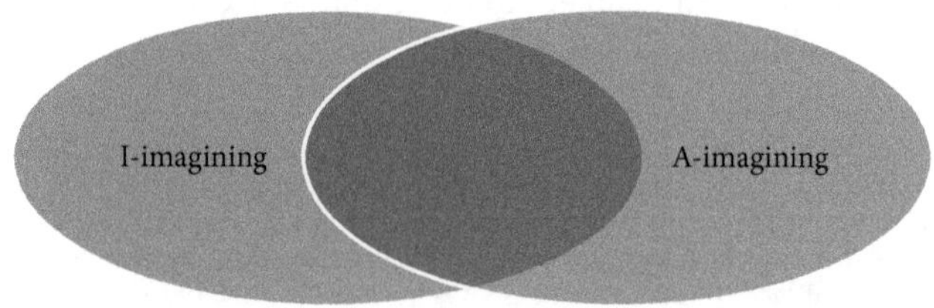

Fig. 3.1 The relationship of imagistic imagining to attitude imagining

3.5 A-imagining without I-imagining

It is common in philosophy to allow for imaginings that lack mental imagery, even if the practice has its dissenters (Kind, 2001). Timothy Williamson warns that, even if many cases of imagination involve mental imagery, "We should not over-generalize to the conclusion that all imagining involves imagery" (2016, p. 117). And many of the philosophers who theorize about a capacity for "propositional" or "attitudinal" imagination hold that it does not (or at least need not) involve mental imagery (Doggett & Egan, 2007; Nichols & Stick, 2003; Van Leeuwen, 2014; Nichols, 2004; Goldman, 2006a). An open question for such conceptions of imagination is how (and whether) to distinguish these non-imagistic imaginings from related acts like supposing, conceiving, and hypothesizing (see, e.g., Weinberg & Meskin (2006b), Stock (2017, Ch. 6), and Arcangeli (2018) for discussion).

The idea that there is a non-imagistic form of imagining is sometimes tied to the occurrence of that-clauses in sentences used to ascribe imaginings. Witness Alvin Goldman's characterization of "S-imagination" (where "S" is for "supposition"):

> S-imagination is typically formulated with a 'that'-clause, 'X imagines that *p*', where *p* can refer, urestrictedly, to any sort of state-of-affairs. To S-imagine that *p* is to entertain the hypothesis that *p*, to posit that *p*, to assume that *p*. Unlike some forms of imagination, S-imagination has no sensory aspect; it is purely conceptual. (Goldman, 2006a, pp. 41–2)

Taken as an *argument* for the existence of non-imagistic imaginings, Goldman's claim is question-begging. Certainly, we at times use the verb 'imagining,' followed by a that-clause, when describing people as imagining. But it is not obvious that, when we do so, such people are in psychological states that have "no sensory aspect." If, in ordinary conversation, I say that Jim is imagining that he is skiing in the Alps, it would be strange to add: "And, of course, his doing so involves no state with a sensory aspect." It is only in the context of a specific heavy-duty folk psychological ontology, wherein ascriptions of folk psychological states involving that-clauses are made true by corresponding amodal, language-like ("conceptual") representations, that we can (arguably) move from the truth of such an ascription to the conclusion the corresponding mental state lacks any sensory aspect. Such assumptions have no place at this stage in the dialectic. If we want to establish the existence of some imaginings—some A-imaginings—that don't involve mental imagery, we need to do so in a more theoretically-neutral manner. As it turns out, this is not so easily done. Nevertheless, I think the balance of considerations tips in favor of there being non-imagistic A-imaginings. I'll sketch two arguments to that end.

The first takes it as a premise that A-imaginings are the mental events we rely upon to guide our pretenses. Consider two children pretending to have a tea party. Jamie pretends to set out plates while Sophia pretends to fold napkins. We are apt to describe them as imagining that they are setting up for a tea party, before we give any consideration to whether they are making use of mental imagery. They certainly *might* form mental images while pretending; they might even attempt to imitate what they "see" in their mind's eye (as suggested by Van Leeuwen (2011)). But they might also simply draw upon their declarative knowledge of what typically goes on at tea parties to act in at-tea-party-like ways. After all, if we just *asked* the children what sort of things go on at tea parties, they would be able to answer. On the face of it, they could do so without forming any mental images. If a pretense *could* at times unfold with only that sort of information being exploited, we have reason to think that not all A-imaginings make use of mental imagery.

A critic might respond that, despite appearances, mental imagery is in fact essential to all such pretenses. But it is hard to see why this would be the case. The use of mental imagery in the guidance of action does not suffice to render the action pretense—as evidenced by the role of imagery in decisions about how to climb a wall, decorate a room, or craft a tool (Arp, 2008). It is unclear, then, why using mental imagery would be *necessary* to pretense, short of a robust neo-empiricism, where mental imagery is essential to action and inference more generally. At that point, the debate no longer concerns the special relevance of mental imagery to A-imagining, but rather to action and cognition in general.

Another critic might object that the case of A-imagining without imagery I described (and others like it) are really just cases of supposition—and not any form of imagination. However, my definition of A-imagining is intended to include supposition within it. Like the *OED* (definition 2), I don't assume any deep differences between supposing and (at least some instances of) A-imagining. Some A-imaginings that lack mental imagery may be richer, or more developed, or more cognitively engaging than others. These differences, occurring along a spectrum, may track an intuitive difference between non-imagistic A-imagining and (mere) supposition. But this is compatible with them all being cases of A-imagining. On my view, supposition, like imagination, will reduce to a more basic collection of other folk psychological states. So, when we reduce A-imagining to beliefs, judgments, desires, decisions, and so on, we will have done the same for supposition.[8]

A second argument for allowing A-imaginings without mental imagery is that we engage in A-imaginings about unobservable entities—such as the theoretical posits of physics, or legal and moral principles—that, presumably, cannot be

[8] Supposition is particularly important to conditional reasoning. Chapters 5 and 6 focus on conditional reasoning and confront the challenge of reducing supposition to other folk psychological states.

represented through the use of mental imagery. For instance, a lawyer might ask a judge to imagine the absurd lawsuits that would follow from setting a precedent that may seem acceptable in a single instance. It is not clear that the judge would need to generate mental imagery in order to comply. Or perhaps a mathematician may imagine different ways of solving an equation without using imagery; similarly, a philosopher may imagine an objection to her argument without forming any mental images. Van Leeuwen makes the same point by appeal to temporal properties: "When I imagine, on reading *Lord of the Rings*, that elves can live forever, I'm fictionally imagining a proposition that I couldn't imagine using mental imagery" (Van Leeuwen 2013, p. 222).

It might be responded that, even in these cases, we imagine the putatively unobservable entities by generating imagery of observable models of those entities—written numerals, people acting out contractual obligations, a printed list of premises and conclusions, ancient-looking elves, and so on. For it is one thing to show that imagery cannot contribute all the contents to an A-imagining; it is another to establish that it provides none of them. Yet here, again, the question seems headed toward a more general dispute about the role of mental imagery in all of cognition. Why expect imagery to be featured in each of these contexts where we describe people as imagining, if it is not in general necessary for the generation of complex thoughts?

Kind (2001), perhaps the most prominent advocate of the view that any cognition worthy of the name "imagining" must involve mental imagery, defends the thesis on the grounds that "no matter what I imagine, my imagining will involve an experiential aspect," and that "without such an experiential aspect, a mental exercise is not an act of imagining" (p. 94). Mental images, she argues, are what account for this experiential aspect. Yet she offers no reason to doubt the claims of others who are happy to allow for imaginings that lack such an experiential aspect; nor, to my knowledge, does she seriously question the kinds of examples raised in their favor. We have, at best, a stalemate.

Fortunately, should it turn out that there are no non-imagistic A-imaginings, we will only have explained *more* than we needed to when we explain A-imagining as I conceive of it. On the other hand, we risk omitting relevant phenomena from our explanation of imagination if we assume that there are no non-imagistic A-imaginings. So I propose to move forward with the working assumption that there are indeed non-imagistic A-imaginings.

The same form of response can be given to those who grant the existence non-imagistic A-imaginings but worry that the notion of A-imagining (as I define it) still pulls in other states—such as supposings, or conceivings—that should be distinguished from (non-imagistic) imagining proper (see, e.g., Arcangeli, 2018). My characterization of A-imagining goes some distance toward accommodating the intuitions that lead some to distinguish imagining from supposing and conceiving, insofar as A-imagining is an especially "rich" and "elaborated" way of dwelling on the possible, fantastical, unreal, and so on (whereas supposing and conceiving may be less involved). But some may think there is a difference in kind between supposition and A-imagining that is missed by trying to see one as a more elaborated version of the other. In favor of maintaining a hard distinction between the two, it is sometimes held that, while we can easily suppose flat contradictions, we cannot imagine them (Kind, 2013; Weinberg & Meskin, 2006b). This seems to point to something more than a difference in degree. Similarly, it might be proposed that, while imaginings tend to trigger emotions, suppositions as a class do not (Kind, 2013, p. 153).

In response, it is not clear to me that we really can suppose obvious contradictions. If someone asks me to suppose that all squares have fifty-two sides, I won't know what to do. Sure, we are told, in logic class, that *everything* follows from a contradiction. We know how to write out proofs where a contradiction appears on one line. But, psychologically speaking, what is it to suppose a contradiction? How can we know when we've done so? I'm really not sure. (NB I address the phenomenon of supposing/imagining for the sake of *reductio ad absurdum* separately in Chapter 7, on hypothetical reasoning.)

But, fine, let's suppose, for the sake of argument, that we really can suppose contradictions. How do these authors know that, when they suppose a contradiction, they aren't also imagining it? Likewise, when they suppose a proposition and register no emotional response, how do they know that they didn't also imagine it? Is it that they can *just tell*, introspectively, which state is which? If that is the answer, then whatever feature it is that allows them to confirm, introspectively, that their supposings are one thing, and their imaginings another, is what *really* underwrites the distinction between the two. If that feature is mental imagery (or the lack thereof) that makes the difference—with imagining always featuring imagery—then we are back to the question of whether there can be A-imagining without mental imagery. If it is not mental imagery that allows one to introspectively descrimiate imaginings from supposings... well then what is it?

3.6 I-imagining without A-imagining

Let's return now to the second question above: are all mental episodes that involve mental imagery, and which are therefore I-imaginings, also cases of A-imagining? One reason to think not is that mental imagery is a prominent feature of ordinary episodic memory (Addis, Pan, Vu, Laiser, & Schacter, 2009; Schacter & Addis, 2007). Episodic memories are memories of specific events from one's personal past. Episodically remember this morning's breakfast and you will likely generate a mental image. Did you *imagine* your breakfast? In one sense—the I-imagining sense—yes, you formed a mental image of something. In another sense—the A-imagining sense—it seems not. In recalling your breakfast, you did not engage in especially rich, elaborated, thought about the possible, fantastical, or unreal. You just remembered your Cheerios.[9] Berys Gaut makes a similar observation in distinguishing (mere) imagery-involving states from imagining in something like the A-imagining sense:

> Imagery is a matter of the having of sensory presentations; but these images need not be instances of imagination. A memory image of the blue front door of my previous house involves a belief about that front door, not an imagining of it (2003, p. 272)

Van Leeuwen concurs:

> Imagery is involved in many beliefs, possibly as a constituent of a larger structure, which the agent takes to represent reality... This often happens with vivid memories. (2013, p. 222)

So, many find it natural to conceive of episodic memories both as image-involving *and* as constituting (many of) our beliefs about our personal pasts. This meshes with the fact that, when we lose the ability to generate imagery, we lose most of our beliefs about our past experiences; that is, we acquire amnesia (Greenberg, Eacott, Brechin, & Rubin, 2005; Rubin & Greenberg, 1998). These I-imaginings—the loss of which causes us to lose many of our most important beliefs—are not good candidates for A-imaginings. Instead of considering elaborate possibilities, fictions, and unrealities in an epistemically safe way, we trigger basic commitments about our own personal pasts.

Nevertheless there remain strong currents of resistance to the idea that mental imagery can have a role within beliefs or "commitments" themselves, even among philosophers who emphasize the importance of imagistic states to human reasoning in general. An attractive view to some will be that we form beliefs about our personal pasts *on the basis of* imagistic episodic rememberings, without those imagistic episodes themselves being beliefs. They may propose, by analogy, that we form beliefs about our current environment on the basis of our perceptual experiences, without our perceptual experiences themselves being beliefs. This view leaves the door open to thinking of all I-imagining—episodic memory included—as, in some sense, flying free of what we believe, and, instead, as misrepresenting no-longer-existent scenarios as present before us (even if we are not taken in by the misrepresentations).

[9] As I am finalizing this book, I've become more aware of a debate among memory researchers over whether episodic remembering is the same kind of process as imagining (Michalian, 2016; Robins, 2020; Debus, 2014; Perrin, 2016). What they mean by 'imagining' in this debate is not always clear. It does not appear to be either A- or I-imagining that they have in mind. I plan to address this debate—and what it is they might mean by 'imagining'—in future work.

Why would one be attracted to this way of thinking about episodic memories, as opposed to viewing them as commitments or judgments of a kind? There are several reasons worth exploring. The first is grounded in a heavy-duty ontological view, popular in some quarters, according to which all *reasoning* takes places in a language-like symbolic format (see Chapter 2). For if reasoning is symbol-crunching of a sort that mirrors the manipulations of symbols in a system of formal logic, then mental imagery—supposing it occurs in a picture-like format—is left to impinge, somehow or other, from the sidelines. It won't then seem absurd to view all imagistic cognition as divorced from one's beliefs and proper commitments. I will consider the motivations and costs of such a view in more depth later (Chapter 4). For now it bears noting that, even on such views, something will need to be said about how I-imaginings interact with non-imagistic beliefs and desires in inference-aiding and (apparently) truth-preserving ways. Once imagery is properly woven into the general fabric of human inference, much of the resistance to viewing imagery as partly constitutive of our beliefs falls away. Moreover, whatever problems there might be in holding that images form proper parts of states that are not wholly imagistic simply reappear when we ask how imagistic states can be featured in sequences of reasoning with non-imagistic states.

Others may find it wrong to posit imagery-involving beliefs for much the same reason it seems wrong to assimilate perceptual states to beliefs. The fact that we can perceive things to be ways we don't believe them to be—as when knowingly viewing an illusion—is commonly seen as reason to distinguish perception from belief. We can also generate I-imaginings of things we don't believe to exist. This may seem to show, by parity of reasoning, that I-imaginings are not beliefs. Yet an easy response is to ask why I-imaginings should be treated *as a single class* when considering their relation to states like beliefs and desires. The fact that some I-imaginings are not judgments does not suggest that *none* are. (Recall that our question here is only whether *some* I-imaginings are simple judgments about past events and, thus, not A-imaginings.)

The similarities of perceptual experiences to I-imaginings may, however, tempt us to treat I-imaginings as a single class. The thought here is that, if perceptual experiences form a single class, and I-imaginings are very similar to perceptual experiences, then I-imaginings likely also form a single class. Here it helps to remember that when we ask whether an I-imagining should be considered a belief or desire, we are just asking whether it tends to guide or motivate behavior in the same way that a relevant belief or desire would. An I-imagining may play such a role even if it has important similarities to perceptual experience—including in the kinds of (fine-grained) properties it represents (Tye, 1991), its phenomenal character, or the neural regions underlying its use (Kosslyn, Thompson, & Ganis, 2006). None of the features that I-imaginings share with perception suggest that all I-imaginings must have a single kind of (non-belief-like) functional role.

After all, many philosophers take belief and desires to be realized in the same representational format—and so to be profoundly similar in *that* sense—and yet to be fundamentally different *kinds* of mental states, with quite distinct functional roles. Once we are clear that the notion of an I-imagining simply picks out processes that make use of mental states that, introspectively, appear to occur in a certain imagistic *format*, there is no reason to expect all such states to be functionally on a par. And if they are not all functionally on a par, we can easily see them as playing a role in a variety of different kinds of states—including beliefs, desires, intentions, and decisions—that we ascribe with ordinary folk psychological terms.

A last reason one might resist the idea that some I-imaginings are simply commitments of a kind—and beliefs, in particular—traces to the intuition that what we imagistically imagine is "up to us." It is, arguably, a platitude about both A- and I-imaginings that what we imagine is (at least in the normal case) determined by what we *intend* to imagine, and not by what is before our eyes. Colin McGinn comments: "I know that my image is of my mother because I *intended* it to be; I don't have to consult the appearance of the person in the image and then infer that I must have formed an image of my mother" (2004, p. 31). Unlike ordinary perceptual experience, where our causal contact with the perceived entity determines the object of our perception, in the case of I-imagining, "the imaginer starts with the object and then constructs an image of it" (p. 31).

If who or what I am imagining is typically determined by my intentions, it seems a short step to the conclusion that an I-imagining can't have the functional role of a belief. Beliefs aren't under intentional control in that way; this, it seems, is why they are suitable guides for navigating the world. If what we are imagistically imagining is entirely determined by our intentions, it is hard to see how imaginings could be guides to anything other than our intentions themselves.

One response here would be to insist that the object of an I-imagining is not, in fact, determined by the imaginer's intentions. It could instead be held that, even if our intentions are what start us rummaging about for a proper image, their doing so does not *guarantee* that the image retrieved is in fact an image of the intended object. For reasons explored later, this is not the path I recommend. For one thing, it leaves us with the question of what it is that makes the image an image of one object, and not another. If we point to its causal history—to the perceptual experience from which it derives (if any)—we seem boxed in to saying that any subsequent use of that image will constitute an imagining of its causal source, regardless of our intentions. Moreover, in many cases—e.g., imagining a standard yellow pencil—it seems unlikely that there will be just one particular object from which the image causally derives.

Fortunately there is a better and more obvious response to make here on behalf of some I-imaginings being beliefs. We can accept, with McGinn, that our intentions typically determine the *object* of our I-imagining. Even so, there is still the question of whether that object is correctly represented by the image we form. So, for example, suppose that I try to recall the hairdo of my twelfth grade English teacher, Mrs. Wells. I end up imagistically imagining Mrs. Wells because it is she whom I intend to imagine. In that sense, it is "up to me" that my image is of Mrs. Wells. My intention determines the object. However, if Mrs. Wells' hair didn't look the way my image represents it as having looked, the I-imagining is non-veridical—the judgment false. (I will come back to the question of the degree and respects in which an image must faithfully represent its object for the imagining to be considered accurate.) My episodic remembering—itself an I-imagining—will be under voluntary control in the sense that I have chosen the *object* of the imagining; but having this kind of control does not entail that the memory is accurate, or that it only carries information about my intentions.

This point connects to an observation made in Chapter 1 in the explanation of the "freedom" of imagination. There is a perfectly good sense in which we are free to make judgments, or bring to mind beliefs, on whatever topic we like. I can *choose to remember* my twelfth grade teacher, my first baseball game, the capital of Arkansas, or whatever. The fact that we get to pick these topics does not, however, entail that the recollections or judgments we make concerning them will be correct. In the case of episodic memory, more is needed: the *way* that my third grade teacher, or my first grade soccer team, or college dorm room, is represented must be faithful to how I really saw them to be. Or consider a standard block rotation task of the sort used in imagery studies; a participant is shown a set of blocks and asked to judge which of several pictures depicts the same block configuration as it would look when rotated 180 degrees (Shepard & Metzler, 1971). Suppose that I answer by visualizing the block figure rotating. My intention will ensure that my I-imagining is of those very blocks; yet it will not ensure that I accurately represent the way they would look if rotated 180 degrees. The imagining ends up being a reliable guide to action and inference only if the blocks really would look the way I imagine them looking when rotated 180 degrees. In this way, the imagining has a functional role and associated correctness conditions of an ordinary judgment. This isn't to say that *all* I-imaginings have the functional role of beliefs, of course—only that having their objects determined by our intentions does not *prevent* them from ever having such a role. And when they do play the role of a judgment—regarding, say, what one had for breakfast—they will not always be good candidates for A-imaginings. This allows for I-imaginings that are not A-imaginings.

There still remains a last source of skepticism about the idea that some I-imaginings have the functional role and psychological force of beliefs. This is the idea that I-imaginings are inherently *simulative*, *recreative*, or *emulative* of perceptual states. As we will see, this view goes hand-in-hand with the idea that I-imaginings are to be analyzed *as a class* when considering their functional role.

And it is also suggestive of a broader view, on which *recreative imagining* is the most general type of imagining—a type of imagining obscured by the A-imagining/I-imagining distinction I have recommended. Is important to see why this influential view should be resisted.

3.7 Against Recreative Imagining

In presenting a view where there are just two overlapping conceptions of imagination—A-imagining and I-imagining—I have suggested that there is no *additional* notion of imagining that ought to guide philosophical inquiry. Currie & Ravenscroft (2002) (hereafter "C&R") appear to challenge this view in arguing for an umbrella notion of imagining—what they term *recreative imagining*—that encompasses both belief-like imaginings and perception-like imaginings. Goldman (2006a) espouses a similar umbrella notion of *enactment imagination* (or "E-imagining"), which he describes as "a matter of creating or trying to create in one's own mind a selected mental state, or at least a rough facsimile of such a state, through the faculty of imagination" (p. 42). Belief-like imaginings, for C&R, are belief-like mental representations put to use in the kinds of activities I have associated with A-imagining. These include pretense, conditional reasoning, and fiction consumption as central cases. C&R's perception-like imaginings are any and all mental episodes that make use of sensory imagery (2002, pp. 24–7). So characterized, these appear to align with I-imaginings, as I have understood them. (C&R consider whether some uses of mental imagery might not be *imagining* in any proper sense and conclude in the negative: "we have been given no reason for thinking that imagery is not imagining... the idea that visualizing is imagining is at least unrefuted" (2002, p. 26).)

While belief-like imaginings and perception-like imaginings are, for C&R, entirely distinct sets of cognitive episodes, they propose that the two kinds of imagining fall together within a single class of recreative imagining. It might be thought that there is no real conflict between the notion of a recreative imagining and my dual notions of A- and I-imagining; the former might even appear to be a useful umbrella notion for capturing what the latter two have in common. However, to lump A- and I-imaginings in this way is to suggest that all instances of each have something important in common—something that would be missed by a view that, like my own, distinguishes A- from I-imaginings, without placing all instances of both within a broader class of imaginings. C&R also don't allow for overlap between belief-like imaginings and perceptual imaginings, in the way I allow for overlap between A- and I-imaginings. This is another reason to suspect that there's a substantive dispute in the offing.

To see what's at issue, we can ask, first, what it is that every perceptual imagining has importantly in common with every belief-like imagining, in virtue of which they are all recreative imaginings. And, second, why is there, for C&R, no overlap in belief-like and perception-like imagining? In answering, we can begin with C&R's most general description of recreative imagination, which they characterize as:

> the capacity to have, and in good measure control the having of, states that are not perceptions or beliefs or decisions or experiences of movements of one's body, but which are in various ways like those states—like them in ways that enable the states possessed through imagination to mimic and…to substitute for perceptions, beliefs, decisions and experiences of movements. (2002, p. 11)

Because forming visual imagery amounts to entering a state that is like visual perception in various ways—"standing in" for it as a "counterpart"—C&R include all uses of imagery within the realm of recreative imagination (2002, pp. 24–7). Like C&R, Goldman agrees that all image-involving states fall within the broad category of E-imagination: "Acts of visual and auditory imagination…are familiar types of E-imagination…The term 'imagery' is commonly applied to these cases" (Goldman, 2006a, p. 42). The notion of a recreative or "E" imagining can be extended broadly to apply to a wide variety of putative counterpart states. Indeed, it has been proposed that practically *every* sort of mental state has an imaginative counterpart, insofar as there is some state or other that serves to "recreate" or "simulate" it (Arcangeli, 2018). This suggests a fundamentally different way of conceiving of imagination—one that doubles our mental ontology with *sui generis* imaginative counterparts.[10] Needless to say, this is not an approach I recommend. I aim to undermine its appeal in the balance of this section.

Earlier I proposed that the use of imagery in episodic memory and visuospatial reasoning (e.g. block rotation tasks) warrants separating at least some I-imaginings from the class of A-imaginings. Arguably, in those cases, imagery does not "stand in for," "mimic," or "substitute for" some perceptual state; such imaginings simply constitute one's judgment on an issue. If there is nothing substantively *recreative* about mental imagery in itself, then, *pace* C&R and Goldman, not all uses of imagery should in fact be included among the recreative (or enactive) imaginings. Even if mental imagery and perceptual experiences were to share the same representational format, this would hardly be a reason to label one a recreation or simulation of the other. Beliefs and desires occur in the same representational format, on most views, without one sort of state recreating the other.

[10] One such putative counterpart state is a counterpart to desires—namely, "i-desires" (Currie, 2010; Doggett & Egan, 2012). These are typically posited to explain phenomena surrounding our appreciation of fictions. I question the need for such in Chapters 9, 10, and 11.

C&R and Goldman might respond that episodic memories are indeed recreative (or E-) imaginings precisely because they serve to stand in for, or mimic, previous perceptual experiences one has had. (Unfortunately, C&R and Goldman never explicitly discuss the role of imagery in episodic memory when arguing that mental imagery is inherently recreative—a curious omission.) Similarly, in cases of visuospatial reasoning, such as block rotation tasks, they might hold that I-imaginings serve to recreate, or mimic, *possible* perceptual experiences one would have when watching the block figure rotate.

Granting these as coherent proposals, we still have the question of whether such recreative imaginings should *also* be considered beliefs or judgments of a kind. This is where the real tension lies in the relation of their proposal to my own. Suppose it is granted that episodic memories are both (occurrent) beliefs about one's past *and* recreative imaginings. Recall that belief-like imaginings are, on C&R's account, states that mimic or stand in for beliefs. If some beliefs (namely, episodic memories) are *also* recreative imaginings (because they recreate previous perceptual experiences), it should be possible for us to "recreate" those episodic-memory-beliefs themselves through the use of belief-like imaginings. That is, if episodic memories *just are* beliefs of a kind, we should be able to generate "belief-like" counterparts to those mental states. We could call these counterpart states episodic-memory-like imaginings. These would be a sub-class of belief-like imaginings and would occur when we merely simulate remembering an experience from our personal past. Of course, episodic memories are themselves *already* recreative imaginings, on C&R's view, due to their involving mental imagery. So this would entail our having recreative imaginings of states that are already themselves recreative imaginings. Episodic memory-like imaginings would be recreative in two ways *simultaneously*: they would mimic, and so serve to recreate, episodic memories; and they would also mimic, and so recreate, genuine perceptual experiences (insofar as they involve imagery).

This is not an incoherent result. But it shows something important: we in fact have two notions of recreation at work. First, there is a *functional* notion, according to which certain states are considered "recreative" because they recreate aspects of the functional role of another state. This is the sense in which C&R's belief-like imaginings are recreative. And, second, there is a *format* notion of recreation, where all mental imagery-involving states are recreative because they recreate the (presumably pictorial, or iconic) format of different perceptual states. A particular mental state—such as the episodic-memory-like imagining just described—can be recreative *in both ways simultaneously* just because these are distinct notions. But once we have separated the two ways of being recreative, we can see that there is no interesting psychological similarity that mental episodes recreative in one way bear to episodes that are recreative in the other.

One way for C&R and Goldman to maintain that recreative or enactive imagining is an important category in its own right would be to reject the proposal that episodic memories are beliefs. Then they could maintain that there are no recreative imaginings that are recreative *only* because they reproduce the format of some other kind of state. (This would, in turn, allow them to reject the idea that there are two distinct, unrelated notions of recreation in play.) To simply stipulate that beliefs cannot have mental images as proper parts would be question-begging in the present context, however. Yet they could argue, instead, that mental image-involving processes—*qua* simulations of perceptual experiences—are invariably recreative in a *functional* sense, just because they invariably recreate aspects of the functional roles of perceptual experiences. Arguing that all image-involving processes are *functionally* recreative (or enactive) of perceptual experience requires that one specify the sense in which imagistic imaginings invariably duplicate the functional role of perceptual experiences. Here it is difficult to see what the relevant resemblances could be. The causes of perceptual experiences and sequences of mental images, respectively, are for the most part entirely different—the former being caused by outward stimuli impinging on our sensory transducers, while the latter are endogenously triggered. Their normal effects are distinct as well: perceptual experiences of an *x* typically lead us to believe in the presence of a nearby *x* in our environment. Generating a mental image of an *x* rarely if ever has that effect. Further, the particular sequence of perceptual states we experience across time depends on the nature of the environment we are perceiving. With I-imaginings, the environment plays no such role; their causes are again endogenous in nature. Moreover, it appears that I-imaginings can play many different functional roles, depending on the uses to which mental images are put. If all ordinary perceptual experiences are functionally on a par—tending to cause belief in the presence of the objects represented, for instance—not all I-imaginings can serve to recreate that same role. So, if all imagistic imaginings are recreative in some sense or other, it is not because they recreate the functional role of perceptual experience.

An alternative route of response for C&R would be to reverse course and allow that some uses of mental imagery—including episodic rememberings, in particular—are not perception-like imaginings. This would also evade the charge that a perception-like imagining can be recreated simply by triggering mental imagery. Yet this leaves them owing a different account of what unifies the class of perception-like imaginings. Since format could no longer be the answer, we would need to look for functional similarities between perceptual imaginings and perceptual experiences. Once again, it is hard to see what these similarities might be, and how they could be robust enough to define the class.

Again, none of this is to deny that visual imagery and visual perception draw on partially overlapping neural networks (Kosslyn, Thompson, & Alpert, 1997; Slotnick et al., 2005); and it *may* even be that they both represent objects by means of a common, non-discursive "pictorial" cognitive format. The point is simply that these are not in themselves reasons to conceive of one as a simulation, or recreation of the other. Mental images are not *wanna-be* perceptual experiences. They are tools for ordinary, stimulus-independent reasoning about the past, present, and future. The notion of "recreative" or "enactive" imaginings favored by those who view I-imagining as inherently simulative does not cut the mind at a natural joint. Nor does it mark any salient commonsense conception of imagination. Instead, it reinforces the misconception that I-imaginings cannot share the functional role of states like judgments, desires, or decisions; and it wrongly suggests that all imagery-involving cognition must occur, in some sense, "offline," detached from our proper commitments.

This concludes my argument for the framework sketched in Fig. 3.1: some A-imaginings are I-imaginings; and some I-imaginings are A-imaginings. But neither is a sub-set of the other. Further, there is no theoretically significant third class of imaginings—recreative imagining—that includes both. We turn, in the next chapter, to look more closely at the role mental images play within different kinds of folk psychological states.

4
Imagistic Imagining Part II
Hybrid Structure, Multiple Attitudes, and Daydreams

4.1 Introduction

This chapter delves further into the nature of I-imaginings and the mental images they employ. I develop a framework where I-imaginings have both imagistic and non-imagistic components. Within this "hybrid" framework—elements of which I've defended elsewhere (Langland-Hassan, 2015, 2018a)—some I-imaginings are shown to be familiar folk psychological states like judgments, desires, and decisions. Establishing that instances of I-imagining can be identified with such states is crucial to this book's larger project of showing how A-imagining (or "attitude imagining") can be reduced to a collectively more basic assortment of folk psychological states. The reason is this: last chapter I argued that some mental events are both A-imaginings *and* I-imaginings: they are A-imaginings insofar as they are cases of rich, elaborated, epistemically safe about the possible, unreal, and so on; and they are I-imaginings insofar as they make use of mental imagery. If one cannot see how I-imaginings can be identified with judgments, decisions, desires, beliefs, and so on, one won't be able to see how A-imaginings that incorporate mental imagery can, either. My aim in this chapter is to make the possibility of such identifications more visible.

One source of resistance to the idea I-imaginings can have instances that are judgments or desires is the idea that mental images occur in a representational format distinct from "propositional" thoughts like judgments and desires (where "propositional thoughts" are folk psychological states whose contents we ascribe with that-clauses). This apparent difference in format can make it difficult to see how the two kinds of mental state could combine to form complex truth- (or accuracy-)evaluable mental states. Now, on my way of speaking, a mental image is simply a kind of mental state that appears, to the person having it, to be image-like, or to have sensory character, and that occurs without a proximal external cause. It remains an open empirical question how we are to understand the format of the mental representations or processes underlying this introspectively familiar phenomenon. This is so even if we are convinced that mental imagery has the same representational format as the processes involved in ordinary perception; for the

Explaining Imagination. Peter Langland-Hassan, Oxford University Press (2020). © Peter Langland-Hassan.
DOI: 10.1093/oso/9780198815068.001.0001

format of perceptual states is itself an open question.[1] Likewise, as I argued in Chapter 2, agnosticism about the representational format of propositional states like belief and desires is also reasonable at this moment in cognitive science. Because I view questions concerning the representational format underlying mental imagery and other folk psychological states as unsettled, I don't think that theories of A- and I-imagining need to be tightly constrained by any (putative) facts about the cognitive formats in which they occur.

And yet: I know that not everyone will share in my agnosticism about cognitive formats. Nor do I want my general arguments concerning I- and A-imagining to rely upon that agnosticism. So, in addition to articulating a hybrid framework for understanding the nature of I-imaginings—where I-imaginings have both imagistic and non-imagistic components—I will also try to motivate it from within the terms of views on which there *is* an important difference in cognitive format between non-imagistic folk psychological states and sequences of mental imagery. I circle back to the "clash of formats" worry, in particular, at the end of this chapter (section 4.10). Before that, I will show how token I-imaginings can be instances of states like judgments, desires, and decisions—and propose that this is compatible with some of the same token instances *also* being daydreams. These points are all important for the larger project of establishing that A- and I-imaginings are themselves heterogeneous classes of mental states and processes—classes that can be fruitfully reduced to a more basic collection of folk psychological states.

4.2 The Relation of Mental Images to I-imaginings

As I stare at the coffee cup on my desk, we have an easy answer for why my visual experience is of *this* cup and no other: the experience is being caused by just this cup. Wiggle the cup and you wiggle the experience. A similar story applies to photographs. The contrasting stimulus-*independence* of I-imaginings forecloses

[1] I don't have space to defend agnosticism about perceptual and imagistic formats here. My main worry is that the space of options is too small in contemporary philosophical debates. It is often assumed that mental imagery and/or perceptual states have to be *either* pictorial/analog/nonconceptual or discursive/language-like. Yet contemporary artificial neural networks give us reason to allow for other possibilities. Consider those used in face recognition (Lawrence, Giles, Tsoi, & Back, 1997; Parkhi et al., 2015). These connectionist networks take images as input and output judgments about whether the image records a face—or even whether it records a particular previously encountered face. Variations on such networks have been used not only to discriminate images, but to *generate* novel photorealistic images as well (Denton, Chintala, & Fergus, 2015; Ledig et al., 2017). As discussed in Chapter 2, such networks do not make use of discrete language-like representations; but neither do they make use of discrete *analog* or *pictorial* representations. The judgment, by a face-detection neural network, that a certain input contains a face arises out of parallel processing, distributed across multiple "hidden layers" of nodes, where the nature of the processing is determined by the strength of connections among the many nodes in the hidden layers. Any claims about the format of perceptual state and mental imagery will need to consider carefully the relevance of these, our most successful, models of perceptual states.

this way of answering the question about their reference. Part of what makes an I-imagining a (mere) imagining is that it is endogenously, as opposed to exogenously, caused. I-imaginings are, in that sense, stimulus independent. We cannot lean on the external world to settle the question of their objects in the same way. Nor can we trace the reference of a mental image to the particular from which it causally derives—my image of my mother being *of* my mother just because it in some sense derives from past sightings of my mother. For it is doubtful that there is a *single* individual from which each token image could be said to causally derive. For instance, it's unlikely that my image of a yellow pencil derives from just one yellow pencil I perceived in the past. Moreover, an important feature of I-imaginings is that they are capable of taking, as objects, things never before perceived.

What, then, determines the objects of our I-imaginings? What, in Wittgenstein's (1953) phrase, makes my image of him an image of *him*? My answer will be that it is an internal, non-imagistic state of the person doing the imagining—one that pairs in the proper way with the mental image. I will motivate this answer by appeal to the theoretical work it can do. Mine is not the only conceivable answer to how mental images come to be images *of* something, of course. And it comes with questions of its own. How, for starters, do *non*-imagistic states come to have objects? While the question is legitimate, I won't try to answer it. In defense of that omission: most in these debates are already committed to the existence of non-imagistic mental states that have objects; relying upon them is not introducing a new tool.

Supposing that we are happy enough with non-imagistic mental states having determinate objects, the question is how we are to understand the relation of such states to the mental images that occur within I-imaginings. I will argue that I-imaginings are *hybrid* states, consisting of a mental image—or sequence of images—paired with a non-imagistic state. The non-imagistic component is what enables the I-imagining, as a whole, to have an object. While mental images may be "purely imagistic," in some sense relevant to their format, I-imaginings *are not*. The precise sense in which mental images are "paired with" non-imagistic states will be explained below, with the general picture being motivated by the explanatory work it can do.

4.3 The Multiple Use Thesis

While the "hybrid" view of I-imagining I will defend may seem counterintuitive to some, general sympathy for such a view is implicit in the widely accepted Multiple Use Thesis concerning mental imagery (Martin, 2002; Noordhof, 2002; Peacocke, 1985). According to the Multiple Use Thesis, the very same mental image—in the sense of a *type* of image—can be used in the fulfillment of multiple different imaginative projects. In Peacocke's terms, "the same conscious, subjective image" will serve to support numerous imaginative projects, including:

> Imagining being at the helm of a yacht; imagining from the inside an experience as of being at the helm of a yacht; and imagining from the inside what it would be like if a brain surgeon were causing you to have an experience as of being at the helm of a yacht. (1985, p. 19)

The difference-maker in such imaginings, Peacocke tells us, are "S-imaginings" where "'S' is for 'suppose.'" S-imaginings account for "the difference between imaginings which, though having a common image, still differ" (1985, p. 25). Although S-imagining is not literally supposing, he remarks, "it shares with supposing the property that what is S-imagined is not determined by the subject's images" (p. 25). The differences in the three yacht-related imaginings are "differences in which conditions are *S-imagined* to hold." While Peacocke never commits to the claim that images can only gain reference by being paired with a non-imagistic component, he has arrived at the same conclusion that a characterization of the full content of an I-imagining will incorporate the contribution of non-imagistic ("S-imagining") states. In specifying that S-imagining is "not literally supposing," he seems to suggest that S-imaginings are, instead, literally parts of sensory imaginings (though parts that are distinct from sensory images themselves). M. G. F. Martin voices a similar idea when considering the multiple uses to which a certain type of image can be put. "Typically," he remarks, "acts of imagining things to be a certain way have both imagistic and non-imagistic aspects" (2002, p. 403). (See also Kung (2010).)[2] Whether or not these theorists literally mean to propose that an imagining, considered as a particular kind of mental state, can have both imagistic and non-imagistic elements, this is indeed the sort of "hybrid" view I will go on to develop.

It is one thing to explain how images acquire objects; it is another to show how image-involving states can, like judgments, be considered *true* or *false* (or, like desires, be considered *satisfied* or *unsatisfied*). (Sometimes images themselves are thought only to be *accurate* or *inaccurate* with respect to their objects, where,

[2] Wiltsher (2016) argues against what he calls the "additive view" of sensory imagination, which he characterizes as the view that "mental imagery often involves two elements," including "an image-like element" and "a non-image element, consisting of something like suppositions about the image's object" (2016, p. 266). He targets, in particular, the views of Peacocke (1985) and Kung (2010). While it might seem that Wiltsher's argument targets my view as well, it does not. Wiltsher himself defends a view where the objects of mental images are determined by relevant non-imagistic "concepts" involved in the generation of an image: "You actively generate an image by deploying a concept, which calls up sensations sufficient for a scenario, and simultaneously dictates what... content is applied to that scenario" (2016, p. 273). In the end, Wiltsher's target is quite narrow; it is the view that mental images are accompanied by "something like *suppositions* about the image's object" that are not, strictly speaking, suppositions (my emphasis). Whatever its merits, the view targeted is not one I defend.

unlike truth and falsity, accuracy comes in degrees.) If at least some I-imaginings are going to be assimilated to judgements, desires, and decisions, we need to see how they can both represent particulars *and* have different kinds of truth or satisfaction conditions. That is the main project of the next section.

4.4 Judgment I-imaginings

This section lays out an approach for seeing some I-imaginings as judgments (where judgments are occurrent beliefs). The more general framework, in which I-imaginings have hybrid structures, will then be applied to other folk psychological states, including desires and decisions.[3]

Let BEL represent the attitude of belief, with whatever follows it inside parentheses representing its content. So, the belief that it is raining can be symbolized as: BEL (it is raining). We understand the BEL part of that symbolization to the extent that we understand the functional (and inferential) role of beliefs in general. Judgments, as I am understanding them, are occurrent beliefs; this is to say that they are mental *processes* in which one arrives at a belief of the same content.[4] Using JUD to stand for the attitude of judgment, we can express the judgment that it is raining as: JUD (it is raining).

Let us use JIG to stand for an image-involving state that is a sub-species of judgment generally—what I will call *judgment I-imaginings* (JIGs). In calling the state a "judgment I-imagining," I am not suggesting that it is a kind of non-serious, imitative, or pretend form of judgment. (JIGs, as I will understand them, are not akin to "belief-like imaginings" as some use that term (see, e.g., Currie & Ravenscroft, 2002; Doggett & Egan, 2007); and Schellenberg, 2013).) Rather, JIGs simply *are* judgments that involve mental images as proper parts; they are a sub-set of all judgments. And they are a sub-set of I-imaginings, as well. The idea, which I will sharpen in a moment, is that, just as I might judge that tomorrow it will rain, I might also judge that the front of my childhood home looked thus-and-so—where "thus-and-so" is replaced by a mental image of the house. Both are ordinary judgments; but only the latter incorporates a mental image and so is also an I-imagining.

We can symbolize a judgment I-imagining by using JIG with a content following it in parentheses. As JIGs are instances of I-imagining, at least some of their constituents will be mental images. This means that, in expressing the content of a JIG, we need to account for the place of the image. My proposal will be that a JIG constitutively involves two components, one of which pertains to the

[3] This section develops, refines, and expands a proposal I have made elsewhere (Langland-Hassan, 2015, 2018a); here, new terminology is adopted to fit the terms used elsewhere in this book.

[4] Characterizing the difference between occurrent and non-occurrent states is not as easy as one might wish. I recommend Bartlett's (2018) treatment of the topic, according to which a state's being occurrent amounts to its consisting in an *activity* or *process* of some kind.

visual (or other sensory) image itself, the other of which lies outside of it and is non-imagistic in nature. Considered together, these components constitute a single judgment-imagining.

I will use **bold** to distinguish the specific portion of an imagining contributed by a mental image. Of course, the fact that psychological contents are here described in natural language should not be taken to suggest that their format is itself language-like. As earlier remarked, I am remaining neutral on questions of cognitive format. Also, it should not be assumed that, for every word included in bold, the relevant image represents that very property. The image whose content is described as **a big brown horse**, for instance, may not itself represent the property of being a horse. The words in bold are simply meant to point the reader toward a general idea of the kinds of (perhaps only superficial) properties represented by the image.

Like visual perceptual states, visual images seem to have a rich and fine-grained content that can be difficult, if not impossible, to capture in the words of a natural language. This is part of the reason I do not pretend to do so with the words in bold. Another reason is that folk psychological platitudes do not put clear limits on the kinds of properties that an image-like thought can represent; and the science of mental imagery is, in my estimation, too young to do so definitively (see fn. 1, above)). Thus I will include an ellipsis as part of the description of such contents to indicate that the words in bold only gesture at the actual full imagistic content. The ellipsis is also meant to convey that the imagistic content may include within it what we would intuitively count as a sequence of images, and not simply a single static image.

Finally, and importantly, I will suggest that the contents of images should be thought of as akin to indefinite descriptions (i.e., descriptions beginning with "a" or "an," or "some"). Among other things, this allows for a natural account of how one and the same image (in the sense of an image type) can be used to imagine many different objects and scenarios. It also entails that, like indefinite descriptions generally—such as "a big brown horse"—mental images are not *by themselves* assessable for truth or falsity (or as being satisfied or unsatisfied).[5]

[5] In saying that mental images, by themselves, fail to represent truth-evaluable propositions, I may seem in agreement with others who say that sensory images are only "as if" they have a direction of fit (Lormand, 2007, fn. 15; Searle, 1983, pp. 13–14), or are "neutral about reality" in that they "do not purport to tell us how the world is" (McGinn, 2004, p. 21). Yet, in other work (Langland-Hassan, 2015), I have taken aim at such proposals. Here is why: these other accounts do not distinguish between the content of an image itself and the *sensory imagining* in which it is featured. On my view, it is crucial to grant that an imagistic (or sensory) imagining can have robust correctness or satisfaction conditions, even if images, taken by themselves, do not. If, on the other hand, the point others are making is simply that mental images—like predicates without subjects—lack correctness conditions *by themselves*, then we may be in agreement. My strong hunch is that there is in fact a deep disagreement, however, insofar as others view sensory imaginings as entirely composed of mental images and do not make suggestions for how a sequence of images can have correctness conditions when a single image does not. Indeed, Lormand characterizes sensory imaginings as being able to "mismatch the world without being in epistemic need of revision" (2006, fn. 15). The notion of a *mismatch* suggests a view where sensory imaginings do in fact represent the world as being a certain way—a way it is not. This is *unlike* the notion of a bare indefinite description which cannot by itself be said to predicate anything of the world one way or the other.

To put this framework into practice, suppose that Joe is engaged in some I-imagining in order to determine whether the couch he ordered will fit through his doorway. He might have an imagining we can express as:

(1) JIG (When the couch I ordered arrives, it will be: **a tan couch-shaped-object fitting through a rectangular doorway**...)

While the image itself only represents (in a fine-grained way) a tan, couch-shaped object fitting through a doorway, the imagining as a whole represents the specific couch he bought as fitting through his doorway. This is thanks to the (non-bold) portion of content that is non-imagistic in nature. Here we see an affinity with Fodor's (1975) idea that images "convey *some* information discursively and *some* information pictorially" (p. 190). The definite description—"the couch I ordered"—occurs as a non-imagistic, descriptive aspect within the imagining—one that helps determine what the image is an image *of*.[6] This non-imagistic component accomplishes two important tasks simultaneously: it generates an object for the image; and it allows the image to be characterized as contributing to a truth- or satisfaction-evaluable state.

In this case, Joe is trying to predict how the couch will look as it comes to his door, in order to determine whether it will fit through. The attitude he takes toward the overall content is that of judging it to be the case. So the mental episode as a whole is veridical if the couch will indeed fit and non-veridical otherwise. Note, however, that for a JIG to be veridical, it is not necessary for the image to represent the object exactly as it looks (or would look), with all the same detail as a comparable perceptual experience. Just as ordinary sentences (e.g., "The brown dog jumped") can be true while leaving out many details (What shade of brown? How high?), so too can an imagining be veridical without going into all the details that a perceptual experience might. To assume otherwise is to mistake the cognitive role of imaginings for that of perceptual experience.

To try another example, suppose that Avery has only seen misleading pictures of the Arc de Triomphe—pictures which made it look silver in color. Setting out on his first trip to Paris, he might engage in the following imagining:

(2) JIG (The Arc de Triomphe is: **a big silver arch**...)

In such a case we can say that Avery has *misimagined* the Arc de Triomphe, just as one might *misperceive* the Arc de Triomphe if somehow, through a trick of light,

[6] David Kaplan advocates a similar approach to placing images within judgments in his "Quantifying In" (1968): "Many of our beliefs have the form: 'The color of her hair is ___', or 'The song he was singing went___', where the blanks are filled with images, sensory impressions, or what have you, but certainly not words. If we cannot even say it with words but have to paint it or sing it, we certainly cannot believe it with words" (p. 208). Kaplan seems to share the view that, within judgments and beliefs, images assign properties to an object that is determined by an element of content *outside of* the image, with images playing a predicative role. Thanks to Neil Van Leeuwen for alerting me to this passage, which he discusses in Van Leeuwen (2013).

one saw it as silver. Taking his first stroll down the Champs Elysées, he comes upon the arch itself and thinks: "It's not at all as I imagined it." Intuitively, he did indeed I-imagine *the Arc de Triomphe* before; he just got it wrong. He imagined *as silver* something that is not in fact silver. That is why it is a *mis*imagining—and, indeed, a misjudgment. He was trying to get it right and failed.

But note that a successful imagining closely related to (2) is also possible—one that involves the same type of mental image. It is possible to successfully imagine the Arc de Triomphe *as silver*, even if one knows it is not silver. For a clear role of many I-imaginings is to represent not how things are or were, but how things could be, or could have been. Such hypothetical and counterfactual imaginings are closely associated with the creative "freedom" of imagination. Knowing full well what the Arc de Triomphe looks like, Jude might imagine the arch *as silver*, just because he is interested in what it would look like painted silver. For Jude, the experience could be symbolized as:

(3) JIG (The Arc de Triomphe painted silver would be: **a big silver arch**...)

Here the imagining still has correctness conditions, but of a different (modal) kind. The content pertains to how the Arc de Triomphe *would look* under certain conditions. And if the arch would not have those characteristics when coated in silver, it is another misimagining. It is a misimagining with a modal content.

With (3) we get a first look at how we might explain some imagery-involving A-imaginings in terms of their being image-involving judgments. When Jude makes the JIG in (3), it is reasonable to describe him as "engaging in rich thought about a merely possible situation, in an epistemically safe way." He is, after all, thinking about a merely possible situation, where the Arc de Triomphe is painted silver; his use of imagery renders it phenomenologically and representationally rich; and he does not diminish his epistemic standing in making this (presumably true) judgment about what the Arc de Triomphe would look like painted silver. This particular A-imagining turns out to be an image-involving judgment (a JIG); it is therefore also an I-imagining.

Imaginings with modal character can also be aimed at the past. The person who imagines what it would have been like if Hilary Clinton had won the 2016 U.S. presidential election may have an imagining with the content:

(4) JIG (Hilary Clinton giving a victory speech on election night would have been: **a smiling and waving Hilary-Clinton-looking woman**...)

This is another plausible example of an I-imagining that is also an A-imagining. Of course, (3) and (4) add more structure to certain acts of imagining than one might have expected, pre-theoretically. But then, there must be some cognitive difference between the person (Avery, in example (2)) who imagines the Arc de Triomphe as silver with the idea that it *is* that way, and the person (Jude, in example (3)) who imagines it counterfactually as being that way. And there must be some difference between the person who, thinking Clinton won, imagines her smiling and waving, and someone who imagines her doing so while knowing it never happened. The above is a proposal for capturing these differences that respects the different roles each imagining plays in guiding the behavior of the imaginer. By adding in the structure here (as opposed to within metacognitive background beliefs about what their respective imaginings aim to depict), we are able to give an account of the contents and correctness conditions of the related I-imaginings that links them to their actual roles in cognition. When these JIGs are false, they decrease our epistemic standing and lead us to say false things; when they are true, they increase our chances of successfully navigating the world. In short, we are able to link the content and resultant correctness conditions of I-imaginings to their successes and failures in allowing us to carry out our goals.

If, instead, we think of the entire act of I-imagining as lacking any correctness conditions—as being only "as if" it has a direction of fit (Lormand, 2007, fn. 15; Searle, 1983, pp. 13–14), or "neutral about reality" in that it "does not purport to tell us how the world is" (McGinn, 2004, p. 21)—we miss the obvious fact that our I-imaginings do in fact guide our actions and inferences to greater or lesser degrees of success. We need a way of seeing how I-imaginings can constitute some of our considered judgments themselves, and holding that they have hybrid structures allows us to do so. At the same time, we can see I-imaginings such as (3) and (4) as episodes of thinking about the merely possible, fantastical, and so on, in an epistemically blameless way. This means they satisfy the criteria for A-imagining. As (3) and (4), being JIGs, are, in addition, judgments, we can see them as image-involving A-imaginings that are reducible to more basic folk psychological states.

Next I want to extend this framework to show how instances of I-imagining can be folk psychological states of other kinds. This meshes with the larger project of showing how both I- and A-imaginings are heterogeneous collections of more basic folk psychological states.

4.5 I-imaginings that are Desires, Decisions, and Intentions

The schematic form used to symbolize JIGs can be coopted to symbolize I-imaginings with other attitudinal forces and other associated functional roles. Very often, these processes are also instances of A-imagining. Recall Walton's "paradigm instance of an exercise of the imagination" recounted in Chapter 1:

> Fred finds himself, in an idle moment, alone with his thoughts. Feeling unsuccessful and unappreciated, he embarks on a daydream in which he is rich and famous. He calls up images of applauding constituents, visiting dignitaries, a

> huge mansion, doting women, fancy cars. But alas, reality eventually reasserts itself and Fred gets back to selling shoes. (1990, p. 13)

Walton is clear that this daydream involves Fred's calling up "images." In line with my proposal in Chapter 1, we can characterize the daydream as sequence of occurrent imagistic desires, using "DIG" to designate a desire-I-imagining:

(5) DIG (I see cheering constituents that are **a crowd of people waving and holding signs bearing my name**; I own a lavish home that is **a gleaming mansion on a hill**; I am greeting visiting dignitaries who are **a well-coifed and fancily tailored group**; I am trailed by doting women who are: **some beautiful model-types**; my garage is: **a large, car-filled museum**.)

Just as JIGs are full-blown judgements, so too are DIGs actual, occurrent desires. They are not imaginative "analogues" to desires, or desire-like states—they are not "i-desires" (Doggett & Egan, 2012) or desire-like imaginings (Currie, 2002, 2010). DIGs are simply desires that have mental images as proper parts. The DIG symbolized in (5) will be satisfied when Fred's fantasy comes true. Until that time, it will play the kind of cognitive role we associate with occurrent, unsatisfied desires generally.

DIGs are important to the explanation of how A-imaginings can be explained in terms of more basic folk psychological states. Much of A-imagining is "mere fantasy"—we think about (and visualize) things we would like to happen, even if we doubt they will occur. One of the more puzzling gaps in recent theoretical treatments of imagination is that few are inclined to call our imagistic fantasies and daydreams what they plainly are: desires! (These include, at times, desires for thus and such *not* to occur—also known as *fears*.) Unlike beliefs and judgments, desires needn't reflect what we think is true or even likely. As Amy Kind observes, there is nothing untoward about desires whose chances of satisfaction are slim to none, or that we cannot presently act upon:

> I might desire that I could introduce my children to their grandfather, who is no longer living; I might desire that my (not yet existing) grandchildren have healthy and happy lives; I might desire that a certain ballot proposition had been defeated in a recent election. In none of these cases is the reasonableness of the desire undercut by the fact that the object of the desire is nonactual.
>
> (2011, p. 425)

Of course, Kind does not propose that such desires are cases of imagining. But why shouldn't we allow that at least some desires are indeed A-imaginings? A-imagining is nothing other than epistemically blameless, rich, elaborated thought about the merely possible, fantastical, fictional, and so on. Many desires fit that bill precisely.

4.6 On the Relation of Desire to A-imagining More Generally

Well, there *are* reasons others haven't included image-involving desires within the class of A-imaginings. But they are not, on reflection, *good* reasons. One reason has been the assumption that all I-imaginings should, like the perceptual experiences they resemble, be analyzed *as a class*. If all perceptual experiences are thought of as representing the world as being some way or other, it will then be natural to think of all I-imaginings as doing so as well. It might, for instance, seem that all imagistic imaginings represent their objects *as present before one*, in the manner of corresponding perceptual experiences, even if they are usually non-veridical in doing so. But, as we have seen, this is simply to mistake a possible sharing of format between I-imaginings perceptual experiences for the view that they must have the same force or "direction of fit" as well. Notions of "force" and "direction of fit" (Searle, 1983) are tied to a state's functional role, not its format. As I-imaginings rarely lead us to believe in the nearby presence of what they represent—and certainly do not do so as a default—there is no good reason to view them as always having essentially the same correctness conditions and direction of fit as perceptual experiences. Moreover, supposing that they do leads to the absurd result that all uses of mental imagery are in some sense misrepresentational.

Another reason people have not thought of DIGs, and desires generally, as possible instances of imagining traces to the specific explanatory contexts in which imagination has been put to work. When we focus on explaining a specific behavior or ability—such as pretend play or understanding other minds—it is natural to conceive of the related imaginings as *guides* to behavior and inference. Desires are thought to *motivate*, but not to guide behavior in the manner of beliefs. Now add the tacit assumption that the class of imaginings constitutes a single cognitive kind, and, *voilà*, we quickly arrive at the conclusion that all imaginings must, in some sense, be "guiding" states with a "mind to world" direction of fit.

Yet problems and puzzles quickly arise when we try to shoe-horn everything we would like to say about imagination into a single kind of guiding state with a well-defined functional role and "mind to world" direction of fit. For there are platitudes about imagining that we would like to uphold—such as that we can imagine whatever we wish—that seem to conflict with what we have to say about the guiding process we have posited to explain pretense behavior. One reaction is to nevertheless seek a way of saying those same things about the process we have posited—showing, for example, how it can be *both* constrained by what we believe *and*, at times, free to represent whatever we choose (Kind, 2016a; Langland-Hassan, 2016). Another, more advisable, reaction is to back up and grant that, while the process we have posited to explain pretend behavior is *an instance* of imagining, there is no reason to think it is the only kind of process that can be an instance of imagining—and, therefore, no reason to say that *it* must have all the features we associate with imagining in other contexts. All we really mean by "imagining," in the relevant folk psychological sense, is engaging in rich, or elaborated, epistemically safe thought about merely possible, fantastical, and fictional scenarios. And this characterization remains silent on whether a variety of functionally-distinct processes fit that bill. Should it turn out, on reflection, that all the token processes we end up counting as A-imaginings are instances of folk psychological states we already believed in and understood independently...well then we should be delighted.

4.7 Decision I-imaginings

With JIGs and DIGs as examples, it is easy to see how a range of other imagery-involving folk psychological states can be symbolized. A person who decides that, later today, he will finally put away the screwdriver that has been sitting on the counter for weeks now, may token the following *decision*:

(6) DEC (Later today that screwdriver will be: **a screwdriver going-back-into-a-toolbox**...)

Imagery-involving decisions of this sort will form part of the larger explanation of creativity I develop in Chapter 12. To preview, writing a story will involve making decisions such as:

(7) DEC (In the story I am writing, the officer who pulls me over to compliment my driving looks like: **a friendly policeman**...)

This is again not to say that *all* image-involving decisions should be counted as A-imaginings. Due to their focus on the here and now, their relatively sparse content, or other contextual factors, some image-involving decisions—like some JIGs and DIGs—will not satisfy the general characterization of A-imagining as rich, epistemically safe thought about the merely possible, fantastical, and so on. Thus, by my reckoning, (6) is *not* an A-imagining, while (7) is, due to its connection to story-telling and fantasy. The difference, however, is not deep one.

4.8 Imaginative I-imagining?

In addition to JIGs, DIGs, and DECs, we could also consider whether to posit an imaginative version of I-imaginings, corresponding to cases where we would say a person has imagined (but not judged, desired, or decided) that *X*, and where their doing so involved mental imagery. Such a posit does no harm to the project of reducing and explaining imagination, so long as we understand these as "light-duty" ascriptions and don't take ourselves to be describing a *sui generis* folk psychological state or cognitive attitude, irreducible to any others. For instance, instead of characterizing Fred's daydream, in (5), as a sequence of desires, we could call it case of imagining that he is rich and famous. We could even symbolize it as:

(8) IMAG (I see cheering constituents that are **a crowd of people waving and holding signs bearing my name**; I own a lavish home that is **a gleaming mansion on a hill**; I am greeting visiting dignitaries who are **some well-coifed and fancily tailored individuals**; I am trailed by doting women who are: **some beautiful model-types**; my garage is: **a large, car-filled museum.**)

What matters for the project of explaining A-imagining is that we can give some characterization of this state in other familiar folk psychological terms, and without appeal to a distinct attitude of imagination. And we have precisely that with (5). Just as we can allow that there is such a thing as suspecting that *p*, without its being something over and above one's believing that it is somewhat likely that *p* (see Chapter 1), we can allow that there are I-imaginings where the attitude is one of imagining, without its being the case that taking that attitude is something over and above one's making a certain judgment, having an occurrent desire, making a decision, or a combination of such.

But are there reasons to think that there are I-imaginings for which no such recharacterization is available? Imagistic daydreams, with their tenuous relation to both outward behavior and folk psychological explanation, are perhaps the most likely candidates. I offered a reductive account of one such daydream from Walton, above. But it will help to consider the issue of daydreams in a bit more detail.

4.9 Daydreams

We should want a theory of imagination to say something about the nature of daydreams. But what are daydreams? How can they be characterized in a theory-neutral way? Because daydreams are not associated with any particular kind of outward behavior or resulting beliefs, it is difficult to know what the constraints might be on theory of daydreams. Here is a quick stab at an initial characterization:

Daydreams: daydreams are A-imaginings that, at least typically, involve mental imagery, and which serve no immediate practical goal.

The kinds of "practical goals" screened off by this characterization are things like taking part in a pretense, arriving at a belief in a conditional, consuming a fiction, or making a creative product—i.e., the main contexts I focus on in the chapters to follow. As with A-imaginings more generally—which are simply rich or elaborated, epistemically safe episodes of thought about the possible, unreal, and so on—there is no reason to think that the folk psychological notion of a daydream picks out a single type of mental state or process. We should expect the mental events that get called "daydreams" to be a heterogeneous group, including DIGs (such as (5), above), JIGs, and DECs at a minimum.

For instance, one way to engage in rich thought about the merely possible, unreal, and fantastical, in an epistemically safe way—to A-imagine—is to make a series of elaborate judgments about what is *not* the case. Let's consider an example of that sort. Suppose that Sebastian arrives at an empty and serene park, expecting it to be full of people enjoying the sunny day. Looking out over the park, he thinks:

(9) JIG (How strange it is that there are no **kids running after each other**;...no **families having a picnic**...no **dog leaping after a Frisbee**...no **couples rowing boats**.)

Here Sebastian makes a series of judgments about what is *not* going on in the park, using a variety of mental images in the process. He doesn't make a single snap judgment—*empty park!*—and move on. He *contemplates* the park's being empty through the use of imagery, thinking about what the park would be like if it were a normally busy weekend. Because he is engaged in some rich, extended thought about a merely possible situation (the park being full of revelers) in a way that is epistemically compatible with his not believing the situation to obtain, it is a good candidate for an A-imagining. And, due to the presence of the mental images within this rumination, it is also an instance of I-imagining. Further, because it serves no immediate practical goal, it is, in addition, a daydream. And, finally, because it is a JIG—one of Sebastian's occurrent judgments—the episode can also be explained in more basic folk psychological terms.

Pre-theoretically, we simply don't consider whether all the mental states entertained during an instance of A-imagining could possibly be judgments. We just remark that Sebastian was imagining the park full of revelers, for instance, without contemplating whether the states in virtue of which he does so could possibly have been judgments. But, in this case, on reflection, we can account for the sense in which his cognition is "about the merely possible, fantastical or unreal" by noting that he is thinking about a rich variety of ways he believes the park *not* to be; this is to consider possibilities for how the park could have been.

This is certainly not to suggest that *all* daydreams could receive this sort of analysis. I will consider some different cases below. It is also not to suggest that all JIGs where negations are judged will be A-imaginings. Not all will be adequately rich and extended, or occur in the sort of contemplative setting where we are inclined to ascribe an A-imagining. So it is no objection to point out that there are cases of judging a series of negations that we would not happily describe as imagining. As earlier noted, on my view, imagining does not form a natural (mental) kind. Whether our folk psychological intuitions pull us toward granting that someone is imagining is a highly contextual matter. Issues of subject matter, duration of the episode, the person's assumed mood, the sort of action she is undergoing, and so on, will all influence our judgments.

With these points in hand, other examples are easily found. Assuming that the following occur in a context where they are not put toward achieving some immediate practical goal, here are some other DIGs and JIGs that are plausible instances of daydreams:

(10) JIG (It would be fun to be **a person flying over the Alps in a jetpack**...)
(11) DIG (The animal I see as I peek through the Jurassic reeds, is **a brachiosaurus eating from the treetops**...)
(12) JIG (The car that might resolve my midlife crisis is **a powder blue, '67 Mustang**...)
(13) DIG (The landscape visible from the cliff I'm standing on is **a vast expanse of turquoise water.**)

An extended bout of daydreaming could involve a sequence of such JIGs and DIGs.

Some may nevertheless remain unconvinced by such examples. They may reply that *their* daydreams are not plausibly seen as JIGs or DIGs. Presumably, such claims will be grounded in their introspective assessments of their own daydreams. It is, in any case, unclear to me what else such an objection might be based upon. The fact that disputes about the nature of daydreams are likely to devolve into disputes about the deliverances of introspection is, I suggest, reason to let one's theory of daydreams follow one's broader theory of imagination, and not the other way around.[7]

4.10 Hybrid Structures Are Not Problematic

A key claim of this chapter is that non-imagistic elements of thought combine with mental images to form I-imaginings with complex contents and different kinds of truth and satisfaction conditions. The idea that I-imagining involves both imagistic and non-imagistic elements working in tandem is not new. Precedents can be found in Fodor's (1975, p. 190) notion of entertaining images "under a description," Tye's (1991, Ch. 5) interpreted symbol-filled arrays, Kung's (2010) images with "assigned" contents, Reisberg's (1996) images set in "reference frames," Johnson-Laird's (1996) "mental models," Peacocke's (1985) S-imaginings,

[7] See section 1.11 for more on the limits inherent in letting introspection arbitrate disputes about imagination.

and in the passages from Kaplan (1968) and Martin (2002) quoted earlier. Nevertheless, it is also commonly held (e.g., among pictorialists) that mental images have an iconic or pictorial representational format, whereas non-imagistic thought (which is sometimes equated with *conceptual* thought) has a language-like format, such that the meaning of a complex representation is a function of the meaning of its discrete, semantically significant parts, together with the syntactical the rules for combining them (as we find, e.g., in Fodor (1975, 1987)). The latter view, as applied to folk psychological ontology, was discussed at length in Chapter 2. As noted at the outset of this chapter, it might be thought that these two formats of representation are like oil and water—they don't mix. If that worry is well founded, then we are left with a significant puzzle about how the two formats manage to interact in sequences of thought.

It should be emphasized, first, that the problem of mixing cognitive formats only arises from within the terms of heavy-duty views of folk psychological ontology that are committed to specific theses about the nature (and format) of the states causally responsible for the dispositions we attribute with folk psychological talk. When a light-duty theorist countenances the existence of JIGs, they merely grant that there are occurrent processes that involve apparently image-like states that lead one to have certain dispositions. For instance, to say that Joe has made the JIG in (1) is just to say that he fulfills a certain dispositional stereotype associated with believing that the couch he ordered will fit through his doorway, and that he does so in virtue of a thought process that seemed to him image-like. As there is no commitment here to the existence of representations in particular formats, there is no question to address as to how distinct formats might combine. However, I nowhere assume the truth of a light-duty perspective and, again, don't want to depend on such an account's being correct. I want instead to explain why, even on a heavy-duty view of folk psychological ontology, there is no special reason to be troubled by the idea that I-imaginings have hybrid structures.

The primary reason for holding that language-like and picture-like formats cannot combine within a single truth- or satisfaction-evaluable mental state traces to the issue of logical form. One of the dreams of cognitive science—especially in its early stages—was that transitions in rational thought could be modeled on the rules for manipulating the variables and connectives of various systems of formal logic. We know that the truth-preserving inferences of formal logic can be captured by a set of (syntactic) rules for manipulating symbols based purely on their intrinsic physical properties—their "shape," as it is sometimes put. In that way, relations of semantic entailment among symbols can be mirrored by relations of causal entailment among those same symbols, based on their intrinsic physical features—as discussed, briefly, in Chapter 2. This is, in essence, how computers work. A tempting thought is that human thought processes might also, in effect, be viewable from two perspectives simultaneously: as unfolding according to physical laws governing the neural realizers of symbols in the brain, yet where this "unfolding" at the same time mirrors the rational relations of semantic entailment we take our thoughts to follow at the personal level (Fodor, 1987). A crucial part of this picture is that thoughts have discrete meaningful *parts*, akin to the parts of a logical expression, such that the meaning of a thought is a function of the meaning of its parts. The meaning of a complex representation can then change if the parts are rearranged in accord with relevant syntactic rules. Without these assumptions—or, if you like, *hypotheses*—there is no clear analogy to be drawn between the operations of a computer and human cognition.

Introducing mental imagery into this picture may be thought to create problems. For if pictorialists are right that mental images represent by depicting their referents, then mental images must lack the language-like compositional structure necessary for the desired analogy of thought to formal logic to hold. In Fodor's (2003, pp. 34–7) term, depictions, and "iconic" representations generally, "lack canonical decompositions," insofar as there is no regimented way of breaking the representation into minimally meaningful parts of the sort that can be recombined, in accord with a set of syntactic rules, to form new truth-evaluable representations. It then becomes unclear how a cognitive system could use this type of representation in processes that mirror those of formal logic, unfolding according a fixed set of syntactic rules for manipulating and recombining a set of discrete symbols.

However, the potential problem here is not special to the present "hybrid" account. *Any* heavy-duty theory that grants a role for depictive (or "iconic") representations in practical reasoning must confront the issue of how such representations inferentially interact with non-imagistic, language-like representations. Little is gained on that front by holding that the two kinds of representation never combine into a *single* truth-evaluable representation. We simply trade the question of how a single complex representation can combine formats for the question of how a truth-preserving inference can occur between two complex representations with distinct formats. To the extent that depictive, iconic representations appear at all in sequences of thought, we have already moved beyond what any simple comparison of human inference to the manipulations of formal logic could explain. The proposal that some human thought involves language-like representations combined with iconic representations faces no challenges not also faced by any attempt to find a place in practical reasoning for mental imagery. Thus, those who take a heavy-duty approach to the ontology to JIGs, DIGs, and the rest, are no worse off than anyone else who countenances both language-like and image-like representations in human cognition.

4.11 Recap

Whether we think of folk psychological ontology in heavy-duty or light-duty terms, there is no barrier to mental images forming proper parts of various folk psychological states, including judgments, decisions, desires, and more. We can symbolize these folk psychological states through the use of an "attitude" operator (such as JIG, DIG, or DEC) next to a sentence, where the sentence's predicative content is accounted for by the contribution of one or more mental images. Let's take brief stock of what this framework allows us to explain:

- We are able to see how some I-imaginings have truth or satisfaction conditions, with related functional and inferential roles. This allows, in turn, for an appropriate connection between the state's content and correctness (or satisfaction) conditions, on the one hand, and the conditions under which the state leads to successful (or unsuccessful) action and inference (or motivates behavior), on the other.
- We have an elucidation of the Multiple Use Thesis (Martin, 2002; Noordhof, 2002; Peacocke, 1985), insofar as we have an account of the precise sense in which an image of a certain type can be used in imaginings of different particulars and scenarios.
- We have an explanation of how an I-imagining can be of or about things other than the causal source of the images involved—a capacity assumed by any theory which grants that we can imagine things never perceived.
- We can see how mental image-involving fantasies and daydreams are in fact cases of judgments and desires.
- More generally, we gain a picture of how I-imaginings—such as elaborated JIGs and DIGs that concern the possible, fantastical, and so on—can also be cases of A-imagining. This enables, in turn, an explanation of those A-imaginings in more basic folk psychological terms. Further, it makes vivid the sense in which both I- and A-imaginings are made up of a heterogeneous assortment of more basic folk psychological states.

These positive proposals are intended to be compatible with either a light-duty or heavy-duty understanding of the mental states involved. In ascribing to someone a JIG (or DIG, or DEC) with a certain content, I am ascribing an occurrent mental process that (as a matter of folk psychological platitudes) is responsible for a person's having dispositions to engage in particular behaviors and inferences, and that is the sort of endogenously-triggered process that tends to be introspectively identified as "image-like," or as having sensory character. Some theorists working with a heavy-duty ontology may add to those claims that the process itself makes use of mental representations that occur in distinct language-like and image-like (or analog) formats. The point of simultaneously maintaining a coherent light-duty analysis is not to avoid refutation by empirical science or to imply that any particular view about the nature of cognitive representation is incorrect. It is instead to offer a framework for explaining imagination that may be useful to a variety of incompatible approaches to understanding the underlying mechanics of cognition.

In the chapters that follow, this hybrid framework for understanding I-imaginings will appear in explainations of the A- and I-imaginings that take place in contexts paradigmatically associated with imagination, including conditional reasoning, pretense, fiction consumption, and artistic creation.

5

Conditional Reasoning Part I

Three Kinds of Conditionals and the Psychology of the Material Conditional

5.1 Introduction

We know that A-imagining involves contemplating possibilities in a rich and epistemically safe way. But there are many things it can be to "contemplate possibilities." In this chapter and the next, I want to focus on one particularly important kind of (often) rich or elaborated thought process during which we contemplate possibilities: *conditional reasoning*. Episodes of conditional reasoning, as I will understand them, are thought processes that result in judgments with an if-then structure. We can reason conditionally about what is or will be the case, given that certain other things are or will be the case—judging, for instance, that *if Henry is at the meeting, then he looking at his phone*, or that *if I go to the block party, then I will try the bean dip*. And we can reason conditionally about what would have been the case, had things been different—concluding, for example, that *if I hadn't had the bourbon, I'd feel better today* or that *if Clinton hadn't used a private email server, she would have won the election*. In linguistically expressing such thoughts, we use if-then statements, otherwise known as conditionals. One of the central hopes for a theory of imagination is that it sheds some light on our capacity to reason with and about conditionals.

I want to set reasonable goals, however. Conditionals generate deep and continuing controversies within both philosophy and psychology. There is currently little consensus in how their truth conditions are to be analyzed, nor in whether all types of conditionals have truth conditions at all. (See Bennett (2003) and Edgington (1995) for lucid overviews of these debates.) Nor is there consensus in experimental psychology concerning the psychological states at work in their appraisal (see Evans & Over (2004) and Johnson-Laird & Byrne (2002) for discussion), or even in the normative standards that ought to apply to judgments about conditionals in experimental contexts (Oaksford & Chater, 2003). My limited goals are twofold: first, to articulate a coherent view—a *how plausibly* story—on which inferring and reasoning with conditionals draws only upon beliefs. (Some of these beliefs will involve mental images as proper parts (see Chapter 4).) My second goal is to show that, correct or not, such a view is preferable to any that posits *sui generis* imaginative states. Doing this much will serve the book's broader

Explaining Imagination. Peter Langland-Hassan, Oxford University Press (2020). © Peter Langland-Hassan.
DOI: 10.1093/oso/9780198815068.001.0001

purpose of explaining imagination, insofar as it shows how the A-imagining that occurs during conditional reasoning can be reduced to patterns of inference involving more basic folk psychological states (beliefs, primarily); this reduction undermines whatever attraction views positing *sui generis* imaginings may seem to have. The questions I leave open—such as the proper analysis of the semantic difference between indicative and subjunctive conditionals, or the mental states that are *in fact* exploited during conditional reasoning—are the kinds of questions that can only be answered by a formal philosophical or psychological theory of conditionals, both of which fall beyond the scope of this book. It will, however, be important to understand the key *questions* in this area, including those surrounding the distinction between indicative and subjunctive conditionals, and the relation of each to the material conditional of formal logic. To date, these crucial distinctions among kinds of conditionals have, for the most part, gone ignored in philosophical discussions of imagination's relation to conditional reasoning.[1] As we'll see, grasping them is essential to understanding the role of imagination in conditional reasoning, and in "modal epistemology" more generally.

5.2 Modal Epistemology?

Before diving in, a few words on the project of *modal epistemology* in general. The questions of modal epistemology are questions of how we arrive at knowledge of possibilities and necessities. These questions differ, however, depending on the sense of 'possible' and 'necessary' in play. At times, we use the term 'possible' in an epistemic sense, to mark what is not ruled out by what we know. For instance, it is possible, for all I know, that 237 × 345 is 84,425. Nothing I believe rules it out. However, I have now carried out the calculation and see that the answer is 81,765. It is now no longer epistemically possible, for me, that 237 × 345 is 84,425. Knowing what is and is not possible in this sense has only to do with knowing our own beliefs; there is nothing especially puzzling about our knowledge of these kinds of ("merely epistemic") possibilities.

Other uses of modal terms have a more objective air. There is another sense in which, even before I did the calculation, it was *not* possible that 237 × 345 is 84,425. In the realm of mathematics, this more objective form of possibility is referred to as *logical* or *conceptual* possibility. But I will follow more recent convention in using the term *metaphysical possibility* to mark the entire realm of objective possibilities. (I will leave open the question of whether there are logical

[1] The most detailed existing discussion I know of is in Williamson (2007, pp. 134–55), though Williamson focuses almost entirely on subjunctive counterfactual conditionals to the exclusion of indicatives and the material conditional.

or conceptual possibilities that are not also metaphysical possibilities, as those controversies won't touch the questions at issue here.) Unlike the multiplication example, some propositions that are not epistemically possible (for me) nevertheless remain *metaphysically possible* in the sense that they *could have* been true. Suppose, for instance, that I count the objects on my desk and see that they are five. It is now *not* epistemically possible for me that there are ten objects on my desk; there being ten is not compatible with what I know. However, it remains metaphysically possible that there *could have been* ten objects on my desk. That is a way the world could have been, but is not.

It is a good question how we know that certain things *could have* been the case—in this more objective, metaphysical sense—given that we know they did not occur. How do we figure it out? Since perception doesn't seem to the point, imagination is often pushed onstage to answer. It is said, following Hume (1738/2012), that imagination is to the possible as perception is to the actual. Perhaps it is not obvious *how* imagination would offer us a window onto the possible-but-not-actual. Unactualized possibilities do not, after all, causally impinge upon our imagination in the way that ordinary perceived objects impinge upon our senses. But, nevertheless, some find it highly intuitive that imagination plays such a role; and they may be satisfied to show that there is nothing incoherent in the idea that imagination (or an idealized version thereof) offers us reliable access to facts about the possible (Yablo, 1993; Chalmers, 2002; Kung, 2010).

An alternative way to approach the question of how we determine what is possible is through examining conditional reasoning. When we say that Hillary Clinton could have won the 2016 election, we typically have in mind certain counterfactual conditions under which she would have won. For instance, if Clinton had not used a private email server, we may reason, she would have won the election. Likewise, if Earth had been struck by a wave of giant asteroids millions of years ago, we may think, it would now be devoid of life. Answering how we come to know the relevant facts about what *would* have happened—and thus what is metaphysically possible but not actual—looks to be part and parcel with coming to know related conditionals. Typically, when we decide that if p then q, we have found q to be metaphysically possible, in the sense that q could have happened. (Note the formal difference, however: it is one thing to say "if p had been the case, q would have been," quite another to say, "it could have been that q.") Some have indeed argued for a tight connection between metaphysical modality and counterfactual reasoning, proposing that our knowledge of the former relies entirely on our ability with the latter (Williamson, 2005, 2007, 2016). While I am sympathetic to that project, I won't defend it or rely on it here. (See Strohminger & Yli-Vakkuri (2017) for more on this debate.) I will instead limit my discussion of modal epistemology to querying the role of imagination in our reasoning with and about conditionals. This includes not only counterfactual subjunctive conditionals ("if p had been the case, then *q* would have been"), but forward-looking hypotheticals in the indicative mood as well, such as: *if John mocks the dean, he will be sorry*, or *if Julia goes on a cruise, she will regret it*. These, too, are judgments about merely possible situations.

Focusing on conditional reasoning may leave my treatment of modal epistemology incomplete by the lights of those who reject an equivalence between conditional reasoning and judgments about possibility and necessity. I think this merely amounts to a difference in aims and interests, however. My aim is to explain the platitudinous facts about imagining that anyone needs to accept—e.g., that it guides pretense, helps us to plan our actions, is used when we make ordinary judgments about what could have (but didn't) happen, underlies creativity and our engagement with fiction, and so on. Explaining imagination's role in conditional reasoning serves that end. Some others who theorize about imagination when doing modal epistemology—such as Chalmers (2002), Yablo (1993), and Kung (2010)—seem to have a different project. They take, as common ground, a set of modal claims—many inspired by the work of Putnam (1975) and Kripke (1980)[2]—and aim to describe a kind of mental process (an idealized form of *imagination*) that could be relied upon (or not) to ground our knowledge of those claims. As these modal claims are *prima facie* surprising to most, explaining our knowledge of them requires considerable revision (and idealization) of the commonsense notion of A-imagining.

I do not pass judgment on that project; I just set it to the side, for the purposes of this book. The question of how and why we infer the conditionals relied upon in everyday life—and the role of imagination in our doing so—is difficult enough. It is a question we need to answer whether or not there are such things as *a posteriori* necessities, and irrespective of any controversial claims about *particular* possibilities (such as that we could have physical duplicates who lack phenomenal consciousness (Chalmers, 1996)). Explaining the imaginings that occur during conditional reasoning is essential to explaining how we get about in the world. That is modal epistemology enough. Maintaining this focus has the added benefit of tethering our inquiry to related literatures on conditionals in the philosophy of language and experimental psychology.

5.3 Conditionals: Metaphysics and Psychology

To begin, we need to distinguish two different, if related, questions we might ask about conditionals. First, we can ask the metaphysical question of what conditionals *are*. Here we are asking for a theory of conditionals themselves. Typically, a theory of conditionals tries to explain what conditionals are by giving a systematic

[2] These include surprising "*a posteriori* necessities," such as that water is necessarily H20, and that Hesperus is necessarily Phosphorus.

account of their truth conditions or semantics. This involves comparing and contrasting different kinds of conditionals with respect to their ability to fit a certain framework for understanding truth conditions (or, alternatively, appropriateness conditions for their utterance). The second question we can ask concerns the nature of the psychological states exploited when reasoning about conditionals, or when coming to infer one conditional as opposed to another. This psychological question is my focus here, as imagination is most naturally, and most commonly, invoked in explanations of how we reason our way to conditional beliefs, as opposed to in theories of their semantics and truth conditions.

Traditionally, most philosophical discussions of conditionals have focused on their metaphysics (Bennett, 2003; Edgington, 1995; Lewis, 1973; Lycan, 2001; Stalnaker, 1968), with experimental psychologists attending more to the nature of the mental processes exploited in assessing and inferring conditionals (Byrne, 2007; Evans & Over, 2004; Johnson-Laird & Byrne, 2002). Yet there is always interplay between the two questions. Philosophical theorizing about the truth conditions of conditionals treads deeply into psychological questions concerning how and why we accept the conditionals that we do. And psychological theorizing about the nature of the mental states exploited in conditional reasoning, and related experimental designs, are inevitably tied up in assumptions concerning the proper semantics for conditionals—assumptions according to which some participant responses to prompts are *mistakes* in need of explanation (Johnson-Laird & Byrne, 2002; Oaksford & Chater, 2003).

In the next section, I canvas some reasons commonly given for distinguishing three different types of conditionals—material, indicative, and subjunctive conditionals—by their different associated truth conditions. If these different kinds of conditionals indeed show systematic differences in their truth conditions—if there are different things that *if-then* means in each case—we can expect those differences to show up in whatever imaginings are at work in generating our beliefs in conditionals. One of the main projects of this and the following chapter is to show how imagination needs to be understood somewhat differently when theorizing about each type of conditional. In each case, I will argue, a reductive account is available.

5.4 The Material Conditional and Its Relation to Indicative and Subjunctive Conditionals

In all the foggy terrain surrounding conditionals, there is nothing clearer than the metaphysics of the material conditional, familiar to systems of formal logic. The material conditional is defined in terms of a simple truth table. Letting the horseshoe ("⊃") stand for the relation of material implication, the truth of '$p \supset$ 'q is a simple function of the truth of p and q. That gives us four possibilities: both p and *q* are true; *p* is true while *q* is false; *p* is false, while *q* is true; and both *p* and *q* are false. The truth table used to define the meaning of '$\supset$' tells us that '$p \supset q$' is true in all these situations save where *p* is true and *q* is false. A material conditional's truth, then, is entirely a function of the truth or falsity of the two propositions flanking the horseshoe. This is the sense in which the material conditional is *truth functional.*

Many of the philosophical puzzles concerning conditionals spring from the observation that what goes for the material conditional does not obviously apply to the conditionals of natural, spoken languages. I will follow convention in distinguishing two classes of conditionals that occur within natural language: indicatives and subjunctives. Indicative conditionals are marked by the indicative mood ("is," "will") in the manner of: *If John is at home, then he is studying.* Subjunctives are marked by the subjunctive mood ("had" or "would") and comprise conditionals such as: *If John had studied, then he would have passed the exam*. The study of "counterfactuals" in philosophy focuses on subjunctive conditionals in the past tense, with formulations such as "If he had dropped the rock, it would have broken his toe." The person asserting such a counterfactual typically doesn't believe the antecedent conditions to hold. However, the subjective mood and the notion of an antecedent thought to be counterfactual don't always march in lockstep. There is, for instance, the doctor who in diagnosing malaria comments: "If he had contracted malaria, these are exactly the symptoms we would expect." For reasons we will come to, it is nevertheless customary to theorize about subjunctive counterfactuals as a class, distinguishing them from indicative conditionals in both the present and past tenses.

Most contemporary theories of conditionals deny that the indicative and subjunctive conditionals of natural language are truth functional in the manner of the material conditional (Bennett, 2003; Edgington, 1995; Lewis, 1973; Lycan, 2001; Stalnaker, 1968). The reasons are easy to see when we observe that the truth table for the material conditional '$p \supset q$' is identical to that for the disjunction: not-*p* or *q* (i.e., $\sim p \vee q$). That is, '$p \supset q$' is true in every situation where '$\sim p \vee q$' is true, and false in every situation where '$\sim p \vee q$' is false. This makes plain that the mere falsity of *p*, or the truth of *q*, is each sufficient for the truth of '$p \supset q$.' Yet, in the case of subjunctive counterfactual conditionals, the antecedent is almost always false, and thought to be false by the person uttering it. If the truth conditions for subjunctive conditionals are the same as those for the material conditional, then almost all counterfactual conditionals must be true. This clashes badly with our actual use and appraisal of subjunctive counterfactual conditionals. We are not, for instance, apt to judge *both* of the following counterfactuals true simply because they have false antecedents:

(A) If Clinton had not used a private email server, she would have defeated Trump

(B) If Clinton had not used a private email server, Trump would still have won.

Pundits clash over which of (A) or (B) is true. But none argue that both are true. So subjunctive counterfactual conditionals appear not to be truth functional in the manner of the material conditional. Some other analysis of their truth conditions is needed.

Similar problems plague attempts to equate indicative conditionals with the material conditional. Let '$\rightarrow$' stand for the indicative conditional relation, such that '$p \rightarrow q$' is an arbitrary conditional in the indicative mood. If '$p \rightarrow q$' has the same truth conditions as '$p \supset q$,' then '$p \rightarrow q$' is true whenever p is false and whenever q is true. But, intuitively, in assessing whether '$p \rightarrow q$' is true, we wish to know more than whether p is false or q is true. We want to know whether a certain connection holds between p and q.[3] This tension comes to the fore in the "paradoxes" of material implication. To pull an example from Stalnaker, if the indicative conditional is logically equivalent to the material conditional, then the following should be a valid argument: "the butler did it; therefore, if he didn't, the gardener did" (1975, p. 136). For the premise ("the bulter did it") is in effect the negation of the antecedent of "if he didn't, the gardener did"; and we know, from the truth table for material implication, that $p \rightarrow q$ is true whenever p is false. Similarly, according to the logic governing the material conditional, any false conditional must have a true antecedent. Staying with Stalnaker's example, it seems absurd to propose that, in denying the conditional "If the butler didn't do it, the gardener did," we must thereby accuse the butler.

Efforts have nevertheless been made to defend the idea that indicative conditionals share the material conditional's truth functionality. It can be replied, for instance, that the oddities we see in the above "paradoxes" are pragmatic in nature and don't touch the logical validity of the inferences (Grice, 1989; Jackson, 1987). In situations where one already knows that not-p, for instance, it is conversationally *inappropriate* to say "$p \rightarrow q$." For there is an implication carried by utterances of $p \rightarrow q$ that the speaker is in doubt as to whether p, just as there is an implication carried by utterances of "p or q" that the speaker is in doubt as to both p and q. This flouting of a pragmatic norm might be thought to explain away the sense that it is logically invalid to infer that $p \rightarrow q$ from not-p. The reason it seems "off" to infer $p \rightarrow q$ from not-p is that it is inappropriate to *say* $p \rightarrow q$ when one already believes that not-p—inappropriate because it would have been more informative for the speaker to have instead said that not-p, just as it is more informative to say that p, instead of p or q, when one believes that p.

Few have been persuaded by such efforts, however. As Dorthy Edgington observes, the problems with analyzing indicative conditionals on a par with the material conditional occur at the level of rational inference, irrespective of any norms to be succinct in conversation. This is particularly evident in the many

[3] Strawson (1986), for instance, analyzes the meaning of $p \rightarrow q$ as, roughly, "There is a connection between p and q that ensures that: $p \supset q$."

everyday contexts where one is confident in the truth of some proposition but lacking in absolute certainty. To take Edgington's example, she is confident that her husband is not home; and she is also confident in the conditional: if he is at home, he will be worried about my whereabouts (because she is working later than usual). Edgington is also confident that the Queen is not at home. Yet there is nothing irrational in her *rejecting* the claim that if the Queen is home, then she will be worried about my whereabouts. On the truth-functional analysis of indicative conditionals, however, confidence in not-*p* ("The Queen is not at home") should always warrant equal confidence in "$p \rightarrow q$." "We need to be able to discriminate believable from unbelievable conditionals whose antecedent we think false," Edgington explains. "The truth-functional account does not allow us to do this" (1995, p. 245).

Another point against equating '$p \rightarrow q$' with '$p \supset q$' traces to differences in whether contraposition succeeds for each. For the material conditional, '$p \supset q$' and '$\sim q \supset \sim p$' are equivalent—that is, true in all the same situations. Yet this isn't always the case with indicatives. Here is an example from Jonathan Bennett: "I accept that even if the Bible is divinely inspired, it is not literally true; but I do not accept that if it is literally true, it is not divinely inspired" (Bennett, 2003, p. 30). Other procedures that are valid for the material conditional but of questionable validity for indicatives include Transitivity and Antecedent Strengthening.[4] But, more generally, the idea that indicative conditionals can be equated with the material conditional, with counterexamples explained away as merely pragmatic, has suffered from the availability of a quite different and *prima facie* more attractive alternative for understanding their nature: the Ramsey test.[5] We will look closely at the Ramsey test in Chapter 6.

I have so far canvassed just a few reasons for distinguishing subjunctive and indicative conditionals from the material conditional. The consensus on these matters is that we cannot tether our investigation of conditional reasoning entirely to principles appropriate to the material conditional. For not all procedures that are valid with respect to the material conditional extend to indicative and subjunctive conditionals. If indicative and subjunctive conditionals are the conditionals of everyday life, then our main interest here should be in the psychological states that allow us to evaluate them. Nevertheless, in the balance of this chapter, I want to focus specifically on the material conditional, asking: if and when we reason in accordance with the logic governing the material conditional, what sort of mental states must we exploit? For even if we do not always, or even typically,

[4] The truth table for the material conditional guarantees that if $p \supset q$ is true, then so will be $p \,\&\, r \supset q$. This does not always hold for indicatives. True: If you jump out of an airplane from 3,000 feet in the air, you will perish. False: If you jump out of an airplane from 3,000 feet in the air and pull the ripcord on your parachute, you will perish.

[5] Though see Jackson (1987) for an attempt to fold the key insights of the Ramsey test into an account that still equates the truth conditions of '$p \rightarrow q$' with '$p \supset q$.'

treat the indicative and subjunctive conditionals of natural language as we would if they had the truth conditions of the material conditional, we might in some cases. Moreover, given the historical interest of philosophers in systems of natural deduction—wherein the material conditional resides—some will no doubt hold out hope for understanding either indicative or subjunctive conditionals by close, if not perfect analogy to the material conditional. So it will be worthwhile to consider the relation between the material conditional and our own psychological states before moving on, next chapter, to focus squarely on the nature of indicative and subjunctive conditionals. In particular, we need to ask whether we have good reason to posit *sui generis* imaginative states as a means to explaining our relationship to the material conditional.

5.5 The Material Conditional and Assumptions: Conditional Proof and *Reductio ad Absurdum*

Suppose that we are presented with the conditional statement "if *p* then *q*" and asked to assess its truth. Intuitively, when we consider whether "if *p* then *q*" is true, we imagine that *p* and see if *q* is also true, or at least likely, given that *p*. This is, at least, one thing we might do. But suppose, further, that in answering we must limit ourselves to deductively valid inferences in keeping with the logic of the material conditional and formal principles of natural deduction more generally. (Of course, we are not so limited in everyday life, where inductive and abductive inferences are also available; the point for now is to focus on how imagination relates to procedures within formal systems of natural deduction.) What can the imagining that occurs in considering "if *p* then q" amount to, if we are limited to psychological states and processes that mirror the steps and inferential principles of natural deduction?

We should first observe that not all assessments of "if *p* then q" will require anything that intuitively seems like imagining that p. If, for instance, we already happen to believe that not-*p*, or that q—or to believe other things from which we can deduce that not-*p*, or that q—we can immediately infer that "if *p* then q" is true, relying solely on inferences among our beliefs. This follows straightforwardly from the truth table by which the material conditional is defined. Likewise, if we happen already to believe that *not-p or q*, we will be warranted in believing *if p then q*. On the other hand, if we already believe that *p and not-q*, we will have immediate reason to reject the conditional. In all these cases, deciding whether to believe the material conditional did not require us to step outside of our beliefs to arrive at a judgment about what would happen if *p*. Intuitively, it did not require us to imagine that *p*.

But what about cases where we have no idea whether *p* or *q* and where we lack any beliefs on the basis of which we might deduce either's truth or falsity? How then might we decide whether to believe "if *p* then *q*," limiting ourselves to psychological states that mirror the steps of a deductively valid proof in formal logic? Could imagination get a foothold here? Are there times when we imagine that *p* so as to see what would follow (deductively) from *p*? Here the method of *conditional proof* suggests itself. Within a system of natural deduction, a conditional proof can be used to assess whether the conditional "A ⊃ C" follows from a set of premises, when A and C are not themselves premises of the proof. A simple example occurs in the context of proving that the hypothetical syllogism (also known as transitivity of implication) is a valid form of inference—i.e., that it is always truth-preserving to infer "A ⊃ C" from "A ⊃ B" and "B ⊃ C." Using the method of conditional proof, we can "assume" the antecedent of the conditional in question and see if, in conjunction with our other premises, we are able to derive the consequent of the conditional. If we are, this serves to prove that the conditional itself follows from the (not-assumed) premises. The assumption of A, together with any steps following it in the sub-proof it initiates, are "discharged" at the conclusion of the proof, insofar as they are not put to use in any further derivations.

On paper, the conditional proof of the hypothetical syllogism looks like this:

1: A ⊃ B (premise)
2: B ⊃ C (premise)
3: A (assumed for the purpose of conditional proof)
4: B (from 1 and 3)
5: C (from 2 and 4)
6: A ⊃ C (from lines 3, 4 and 5, by conditional proof; steps 3–5 are discharged)

Here we have a deductive method for arriving at a new conditional, when the antecedent and conclusion are not among the non-discharged, non-assumed premises. If we were to *psychologize* this procedure, understanding each step as a token mental state in a sequential process of reasoning, we could ask what *kind* of state corresponds to each step. A natural picture suggests itself: Steps 1 and 2 correspond to beliefs—beliefs on the basis of which we wish to know whether we may infer the conclusion in step 6. Steps 3, 4, and 5, on the other hand, might be thought to correspond to mere suppositions or *sui generis* propositional imaginings (or, indeed, "assumptions"). For they serve to register the (mere) assumption of A and the determination of what follows from that assumption, given the two not-assumed premises. The fact that the assumed steps are later discharged—and thereby, in a sense, *quarantined* from any further derivations—meshes with the idea that their contents are not preserved among one's beliefs; it also seems to fit with the psychological platitude that we can imagine, suppose, or assume things we do not believe.

Another context where psychologizing the procedures of a system of natural deduction seems to suggests a role for imaginative states are proofs via *reductio ad absurdum*, where we "assume true" a particular proposition in order to show that its acceptance would lead to a contradiction. When constructing a *reductio* of *p*, we typically will not believe that *p*, after all. Thus, were we to carry out a *reductio* "in our heads"—assuming that *p* in the process—it may seem that we must exploit a mental state *other than* one of our beliefs to record the assumption. Here again we seem to have reason to posit *sui generis* imaginative states, corresponding to the "assumed" step(s) in a *reductio*.

5.6 Psychology and Systems of Natural Deduction

We are considering whether the methods of conditional proof and *reductio ad absurdum* within systems of natural deduction give reason to posit *sui generis* imaginative states. A first question to ask about these cases is whether, in order to arrive at the kinds of conclusions allowed by conditional proof and *reductio ad absurdum*, we *must* exploit mental states that correspond in a roughly one-to-one way to the steps of such proofs—positing something like *sui generis* "imaginings" or "supposings" wherever an assumption appears. Is it in some sense a priori, or *necessary*, that such mental states are used to arrive at the all the deductively valid inferences that we in fact can make? Here the answer is a clear no. Prior to the development of systems of natural deduction in the 1930s (Gentzen, 1934; Jaskowski, 1934), "axiomatic" systems of formal deduction—such as those developed by Frege (1879) and Ackermann & Hilbert (1928)—held sway. All the theorems that can be proven in systems of natural deduction can be proven in axiomatic systems as well.[6] Yet axiomatic systems don't employ "assumptions" within proofs at all; instead they contain a set of basic assumptions (the axioms) and, typically, employ a single inference rule of *modus ponens*. If we were to psychologize each step of an axiomatic proof—mapping it to a particular mental state—each step could be seen as corresponding to a suitable belief, insofar as each step is either a premise or an axiom. Sound axiomatic systems can do all the same work as sound systems of natural deduction that employ assumptions; indeed, many logic textbooks teach a method for converting proofs of one kind into proofs of the other.

However, axiomatic proof systems are notoriously complex and unwieldy. A fairly straightforward proof within a system of natural deduction may require dozens of steps in an axiomatic system—with each step containing long strings of linked propositions. The byzantine complexity of axiomatic systems is one reason more "natural" systems were sought. One might argue, therefore, that axiomatic proof systems do not represent a *plausible* alternative to systems of natural

[6] Pelletier (2000) provides a helpful history of the transition from axiomatic systems to systems of natural deduction, and the spread of the latter throughout North America in the 1950s and 1960s, thanks to its adoption in influential logic textbooks.

deduction, provided that we are looking for models that may closely correspond to our actual psychological processes when evaluating conditionals.

While the objection has merit, it would be an error to conclude from the difficulties we may have in understanding a theory that specifies the nature of our cognitive workings that we do not, in fact, make use of the states or processes that the theory describes. The challenges one may experience in understanding the nature of artificial neural networks, or of Bayesian updating, do not, for instance, tell against the hypothesis that our minds exploit processes well modelled by artificial neural networks, or that calculate Bayesian probabilities. We may reason in accordance with principles, or through the use of computational processes, that we are in no position to articulate and that we would struggle to comprehend. So much is a working assumption in computational cognitive science. The comparative complexity of axiomatic systems does not, then, render them otiose as hypotheses about our cognitive underpinnings.

Now, I do not, as it happens, think that any axiomatic proof system *is* a faithful model of our thought processes. They were never created to be such. Nevertheless, they serve as a helpful reminder that there is in principle no difficulty in the idea that deductive inferences—including inferences in favor of new conditionals—can take place without the use of mental states whose contents mirror those of the assumptions or suppositions in systems of natural deduction.

Such reminders aside, we can still ask the more pressing question of whether the theory that we exploit mental states mirroring the steps and inferential rules of systems of natural deduction remains a *plausible* theory. Is there good reason to think that, when evaluating conditionals, we enter into mental states that mirror the steps of proofs within natural deduction—assumptions (or "suppositions") included? Here again the answer is no. As Jonathan St. B. T. Evans comments in a review article summarizing the last forty years of psychological research on human reasoning, "few reasoning researchers still believe that [deductive] logic is an appropriate normative system for most human reasoning, let alone a model for describing the process of human reasoning" (2002, p. 978). While in the late 1960s, it was still common among psychologists (under the influence of Piaget) to hold that adult human thought processes unfolded in ways that mirror the steps of deductive logical proofs, "it soon became apparent that…participants performed very poorly" on abstract deductive reasoning tasks aimed to reveal those capacities (p. 980). These tasks were specifically devised to abstract away from potentially biasing contextual information, so as to allow participants to focus on logical structure. In a typical example, participants are asked to assess whether "not-A" must follow from "If A then B," and "not-B." It is now common coin among psychologists studying human reasoning that people make widespread and systematic errors in their judgments concerning the validity of different forms of deductive inference (see Manktelow (1999) for a review).

Perhaps the most famous and robust paradigm in this literature—the Wason selection task (Wason, 1968)—concerns the evaluation of conditionals. In a typical version of that task, participants are shown four cards and told that each has a letter on one side and a number on the other. Only the letter side is visible on two cards, while the only number side is visible on the others. Participants are asked which cards they would need to overturn in order to evaluate the truth of the conditional: "If there is an even number on one side of a card, there is a vowel on the other." The interesting—and very robust—result is that over 90 percent of participants fail to suggest turning over a card that shows a consonant, despite the fact that, should there be an even number on the other side of that card, the conditional is falsified. One way to put the apparent implication is that, when evaluating conditionals, most people fail to consider the relevance of situations where the consequent is falsified. And yet, if people were hard-wired to reason in accordance with the principles of natural deduction, it is hard to see why they should so often fail to recognize the importance of such situations to the truth of the conditional they are to evaluate.

In another well-known and equally robust result from this literature, while participants reliably affirm that *modus ponens* (if *p* then *q*; *p*; therefore, *q*) is a valid form of inference, only about 60 percent of undergraduate university students answer that *modus tollens* (if *p* then *q*; not-*q*; therefore, not-*p*) is valid (Evans, Newstead, & Byrne, 1993). Further, participants frequently endorse fallacies, such as "denying the antecedent" (viz., "if *p* then *q*; not-*p*; therefore, not *q*") and, especially commonly, affirming the consequent (viz., "if *p* then *q*; *q*; therefore, *p*") (Evans, Clibbens, & Rood, 1995). Such results have spurred psychologists to posit psychological processes that would explain them. These processes have properties at odds with systems of natural deduction, insofar as they are specifically designed to explain the ways in which human judgments systematically diverge from the patterns allowed by systems of natural deduction. One of the most influential proposals of this sort is Johnson-Laird's (1983) and Johnson-Laird & Byrne's (2002) "mental models" hypothesis, which we will consider in some detail below.

For now, two important points can be made in summation. First, there is no necessary entailment that our thought processes, when evaluating conditionals, mirror the steps of a system of natural deduction—including its use of "assumptions." When we follow along with a request to "assume that *p*"—be it in ordinary conversation, or when assembling a *reductio*—there are a variety of things we may be doing that are not entering into a *sui generis* mental state of assuming, supposing, or imagining with *p* as its content. We saw that there are well-developed alternative logics that incorporate no assumptions. While there is no reason to think that these systems describe our thought processes as they actually occur, they serve as exemplars for the in-principle dispensability of "assumptions" and "suppositions" at the level of cognitive processing. (We will consider other possibilities of this sort below and in the chapter to follow.) Second, systems of natural deduction are not, in general, descriptively adequate with respect to ordinary human reasoning. While it certainly *could be* that we nevertheless, at times, make use of *sui generis* imaginative states when evaluating conditionals, the important role that assumptions play in systems of natural deduction give us no reason to posit such states, for the simple reason that such proof systems are not themselves descriptively adequate with respect to human reasoning.

5.7 Conditional Proof and *Reductio ad Absurdum* Revisited

And yet, even if systems of natural deduction are not descriptively adequate with respect to human reasoning, one might think that some *pieces* of them are, some of the time, for some people. In particular, if one can't really see how to do without assumptions when deductively inferring a conditional, or conducting a *reductio*, it may be tempting to hold on to the idea that assumptions play a role in the mind comparable to the role they play in natural deduction. For this reason, it will be worthwhile to show how the methods within natural deduction that seem to cry out for mental states of "assuming" (or "supposing" or "imagining") can be reconceived so as to involve only belief. We've already seen that such reframings are possible, in principle, by reflection on axiomatic proof systems. However, knowing that assumptions are eliminable in principle may leave one skeptical that they can be avoided in practice. Thus, in the examples below, I will limit myself to mental states and inference rules that, like those of natural deduction, translate smoothly to the terms of ordinary folk psychology. This will help to reinforce the point that any apparent practical need for cognitive equivalents to "assumptions" (via *sui generis* imaginative states) is illusory.

5.7.1 Conditional Proof without Assumptions

Let's return, first, to the assumptions within a conditional proof. The role of a conditional proof is to *prove* that a certain conditional follows from specific premises that are not themselves assumptions (and that will not be discharged). For instance, the conditional proof we considered above is a proof that $A \supset C$ follows from $A \supset B$ and $B \supset C$. This proof just serves to establish that transitivity of implication holds for material conditionals—that if we know that both $A \supset B$ and $B \supset C$, we will always acquire a true belief in judging that $A \supset C$. An inferential procedure that takes the first two material conditionals as premises and outputs the third as a conclusion will be truth-preserving. This suggests an obvious alternative for understanding the transitions in psychological states that actually occur when we infer that $A \supset C$ from $A \supset B$ and $B \supset C$. Supposing we believe that

A ⊃ B and B ⊃ C, we may infer directly from those beliefs that A ⊃ C. The inference rule followed would be transitivity of implication. So, to explain our ability to come to know A ⊃ C on the basis of knowing A ⊃ B and B ⊃ C, we need only posit an ability to reason in conformity with transitivity of implication.

Of course, it remains *possible* that we might, instead, break the inference into additional steps "in imagination"—steps mirroring the steps of a conditional proof—representing that A, B, and C via *sui generis* imaginative states, before concluding that A ⊃ C. This would be, in effect, an alternative method for carrying out the same computation of deriving A ⊃ C from the inputs of A ⊃ B and B ⊃ C. This latter method modelled on the method of conditional truth has the virtue of not requiring use of the inference rule of transitivity of implication. Yet it has the vices of both requiring additional inferential steps and the interaction of two different kinds of mental states (beliefs and *sui generis* imaginings). If we really did, at the psychological level, carry out an inference mirroring the steps of this conditional proof, we would need to keep in mind five premises at once—two of which involve conditionals—in order to arrive at the conclusion. The alternative method, which moves directly from two premises to the conclusion, has the virtue of requiring fewer steps and of only employing beliefs. It has the corresponding vice of requiring use of an extra inferential rule: transitivity of implication. From my vantage, this method appears simpler overall; from any vantage, it is at best a toss-up. This case of conditional proof gives no reason to posit *sui generis* imaginative states.

Stepping back, it's easy to see that any case of conditional proof at all can be reconceived without assumptions—even while still working within a framework that otherwise mirrors closely the steps of a proof within a system of natural deduction. The method of conditional proof simply serves to show that it is truth-preserving to infer a certain conditional from a certain set of (not-to-be-dischared) premises. Doing without the assumptions requires exploiting an additional inferential rule in their place—one that takes us from the main premises to the conclusion. Granted, it may seem extravagant to posit a new rule for each species of inference (to a conditional) we might wish to make. But, as a practical matter, most of us will be unable to conduct many different species of such proofs "in the head" anyway—whether we think of them as involving assumptions or not! If our inferential capacities are limited, in practice, we needn't attribute to ourselves a grasp of all the inferential rules we might need, in principle.

5.7.2 *Reductio* without Assumptions

Similar points apply to the case of *reductio ad absurdum* in systems of natural deduction, where we "assume" that *p* as a means to establishing that *not-p*. When we carry out a *reductio* "in our heads"—assuming that *p* in the process—it may seem that we exploit a mental state *other than* one of our beliefs to record the assumption. Here again we seem to have reason to posit *sui generis* imaginative states. Perhaps we assume that *p* by tokening an imaginative state with the content *p* and then appreciate the contradiction that follows "in imagination."

To see why psychologizing this procedure needn't involve *sui generis* imaginative states after all, it will help to consider a couple of concrete examples. I offered one style of *reductio* above in passing, when dismissing the thesis that subjunctive (counterfactual) conditionals have the same truth conditions as the material conditional. We know that the material conditional is true whenever its antecedent is false. Therefore, if counterfactual conditionals have the same truth conditions as the material conditional, then all counterfactual conditionals with false antecedents are true. But that is absurd, because it is clear that many counterfactuals with false antecedents are false (e.g., "If I had dropped a feather on my toe, it would have left a bruise"). Therefore, we are warranted in rejecting the claim that counterfactual conditionals have the same truth conditions as the material conditional. Writing the proof out in steps, it might look like this:

1. Counterfactual conditionals have the same truth conditions as the material conditional. (Assumed for *reductio*)
2. The truth conditions for the material conditional mandate that a material conditional is true whenever its antecedent is false. (Premise)
3. All conditionals with the same truth conditions as the material conditional and with a false antecedent will be true. (Lemma, from 1, 2)
4. Therefore, all counterfactuals with false antecedents are true. (Lemma)
5. Not all counterfactuals with false antecedents are true. (Premise)
6. Steps 4 and 5 generate a contradiction; reject 1, 2, or 5.

If we were to psychologize these steps as a means to understanding how the computation is carried out psychologically, steps 1 and 4 would correspond to *sui generis* imaginative states; for we can assume that the person carrying out the inference does not belief those propositions. (Those propositions are not "in" their Belief Box.) The other steps, presumably, correspond to beliefs in one's knowledge store.

The purpose of a *reductio* is to arrive at an answer as to whether to a particular proposition (to be rejected) is true. Put in terms of an input and output, and of a process that mediates between them, the input can be seen as a question, namely: is it the case that *p*? The output of a successful *reductio* returns the answer: "No." Staying with the example above, let us suppose that the process begins by the subject registering the question "Is it true that counterfactual conditionals have the same truth conditions as the material conditional?" The system searches its knowledge store for information relevant to answering and, in particular, locates 1, 2, and 3:

1. All material conditionals with false antecedents are true, as a matter of their truth conditions. (Premise)
2. If counterfactual conditionals have the same truth conditions as the material conditional, then all counterfactual conditionals with false antecedents are true. (Premise)
3. Not all counterfactuals with false antecedents are true. (Premise)
4. Therefore, counterfactual conditionals do not have the same truth conditions as material conditionals. (Conclusion, from 2, 3 *modus tollens*)

This reasoning process answers the same question as the one modelled on *reductio ad absurdum*. It takes, as input, the question of whether counterfactual conditionals have the same truth conditions as the material conditional and gives, as output, the answer: No. And it makes use of essentially the same stored information. However, it does not call upon any internal states that are not beliefs—no "merely assumed" representations. Nor does it exploit any unusual rules of inference. For all we know a priori, when humans carry out the kind of reasoning associated with this style of *reductio*, they are, at the psychological level, making inferences from among their beliefs, in the manner of 1–4, using *modus tollens*.[7]

This style of *reductio*, while common, is not a *reductio* in the strict sense. It relies upon a strong prior belief (in 3) that conflicts with an entailment of the proposition in question. More formal arguments by *reductio* work simply by showing how a contradiction follows from a certain premise—a premise that is then rejected because of its entailment of a contradiction. Such arguments do not rely upon one's having a prior conviction that the denial of a certain proposition (e.g., step 3) would be unacceptable. These might seem more clearly to necessitate *sui generis* imaginative states as such cases don't lend themselves to reformulation as instances of *modus tollens*. Let us consider an example of this kind, which I adopt from Rescher (2018). Suppose that we are uncertain whether it is possible to divide a non-zero number by zero to get a well-defined quantity, Q. A classical *reductio* of

[7] I hear the following objection: "Let A be 'Counterfactual conditionals have the same truth conditions as material conditionals' and let B be 'All counterfactual conditionals are true.' It is precisely by representing that A, in imagination, that we come to infer, in imagination, that B! And it is again only by representing that B, in imagination, that we are able to see that it conflicts with our belief that not-B."

The heart of the objection is that it is only by representing that A, in imagination, that we are able to *dwell upon* A so as to see that B follows from it; and then it is only by representing that B, in imagination, that we are able to *dwell upon* it so as to see that it (absurdly) conflicts with our stronger prior belief that not-B. But this objection leads nowhere. Imagination is not required to dwell upon questions generally. When asked, we may dwell upon the question of our favorite pizza topping. Turning our attention to that question does not require us to enter into any *sui generis* imaginative states. The same goes for turning our attention to the question of what would happen if A, or the question of whether anything we believe conflicts with B. (I expand on this point in section 8.8.) Whether *answering* the question we have so posed requires *sui generis* imaginative states is the better, more difficult question I am considering at length.

the proposition that this is possible would begin with the assumption whose truth we wish to assess:

(1) $x \neq 0$ and $x \div 0 = Q$ (Assumption)

By familiar principles linking multiplication and division, we can then derive (2):

(2) $x = Q \times 0$
(3) Any number multiplied by 0 is 0. (Premise)
(4) Therefore, $x = 0$.

Step (4) contradicts our assumption in (1) that $x \neq 0$. It is the assumption of (1) itself, together with bedrock principles of arithmetic, that leads to a contradiction of (1) with (4). Noticing the contradiction, we can either reject the bedrock principles of arithmetic or reject (1) on the grounds that its truth entails a contradiction. As written, steps (1), (2), and (4) are all suggestive of states that are not believed and would need to be "merely imagined." Our question is whether this same computation can be carried out through a belief-only reasoning process. We need to start by clarifying the nature of the reasoning: it takes, as input, the question: When $x \neq 0$, and x is divided by 0, can x be Q? As output, it gives the answer: No. On reflection, we can see how the relevant reasoning could instead exploit transitivity of implication, discussed above on the topic of conditional proof. We can rely upon background knowledge of arithmetic principles to infer as follows:[8]

Revised reductio
(1) If $x \neq 0$, and $x \div 0 = Q$, then $x = Q \times 0$

This inference is made on the basis of the same knowledge that allows us to have (2) as a premise in the *reductio*, as initially written. Then, recalling the principle that 0 multiplied by any number is 0, we can infer:

(2) If $x = Q \times 0$, then $x = 0$.

Finally, by transitivity of implication for the material conditional, we are able to conclude:

(3) If $x \neq 0$ and $x \div 0 = Q$, then $x = 0$. (1,2 by transitivity of implication)

When we arrive at (3), we see that something has gone wrong. Our conclusion has the form: if not-A & B, then A. This conditional is not itself a contradiction. By the logic of the material conditional, (3) will be true whenever "$x \div 0 = Q$" is

[8] Whether we actually do so will of course depend upon our facility with mathematics—as it will no matter how we understand the algorithm. The point is to show that there is no practical computational limit imposed by working only with beliefs.

false—i.e., it will always be (vacuously) true. But recall the question that started the computation: when $x \neq 0$, and x is divided by 0, can x be Q? We have found, in (3), that if $x \neq 0$ and $x \div 0 = Q$, then $x = 0$. It is now clear that the truth of the antecedent implies its own falsity. Or so we believe, if we believe (3). This is reason to reject the truth of the antecedent itself—just as step (4)'s contradicting step (1) in *Classic Reductio* gives reason to reject (1). We have our answer to the question that began the computation: No, it can't be that $x \neq 0$, and $x \div 0 = Q$.[9] The same function computed in *Classic Reductio* has been computed without the use of *sui generis* imaginative states, while limiting ourselves to the tools of natural deduction itself. Further, doing so hasn't forced us into computations of obviously greater complexity.

With these examples, I don't claim to have established that every conceivable *reductio* could receive this kind of treatment. But then, we already knew, from reflection on axiomatic proof systems, that it is *possible* to make do without assumptions within a formal system for deduction. What I have aimed to show, in this section, is that *even when working within the general terms of a system of natural deduction*, the denier of *sui generis* imaginative states has ample room to maneuver when faced with explaining deductive inferential patterns that appear to require something like a cognitive state of "assuming," "supposing," or "imagining." The apparent need for "assumptions," even within those systems, is *only* apparent, if we allow ourselves a few tweaks. We have also seen that systems of natural deduction are themselves limited in their capacity to model the actual inferential patterns of human thought—including, especially, thought about conditionals and hypothetical entailment. The combined upshot is that the occurrence of assumptions within the steps of proofs in systems of natural deduction gives us little reason to posit corresponding *sui generis* imaginative states.

5.8 Mental Models?

I noted earlier that a number of psychologists advocate a "mental models" approach to the psychology of conditional reasoning, developed most prominently by Philp Johnson-Laird and colleagues (Byrne, 2005; Johnson-Laird, 1983; Johnson-Laird & Byrne, 2002). The authors who posit mental models sometimes describe the use of such states as "imagining," and hold that they are exploited when people consider whether various forms of reasoning are deductively valid.

[9] We get a similar result when interpreting the conditional in (3) in line with the Ramsey test, discussed next chapter. On that view of conditionals, (3) should only be believed if "$x = 0$" has a high probability within a belief set containing "$x \neq 0$" and "$x \div 0 = Q$." Obviously, "$x = 0$" will not receive a high degree of probability within any belief set containing "$x \neq 0$," and so (3) will be rejected. We will not, in turn, believe the antecedent of (1)—"x is not 0, and $x \div 0 = Q$"—because we see that any belief set that contains it must contain (3) as well, which has been rejected.

So it is worth exploring whether these theorists are in fact committed to the kind of *sui generis* imaginative states that I've claimed we needn't countenance. The reader is forewarned that translating the terms of psychologists into those familiar to philosophers is not always straightforward. Before beginning, let me preview my conclusion: psychologists positing mental models often hold that the models consist in sequences of mental imagery; they therefore assume that uses of mental models are cases of I-imagining, in my sense. However, when we consider the attitude or force of those imagistic model-states, the most natural interpretation is that they are judgments or beliefs. Specifically, the mental models are *proper parts of* judgments or beliefs. Thus, these theorists are not committed to anything like a *sui generis attitude* of imagining. Their views are compatible with reducing A-imagining to a collection of more basic folk psychological states.

Johnson-Laird and Byrne ("JLB") see their theory—which extends beyond reasoning with conditionals to include inductive and deductive inference generally—as differing from what they call "formal rule theories." Formal rule theories, by their reckoning, are classical computational approaches according to which "individuals reason using formal rules of inference like those of a logical calculus" (2002, p. 646). They propose that instead of using quasi-logical formal rules of inference, reasoners "imagine the possibilities under consideration—that is, [they] construct mental models of them" (p. 647). The "underlying deductive machinery" at work in conditional reasoning, they argue, "depends not on syntactic processes that use formal rules but on semantic procedures that manipulate mental models" (p. 647). They support their theory with experiments showing that people reason about conditionals in ways that would be expected if they were using mental models of a specific sort (and not "formal rules").

How do mental models relate to things philosophers are accustomed to theorizing about—such as propositional imaginings, or sensory imaginings? JLB's broad characterization of mental models doesn't clarify matters. Mental models, they propose:

> can be constructed from perception, imagination, or the comprehension of discourse. They underlie visual images, but they can also be abstract, representing situations that cannot be visualized. Each mental model represents a possibility. It is akin to a diagram in that its structure is analogous to the structure of the situation that it represents, unlike, say, the structure of logical forms used in formal rule theories. (2002, p. 647)

On the one hand, mental models can "underlie visual images" and so, perhaps, are imagistic in nature.[10] This seems to fit with their idea that, unlike "logical

[10] Elsewhere: A model "may take the form of a visual image" (Johnson-Laird, Byrne, & Schaeken, 1992, p. 421). "The end product of perception is a model of the world (Marr, 1982)" (1991, p. 421).

forms," a model's structure "is analogous to the structure of the situation that it represents." On the other hand, these models can also be "abstract, representing situations that cannot be visualized." In that case, it is unclear how we are to understand the structural isomorphism between the representation and its content. JLB invoke imagination (as well as perception, and language comprehension) as a kind of faculty that *constructs* mental models; but they say little else about the faculty. More often, when they speak of imagining, they appear simply to have in mind the occurrent use of mental models—whatever *their* nature.

We are able to get a clearer picture of the relation between mental models and folk psychological states like belief by looking at the role mental models play in JLB's theory. "By definition," they tell us, "a mental model of an assertion represents a possibility given the truth of the assertion. Hence, a set of mental models represents a set of possibilities" (p. 653). Of course, actualities are possibilities; thus, when representing actualities, beliefs represent possibilities. So, the fact that a mental model represents a possibility is not at odds with its being a constituent of a belief. In the case of what they call "basic conditionals,"[11] JLB hold that there are three possibilities where the conditional "if *a* then *b*" is true, mirroring the three rows of the truth table for the material conditional where a conditional is true.[12] In one such possibility, *a* and *b* are both true; in another, *a* is false while *b* is true; in the third, both *a* and *b* are false. To represent that set of three possibilities, JLB propose, one needs to generate three separate mental models: one mental model representing *a* and *b* as both being the case; another representing not-*a* and *b*; and a third representing not-*a* and not-*b*. JLB use quasi logical notation in symbolizing these "models" as follows:

a b
not-*a* *b*
not-*a* not-*b*

Anyone who explicitly represents what they call the "core meaning" of a basic conditional will generate all three mental models simultaneously, on their view. However, they claim, reasoners typically do not *explicitly* represent all three mental models when considering a conditional. Rather, they often represent some of the possibilities only "implicitly"—in particular, those where the antecedent is

[11] Basic conditionals, for Johnson-Laird and Byrne, "are those with a neutral content that is as independent as possible from context and background knowledge, and which have an antecedent and consequent that are semantically independent apart from their occurrence in the same conditional" (2002, p. 648).

[12] In contrast to Evans & Over (2004), who posit a role for mental models in conditional reasoning while espousing the Ramsey test (see Chapter 6) as a criterion for a conditional's acceptability, JLB hold that the truth conditions for conditionals are in fact those of the (truth-functional) material conditional—even if we do not use "formal rules" when assessing them. See Barrouillet et al. (2008) for further discussion.

false. To represent the model implicitly is to be *disposed* to generate the model explicitly, should one be triggered in the right way.[13] On their theory, very often the only model explicitly represented (read "explicitly represented" as *occurrently tokened*) when someone thinks about a conditional is the first of the three mentioned above, where the antecedent and consequent both hold. They symbolize this tendency—where one model is explicitly represented, with others represented only implicitly—by showing a model of the first situation (true antecedent and consequent), with an ellipsis below it:

a b
...

The ellipsis symbolizes that one is disposed to generate certain other models, but is not yet doing so. JLB argue that our tendency to generate just one of the three models in the set corresponding to a conditional (with the others "footnoted") serves to explain various experimental results on conditional reasoning. One is that *modus ponens* is an easier inference form to process than *modus tollens*; a second is that people are more likely to fall into the error of affirming the consequent than denying the antecedent (pp. 666–9).

Whether their theory is fact well supported by such findings needn't concern us here. Our interest is in the nature of mental models themselves—in whether we would need to countenance something like *sui generis* imaginative states if we wished to avail ourselves of JLB's theory. We now have enough pieces of the theory on the table to see that we do not. For it is not only conditionals that are represented via mental models on their theory; practically any other kind of assertion is as well. Consider the inclusive disjunction: either *p*, or *q*, or *p* & *q*. According to JLB, a person who explicitly represents (and occurrently judges) such a disjunction to be true forms the following set of mental models:

p
q
p q (p. 653)

Three distinct mental models are tokened as a means to representing the single proposition that *p*, or *q*, or *p* & *q*. Do we *imagine* these three "possibilities" when we explicitly represent the inclusive disjunction? Perhaps we do so in the

[13] JLB explain this as follows: "Basic conditionals have mental models representing the possibilities in which their antecedents are satisfied, but only implicit mental models for the possibilities in which their antecedents are not satisfied. A mental footnote on the implicit model can be used to make fully explicit models...but individuals are liable to forget the footnote and even to forget the implicit model itself" (2002, p. 654).

imagistic sense of imagine, supposing we use mental imagery in the process. But the question we are interested in is whether we generate a *sui generis* imaginative state in doing so—some state that cannot be viewed as a belief. (We've already seen, in Chapters 3 and 4, that there is no barrier to beliefs having mental images as proper parts.) Here the answer must be no. What JLB have given us is an account of what it is to believe an inclusive disjunction—or, perhaps better, to *occurrently* believe or *judge* an inclusive disjunction to be true. Namely, it is to think about these three possibilities simultaneously, via the use of this set of three mental models. To judge the proposition that *p, or q, or p &q* is, for JLB, nothing other than to token these three mental models. Mental models appear to be the constituents of beliefs, then, and not *sui generis* states that stand apart from them. Indeed, for JLB, the only difference between representing "if A then C" and the conjunction "A and C" lies in what is *implicitly* represented—i.e., the models we are *disposed* to generate, when triggered in the right way. In explaining the role of the ellipsis in their account, they note that "the ellipsis denotes the implicit model, which has no explicit content, and which distinguishes a conditional from a conjunction, *A and C*" (p. 655). So, on their account, there is often no *explicit* cognitive difference in what is represented when one represents a conditional and when one represents a simple conjunction. In both cases we explicitly "imagine" the same possibility where *a* and *c* hold, the only difference lying in certain "implicit" models (with "no explicit content") being available—if they are triggered in the right way—in the case of the conditional. This helps to clarify that simply judging that A and C often involves the same explicitly represented mental models as judging that if A then C; there is obviously no clash here with mental models serving to realize beliefs.

We can, when prompted, go on to explicitly represent the other two (normally implicit) models that differentiate believing the conditional from believing the conjunction. But this still amounts to believing (now *completely explicitly*) the conditional. We still have not in any sense stepped outside of what we really believe. Thus, JLB do not have anything like the notion of a cognitive attitude of imagination in mind when they speak of "imagining possibilities." They are better seen as making a claim about the nature of judgments. They are saying that *what it is* to judge "if *p* then *q*" is to generate one or more of the three mental models listed above (and that, typically, we generate just one, which explains various experimental results). There is no notion of a *sui generis* imaginative state at work. They do suggest that these models are often imagistic in nature. But, again, there is no tension in the idea that some beliefs and judgments have mental images as constituents. So, despite appearances—and despite JLB's own affinity for characterizing uses of mental models as "imagining possibilities"—there is nothing in their theory of mental models and conditional reasoning that stands in the way of explaining conditional reasoning entirely in terms of sequences of (sometimes imagistic) beliefs.

5.9 Summary

Let's recap. I distinguished three kinds of conditional—material, indicative, and subjunctive—and explained, briefly, why most take the conditionals of natural language (indicatives and subjunctives) to behave differently than the material conditional. Nevertheless, we may at times reason in accord with the material conditional. Philosophers, especially, are often inclined to characterize human thought in such terms. So it is worth considering whether systems of natural deduction, in which the material conditional occurs, give us reason to think that imagination cannot be explanatorily reduced to a collection of more basic folk psychological states. The best reasons appear to lie in two species of deductive reasoning that involve "assuming true" a proposition one does not believe: the method of conditional proof, and arguments via *reductio*.

In response, I first noted that the existence of axiomatic proof systems shows that there is no *in principle* difficulty in doing without "assumptions" (or corresponding *sui generis* imaginative states). Second, I discussed empirical work that casts strong doubt upon the claim that human reasoning mirrors the steps of a proof in a system of natural deduction. Even when contextual features are removed from reasoning tasks, so as to highlight their abstract structure, ordinary participants do not evaluate conditionals as they would if the logic of the material conditional were mirrored in their inferential architectures. This robust finding has led psychologists to seek means other than systems of natural deduction for modelling the psychological processes at work in "abstract" conditional reasoning tasks, such as judging the validity of a pattern of inference, or assessing the truth conditions of an artificially concocted conditional (as in the Wason selection task). Third, looking more closely at a few deductive proofs that make paradigmatic use of assumptions, I showed that the same conclusions can be reached without the use of assumptions, while still limiting oneself to a framework similar to that of natural deduction. This helps to further chip away at the sense that assumptions—conceived of as a *sui generis* mental states akin to "imaginings"—are especially valuable theoretical posits. The discussion concluded with a close look at the notion of a "mental model" as it appears in the influential work of Johnson-Laird and Byrne. Mental models, I argued, are best viewed as constituents of occurrent judgments—and, possibly, desires as well—and not as *sui generis* imaginative states.

Having seen that the material conditional, as it functions within systems of natural deduction, does not give us reason to posit *sui generis* imaginative states, we can now turn to see how matters stand with respect to the indicative and subjunctive conditionals of natural language.

6
Conditional Reasoning Part II
Indicatives, Subjunctives, and the Ramsey Test

6.1 Introduction

Last chapter I focused on the material conditional and its place within systems of natural deduction. I argued that nothing in the evaluation of such conditionals gives good reason to posit *sui generis* imaginative states. Even when experimental prompts abstract away from context to encourage participants to reason purely deductively, participants' conclusions concerning conditionals systematically deviate from the norms appropriate to the material conditional. It would be surprising, then, if systems of natural deduction were nevertheless good models for our actual psychological states and inferential processes. At the beginning of last chapter, I also noted that the indicative and subjunctive conditionals used in everyday life are evaluated differently than the truth-functional material conditional. The way we arrive at beliefs in such conditionals demands a different account, whatever we say about the material conditional. This chapter considers what that account should look like, and whether there is good reason to think that *sui generis* imaginative states will have a role within it.

The Ramsey test looms large in contemporary discussions of indicative and subjunctive conditionals and, as we will see below, inspires some of the best-developed and most influential theories of the role of imagination in conditional reasoning (Nichols & Stich, 2000; Currie & Ravenscroft, 2002; Williamson, 2016). I will explain what the Ramsey test consists in presently (section 6.2). A key argument of this chapter is that, regardless of whether the Ramsey test records an important insight about the nature of conditionals, it gives us no reason to posit *sui generis* imaginative states. Indeed, even if the Ramsey test provides a cogent analysis of how we assess conditionals, a view where such reasoning only involves beliefs is still preferable.

6.2 The Ramsey Test and Its Psychology

Often, when faced with whether to accept 'if *p* then *q*,' we simply consider the likelihood of *q*, on the supposition that *p*. This is to calculate the *conditional probability* of *q*, given *p*. If *q* appears likely in the event that *p*, we are inclined to

Explaining Imagination. Peter Langland-Hassan, Oxford University Press (2020). © Peter Langland-Hassan.
DOI: 10.1093/oso/9780198815068.001.0001

believe that if p then q; if not, then not. If it's true that our degree of belief in a conditional is simply a function of the probability we assign to q, in the event that p should occur, it's no wonder that analyzing indicative and subjunctive conditionals on a par with the material conditional creates "paradoxes" of the kind discussed last chapter. For if indicatives and subjunctives had the same truth conditions as the material conditional, we should be *equally* interested in the probability of not-p when considering whether to accept 'if p then q' as we are in the conditional probability of q given p. That is, our confidence in the truth of 'if p then q' should raise as a function of our confidence in 'not-p.' Yet, in general, it does not. As we saw last chapter, Edgington's increasing confidence that the Queen is not home doesn't make her increasingly confident that, if the Queen is home, then she is worried about Edgington's whereabouts. It does, however, sound plausible to say that Edgington's inclination to believe the (indicative) conditional, 'if the Queen is home, then she is worried about my whereabouts,' raises as a function of how likely Edgington takes it to be that the queen will be worried about Edgington's whereabouts, in the event that the Queen is home.

In the case of subjunctive conditionals, where we typically believe the antecedent to be false, the point is even clearer. Our degree of belief in the conditional does not match what it ought to be if the conditional had the truth conditions of a material conditional. After all, we may reject a subjunctive conditional—'if I'd had a healthy breakfast, I would have won the presidential election'—despite knowing that its antecedent is false. All material conditionals with false antecedents are true, however. As with indicative conditionals, it may seem, instead, that we will accept a subjunctive counterfactual to the extent that we find the consequent likely, had the antecedent occurred (though we will see counterexamples to this shortly).

Philosophers and psychologists have thus explored an alternative theory of both indicative and subjunctive conditionals, tracing to Frank Ramsey. In a brief and now very famous footnote, Ramsey offered the following characterization of what occurs when we consider whether to accept a conditional:

> If two people are arguing 'If A will C?' and are both in doubt as to A, they are adding A hypothetically to their stock of knowledge and arguing on that basis about C... We can say they are fixing their degrees of belief in C given A.
>
> (1929, p. 143)

Ramsey's proposal is that, when deciding whether to accept 'If A then C,' we are deciding how strongly we ought to believe that C, in the event that A—we are "fixing [our] degrees of belief in C given A." Stalnaker (1968) cites Ramsey's idea in developing his own influential theory of conditionals, applying it to both indicatives and subjunctives. (For reasons we will see, this lumping of the two under a single analysis is relatively uncommon, with the Ramsey test more commonly applied only to indicatives.) Stalnaker characterizes the psychological process of assessing a conditional as follows:

> First, add the antecedent (hypothetically) to your stock of beliefs; second, make whatever adjustments are required to maintain consistency (without modifying the hypothetical belief in the antecedent); finally consider whether or not the consequent is then true. (1968, p. 102)

Often, when we evaluate a conditional (such as a counterfactual), we already *disbelieve* the antecedent. In such cases, Stalnaker adds, "you cannot simply add it to your stock of beliefs without introducing a contradiction" (1968, p. 102). This is why he goes beyond Ramsey in specifying that "adjustments" must be made to one's stock of beliefs to accommodate the antecedent. Of course, in such cases, we do not literally come to *believe* the antecedent during hypothetical reasoning. Nor is it obvious what it could mean to add a proposition to one's stock of beliefs *only hypothetically*. After all, *something* really needs to be done in carrying out the Ramsey test, if it is to be seen as a bit of reasoning by which we decide whether, and how strongly, to believe a conditional. We *really* need to add the antecedent to our stock of beliefs *only hypothetically*. What could this involve?

Several philosophers see imagination as the crucial ingredient. Currie and Ravenscroft (2002) ("C&R") suggest that there is "nothing new" in their suggestion that imaginative states are belief-like because "philosophers interested in belief dynamics assume that imagining is belief like... when they offer the Ramsey test as a way of deciding whether you should accept a conditional" (2002, p. 12). In cases where we don't believe that *P*, but wish to determine whether we should accept 'If *P* then *Q*,' we can simply add *P* "in imagination... since imagination preserves the inferential patterns of belief" (p. 12). This is what C&R think Ramsey and his followers have in mind when they speak of disputants "adding A hypothetically to their stock of knowledge." If *Q* then "emerges as reasonable" one knows that 'If *P* then *Q*' should be believed (p. 12).

In a similar spirit, Nichols & Stich (2000) ("N&S") hold that, in order to form beliefs in conditionals relevant to pretending that *p*—e.g., "If we were at a tea party, then pastries would be served"—one must first represent that *p* in the Possible Worlds Box (hereafter, the "PWB," and aka the "Imagination Box") and see what inferences come to be made on that basis "in" the PWB. It is then by importing the latter representations—e.g., *q1* & *q2* & *q3*...—into our Belief Box as consequents of a conditional with *p* as its antecedent that we arrive at beliefs of the form: "If it were the case that *p*, then it would be the case that *q*1&*q*2...&*q*n" (2000, p. 128). As with C&R, the idea is that, in order to find out what would happen if *p*, we need to represent (in the PWB, or with *sui generis* belief-like imaginative states more generally) that *p* and see what we infer "in imagination." This is, putatively, a way of finding out what one *would* infer, *were* one to in fact believe that *p*; it is a way of adding *p* to one's stock of beliefs "only hypothetically." And it is available to us just because the relevant form of imagination is belief-like in its inferential properties. In N&S's terms, imagination's being belief-like amounts to the same "inference mechanisms" operating on representations in the PWB as in the Belief Box—a feat made possible by the representations in each box occurring "in the same code."

Finally, while Williamson (2016) does not place the same emphasis on imaginative representations having a certain format or "code," his account of imagination's role in conditional reasoning is also inspired by Ramsey's observation that "how we evaluate conditionals is closely tied to how we update our beliefs on new information" (2016, p. 118).

6.3 From Belief Conditions to Truth Conditions

Before evaluating these proposals concerning the psychological implementation of the Ramsey test, we should pause to consider the relationship of the Ramsey test to theories of conditionals more generally. As noted, Stalnaker endorses the Ramsey test as an account of what we do when *considering* a conditional (both indicative and subjunctive)—an account of the psychological conditions under which we will *believe* a conditional. The question still to be answered for a theory of conditionals, he notes, is how we are to "make the transition from belief conditions to truth conditions; that is, to find a set of truth conditions for statements having conditional form which explains why we use the method we do use to evaluate them" (1968, p. 102). To that end, he appeals to the notion of a *possible world*, which is to serve as an "ontological analogue" to a hypothetical set of beliefs. Stalnaker's idea is that, for any hypothetical set of (consistent) beliefs, there is a possible world where those beliefs are all true. He then defines a conditional's truth conditions in terms of such possible worlds—applying it to both indicatives and subjunctives—as follows:

> Consider a possible world in which *A* is true, and which otherwise differs minimally from the actual world. *'If A, then B' is true (false) just in case B is true (false) in that possible world.* (p. 102)

By this criterion, the truth or falsity of 'If A then B' doesn't hang at all on the actual truth value of A. Instead, it hangs on whether, in whichever possible world where A is true (i.e., in whichever "A world") that is otherwise most similar to the actual world, B is true as well. (Lewis (1973) develops a similar and equally influential approach to the truth conditions of counterfactuals.) An immediate advantage is that not all counterfactual conditionals come out true. "If Jeremy had asked Alice to dance, she would have agreed" is true just in case, in the possible world most similar to our own where Jeremy asks Alice to dance, she agrees.

How are we to *know* whether B is true in the A world most similar to our own? Here we are brought back to the Ramsey test. Adding A "hypothetically" to our set of beliefs and adjusting the set minimally for consistency with A constitutes an effort toward mentally representing a minimally different possible world where A is true. If we judge B to be likely from within that hypothetical set of beliefs, our confidence in the truth of 'If A, then B' should rise correspondingly. Such is Stalnaker's influential suggestion for linking the Ramsey-inspired epistemology to the metaphysics of conditionals. Notably, this theory still allows us to *misjudge* the truth value of a conditional. The A world that is *in fact* most similar to our own can easily differ from the possible world corresponding to a particular person's idiosyncratic belief set when it is revised to accommodate A.[1]

6.4 A Difference for Subjunctives

But there is a more profound way in which gaps can open between the Ramsey test and a conditional's truth value—one that has importance to theories of imagination. Earlier I mentioned that philosophers often approach the truth conditions of indicative and subjunctive conditionals differently, with Stalnaker (1968) being an exception. Why think that the mood difference between past-tense subjunctive conditionals ("If he had asked Sally to dance, she would have accepted") and past-tense indicative conditionals ("If he asked Sally to dance, then she accepted") warrants any difference in the treatment of their epistemology or metaphysics? A series of examples from Adams (1970) is telling.

[1] Bill Lycan (2001) offers an example where the two diverge: "If I finish this chapter today, Norway will have an unusually early autumn in 2055." The Ramsey test can explain why he does not believe this conditional, even if he suspects he will not finish the chapter today. For when he considers the belief set that results from adding "I will finish this chapter today" to his own stock of beliefs and revises for consistency, the proposition that Norway has an early autumn in 2055 does not emerge as likely. However, Lycan notes:

> Suppose that unbeknownst to us and even the world's most competent physicists, there are arcane laws of nature *L* such that the conjunction of *L* with my finishing this chapter today entails Norway's having the early autumn... Stalnaker or Lewis would count the conditional as straightforwardly true, since a world in which I finish the chapter but Norway fails to have the early autumn would have to differ from our world in its laws of nature (a large difference). (2001, p. 70)

On both Stalnaker (1968) and Lewis's (1973) theories, the truth of a conditional hangs on what is true at the "closest" or "most similar" possible world where the antecedent is true; and, as Lycan notes, differences in the natural laws governing a world are generally held to be among the most significant differences there can be. In this case, our denial of the conditional after applying the Ramsey test is "just a case of perfectly well justified false belief."

Consider this famous pair of conditionals that differ only in mood:

(1) If Oswald didn't kill Kennedy, then someone else did.
(2) If Oswald hadn't killed Kennedy, then someone else would have.

Most judge (1) to be true and (2) false. The difference in mood seems to generate a difference in truth value. Examples are easily multiplied. (It seems obvious that, if a meteor did not lead to the dinosaurs' demise, then something else did. It is less obvious that, if a meteor hadn't led to the dinosaurs' demise, then something else would have.) The recognition that subjunctives and indicatives have different truth conditions is the departure point for much contemporary theorizing about conditionals. Like any orthodox view, it can be questioned (see, e.g., Edgington 2008; Lassiter, 2017). But I won't do so here; my aim instead is to explain the relevance of this common view to theories of imagination.

My focus will be on the different epistemologies pertaining to each kind of conditional. Our tendency to accept (1) could reasonably be thought to derive from an application of the Ramsey test. We add 'Oswald didn't kill Kennedy' hypothetically to our stock of beliefs and make the minimal adjustments needed to maintain consistency (viz., we remove the belief that Oswald killed Kennedy). We then consider whether 'someone else killed Kennedy' should also be a member of that set—that is, we determine how *probable* that proposition is, from within the terms of our hypothetical stock of beliefs. The probability will be high. For still within that set remains the proposition that Kennedy was killed. Any *minimal* adjustment to one's set of beliefs—made only to preserve consistency—must leave that one in place. And indeed it is crucial to the relevance and reliability of the Ramsey test that our adjustments *be* minimal. Practically any consequent could appear to follow with probability from the truth of any antecedent, given *arbitrary* adjustments to a surrounding stock of beliefs, after all. A version of the Ramsey test that allowed for *more than* minimal adjustments to one's belief set would not be a reliable method for arriving at the truth of (1).

N&S—who are more explicit than C&R and Williamson in their explanation of how, precisely, we implement something like the Ramsey test—hold that when considering whether to accept 'if *p* then *q*,' we represent *p* in imagination and combine it there with representations of *all the other contents we believe*,[2] making only minimal adjustments for consistency. They posit an "UpDater" mechanism that is responsible for these adjustments—one that works either by deleting incompatible representations from the PWB, or by filtering them out before they arrive in the PWB. This gives us, in imagination, a set of representations consistent with a conditional's (not believed) antecedent that is otherwise coextensive

[2] "Let us assume that in addition to the pretense initiating premise, the cognitive system puts the entire contents of the Belief Box into the Possible Worlds Box" (Nichols & Stich, 2000, p. 123).

with our beliefs. We then let the relevant inferences unfold "in" the PWB (2000, pp. 122–5). In the present case, one such inference will be: someone other than Oswald killed Kennedy. We will then come to believe that, if Oswald didn't kill Kennedy, then someone else did.

Subjunctive conditionals present a problem for this method, however. Recall (2): 'If Oswald hadn't killed Kennedy, then someone else would have.' When I add 'Oswald didn't kill Kennedy' hypothetically to my set of beliefs and revise only for consistency, it will still emerge as reasonable that someone else did. For within that stock of beliefs remains the belief that Kennedy was shot. Lest I succumb to conspiracy theories, I would be wrong to infer that, if Oswald hadn't killed Kennedy, someone else would have. Nor am I inclined to make the inference.

For these reasons, it is thought by many that the Ramsey test is not the method we in fact use when considering subjunctive conditionals.[3] If that is so, then theories of imagination that aim to explain conditional reasoning in Ramseyan terms—showing how general principles governing the updating of beliefs apply *mutatis mutandis* to *sui generis* imaginative states—cannot extend themselves to explaining our reasoning about subjunctives. This is a significant limitation on these approaches. Imagination is a dear friend of the subjunctive mood. One of the key platitudes surrounding 'imagining,' in the A-imagining sense, is that it is a kind of cognition involved in considering how things *could have been*, had something else not occurred. Philosophers, in particular, are interested in the role imagination plays in our understanding of counterfactuals, linking them to our understanding of causation and natural laws. If we analyze imagination as a faculty which, by default, moves forward inferentially from a proposition as one would if one believed the proposition, imagination becomes ill-suited to explain counterfactual reasoning. Yet this appears to be precisely what theorists such as Nichols & Stich, Currie & Ravenscroft, and Williamson have in mind when they propose that "left to itself, the imagination develops the [possible] scenario in a reality-oriented way, by default" (Williamson, 2016, p. 116).

This does not mean that there is no possible explanation to be had for reasoning about subjunctive conditionals from within the terms of such accounts—only that they will require significant amendment to explain how belief-like *sui generis* imaginative states are used in reasoning about subjunctive conditionals. It has been proposed, for instance, that subjunctive counterfactuals simply require us to "rewind time" back to when the antecedent occurs, revising all beliefs concerning matters subsequent to that time. We then "re-run" the tape forward from there, as it were, assessing whether the consequent is probable in *that* context

[3] Problems have also been noted in extending the Ramseyan approach to indicatives, though these appear less pervasive. Counterexamples trade on cases where the truth of indicative conditional's consequent would require the agent considering the conditional not to know its truth. An example of this attributed by van Frassen (1980, p. 503) to Richard Thompson is: "If my business partner is cheating me, I will never realize that he is" (Bennett, 2003, pp. 28–9).

(Edgington, 2008). This is a version of what Lassiter (2017) calls, the "Rewind, Revise, Re-run" heuristic: "Rewind to the antecedent time, Revise to make the antecedent true, and selectively Regenerate following events that depend causally on the antecedent" (p. 527). This is one way of preserving a "suppositional" account of subjunctive counterfactuals—one where we "assume true" a certain set of propositions and assess the probability of another (the consequent) from within the terms of that set.

Note, however, that on this view we are no longer able to make use of our existing belief set minus one or two, together with our ordinary inferential procedures taken "offline." Instead we need to mentally rewind world history to a certain point—knowing what to edit out from our beliefs in the process and what to let stand—and then let it play forward again, calculating the consequences of the antecedent's having been true. Any heavy-duty suppositional account, like that of Nichols & Stich (2000), will need to posit additional features of cognitive architecture to accommodate these time-relative adjustments to one's belief set. Thus, evaluating subjunctive conditionals will require not simply the "offline" reuse of ordinary inference procedures—whatever they may be—but some mechanism capable of determining the historical time represented by each of our beliefs. This is like having to posit a special mechanism for weeding out all and only beliefs about events occurring in Europe, or events occurring during the summer. There is nothing incoherent in the idea of such a mechanism. But its addition, as a posit, is a significant cost to the theory.

I will analyze the Ramsey test in more depth soon when considering indicative conditionals. Those deeper reflections, aimed at undermining the assumed link between the Ramsey test and *sui generis* imaginative states generally, will apply *mutatis mutandis* to subjunctive conditionals. Supposing, until then, that we wanted to avoid a Ramseyan/suppositional account of subjunctive conditionals, how *else* might we understand the psychology of evaluating subjunctives? Let '□→' stand for the if-then relation of subjunctive conditionals. On the Stalnaker/Lewis account of subjunctive conditionals, which remains the most influential, to judge 'p □→ q' true is (roughly) to judge that the closest (i.e., most similar to our own) possible worlds where *p* are also worlds where *q*. The question then becomes how we go about judging the relative location of possible worlds with respect to our own. How do we decide that all possible worlds where Oswald doesn't shoot Kennedy and Kennedy is still assassinated are further from the actual world than those where Oswald doesn't shoot Kennedy and no one else does?

On the one hand, we do not have a complete mystery here. Most will agree that a world where the laws of nature are the same as our own is closer to our own than one where the laws are very different (Lewis, 1973). And specific cases seem easy to judge: a world where Donald Trump was never elected president seems closer than any where a centipede was elected president (unless, of course,

Trump's not winning would have required an unobvious adjustment in natural laws not required by a centipede's victory...). Proceeding from uncontroversial cases, we can make efforts to systematize those nearness judgments, showing how certain principles (such as sameness of natural laws) drive many of them. In the end we seem destined to arrive at a set of norms, heuristics, and rules of thumb for making relative location judgments. Without question, this is a complex form of reasoning that depends, crucially, on what we take to be true in the actual world. Our ignorance about the actual laws of nature will spill over into ignorance about the relative closeness of other possible worlds. But there is no reason to think that engaging in this sort of complex reasoning would require us to set aside, or step outside of, our beliefs. The process is *fueled by* belief. Based on what we believe true of our own world—and what we take "closeness" to depend upon—we reason that a possible world where A and B are true is closer to our own than any where A and not-B is true, and so judge that that "A □→ B" is true. It was only the Ramsey test—with its metaphorical talk of adding a proposition hypothetically to an existing stock of beliefs—that gave the impression of our needing to somehow step outside of our beliefs through the use of *sui generis* imaginative states to engage in this complex reasoning.

6.5 The Ramsey Test and the Psychology of Indicative Conditionals

Whatever difficulties subjunctive conditionals may present to theories of imagination modelled on the Ramsey test, such views would remain attractive if they still offered the best account for our reasoning with indicatives. These accounts—specifically, those of N&S, C&R, and Williamson—all posit *sui generis* imaginative states. Their success at explaining our reasoning with indicative conditionals would give reason to doubt my claim that we can fruitfully explain the A-imagining at work in conditional reasoning entirely in terms of beliefs. We need to look more closely now at how such theories propose to explain indicative conditional reasoning, to assess whether that reasoning could instead be implemented entirely within one's beliefs.

To begin, it is important to see that one can endorse the Ramsey test as an adequate account of the epistemology of indicative conditionals without thereby committing to the existence of *sui generis* imaginative states. The Ramsey "test"—with its language of adding propositions hypothetically to one's stock of beliefs—can be seen as an artful way of expressing the *theory* that, when evaluating an indicative conditional, people calculate the probability of the conditional's consequent given the antecedent. Taken as a theory about how people evaluate indicatives (or *should* evaluate them), it is at odds with the theory that people evaluate indicatives as though they are truth-functional in the manner of the material conditional. The latter theory predicts that people will evaluate indicatives by consulting the truth or falsity of their antecedents and consequents and matching those values to the corresponding row of the truth table for the material conditional. This debate about what people are actually up to when evaluating indicatives can march forward without either side committing to a view about *how* people go about judging conditional probabilities (when they do).[4]

And so it does in the book *If*, by psychologists Jonathan St. B. T. Evans and David Over (2004). Evans & Over hold that the Ramsey test captures the psychology of indicative conditionals to the extent that people's judgments concerning the probability of a conditional are shown, in experimental settings, to mirror their judgments about the conditional probability of the consequent, given the antecedent.[5] "The majority of people judge the probability of 'if p then q' to be at least close to the conditional probability of P(q|p)," they explain. This is "precisely what we would expect if people were conforming to the Ramsey test" (2004, p. 154). Yet they also stress that "the Ramsey test does not tell us *how* people make conditional probability judgments," where answering *how* would be to provide an account of the psychological mechanisms or processes by which the inference is made (p. 169, emphasis added). They add:

> Trying to answer the question of how the Ramsey test is implemented is a problem...there is no one answer to the question. There are rather many answers that will refer to many psychological processes. (p. 25)

And again:

> The Ramsey test is a high-level description of many processes that contribute to hypothetical thought. Describing fully the processes that can make up a Ramsey test of a conditional is a formidable challenge for psychological research on conditionals and in judgement and decision making. (p. 158)

We can see N&S, C&R, and Williamson as making specific (and indeed ambitious) proposals for how the reasoning behind the Ramsey test occurs—proposals that invokes *sui generis* (or "offline") imaginative states. They are not merely

[4] It is possible to hold that, while people in fact treat indicative conditionals as though their probability is equivalent to the conditional probability of the consequent given the antecedent, such conditionals nevertheless have the truth conditions of the material conditional. This would require holding that the proper normative account of indicative conditionals does not mesh well with how indicatives are in fact treated by ordinary reasoners.

[5] Johnson-Laird & Byrne (2002) adduce their own set of experiments where participants do not accept or reject conditionals based on the probability of the consequent, given the antecedent, to argue that the Ramsey test gives an incorrect account of our actual psychological engagement with conditionals.

concurring with Ramsey, and Evans & Over, that indicative conditionals are evaluated differently than material conditionals.

I want now to explore whether some approach along those lines proposed by N&S, C&R, and Williamson *must* be true. Having answered in the negative, I'll then evaluate whether such proposals are likely simpler or more powerful than any that appeal exclusively to belief. Again I will reply in the negative. "Belief-only" approaches are in fact more parsimonious, as they require nothing over and above what theories that posit *sui generis* imaginings themselves require—while doing without the *sui generis* imaginings.

6.6 A General Argument Against the Need for *Sui Generis* Imaginative States in Conditional Reasoning

Before we can find a belief-only approach to conditional reasoning plausible, we need to see how one is possible. That is the project of this section. Judgments in favor of conditionals are, for those espousing the Ramsey test, judgments concerning the high probability of the conditional's consequent, given its antecedent. Is it possible to judge, and thereby come to know, that the conditional probability of *q* given *p* is high, using only one's standing beliefs? In at least some cases, the answer is obviously yes. Evans and Over note that "there must always be some conditionals, of the form 'if p then q', that people consider probable *to the extent that they have learned that q type events follow p type events*" (2004, p. 8, emphasis added). If I believe that every time I have gone to the grocery store there were flowers for sale, it seems I can reasonably infer from my beliefs alone that if I go to the grocery store, I can buy flowers there. The inference would be something along the lines of:

1. Whenever I've gone to the grocery store, flowers have been for sale.
2. There is no reason to think conditions have changed.
3. Therefore, the probability that I can buy flowers, in the event that I go to the grocery store, is high.
4. Therefore, if I go to the grocery store, I can buy flowers there.

I did not, in conducting this reasoning, need to imagine that *I am at the grocery store* and see what emerged as likely. Williamson, N&S, and C&R will likely agree that simple inferences of this kind can be made without use of a PWB or an "offline" imaginative exercise. The more difficult question is whether there are nevertheless *some* more complex judgements in favor of conditionals that could not be carried out in this "belief-only" way. Evans & Over seem to think that there are, noting that people are not restricted to reasoning of the sort just described, "but can also use, for example, mental models of complex causal relationships to make probability judgments about conditionals . . . probability judgments that are generated theoretically and not just on the basis of past experience" (2004, p. 9).

We already looked closely, last chapter, at the notion of a "mental model" as it appears in the work of Johnson-Laird and colleagues. Properly understood, mental models are constituents of ordinary beliefs (or so I argued). Here I want to focus on whether there is any reason, in principle, to think that *some* judgments in favor of conditionals simply couldn't be construed as justifiably flowing from a set of preexisting beliefs—and if, instead, there are some that require the use of *sui generis* imaginative states. As a means to arguing that there is no such barrier on belief-only approaches, I will defend the following entailment:

RT Entailment: If an application of the Ramsey test, via *sui generis* imaginative states, would lead *S* to justifiably infer 'if *p* then *q*,' then *S already has*, prior to triggering the *sui generis* imaginative states, beliefs on the basis of which she can justifiably infer 'if *p* then *q*.'

To deny the RT Entailment, one needs to hold that an application of the Ramsey test, through the use of *sui generis* imaginative states, would lead *S* to reasonably infer 'if *p* then *q*,' *despite the fact* that *S* did not, prior to conducting the Ramsey test, have beliefs that warranted inferring "if *p* then *q*." (That would be to affirm the antecedent of the RT Entailment while denying its consequent.) The problem here is that the objector would *also* need to hold that there were no additional beliefs *S* needed to gain, so as to be warranted in inferring 'if *p* then *q*.' After all, the only thing that ensures that a person's Ramsey test will return *q* as likely after *p* is added hypothetically to her stock of beliefs "in imagination" is the stock of beliefs itself: do they, or do they not, contain other information that, when combined with *p*, make *q* emerge as likely? So, prior to imagining that *p* in the service of any Ramsey test that results in one's judging that *if p then q*, one's stock of beliefs must already be such that, were *p* imagined, *q* would emerge as likely. If that is not true of one's stock of beliefs, then imagining that *p* will not cause *q* to emerge as likely, and 'if *p* the *q*' will not be inferred.

Thus, the person denying the RT Entailment is in the absurd position of holding that one can lack justification for inferring 'if *p* then *q*,' despite there being no further beliefs one needs to gain before justifiably inferring 'if *p* then *q*.' What else *does* the person need to do before justifiably inferring 'if *p* then *q*'? The RT Entailment-denier will propose that *S* has to carry out a very specific psychological procedure of adding *p* hypothetically to her beliefs—via an offline imaginative exercise, use of the PWB, *sui generis* imaginative state, or similar—before justifiably inferring 'if *p* then *q*.' That claim is both adventurous and question-begging. In every other situation where a person has all the beliefs she needs to justifiably infer a proposition, we do not hesitate to conclude that she can use those beliefs—without aid of some other type of content-bearing mental state—to arrive at the inference. We may not yet be able to articulate the specific inferential rule, heuristic, or process that would be used in each case. But neither has the defender of *sui generis* imaginative states articulated such for imagination—appealing, as they do, only to "belief-like" or "reality-oriented" inference patterns. To the extent that questions remain open about the principles governing such inferences, they apply to theories invoking imaginative states as well.

So, the RT Entailment is hard to deny. If the Ramsey test rightly captures a normative standard for when we are justified in inferring a conditional, then *sui generis* imaginative states are never needed to provide justification for those beliefs. Nevertheless, it may be that such states provide a necessary *tool* for inferring conditionals—that they are not normatively but, rather, *psychologically necessary* for arriving at (at least some of) our beliefs in conditionals. This is the idea I want to explore now.

6.7 It Is Simpler to Just Use Beliefs—Considering an Example from Williamson

We have seen that there is no normative barrier to doing without *sui generis* imaginative states when carrying out the mental calculations needed to reason in accord with the Ramsey test. Beliefs will serve just fine, in principle. But it might still seem that such reasoning would be less cognitively demanding, faster, and, indeed, only psychologically feasible were we to use imaginative states that are distinct from our beliefs—that it is some cognitive limitation of our own that prevents us from being able to rely solely upon beliefs in all cases of conditional inference. In developing and responding to this objection, I will look in some detail at an example provided by Williamson (2016) in his explanation of imagination's role in conditional reasoning. Aside from the fact it is adduced in favor of there being "offline" imaginative states at work in conditional reasoning, there is nothing exceptional about the case. My argument will be that, in cases such as these, there are always background beliefs in generalizations that can serve as sufficient fuel for the inference, without need of *sui generis* imaginings. Further, it is no more cognitively demanding or time-consuming to make use of those background beliefs; for the very same background beliefs are needed on approaches that invoke *sui generis* imaginings as well.

In analogizing conditional reasoning to ordinary, non-conditional inference, Williamson describes a shepherd who is told that the sheep have broken out of their pen. On the basis of that testimony, the shepherd infers that the sheep have gone down to the river. "Presumably," Williamson writes, "even if the shepherd had not been given the testimony, he could still have reached the indicative conditional conclusion 'If the sheep have broken out of the pen and disappeared, they have gone down to the river.'" Williamson thinks of the two different inferences—one from testimony, the other only hypothetical—as involving "online" and "offline" processes, respectively:

> If we regard the shepherd's updating of his beliefs in the first case [involving testimony] as an online process, then we can regard his evaluation of the conditional in the second case as the corresponding offline process. If he accepted the conditional on the basis of an imaginative exercise...then that imaginative exercise is the offline analogue of online updating. Very roughly, the online and offline processes take the same input—'The sheep have broken out of the pen and disappeared'—and deliver the same output—'The sheep have gone down to the river'—by the same means. One process is online and the other offline in virtue of the different sources of the input. (p. 118)[6]

Williamson's proposal is openly inspired by the Ramsey test (2016, p. 118) and similar to N&S's theory of hypothetical reasoning, if less explicit in its details. For Williamson, the imaginative reasoning process takes place "offline," even if it is an "analogue" of "online updating" (p. 118). Like N&S, Williamson hypothesizes that during an imaginative episode "various offline cognitive procedures add further conclusions to a pool that starts with the initial supposition." He adds, importantly, that "most of the procedures are non-deductive" (p. 120). The inferences that, for Williamson, occur "offline" nevertheless mirror the broadly inductive or abductive inferences we would make were we to believe the supposition. "Left to itself," Williamson explains, "the imagination develops the scenario in a reality-oriented way, by default" (p. 116). The idea that imagination has a "default" mode where it develops scenarios in a "reality-oriented" way is again similar to N&S and C&R's claim that imagination is belief-like in preserving the inductive and deductive inference patterns that characterize transitions among beliefs. Unlike N&S and C&R, however, Williamson explicitly allows that this kind of "reality-constrained" imagining can incorporate imagistic states, in addition to language-like states.[7]

[6] Williamson explains that during most imaginings the cognitive processes will take "a mix of online and offline input." Yet, in the block quotation above, he remarks that "one process is online and the other offline in virtue of the different sources of the input." If the difference in type of input is to constitute the difference between online and offline processes, it is not clear how one of those processes can involve "a mix" of input types (the process itself would then be "mixed" between an online and offline process). What Williamson seems to mean is that, usually, the states used by our offline imaginative processes involve a mix of *contents*, insofar as some of the contents are believed and some are not believed. Understood in that way, he arrives at N&S's view, where the majority of the representations in one's Belief Box are duplicated within imagination, with a few premises inserted that are not also believed. (Subsequently, on N&S's view, the contents that conflict with the new solely-imagined premises are said to be weeded out by the UpDater mechanism.) The presence of all this information "in imagination" is needed to explain how non-deductive, belief-like inferences—inferences entirely shaped by one's contingent beliefs—can unfold in imagination, without imagination being "online." It is also one of the significant *costs* of this approach to conditional reasoning.

[7] A difficulty in interpreting Williamson on the psychology of conditional reasoning is that, in some of his examples, he seems to favor a view where the knowledge relied upon in counterfactual reasoning is sensory in nature and "may be stored in the form of some analogue mechanism, perhaps embodied in a connectionist network, which the subject cannot articulate in propositional form" (2007, p. 145). (This seems to apply to his stream-jumping case (2016, p. 118), and the

With this general picture in place, we can map out the reasoning that Williamson takes to occur when the shepherd reasons hypothetically about the sheep breaking out of their pen:

Offline Sheep Counting

1. The shepherd registers the question, "Where are the sheep likely to be if they have broken out of their pen and disappeared?" and begins relevant processing.
2. The shepherd represents, "in imagination" (or "in the PWB" or "offline"), that the sheep have broken out of their pen and disappeared.
3. Beliefs about the dispositions of the sheep and their typical behaviors are accessed, and their contents are copied into imagination (or "in the PWB" or "offline") so as to be "mixed" with the representation that the sheep have broken out of their pen. Such contents include propositions such as that the sheep like to drink water and frolic in the river and that the sheep have, in the past, run down to the river when their pen was left open.
4. It is inferred, "in imagination" (or "in the PWB" or "offline"), that the sheep have gone down to the river. (The principle or process by which this inference is achieved is important to consider—we will return to it.)
5. On the basis of this processing in imagination, the following conditional is inferred and takes up residence in one's Belief Box: "If the sheep are out of their pen and have disappeared, then they have gone down to the river."

First, a few notes on step 3. This "mixing" of what is imagined with contents that are believed is necessary for the imaginative episode to develop "in a reality-oriented way" and, especially, for it to develop in ways that mirror what would be one's inductive inferences were one to believe the antecedent. We saw that N&S, in their explanation of how the mixing occurs, propose that the entire contents of one's Belief Box are copied into one's PWB and then revised for consistency with the conditional's antecedent. With all of that information in the PWB, the same "inference mechanisms" that operate on belief can then operate within the PWB to draw out inductive and abductive inferences that mirror those that would be

rock-rolling-down-the-hill case, from Williamson (2007, p. 143).) Yet, in other examples, he seems to have in mind processing that involves articulable inference rules and propositionally stored knowledge. (This seems to apply to his sheep escaping from the pen case (2016, p. 119), and the case of counterfactual reasoning about who would have won a general election in Britain in 1948, had there been one (2007, p. 150). There can be no clarity on the distinction between the two kinds of reasoning at work in each case until the distinction between "analogue" and "propositional" forms of thought is clearly drawn, which Williams does not do. He holds that each rely on a more general ability "to predict the future" (2007, p. 150). On the face of it, accurately predicting the future requires lots of knowledge about the past; it does not, however, require—or even suggest—*sui generis* imaginative states or "offline" processing.

drawn were one to believe the antecedent. Williamson does not offer details on how the mixing occurs, other than that "the imagination develops the scenario in a reality-oriented way, by default" and takes "a mix of online and offline inputs."

As we saw when considering the Ramsey test in its application to indicative and subjunctive conditionals, we will not infer offline what we would have inferred from an antecedent, online, unless most our beliefs are made relevant to the inference.[8] Thus, as N&S recognize, the amount of information that must be brought to bear in any "offline" inference of the sort Williamson imagines is vast, provided that the imagining is indeed to develop the antecedent in a "reality-oriented way." Step 3, above, only highlights a fraction of the background beliefs that will be relevant to the inference moving forward.[9]

Now let's consider the nature of the inference made in step 4, where the shepherd infers, in imagination, that the sheep have gone down to the river. We know that it is supposed to be the same type of inference that the shepherd would have made had he instead come to believe, through testimony, that the sheep had broken out of their pen. Certainly, it is not a *deductive* inference that the sheep have gone down to the river. Rather, like most acts of conditional reasoning, the shepherd's inference is based on past experience. Williamson agrees that the inferences that take place during "imaginative exercises" usually "depend somehow on past experience, and go beyond it non-deductively" (p. 119). Thus, the shepherd's reasoning in step 4 appears to be something like an inductive inference, made in light of the information brought to mind in step 3 (though, as we will see, Williamson is not entirely happy calling the inference "inductive"). The issue I want to consider now is whether we can follow Williamson and N&S in understanding the shepherd's inference as essentially inductive in nature, drawing on beliefs about how things have typically gone in the past, while rejecting their claim that the reasoning makes use of states that are not beliefs. We know, from the arguments above, that such a position is coherent in principle. To assess whether it is *psychologically* plausible, it will help to dig into the details of a specific example.

Consider, first, how we might generate a "light-duty" (see Chapter 2) explanation of the shepherd's coming to infer the conditional about the escaping sheep. To do so, we just need to think about what the shepherd himself might say when asked to justify his inference. Suppose we ask him, "Where are the sheep likely to be, if they have broken out of their pen and disappeared?" He thinks a moment

[8] Recall, for instance, the indicative conditional "If Oswald didn't kill Kennedy, then someone else did," which most judge to be true. If, in deliberating on whether to accept this conditional, we fail to "mix" the proposition that Kennedy has been killed with the proposition that Oswald didn't kill Kennedy, we will wrongly judge the conditional to be false.

[9] One might wonder whether an account such as Williamson's could make do with only a small sub-set of one's (relevant) beliefs being copied into imagination, as opposed to most of them. I will address this response below.

and replies: "If they have broken out of their pen and disappeared, then they have gone down to the river." "Why do you think that?" we ask. "Well, the sheep love going down to the river for a drink and a frolic," he replies. "That's where they tend to go when out of their pen and left to their own devices." From these expressed beliefs alone—with nothing occurring "offline"—he can reasonably infer that if the sheep have broken out of their pen, then they have gone down to the river. Who are we to gainsay him for doing so?

The shepherd is not revealing to us the specific computational process he has exploited, or making any heavy-duty claims about the nature of beliefs themselves. His is a superficial, light-duty folk psychological explanation for how and why he came to infer the conditional that he did. But it is significant in itself. If we were inclined to describe him as having imagined his way to the answer, we now see that this case of imagining can alternatively be described as a case of drawing inferences from his standing beliefs in past regularities and tendencies. Further, as we saw in Chapter 2, superficial folk psychological explanations are often suggestive of a heavy-duty counterpart. That is again the case here. We can think of the shepherd's prior beliefs as mental representations that are causally implicated in the generation of a new belief in a conditional. Those beliefs are activated, so as to take part in a chain of reasoning, when the shepherd's cognitive system registers the question of the sheep's likely whereabouts when out of their pen.[10] With these points in mind, we can map out the psychological processes as follows:

Online Sheep Counting

1. The shepherd registers the question, "Where are the sheep likely to be if they have broken out of their pen and disappeared?" and begins relevant processing.
2. Beliefs about the sheep's preferences and tendencies are accessed from the Belief Box, such as "The sheep like to drink water and frolic in the river" and "The sheep have, in the past, gone down to the river when their pen was left open."
3. From these beliefs, the following conditional is inferred and takes up residence in one's Belief Box: "If the sheep are out of their pen and disappeared, then they have gone down to the river."

Note, first, that steps 1 and 2 are the same as steps 1 and 3, respectively, in *Offline Sheep Counting*. The episode requires the shepherd to begin by registering a

[10] As discussed earlier (in Chapter 5, fn. 7), simply registering a question, so as to reason about its answer, does not suggest a role for *sui generis* imaginative states. For instance, we do not need to imagine simply in order to ask ourselves "What is the capital of Ohio?" or "What kinds of things are sold at Starbucks?" Whether *answering* these self-put queries requires *sui generis* imaginative states is the point at issue. (See also section 8.8.)

particular question and searching his memory for information relevant to answering. Again a handful of beliefs of particular relevance are accessed. However, in *Online Sheep Counting*, there is no "mixing" of states in imagination (or the PWB), no tokening of a mental representation with the content "The sheep have broken out of the pen and disappeared." Instead, the two standing beliefs cited in step 2 serve as the mediating states that take us from "Where are the sheep likely to be, if they have broken out of their pen?" to an inference in favor of the conditional "If the sheep are out of their pen and disappeared, then they have gone down to the river." Again the inference is not deductive in nature, but based on past experience—it is, we can say, *broadly* inductive, so as to leave open the precise inductive inference rule deployed.

The alternative I have just described is certainly simpler than the "offline"/PWB version in one respect: it does not require the interaction of two different kinds of mental states (*sui generis* imaginings, and beliefs); nor, for that matter, does it require the wholesale copying of one's Belief Box into some other area of the mind, and the subsequent adjustment of that copied set for consistency with the hypothetical antecedent. Supposing both alternatives are live options, why prefer more complex account?

One response may be that we have yet to carefully consider the *inference rules* that govern the transitions among states—either within the Belief Box, in step 3 of my proposed account, or "offline" (or in the PWB), in step 4 of the Williamson/N&S account. If the kinds of rules or heuristics used on the belief-only account were much more complex or difficult to implement than those used on the two-attitude/offline accounts, that would be a point in favor of the latter. But there is no reason to think that the inference rules exploited on the two-attitude/offline accounts would be of a different kind. The key inferences are not deductive on either picture; so, in neither case are there easily stated rules to be imported from systems of natural deduction. In both cases, the inferences are inductive or abductive in nature. On the *sui generis* imaginings and "offline" views, after registering the question, "where have the sheep gone, if they have broken out of their pen?" we move, in imagination, from the propositions that (a) the sheep have broken out of their pen and disappeared, (b) the sheep like to drink water and frolic in the river, and, (c) the sheep have, in the past, gone down to the river when their pen was left open, to the (imagined) conclusion that (d), the sheep have gone down to the river. From there we arrive at the belief (e) that if the sheep have broken out of their pen, then they have gone down to the river. These inferences are inductive, abductive, or probabilistic; it is difficult to extract a schematic inferential principle that is deployed (as is indeed the case with *all* inductive inferences, as Goodman (1983) showed).

On the belief-only view, after registering the question, "where have the sheep likely gone, if they have broken out of their pen?" we move from (a) the sheep like to drink water and frolic in the river, and (b) the sheep have, in the past, gone down to the river when their pen was left open, to the conclusion that (c) if the sheep have broken out of their pen, then they have gone down to the river. Again the inference is inductive at heart, with the precise schematic inference rule or heuristic that is followed being a matter for empirical investigation. But there is no reason to think that such inferences are easier to carry out "offline" ("in imagination") than online—and, indeed, no reason to think that the inferences would be of a different sort, were they to occur offline, instead of online. So the only salient difference between *Offline Sheep Counting* and *Online Sheep Counting* is that the offline version builds in states and inferential steps that aren't necessary in the online version.

The online account is clearly preferable.

Perhaps anticipating this sort of objection, Williamson shows ambivalence when considering whether the kinds of inferences that take place during his "imaginative exercises" are simply inductive in nature:

> Could someone argue that what have here been called 'imaginative exercises' are really just inductive inferences? Most of them depend somehow on past experience, and go beyond it non-deductively. If that suffices for a cognitive process to be an inductive inference, then they are inductive inferences. (2016, p. 119)

Yet he qualifies this point, asserting that the inferences:

> Do not depend on the subject's *remembering* the relevant past experiences. What matters is whether they have made the subject skillful enough in performing the imaginative exercise itself. It is irrelevant to the process whether the subject can assemble the particular premises of the supposed inductive inference. Nor is it remotely clear in the given cases how to fill in the 'F' and 'G'in the conclusion of the supposed inductive inference, 'All Fs are Gs' (or 'Most Fs are Gs', for that matter)...the imaginative exercises are inductive inferences only in a sense so loose as to be entirely unhelpful. (p. 120)

On the one hand, we can agree with Williamson that in calling the relevant inferences inductive, we do not arrive at a deep understanding of the inference rules and principles that underlie the reasoning. It is less clear why Williamson finds it *more* helpful to describe the inferences in terms of a skillful "offline" imaginative exercise—as though those notions are more perspicuous. By definition, the idea of an "offline" inference, or thought-transition, is clear *only* to the extent that we already understand the kinds of inductive or probabilistic inference rules and heuristics that drive the ordinary "online" inferences that the "offline" processes supposedly mirror. Consider again the scenario where, on the basis of testimony, the shepherd comes to *believe* that the sheep have broken out of their pen and disappeared. The shepherd then infers that the sheep have gone down to the river.

This is not a deductive inference, obviously. Here, too, it is unlikely that the shepherd makes use of a formal inductive premise of the form "All observed Fs have been Gs." Nevertheless, the inference is, in some sense, inductive or probabilistic. Would Williams would find it "entirely unhelpful" to call it inductive, because doing so does not give us a clear picture of the nature of the inference rule deployed? In that case, neither do we have a clear picture of what an imaginative exercise involves, as it must (on his picture) make use of the very same sort of process or inference rule. Invoking the notion of an imaginative exercise won't move us any further forward than the loose appeal to induction he disparages.

6.8 Mental Imagery and Conformations of the Brain?

The arguments so far considered speak mainly to those who see in the Ramsey test a validation of the idea that conditional reasoning involves use of *sui generis* belief-like imaginative states. Some of what Williamson says about imaginative exercises is suggestive of a less intellectualist picture, where it is not so much a set of belief-like imaginings (copied from one's actual beliefs) that is relevant to the conditionals one will infer, but rather the way one's brain has been hard-wired through past experience. Recall that, in questioning the view that imaginative exercises are inductive inferences based on past experiences, Williamson holds that the exercises "do not depend on the subject's *remembering* the relevant past experiences." What matters, he tells us, "is whether they have made the subject skillful enough in performing the imaginative exercise itself" (p. 120). Here Williamson seems to have in mind a picture where people are able to generate imaginative states (including sequences of mental images) that represent likely ways a certain scenario would unfold, and where their doing so does not depend upon an ability to exploit their beliefs in a stepwise inference. In earlier work, he offers similar remarks in an explanation of the relation between our beliefs and the counterfactual judgments we are inclined to make:

> Very often, the background knowledge needed to evaluate a counterfactual consists not of specific items of information acquired on specific occasions but of a more general sense of how things go, honed over long experience. Such a sense is typically not presented to the subject in usably verbal form...Of course, underlying the inarticulate sense of how things go must be some conformation of the brain, but the latter does not constitute a theory from which the subject can infer the counterfactual or its negation. (2005, p. 14)

Here Williamson is addressing subjunctive counterfactuals as opposed to indicatives; yet he shows a similar inclination to move away from talk of "reasoning" towards a "conformation of the brain" that allows one the requisite "skill" to arrive at what otherwise look to be paradigmatic *inferences*.

Williamson is welcome to invoke the brain and its conformations here, but doing so does nothing to support the idea that conditional reasoning occurs "offline." At bottom, the proposal is for a kind of reasoning that is "honed over long experience," dependent on the shape of the brain, and difficult to put into words. If there is such reasoning, its relation to imagination is obscure. Williamson *may* simply mean to pick out reasoning that involves mental imagery.[11] But, in that case, "offline" imaginative exercises are simply I-imaginings, as I have defined them. And we have already seen (in Chapters 3 and 4) that there is no conflict in I-imaginings reducing to more basic folk psychological states.

Note that to remove beliefs from one's picture of conditional reasoning—opting instead for a notion of "imaginative skill"—is to remove whatever explanatory value the Ramsey test may have had in shedding light on the nature of that reasoning. For the Ramsey test *does* explicitly appeal to the notion of a belief set, and of adding propositions to it hypothetically. Once it is divorced from the notion of belief, the posit of an "offline" imaginative process can no longer be explicated by appeal to the online inferential procedures it supposedly mirrors. Inferences hold among beliefs, after all, not perceptual experiences; and perceptual experiences, presumably, would be the online counterparts to "offline" mental imagery, on Williamson's picture.[12] It is possible to propose something *like* purely imagistic inference rules, appealing to mechanisms involved in sensorimotor planning and prediction (Langland-Hassan, 2016; Van Leeuwen, 2011). One could even propose that it is through the use of imagistic states that we compute the conditional probability of a consequent given an antecedent. But this raises again the question of whether the imagistic states mediating those predictive computations are themselves properly viewed as judgments, *sui generis* imaginings, or something else.

Alternatively, one could reject the Ramsey test with its suggestion that, in evaluating an indicative conditional, we calculate the conditional probability of the consequent given the antecedent. In that case, an alternative theory of the computation undertaken when evaluating a conditional is required before we can move forward with an account of the particular mental states and inference rules used in carrying it out. After all, if we don't know *what* we are trying to determine when evaluating a conditional, we certainly can't know whether our doing so requires states other than beliefs.

[11] Though we also saw, in Chapter 3, that Williamson warns us not to "over-generalize to the conclusion that all imagining involves imagery" (2016, p. 117).

[12] Not surprisingly, when commenting on the nature of the inference rules that are used during imaginative exercises, Williamson moves back to a belief-inspired picture, according to which, "the deductive aspect of the whole process will look something like the method of tableaux in first-order logic, by which the consequences of the initial premises are teased out" (2016, p. 120).

6.9 Two Objections Considered

I will end this chapter by considering two objections to the line of argument I've so far developed. The first asks whether views positing *sui generis* imaginings must really be committed to the claim that, when we imagine, most of what we belief is "copied into" imagination. The second holds that there are specific acts of counterfactual reasoning—philosophical thought experiments being prime examples—where we infer a new generalization, and where our doing so requires focusing on the details of a hypothetical case. This may be thought to create difficulties for the kind of "belief-only" account I've sketched above, which relies upon our having pre-existing background beliefs in relevant generalizations. I will address these objections in turn.

6.9.1 Would We Really Have to Copy So Much into Imagination?

The first objection holds that I have overstated the requirements of theories invoking "offline" states or *sui generis* imaginings. Following Nichols & Stich (2000, pp. 124–5), I have noted that, in order for the inferential characteristics of offline imaginative states to mirror those of one's beliefs, most of one's beliefs would need to be transferred into imaginings as well. This has the odd result that we imagine almost everything we believe whenever we engage in conditional reasoning. A simpler alternative is desirable.[13] The objector may hold that it is not really necessary that we copy all, or nearly all, of our beliefs into imagination when evaluating conditionals. Perhaps only a handful of relevant beliefs need to be tokened offline, via imaginative states, in order for the resulting inductive or abductive inferences to be suitably sensitive to our background knowledge.

While I agree that only a handful of beliefs may at any time inform a certain inference—be it online or offline—the objector faces the question of the mechanism by which only some beliefs are judged relevant to the inference at hand, so as to be copied, or not, into imagination. The problem here is that there are innumerable ways for a belief to end up being relevant (or not) to a certain inference. It is not inconceivable that there would be a sophisticated mechanism or process capable of revealing such relevance—at least in a rough-and-ready way. (Add this to the view's list of posits.) But if we are in a position to highlight for ourselves the

[13] Nichols and Stich offer two possibilities for thinking about how propositions end up in the Possible Worlds Box (2000, pp. 124–5): on the first, all of one's beliefs are copied into the Possible Worlds Box, with the UpDater mechanism then weeding out the representations that conflict with the imagined antecedent; on the second, the UpDater acts as a "filter" only letting into the PWB representations that do not conflict with the imagined antecedent. Note that, even on the second alternative, most of one's beliefs still end up in the Possible Worlds Box, since most of one's beliefs will be consistent with most of the antecedents we in fact consider.

beliefs that are relevant to assessing a certain conditional, so as to import them into imagination, why, in addition, would we need to token the antecedent of the conditional "offline" during conditional reasoning? Why not move straight from those beliefs identified as relevant to accepting or rejecting the conditional?

6.9.2 Thought Experiments—Hard Cases for Me?

A second objection is that, at least in *some* cases, we arrive at the beliefs in the conditionals we do without relying on any background beliefs in generalizations; instead, it may be claimed, it is only by imagining a very specific scenario that we come to infer some new conditional—or, indeed, some new generalization. Such cases would challenge my claim that when we infer a new conditional of the form 'If *p*, then *q*,' it is by drawing upon preexisting beliefs in generalizations and regularities relevant to *p*. Philosophical thought experiments would seem to be vivid examples where the details of a carefully constructed case are used to induce belief in a new conditional. In such cases, it may seem that it is precisely by imagining a very specific scenario that we first arrive at a belief in a new generalization of the sort we can then apply to future cases. Here it may seem that it is *only* by representing a certain content as true, in imagination, that one comes to believe an important new generalization—as when, for instance, we imagine a Gettier (1963) case and infer, on that basis, that justified true belief is not sufficient for knowledge. It is with this thought in mind, no doubt, that imagination—considered as a *sui generis* mental state or faculty of some kind—is invoked in discussions of the epistemic role and psychological nature of thought experiments.

In response, it is quite true that we at times come to believe a new generalization by considering a specific counterfactual scenario; and it is also true that the details of an imagined scenario are crucial in helping us to do so. But these facts pose no challenge to the idea that we only exploit existing beliefs in the process of inferring the new conditional and generalization. When imagining that *p* as a means to arriving at a new conditional with *p* as its antecedent—and whatever new generalization that may bring with it—all that matters is that we have beliefs in *some* generalizations relevant to determining what would happen if *p*. The value of a good thought experiment lies in its power to reveal conflicting background beliefs we didn't know we had—and to force us to resolve them. To engage with a thought experiment is to think about what else would be true in the kind of situation described in the thought experiment, and to be pulled in opposing directions.

It will help to look at some examples. Consider, first, Searle's (1980) famous "Chinese Room" thought experiment. It might seem to be a case where, by imagining a specific scenario, we (rightly or wrongly) come to believe a new generalization about the relation between computing and thinking. When considering Searle's thought experiment, we ask ourselves: "If the system Searle describes were created, would it *understand* Chinese?" Suppose that the antecedent of this question contains within it all the specifics of Searle's thought experiment; we consider all those details when asking ourselves the question. If we react to his story in one way or the other, it will only be because considering his story brings to mind various background beliefs we have about, e.g., manipulating symbols, understanding a language, responding sensibly to prompts, and so on. Perhaps one such generalization is "The ability to respond appropriately to language prompts constitutes understanding that language"; perhaps another is "understanding requires consciousness"; perhaps a third is "non-biological systems lack consciousness." Many philosophical thought experiments (Searle's included) work by alerting us to the fact that two or more believed generalizations might be in conflict, by showing them to point in opposite directions with regard to a particular case. Indeed, anyone *without* beliefs in conflicting generalizations of this kind will fail to find the thought experiment interesting. The end result, for most, is revision of one of the formerly believed generalizations—or continued puzzlement. All of this is quite consistent with the claim that coming to believe "if *p*, then not-*q*" does not require first entering into a state with the content *p*.

Now consider a standard Gettier case. Jones looks at a broken clock that reads 4:15 p.m. and forms the belief that it is 4:15 p.m. Coincidentally, the belief is true. We ask ourselves: what should we say about this case? Does Jones know the time? On the basis of other cases we've considered (pre-Gettier), we've come to believe that justified true belief is sufficient for knowledge. Looking at a clock seems a good way to acquire a justified belief about the time. On the other hand, we also *already* think that a belief is not knowledge when it is only coincidentally true; our having that belief is what originally led us to include justification within the set of sufficient conditions for knowledge. But now, in considering the story about Jones, it seems that our existing beliefs force us to say that his belief is true and justified, yet *also* coincidentally true. The details of the case help us to discover a dark spot in our previous belief set: we didn't realize that the belief that knowledge is justified true belief conflicts with the belief that knowledge cannot be coincidental. Now we see the conflict and have to reconfigure. Nothing in this reasoning requires a *sui generis* state of imagining.[14]

[14] True, within all this, we need to consume the fiction we are told about Jones (and about the Chinese room). It is commonly held that we use imagination when engaging with fictions generally. Chapters 9, 10, and 11 deal with puzzles specific to fiction. For now, I assume that simply comprehending what is going on in a fiction does not *require* imagination—that, in reading about Jones, we may simply form beliefs of the form: in the Jones fiction, thus and such. This is all that is required by the present arguments.

6.10 Recap

This chapter began with some familiar distinctions between indicative and subjunctive conditionals, using them to raise questions concerning the relevance of the Ramsey test to the psychology of how we evaluate conditionals of each sort. We saw that, when applied to subjunctive conditionals, conducting something like the Ramsey test cannot simply amount to adding a proposition hypothetically to one's belief set and revising for consistency. Accounts of imagination's role in conditional reasoning that take inspiration from the Ramsey test will require significant amendment.

I then put forward a general argument to the effect that, in any situation where the Ramsey test would take one to a true belief in a conditional, we must already have beliefs that would, by themselves, justify our inferring the conditional. So there is no normative requirement for imaginative states that would allow one to implement the Ramsey test. Next I considered whether *sui generis* imaginative states might be valuable psychological tools for arriving at beliefs in conditionals, by considering cases where imagination has been invoked to explain conditional reasoning—focusing, in particular, on Williamson's example of sheep getting out of their pen. I showed that an account involving beliefs alone is more parsimonious than Williamson's, which appeals to offline "imaginative exercises." The "belief only" account makes do without *sui generis* imaginings and requires nothing not also needed on the account involving offline imaginative exercises. Matters don't change, I argued, if we conceive of imaginative exercises as exploitations of a "skill," as opposed to inferences of a kind.

Finally, I looked at cases that might seem especially challenging for the sort of view I've advocated: philosophical thought experiments. In those cases, it might seem that we don't rely upon background generalizations when inferring a new conditional; imagining the details of the case seems to be what matters. Granting that the details matter, I argued nevertheless that, when we infer a new conditional (or generalization) in light of a thought experiment, it is because the details of the case highlight for us a conflict, or dark spot, in our preexisting beliefs. We think about what else would be true of the situation described and notice that we're pulled in opposing directions. A new belief in a conditional or generalization arises when we decide how to resolve the conflict. Understanding how all this occurs isn't aided by positing *sui generis* imaginative states.

7
Pretense Part I
Metaphysics and Epistemology

7.1 Introduction

The project of this and the following chapter will be to explain pretense and the imagining it involves, without invoking any folk psychological states other than beliefs, intentions, desires, judgments, decisions, and the like. The specific mental states to which I appeal—judgments, intentions, and desires with particular contents—are ones that those who posit a *sui generis* cognitive attitude of imagination to explain pretense must *also* allow pretenders to have. So the reductive approach here has parsimony on its side (in the sense explained in section 2.7). It doesn't just do without a *sui generis* attitude of imagination; it also does not add any states not also appealed to in theories that invoke *sui generis* imaginings. I will do my best to lend credence to the view by showing how it can be applied to a number of paradigmatic cases of pretense, including those typically cited in support of positing *sui generis* imaginative states. Because some pretenses require hypothetical and counterfactual reasoning on the part of the pretender, I'll also be arguing that the kind of conditional reasoning that occurs during pretense does not require *sui generis* imaginative states. More general arguments about the role of imagination in conditional reasoning were already put forward in the previous two chapters. Now we'll be able to see the "belief-only" approach defended there in action.

7.2 Metaphysics, Epistemology, and Psychology: Three Questions about the Relation of Pretense to Imagination

It is common to draw a distinction between imagining and pretending (Currie & Ravenscroft, 2002; Langland-Hassan, 2014b; Nichols & Stich, 2000; Picciuto & Carruthers, 2016; Van Leeuwen, 2011). Unlike imagining, pretending seems to require some form of outward behavior on the part of the pretender—behavior connected to what is being pretended. For instance, while I can imagine that I am running a marathon while sitting in my office, I cannot pretend that I am running a marathon while doing the same—not unless sitting in my office is in some way tied in to the pretense (as it might be if I were pretending to take a breather in my

Explaining Imagination. Peter Langland-Hassan, Oxford University Press (2020). © Peter Langland-Hassan.
DOI: 10.1093/oso/9780198815068.001.0001

office while running a marathon). By contrast, I don't owe an account of how sitting in my office ties in to what I am imagining when I say that I am imagining that I am running a marathon. Likewise, I might pretend to be a dead cat simply by lying on the floor. While this does not involve "outward behavior" in the *movement* sense, I still have at hand an account of how my lying on the floor ties in to the pretense that I am a dead cat—an account I don't owe when I am simply imagining that I am a dead cat.

With this distinction in place, there are three questions we can ask about the relationship of imagining to pretending. I will call them the *metaphysical, epistemological,* and *psychological* questions, respectively. Each has received a good amount of discussion, even if they are not always recognized as *distinct* questions. The metaphysical question concerns *what it is to pretend*: what features, mental or otherwise, make it the case that a person is pretending, as opposed to not pretending? To answer is to give some non-trivial set of necessary and sufficient conditions, or something approaching such, that sheds light on the nature of pretense by identifying features that distinguish pretense from other kinds of non-pretend actions. (See Austin (1979), Langland-Hassan (2014b), and Picciuto & Carruthers (2016) for attempts.) The metaphysical question is relevant to the project of explaining imagination for the following reason. Suppose that, when we try to specify what it is that qualifies someone as pretending, we are unable to do so by appeal to their beliefs, desires, decisions, and intentions alone. Suppose that there could always be someone else with the same beliefs, desires, and intentions who was not pretending. (Or, in a similar vein, suppose that the beliefs, desires, and intentions that qualify someone as pretending must make use of a primitive *concept* of pretense (Leslie, 1994), where that concept cannot be explicated without appeal to a *sui generis* mental state of imagining). In that case, it might seem that the only way to capture the difference between sincere and pretend action is by appeal to a *sui generis* imaginative (or "make-believe") mental state that is exploited during pretense (see, e.g., Picciuto & Carruthers, 2016).

On the other hand, if we can explain what it is to pretend without appeal to *sui generis* imaginative states, the question of whether we *ever* need to exploit *sui generis* imaginative states during pretense takes on additional force. A desideratum on this analysis is that it reveal what is common in a variety of different kinds of pretense, including childhood games of pretense, deceptive pretenses (as when prisoners dress as guards to escape jail), and the theatrical pretenses of actors on a stage.

The epistemological question concerns how people—especially young children—are able to determine that *someone else* is pretending, so as to join in the pretense. This is a question of concern especially among developmental psychologists interested in how and when children develop a theory of mind (Friedman & Leslie, 2007; Friedman, Neary, Burnstein, & Leslie, 2010; Leslie, 1987; Lillard, 1993; Richert & Lillard, 2004). Imagination enters the picture on the assumption that recognizing that someone is pretending requires judging that person to be imagining something or other.[1] The link to imagination then becomes especially significant for our purposes if no account of what it is to understand someone as imagining can be given in more basic terms.

Finally, the psychological question concerns the mental tools and resources by which people are able to pretend. This question has received the most discussion of the three among philosophers, with imagination universally held to be a central resource. Of course, it is a mere platitude that a person who is pretending that *p* is, at least often, imagining that *p*. There are two deeper questions at issue. First, whatever we take imagining to be, is it *necessary* that we imagine while we pretend? Or is it, instead, only something we *very often* do while pretending? While some will hold that any action *not* guided by imagination is *ipso facto* not pretense (Picciuto & Carruthers, 2016), others defend a more moderate position where imagination typically guides pretense, even if other kinds of states are at times sufficient to drive pretense as well (Currie & Ravenscroft, 2002). Second, does the imagining in question involve a *sui generis* imaginative state, or is such imagining instead explicable in more basic folk psychological terms?

It is important to appreciate the difference between the metaphysical and psychological questions, given that answers to each will likely appeal to specific types of mental states. An analogy might help. We can ask the metaphysical question about firefighters, querying what makes a person a firefighter—viz., what distinguishes firefighters from those working in other fields. And we can also ask the equivalent of the psychological question about firefighters, which becomes a question concerning *the tools typically relied upon* in firefighting (such as hoses, ladders, and water). We can answer the metaphysical question about firefighters without mentioning hoses, ladders, and water. Yet any adequate account of the *tools relied upon* in firefighting will inevitably mention them. Similarly, even if one can give an account of what it is to pretend that makes no appeal to imagination—as in Langland-Hassan (2014b) and Austin (1958)—it may be that many or even all *actual* pretenses rely upon *sui generis* imaginings as a cognitive tool. For it may be that, given the nature of the human mind, the only way *we* are able to pretend—or the easiest way for us to do so—is by exploiting *sui generis* imaginative states, even if some other intelligent creatures could pretend without the use of such states (just as firefighters of the future might make no use of hoses, ladders, and water). Nevertheless, while the metaphysical and psychological questions are indeed distinct, answers to one will influence answers to the other, in ways I'll endeavor to explain. This is why it is important to see them as distinct questions.

I will address the metaphysical question first, the epistemological second, and will conclude (in Chapter 8) with the psychological question, which is the thorniest.

[1] A view along these lines is defended by Leslie (1987) and Friedman & Leslie (2007). In their terms, recognizing pretense requires use of a *sui generis* PRETEND concept. Their notion of a PRETEND concept plays much the same role as the notion of a *sui generis* attitude of imagination in other accounts. See Nichols & Stich (2000) for discussion of that link.

7.3 The Metaphysical Question: What Is It to Pretend?

I have written at length on the question of what it is to pretend elsewhere (Langland-Hassan, 2014b). I will briefly summarize the conclusions I came to below, without repeating the full arguments that led to them. The take-away from that discussion is that we can give a substantive account of what it is to pretend without invoking the notions of pretense or imagination in the account itself. If that is right, then the project of explaining imagination in more basic folk psychological terms is not put in jeopardy by a need to invoke a *sui generis* notion of imagination in explaining what it is to pretend.

Note that my project is not only to show that pretense does not call for a *sui generis* attitude of imagination (or of pretend); it is also to show that we can explain pretense without appealing to a sui generis *notion* or *concept* of imagination (or of pretend). Alan Leslie, author of some of the most influential work on pretense in psychology, concurs with me on the first point while diverging on the second. Partly to account for results in developmental psychology, he argues that "pretense representations" can be "decoupled" from their ordinary cognitive role through use of a primitive (and innate) concept PRETEND (Leslie, 1987, 1994). Suppose, for instance, that a mother and daughter are pretending that an empty cup is full of tea. Leslie's idea is that, instead of a child's confusedly thinking of her mother as representing that an empty cup is full, her mother-directed thought has the structure: Mother *pretends* of the empty cup "it is full" (1994, p. 220–1). This pretense-guiding thought can still have the force of a belief; it need not be seen as a representation toward which the child takes an attitude of imagining. In this way, Leslie's theory is an important predecessor to my own. However, there is a key difference, revealed in Leslie's claim that the concept PRETEND is *primitive*. Here he explains this notion of primitiveness:

> My assumption is that there is a small set of primitive informational relations available early on, among them BELIEVE and PRETEND. These notions are primitive in the sense that they cannot be analyzed into more basic components such that the original notion is eliminated. (1994, p. 218)

Leslie uses the notion of belief to clarify the sense in which these "informational relations" are primitive:

> While one can paraphrase 'John believes that *p* is true' in a number of ways, one does not thereby eliminate the notion *believes*. For example, one can say '*p* is true for John', but that just gives another way (and alternate set of sounds for) saying 'John believes that *p* is true' (p. 218)

Whether or not belief is a primitive notion, it would be bad news for my project if Leslie were correct that pretending (or imagining) does not admit of any elucidating explanation in more basic folk psychological terms. For then there could be no explanation of pretending (or imagining) in such terms. It is no comfort to me to do without a *sui generis* attitude of pretense (or imagination) at the cost of positing a *sui generis* concept thereof. For that reason, I place Leslie in the opposing corner.

As earlier noted, I've argued elsewhere (2014) that the question of what it is to pretend can indeed be answered without appeal to the notions of pretense or of imagination—and that, therefore, those notions are not primitive after all. Evidently unaware that I'd put this matter to rest, Picciuto & Carruthers (2016) have recently argued, to the contrary, that no action can possibly be a case of pretense if it is not guided by one's imaginings. Further, they hold that such imaginings are a *sui generis* type of mental state to be sharply distinguished from one's beliefs, desires, and intentions (2016, pp. 316–17).[2] If they are correct, there can be no explanation of pretense in folk psychological terms that makes no mention of imagination. It will be instructive to consider their reasoning.

Picciuto & Carruthers begin by distinguishing merely "acting as if" *p* and pretending that *p*. In one sense of acting "as if," I am now acting as if I am writing a sentence—for I am acting *as would be appropriate if* I were writing a sentence. That's a good thing, as writing a sentence is exactly what I aim to be doing. But I am not pretending to write a sentence. Likewise, we cannot simply characterize pretending as "non-serious" action. A moment ago, I was acting non-seriously when I picked up my phone to scroll through my Twitter feed. It was non-serious action in the sense that I was just wasting time, procrastinating, not doing anything that mattered much to me. But I wasn't pretending to check Twitter. So it was not non-serious action in the right sense. If it turns out that all our attempts to characterize pretense in other terms similarly fail, we might be tempted to conclude, with Leslie (1994, p. 218), that pretense involves use of a primitive psychological state—one as difficult to describe in more basic folk psychological terms as belief itself.

For Leslie, this primitive state is one that involves use of the innate concept PRETEND. Picciuto & Carruthers (hereafter, "P&C") instead view *imagination* as the crucial cognitive ingredient for pretense, where pretending involves having one's actions guided by one's imaginings (2016, p. 317). Stich & Tarzia (2015) likewise propose that pretense occurs when a person acts out "a sequence of events that is saliently similar to the events represented in the PWB" (p. 6), where the PWB is the "box" found in the cognitive architecture of Nichols & Stich (2000)

[2] Picciuto & Carruthers' (2016) arguments for seeing imagination as a *sui generis* cognitive attitude are all of the sort explored in Chapter 1.

that corresponds to uses of "propositional imagination."[3] However, as P&C themselves recognize, we do not yet have a sufficient characterization of pretense in noting that it is action guided by imagining. For, very often, our imaginings guide non-pretend actions. Paused at a corner, I may imagine myself pulling into traffic to determine whether I can make it across the street before an oncoming car approaches. A detective may imagine interviewing a suspect while in the act of interviewing that subject, in order to plan questions and anticipate responses. I might imagine tying my tie as an aid to actually tying my tie. There is no pretending to pull into traffic, no pretending to interview a suspect, no pretending to tie a tie in these cases. The imaginings are still guiding action, however. Hence the added parenthetical within Picciuto & Carruthers' formal definition of pretense:

> To pretend that *P* is to act as if *P* (without believing it) *while imagining that P*. A child who pretends that the banana is a telephone needs to suppose that the banana is a telephone, or to imagine the banana *as* a telephone, and act accordingly. (p. 317, italics in original)

So, pretending that *P* is not *simply* a matter of having one's actions guided by an imagining that *p*; one must also act as if *p* "without believing it." This explains why my tie-tying is not pretense. For, in that case, I believe that I am tying a tie. The same goes for the interviewing and driving examples. Yet this amendment solves one problem by creating another: it forecloses the possibility of pretending that *p* while one believes that *p*. A datum driving the debate about pretense over the last twenty years is that we can, in fact, pretend that *p* while believing that *p* (Nichols, 2006a). A commonly cited example occurs within Leslie's (1987) tea party pretense, discussed in more detail below, where a child both pretends *and* believes that a certain cup is empty. Other examples are easy to find. Suppose that I draw a card that says 'philosophy professor' during a game of charades. I then go on to pretend that I am a philosophy professor—rubbing my chin, nodding in recognition of a profundity—while believing that I am one. This difficulty is not addressed by P&C. I will return to it shortly. First, however, I want to show why P&C never give us good reason to think that pretending *always* requires imagining.

Picciuto & Carruthers are clear that imagining (or, equivalently in their usage, *supposing*) not only serves as a tool for guiding a pretense, but is essential to

[3] On the one hand, it is not clear that Stich & Tarzia mean to be giving a criterion for what is to pretend with this characterization; they likely see themselves as offering an empirical hypothesis concerning (just some of?) the cognitive states employed during pretense. On the other, they never give any indication that something *more* is needed to transform an ordinary imagination-guided action into pretense.

pretense: "pretending only lasts for as long as imagination actively guides one's movements" (2016, p. 317). Remove imagination as a guide, they propose, and one's actions are no longer pretense. "A child might set out on Halloween night not only dressed as a witch but pretending to be a witch," they explain:

> Yet as she walks around the neighborhood chatting with her friends, she may no longer be imagining herself as a witch. In that case, although she is dressed as a witch she is not pretending to be a witch. (2016, p. 317)

For P&C, when imagining stops, so does pretense. Their reasons for holding this are not clear. Suppose, for the sake of argument, that we accept P&C's claim that pretending that *p* requires one to act as if *p* while believing that not-*p* (setting aside our ability to pretend that *p* while believing that *p*). Why, then, do we need to *add* that the person's action is guided by an imagining? Why can we not just say that a person acts as if *p* while believing that not-*p*? One possible reason traces the fact that we might *unintentionally* act as if *p*. After stubbing my toe on a bar stool, for instance, I might hobble around, swearing. In such cases I am (unintentionally) acting as if I am an angry, peg-legged pirate, while not believing that I am one. But neither am I pretending to be one. On the other hand, if my hobbling and swearing is guided by an imagining that I am a peg-legged pirate, the problem appears solved.

Yet we needn't have introduced imaginings to solve the problem. We can make do with intentions instead, holding that pretending that *p* is intentionally acting as if *p* while not believing that *p*. This does all the same work in terms of discriminating relevant cases. When I stub my toe on the bar stool, my hobbling and swearing is not done with the intention of acting as if I am a pirate. P&C will need to appeal to some such intention in any case; pretense is always an *action*, on their account, and actions require motivating intentions.

P&C may respond that their concern is with the states that *guide* pretense, as opposed to the intentions that initiate them. They emphasize that "when pretending one performs an action of one sort (holding a banana to one's ear, say) not only *while* imagining it as an action of a different sort (talking on a telephone), but *because* one does so" (p. 317, emphasis in original). Supposing this were true, P&C could respond that, while an intention to act as if *p* (while believing that not-*p*) is what initiates the process of pretense, pretending only occurs insofar as that intention triggers imaginings which then serve to guide the pretense. It would then remain correct to characterize pretense as *essentially* connected to imagination.

But this simply gives us a better view of the question at issue: why should it be that *only* an imagining can guide an episode of pretense? After all, beliefs guide behavior, too; and we have plenty of them. Granted, when I pretend that *p*, the beliefs that guide the pretense will not include the belief that *p* (supposing, for the sake of argument, that pretending that *p* really requires one not to believe that *p*). But there is no reason such a pretense cannot be guided by *other* beliefs. I gave some examples of such in Chapter 1: Uncle Joe pretends that the mud pie is delicious by retrieving beliefs about how people act around delicious desserts; a child pretends that a banana is a telephone by noticing a similarity between telephones and bananas. Consider P&C's own example of the child out on Halloween. We can agree that she is no longer pretending to be a witch when she simply walks around in the witch outfit, chatting with her friends. But suppose that, after this respite in the pretense, she resumes acting on the intention to make herself witch-like, while not believing herself to be a witch. Does she need to elicit a *sui generis* imaginative state to carry this out? It is hard to see why she would. She already knows a lot about how witches are supposed to act. She has numerous beliefs about the stereotypical behaviors of such characters—that they cackle, ride around on brooms, stir cauldrons, and so on. Those beliefs suffice for her to act on her intention of making herself saliently witch-like. In so doing, she is once again pretending to be a witch.

It might be responded that, in order for her to know how to make herself witch-like, she must make use of a *sui generis* imaginative state—one with the content "I am a witch"—that allows her to consider what would occur in such a situation. This is the key idea behind views that hold that *sui generis* imaginings are a central *tool* for many pretenses (Currie & Ravenscroft, 2002; Nichols & Stich, 2000). I will consider that idea in depth when addressing the psychological question about pretense. In the context of addressing the metaphysical question, however, this idea only has relevance if it simply isn't possible to have relevant pretense-guiding beliefs without exploiting *sui generis* imaginings in the process. But, surely, before our trick-or-treater ever put on her costume, she already knew that witches fly around on booms and that they cackle, cast spells, pet black cats, and so on. This is why she wanted to *be* a witch! These beliefs ought to be sufficient resources to guide her efforts in acting saliently witch-like. There is no need for her to contemplate possible worlds where she herself *is* a witch.

Will such a belief-guided pretense be emotionally disengaged, or depressingly un-childlike (Velleman, 2000)? I think not. But I'll set the question of one's emotional "immersion" in (some) pretenses to the side. (The question is revisited, in depth, in Chapters 10 and 11 on our immersion in fictions.) Our question now is whether pretense is *possible* when guided by such beliefs. It is hard to see why it would not be.

On the kind of cognitive architecture for pretense proposed by Nichols & Stich (2000) (and cited approvingly by Carruthers (2006)), *sui generis* imaginings play a central role in guiding pretense by allowing one to generate relevant conditional *beliefs*—beliefs of the form 'if *p* then *q*'—that, in turn, guide the pretense behavior. (Imaginings, on this sort of view, do not *directly* guide action, as they occur "offline" and therefore have no direct links to action-generating systems (Nichols & Stich, 2000, pp. 125–8).) On this sort of picture, there is no reason a person cannot store such beliefs and use them *again*, at a later date, to guide another pretense of the same sort—this time without triggering the imaginings that were (supposedly) needed to generate the beliefs in the first place.

Even if it is clear that not all pretenses require *sui generis* imaginings, a positive case remains to be made that pretense can proceed through the use of beliefs, desires, and intentions alone. Intentionally acting as would be appropriate if *p* while not believing that *p* may be sufficient for pretense; but it appears not to be necessary. As earlier noted, we are able to pretend what we believe. The door remains open for imagination to reveal itself as a crucial ingredient in any comprehensive characterization of what it is to pretend. Moreover, given that we can pretend both what we believe *and* what we disbelieve, it might seem that whether we are pretending cannot hinge on our beliefs themselves. Of course, we have already seen that merely acting on an imagining is not sufficient to render an action pretense. But one might propose, instead, that pretending occurs when one acts on an imagining *with the intention to pretend.*

Emphasizing the role that mental imagery plays in guiding pretense, Neil Van Leeuwen argues that "if an explicit desire or intention to *pretend* causes the [action-guiding] image, the process that follows will be full pretense" (2011, p. 76).[4] Such a characterization still doesn't gain ground on the metaphysical question, however, as it simply pushes the question back to what it is to intend to pretend. How, for instance, does this intention differ from the intention to make oneself saliently like some other thing, or the intention to mirror in one's actions characteristics of what one is imagining (as when we imagine tying a tie in order to really tie a tie)? Neither intention appears sufficient to transform an act into pretense. Further, Van Leeuwen still only offers a sufficiency condition for pretense; unlike P&C, he does not suggest that an act is pretense *only* if it is caused by an intention to pretend and guided by a mental image. So the depth of the connection between the intention to pretend and pretense remains unclear.

7.4 What It Is to Pretend

The relationship of imagination to the metaphysics of pretense remains obscure.[5] It still remains to give a positive account of what it is to pretend that doesn't appeal to a *sui generis* state of imagination. That is the project of this section. I'll begin with a general criterion for what it is to be involved in a *Pretense Episode*. With that in place, I'll then define what it is to pretend any arbitrary proposition.

[4] The sort of imagistic imagining that Van Leeuwen has in mind here would by my—and, I suspect, his—reckoning also qualify as an attitude-imagining.

[5] This section greatly condenses some arguments made in Langland-Hassan (2014b).

My definition of a Pretense Episode begins with the intuitive idea that, when pretending, we act as though something is the case that we do not believe to be the case:

Pretense Episode: An agent takes part in a Pretense Episode when (and only when) she intentionally makes some *x y*-like, while believing that *x* is not, and will not thereby be made into, a *y*.

Before addressing the worry that we can pretend what we believe, let's consider a few examples of how we might fill in the *x*s and *y*s. If I intentionally make myself pirate-like, while believing that I am not, and will not thereby be made into a pirate, I am engaged in a Pretense Episode—one of pretending to be a pirate. I am the relevant *x* here; a pirate is the relevant *y*. If I intentionally make a pencil on my desk rocket-like by throwing it across the room tip-first, and do not believe it will thereby become a rocket, I am engaged in a different pretense episode—one of pretending that the pencil is a rocket (the pencil being *x*, and a rocket being *y*). In this way we can account for the kind of "object substitution" pretenses highlighted by Friedman & Leslie (2007), which do not, strictly speaking, involve making *oneself* act like some type of thing one believes oneself not to be; for one need not be the relevant *x* that is intentionally made *y*-like. Notice also that, unlike Austin's (1958) characterization of pretense,[6] a Pretense Episode requires no intention to *deceive* someone with one's actions; nor does it require any public performance. I can pretend to be a pirate in the privacy of my own home, just as a child can pretend to be Luke Skywalker while playing, by himself, in the backyard.

However, this definition of a Pretense Episode seems to clash with the datum that we can pretend that *p* while believing that *p*. Earlier I gave the example of pretending to be a philosophy professor while believing myself to be one. Leslie (1987) recounts a case of a child pretending that a cup is empty while believing it is empty.[7] Yet we can accept this datum without succumbing to the too-strong conclusion that what we pretend is in no way constrained by what we believe.

[6] According to Austin, "To be pretending…I must be trying to make others believe, or to give them the impression, by means of a current personal performance in their presence, that I am (really, only, &c.) *abc*, in order to disguise the fact that I am really *xyz*" (1958, p. 275). This immediately rules out solitary pretenses—a child pretending on her own, in the backyard, to be a superhero. And it also seems to overlook the many pretense games we take part in just for fun, without any implicit aim at generating a false belief. Austin seems alive to this worry, granting that when, during a party game, he pretends to be a hyena, "there is no question of my trying to convince you *seriously* that I am something other than myself." Why, then, is it a pretense, on his account? His answer is that "on the party level, my performance [is] convincing" (1958, p. 274). However, it is unclear what it could be for the performance to be convincing "on the party level," if it does not cause anyone to believe he is a hyena.

[7] In this example, the child is having a pretend tea party using two (empty) cups. The cups are both pretend-filled with tea by the experimenter. The experimenter then takes one of the cups, turns it upside down, and shakes it. The child is then asked, as part of the pretense, which cup is now empty. Her pointing to just one of the cups is taken as evidence that she is pretending that the one cup is empty; and she also plausibly believes that it is empty.

Instead we can note that instances where we pretend something we believe will always occur in the context of a larger pretense where *something* is pretended that is not believed. That is, pretending what we believe will always occur the context of a related Pretense Episode. I will offer two arguments for this claim. The first appeals to the absurdity of pretenses where, *per impossible*, a person pretends a set of propositions *all of which* he believes; the second is an inference to best explanation, appealing to the fact that, for any clear case of pretense, there is always some pretended proposition the person does not believe.

Taking the absurdity argument first, consider the following cases, which I will call "Hand" and "Standing":

Hand: Waving my hand in the air, I say: "Look, I am pretending that I have a hand!" You say, "Pretending that you have a hand and *what else*?" "Nothing else," I say, "just pretending that I have a hand."

Standing: Standing before you I say: "Look, I am pretending that I am a person standing up!" You respond: "A person that is standing up who is...?" "No," I say, "just a person who is standing up. A person with arms and legs and so on."

In both cases I speak falsely. I am not pretending what I say I am. I *cannot* be pretending these things. At least, I cannot pretend these things without *adding* to each pretense something that I do not already believe. Waving my hand in the air, I can pretend that I have a hand *that is on fire*. This is, *ipso facto*, to pretend that I have a hand. But, I cannot *merely* pretend that I have a hand—not so long as I believe myself to have one. And, standing before you, I can pretend that I am a soldier standing at attention, and thereby pretend to be a person standing up. But I cannot *merely* pretend that I am standing up, while I am doing so (provided, again, that I believe myself to be standing). Pushing the point to its logical limit: we cannot pretend the world is exactly the way we believe it to be. So it is one thing to say that we can pretend what we believe; quite another to propose the absurd—that we can pretend a set of propositions *all of which* we believe.

And, indeed, when we look at specific pretenses where something is pretended that is believed, we find that there are always other propositions being pretended that are disbelieved. In Leslie's (1987) tea party example, the child pretends that a cup that has been turned over and shaken during the pretense is empty while believing it is empty; yet the child *also* pretends that she is at a tea party while believing she is not at a tea party. Put in terms of the Pretense Episode criterion, the pretender is *x*, and *y* is someone at a tea party. The child tries to make *x y*-like while believing that *x* is not, and will not in the process, become a *y*. During the game of charades where I pretend to be a philosophy professor (and believe myself to be one), I act as though I am a person having deep thoughts. I am *x*, and a person having deep thoughts is *y*. I am making myself *y*-like while believing I am not a *y*, and that I will not become one in the process. (The *proviso* that I "will not become one in the process" serves to screen off non-pretenses where we make ourselves like some other kind of thing with the idea that we will become that sort of thing in the very process of the action—e.g. as when copying someone so as to genuinely be like them. See Langland-Hassan (2014b, pp. 411–14) for more on this subtle distinction between copying and pretending.)

Once a Pretense Episode is afoot, any number of propositions can be pretended that are also believed, so long as they are pretended as part of that Pretense Episode. When the child in Leslie's experiment pretends that the empty cup is empty, her doing so forms part of the Pretense Episode that is initiated by her intentionally acting as though she is at a tea party (while not believing she is at one). When I pretend that I am a philosophy professor, my doing so is part of the Pretense Episode that is initiated by my intentionally acting as though I am having deep thoughts (while not believing that I am). To determine whether an action is carried out "as part of" a Pretense Episode, we have look at the purpose of the action in question and compare it to the purpose of the action that initiated the Pretense Episode. When they are both undertaken for the same general purpose, they are both actions undertaken as part of the same Pretense Episode. The most common purposes that drive pretense are to play a game (as in childhood pretense), to deceive, or to entertain (as in the theatrical arts). So long as we can characterize such purposes without appeal to the notion of pretense (or imagination), the account avoids circularity.

So, for instance, the child's purpose in acting like she is at a tea party is to play a game.[8] If pointing to the cup and saying it is empty is done with the purpose of playing that game, the action is part of that Pretense Episode. By contrast, if the child checks the cut under a bandage on her finger during the pretense just because it is itching, that action is not done for the purpose of playing the game—and so is not a pretended action. Similarly, suppose that John is a security guard at First National Bank. He then pretends, as part of a heist, to be a security guard at Ultimate Savings Bank. He is engaged in pretense because he is acting like a security guard at Ultimate Savings Bank, while believing that he is not one. His purpose for acting in this way is to deceive people into thinking he works at Ultimate Savings Bank. Now, he is also acting like a security guard while believing that he is one. This action qualifies as pretense because it is carried out for the same purpose as the action that initiates the Pretense Episode—namely, that of deceiving people into thinking he is a security guard at Ultimate Savings Bank.

We can now define what it is to pretend any arbitrary proposition that q is r:

Pretending that q is r: An agent is pretending that q is r if she intentionally makes q r-like, as part of a Pretense Episode.

[8] The very notion of a game does not presuppose the notion of pretense. Most games—checkers, baseball, croquet—require no pretense at all.

This criterion applies to a wide array of pretenses—indeed, it aims to cover them all—including *deceptive* pretenses (such as the bank heist just mentioned), pretense games undertaken *for fun* (such as a game of charades, or child's play), and *theatrical* pretenses, where actors pretend to be characters they are not, for purposes of artistic expression. It also sheds light on the close relation between copying an action and carrying out the action as pretense. Suppose that I copy the way Gottfried knots his tie because I like the shape of the Full Windsors he wears. I am intentionally making my tie (*x*) Full Windsor-like (*y*-like). Yet it is not pretense, because I think that I will indeed have success in knotting it into a Full Windsor. I think that *x* will, in the process, become a *y*. If, on the other hand, I am quite sure that I will not succeed in completing a Full Windsor knot, yet carry through with intentionally making the tie Full Windsor-like anyway, then my action shades back toward pretense.

A potential counterexample worth considering trades on imprecision in the intentions we might ascribe. Neil Van Leeuwen (personal communication) suggests a case where he intends to make some wire horseshoe-like, as a means to creating a croquet wicket. Acting on that intention, it seems he intentionally makes the wire horseshoe-like without believing it will become a horseshoe in the process—and also without pretending that the wire is a horseshoe. My response is that the intention ascribed (to make the wire horseshoe-like) is too broad. After all, he doesn't intend to make the wire saliently horseshoe-like *in whatever respects possible*. He won't be satisfied if, for instance, he simply succeeds in making the wire *stiff* like a horseshoe, or *associated with luck* like a horseshoe. (This distinguishes him from the girl on Halloween who wants to make herself witch-like in whatever salient respects possible.) There's really only one way that he wants to make it horseshoe-like: he wants to make it horseshoe-*shaped*. His (quite narrow) intention is to make the wire horseshoe-shaped; and he believes he will succeed in that endeavor. That is why it is not pretense.

There is still some open texture here between what will constitute sincere efforts at imitation and copying and what will be pretense, as further explored in Langland-Hassan (2014b). This is to be expected, as copying and imitation are already intuitively close to pretense. What we want from a criterion for pretense is that it identify the most salient features of pretense and not include as pretense, or as pretense-related, lots of acts that bear no family resemblance.[9] And this it appears to do. While I have focused on childhood games of pretense, it is easy to see how the account extends to deceptive and theatrical pretenses. Prisoners pretending to be security guards in order to escape jail are intentionally making themselves security-guard-like while believing they are not security guards; the

[9] In just the same way, our analysis of what it is to be a chair can be accurate, even if there are borderline cases (e.g., love seats); the point is to avoid a definition that includes many things—screwdrivers, toasters—that bear no salient family resemblances, while shedding light on what it is to be a chair.

actor pretending to be Julius Caesar is intentionally making himself Caesar-like while believing that he is not Caesar. The present criterion thus gives good reason to think that pretense does not, as matter of metaphysics, require anything over and above beliefs, desires, and intentions of various kinds. Nor need we invoke the notion of *imagination* or of *pretense* within the contents of those states to capture why it is that their possessors qualify as pretending. Finally, the specific beliefs (about how to make some *x* *y*-like, and that *x* will not become a *y*) and intentions (to make *x* *y*-like) are states that all sides will in any case have to grant pretenders possess. There is no reason to go further and invoke, in addition, a distinct state of imagining when characterizing what it is to pretend.[10]

7.5 Answering the Epistemological Question

How do we recognize pretense in others?[11] Our answer to the metaphysical question offers a quick response to the epistemological one. When we notice that someone is intentionally making some *x y-like* without their believing that the *x* is a *y*, and without their believing that the *x* will become a *y* in the process, we can safely judge them to be engaged in a pretense episode. We can then determine that other specific propositions are pretended by determining that some *q* is made *r*-like as part of that pretense episode. The question of how a person detects pretense reduces to the more general question of how we detect another person's intentions and beliefs.

There is a wrinkle in this answer, however. We know that children are able to distinguish pretend play from sincere action by two years of age, or younger (Harris & Kavanaugh, 1993; Lillard, 1993; Onishi, Baillargeon, & Leslie, 2007).

[10] A referee observes that my characterization of pretense may focus too narrowly on the intentions of pretenders, insofar as there may be propositions pretended whose specific contents never find their way into the minds of those pretending. For instance, according to Walton (1990), many pretenses are governed by certain *principles of generation*, which are "rules about what is to be imagined in what circumstances" (p. 40). In one of his examples, two boys agree that any stump in the woods will count as a bear. With that principle in place, they can be construed as pretending that there is a bear at each specific location where a stump happens to be, even if they have no idea where most of the stumps are located (and so no intentions to pretend—or imagine—that bears are at thus and such specific locations). Such principles can easily be woven into the general account I have sketched. Like any other kind of game, games of pretense may at times have game-specific governing rules that generate truths about what is being pretended. The point remains that no pretense can get off the ground without the necessary and sufficient conditions I've identified in place, and that we needn't invoke *sui generis* notions of imagination or of pretense to understand what is being pretended in any situation. Principles of generation can be understood as rules concerning what should be considered true in a certain game of pretense (as opposed to rules about what is to be imagined). To accommodate the truths that they generage about what is being pretended, we can expand the second aspect of my definition of pretense as follows: *Pretending that q is r*: An agent is pretending that *q* is *r* if she intentionally makes *q* *r*-like, as part of a Pretense Episode, or if there is a principle of generation in place within the Pretense Episode, according to which *q* is *r*.

[11] This section summarizes, expands, and refines several points made in Langland-Hassan (2012).

Yet there is evidence that children cannot reliably apply mental state concepts like BELIEVES and INTENDS to others until about the age of four (Wellman, Cross, & Watson, 2001). This evidence lies primarily in their performance on various iterations of the "false belief task" (Gopnik & Astington, 1988; Hogrefe, Wimmer, & Perner, 1986; Wimmer & Perner, 1983). If such children can nevertheless recognize pretense in others, this suggests they are not doing so by attributing beliefs and intentions of the sort just suggested. A few comments are in order.

First, more recent studies have cast some doubt upon earlier findings that young children lack mental state concepts like BELIEVES and INTENDS. Studies that use looking-time as a proxy for surprise (Onishi & Baillargeon, 2005; Scott & Baillargeon, 2009), or an "active helping" paradigm to assess knowledge of another's epistemic state (Buttelmann, Carpenter, & Tomasello, 2009), suggest that even pre-verbal infants can understand others as having (false) beliefs. As a result, there is now little consensus concerning when children acquire an adult-like theory of mind. Supposing that infants and young children really are able to reliably discern the beliefs and intentions of others, we could explain their ability to recognize pretense by appeal to their ability to recognize the relevant beliefs and intentions. On the other hand, given the conflicting nature of the evidence concerning theory of mind abilities in children younger than four, it would be preferable to explain how pretense games are recognized without relying on the claim that children exploit a well-developed, adult-like theory of mind. And, in any case, I doubt that most pretenses *are* recognized via detection of the mental states that define them.

One alternative proposal is that children recognize another's pretense by noticing that "the other person is *behaving in a way that would be appropriate if p were the case*" (Nichols & Stich, 2000, p. 139, emphasis in original). To understand that Mommy is pretending that the banana is a telephone, it might seem that the child need only discern that Mommy is "behaving in a way that would be appropriate if the banana were a telephone" (p. 139). In recognizing this, the child need not attribute to Mommy any mental states. Unfortunately, as noted by Friedman & Leslie (2007) ("F&L" hereafter)—and later acknowledged by Stich and Tarzia (2015)—this simple behavioral criterion has serious shortcomings. The first is that it fails to distinguish cases of acting in error as if *p* (because one falsely believes that *p*) from pretending that *p*. A second is that it suggests that children will over-interpret people as pretending that *p* whenever they happen to note a similarity between the person's actions and the actions that would be appropriate if *p*. That is, people who act as if *p* without *intending* to do so will nevertheless be interpreted as pretending that *p*.[12] A third is that we typically act

[12] Notably, Lillard (1993) showed that children *do* sometimes make this kind of error. However, F&L might reply that *pervasive* confusions of this kind do not occur, despite the fact that one's actions are almost always appropriate to some other kind of action than what one intends.

as would be appropriate if *p* when we correctly believe that *p*, intend to act as though *p*, and are in no way trying to pretend! This was noted above when considering the necessary conditions for pretense itself. Right now, you are acting as would be appropriate if you were reading this sentence. This is not sufficient for your pretending to read the sentence. If recognizing that someone is pretending that *p* were just a matter of recognizing that they are acting as would be appropriate if *p*, almost any sincere act could potentially be confused for an act of pretense. F&L levy this critique as a means of motivating their own theory, according to which both pretense and pretense recognition require use of a primitive, innate mental state concept of PRETEND (Friedman & Leslie, 2007; Friedman, Neary, Burnstein, & Leslie, 2010).

However, we can preserve a non-mentalistic account of how children recognize pretense if we simply highlight the relevance of *manner cues* and the notion of a *game*. The relevant manner cues include winks-and-nods, characteristically unusual tones of voice, exaggerated gestures, stopping actions short of normal goal points, and so on. When such cues are detected *together with* some behavior that would be appropriate if *p*—particularly when it is salient that not-*p*—a child (or adult, for that matter) can reliably infer that a certain kind of game has been initiated. It is a game where people act like something is the case that is not the case. In determining that someone is pretending that *p*, then, a child looks for three things together: some of a particular cluster of manner cues, some behavior that would be appropriate if *p*, and its being clear that not-*p*. Through experience and positive reinforcement, the child learns that when these conditions are met, the right thing to do is to follow along with the adult in acting in ways that would be appropriate if *p*, even if (as is usually the case when such cues are detected) *p* is obviously not the case. These are the rules of the game, and they can be learned in the same way the child learns the rules to any game—such as kickball, or freeze-tag—that does not require the representation of another's mental states.

However, F&L are well aware that (what they call) "behavioral theorists" would like to appeal to manner cues for help. They argue that behavioral theories cannot appeal to such cues because the very cues that enable one to reliably distinguish episodes of pretending that *p* (the winks, the nods, the exaggerated expressions, the stopping short of completing an action) will not themselves be behaviors that would be appropriate if *p* (2007, p. 112). In their view, this clashes with the behavioral theorist's claim that recognizing a pretense that *p* involves recognizing that someone is acting as would be appropriate if *p*.

But the behavioral theory has ample room to maneuver here. Once the account is amended to include the detection of manner cues together with *some* behavior that would be appropriate if *p*, the fact that some of the manner cues themselves will involve acting in ways that would *not* be appropriate if *p* poses no problem. For to act as would be appropriate if *p*, in the behaviorist's sense, does not require that one act *exactly* as would be appropriate if *p*, but rather that one act *in some salient respects* as would be appropriate if *p*.[13] Suppose that we are pretending that containers of mud are chocolate cakes. We can agree with F&L that the knowing looks and the stopping-short-of-eating are *not* behaviors that would be appropriate to engage in with chocolate cake. Yet, in concert with *some* salient behaviors that it would be appropriate to engage in with chocolate cakes (e.g., cutting them up, saying "Mmm, I love chocolate cake"), the manner cues enable the child to recognize the context as one where she should also act in ways that would be appropriate if the mud containers were chocolate cakes. With this in mind, we can summarize the revised behavioral heuristic as follows:

Behavioral heuristic: a person can be reliably recognized as pretending that *p* by being recognized as acting in some salient ways that would be appropriate if *p*—typically while it is obvious that not-*p*—and while offering some of a familiar cluster of manner cues, which serve to draw attention to the subject matter of the pretense.

Friedman and Leslie might nevertheless press their case by arguing we have secretly attributed the child the concept PRETEND in giving the child the ability to "look for" combinations of specific manner cues together with instances of acting in ways that would be appropriate if *p*. (As they emphasize, "one must guard against secretly interpreting act-as-if as act-as-if pretending" (2007, p. 119).) In one sense, we certainly *have* ascribed the child the concept PRETEND, to the extent that being able to detect and play such games constitutes understanding pretense. In *this* (behavioral) sense of 'pretend,' the child fully understands that the parent is pretending—and indeed that the parent is acting as if pretending. The important point is that we have not thereby given the child the concept of a mental state. Rather, we have given the child the concept of a kind of *game*, the recognition and playing of which does not require an understanding of mental states. Only by begging the question in favor of their own account can F&L hold that understanding someone is acting as if pretending *necessarily* involves understanding that person as being in certain mental states.

Recognizing that someone is pretending does not, then, require the possession of mental state concepts, nor the attribution of beliefs, intentions, or imaginings to others (at least, not in the case of the pretenses that children reliably recognize). Stich & Tarzia (2015) reach the same conclusion in their own response to F&L—which, they note (fn. 10, pp. 5–7), builds on a strategy outlined in Langland-Hassan (2012). However, instead of holding that pretense is recognized

[13] Compare: we easily recognize the actor playing Hamlet as behaving in ways that would be appropriate if he were Hamlet, while recognizing that he is also behaving in ways that would *not* be appropriate if he were Hamlet (e.g., ignoring the 500 people watching him from the theater). Recognizing the two together enables us to recognize that he is merely pretending to be Hamlet. There is no difficulty in the matter.

by means of recognizing behavior that would be appropriate if *p* (together with relevant manner cues), Stich & Tarzia find a necessary role for the PWB (i.e, the "possible worlds box" of Nichols & Stich (2000)). Here they describe the process of pretense recognition with respect to a case where a father pretends to be sleepy:

> Once the child has hit upon a pretense premise that enables her to understand what Daddy is doing (he is behaving in a way that is similar, in salient ways, to what he is represented as doing in the imaginary world of the PWB) she can, if she wishes, join in the pretense game by giving Daddy a good night hug and kiss.
> (Stich & Tarzia, 2015, p. 7)

My only qualm is that the appeal to a PWB here is gratuitous. Stich & Tarzia specify that the child does not know what sort of processing to get going in her PWB until she *first* determines what sort of actions Daddy is mirroring with his own. Only then can she put "Daddy is very sleepy" (as opposed to some other proposition) into her PWB, allow other inferences to unfold therein, and, finally, judge Daddy to be acting in ways that are saliently similar to how he is represented as being in her PWB. Simply determining what the pretend premise is, together with noticing relevant manner cues, will suffice for the child to have determined Daddy to be pretending. So we need not bring the theoretical notion of a PWB into the characterization of how pretense is recognized. Even if children *in fact* notice thus and such occurring in their PWB when they recognize pretense—a fact I will dispute next chapter—their doing so is inessential to explaining how pretense is recognized.

7.6 Summary

This chapter began by distinguishing the importantly different metaphysical, epistemological, and psychological questions we can ask about pretense. I then argued, with respect to the metaphysical question, that we needn't invoke *sui generis* imaginative states in order to give an informative analysis of what it is to pretend. We can characterize someone as pretending (or not) simply by describing their active intentions and beliefs, none of which need incorporate the concepts of pretense or imagination. This analysis of pretense has the added benefit of allowing us to see what childhood games of pretense, deceptive pretenses, and theatrical pretenses all have in common.

I next moved to the question of how pretense is recognized in others, focusing in particular on how young children recognize and learn to take part in pretense. There I explained how the kinds of pretenses children are able to detect can be recognized by noticing certain behavioral features—including stereotypical manner cues—of the people pretending. We need not, as some have argued, deploy a primitive mental state concept of PRETEND in recognizing someone as pretending. While a full metaphysical analysis of the essence of pretense will, if I am right, invoke the mental states of belief and intention, we need not suppose that people are only able to recognize pretense in others by recognizing and attributing those states. Like many things in nature whose essence lies below the surface, pretenses can be distinguished (as reliably as we *do* distinguish them) by their superficial features.

I move on in the next chapter to address the third, *psychological* question concerning pretense—viz., what sort of mental states do we in fact rely upon in order to pretend? Even if my accounts of what it is to pretend and of how pretenses are recognized are correct, it might still be that we usually make use of *sui generis* imaginative states in carrying out a pretense. I will argue that this is not so.

8

Pretense Part II

Psychology

8.1 Introduction

Last chapter, I introduced three distinct questions one might ask about pretense, labelling them the 'metaphysical,' 'epistemological,' and 'psychological' questions. So far we have addressed the first two. In tackling the metaphysical question, I argued that we can explain the difference between a person who is pretending and a person who is not without making any appeal to a *sui generis* state or concept of imagining (or of pretense). In response to the epistemological question, I argued that people—young children included—can recognize pretense in others without attributing mental states of believing, intending, or imagining to those judged to be pretending. Thus, the ability of young children to recognize pretense in others gives no reason to think they make use of the primitive mental state concept of PRETEND (or of IMAGINE) (*pace* Leslie (1987) and Friedman & Leslie (2007)).

We can turn now to the psychological question. This is a question about the mental states and processes that humans typically exploit in carrying out a pretense. Whether or not *sui generis* imaginings are strictly *necessary* for pretense, the vast majority of philosophers and psychologists working on pretense have considered imagination to be its cognitive engine (Carruthers, 2006; Doggett & Egan, 2007; Friedman & Leslie, 2007; Harris, 2000; Leslie, 1987; Liao & Gendler, 2011; Nichols & Stich, 2000; Schellenberg, 2013; Stich & Tarzia, 2015). If they are right, then any suitable answer to the psychological question will invoke *sui generis* imaginative states. The relevant kind of imagining in these discussions is A-imagining—the sort of imagining that allows us to engage in epistemically safe, rich, and elaborated thought about the possible and fantastical—even if some highlight the importance of visual imagery within such A-imaginings (see, e.g., Van Leeuwen, 2011).

Pretending requires an ability to act as though things are ways we believe them not to be. It stands to reason that doing so will require a general ability to have rich, elaborated, and epistemically safe thoughts about the possible, fantastical, unreal, and so on. So if we want to understand the nature of such A-imagining, we can start by asking what sort of mental states and capacities a person must exploit in order to pretend. If, after considering several paradigmatic pretenses,

Explaining Imagination. Peter Langland-Hassan, Oxford University Press (2020). © Peter Langland-Hassan.
DOI: 10.1093/oso/9780198815068.001.0001

these states turn out simply to be beliefs, desires, and intentions of different kinds, then a case can be made that these *just are* the relevant A-imaginings that, intuitively, are relied upon during pretense. That is the case I'll be making over the next several sections.

8.2 The Question of Quarantining from a Light-Duty Perspective

When someone pretends, there is a sense in which they maintain two separate accounts of what is happening. There is the world as it is believed it to be. And there is the world as it is pretended to be. Suppose that Sally is pretending to be a lion. In the real world, Sally takes herself to be a five-year-old girl living in Massapequa, Long Island. In the pretend world, she is a mother lion on the Serengeti. In order for her successfully to carry out this pretense—and for it to remain pretense—she needs to keep a clear account of what is real and what is pretend. Metaphorically speaking, she needs to *quarantine* her take on how the world is imagined to be from her take on how it is believed to be. For many theorists, imagination plays a central role in explaining how this takes place. Sally imagines one thing (that she is a lion) and believes another (that she is a girl). It is in virtue of her only imagining the former (disbelieved) content that the state is "quarantined" from her proper beliefs. Before delving into a critical examination of those accounts, it is important to consider how the challenge of explaining this double-bookkeeping differs as a function of one's view on folk psychological ontology.

Recalling the distinctions of Chapter 2, if we are light-duty theorists, maintaining this double-bookkeeping amounts to Sally's having and manifesting two different sets of dispositions: dispositions to act like a five-year-old girl (ascribed, in part, by attributing her a belief that she is a girl) and dispositions to act somewhat lion-like (ascribed by saying that she is imagining that she is a lion). Having the latter set of dispositions does not amount to being disposed to act *exactly* like a lion—only to mirror some salient qualities of lions in one's behavior. There is no conflict in Sally's having both sets of dispositions simultaneously. For one thing, acting saliently lion-like is a fairly normal thing for a five-year-old girl to do, as is engaging in games of pretense generally. Dispositions to act like a five-year-old girl include among them dispositions to act saliently lion-like, robot-like, at-a-tea-party-like, witch-like, and so on, for any ordinary pretense. It is, in fact, only atypical children—for instance, those with autism spectrum disorder—who lack any such dispositions to pretend. So, from a light-duty perspective—where folk psychological state ascriptions *merely* serve to ascribe relevant dispositions, and not concrete mental representations—there is no potential clash between believing that one is a child and imagining that one is a lion. There is no interal state that needs to be quarantined from another, conflicting one. Even *prima facie*, pretense generates no need for quarantining, on a light-duty view.

It is only once we move to a heavy-duty folk psychological ontology that we get the appearance of a greater puzzle. In offering solutions to that puzzle, heavy-duty theorists take themselves to be giving a more substantive explanation of pretense than the light-duty theorist can provide. For they are no longer merely describing the dispositions characteristic of those engaged in pretense; they are advancing hypotheses concerning the casual bases for those dispositions—hypotheses that invoke mental representations of a certain sort. In Chapter 2, I aired some skepticism concerning the general project of explaining folk psychological dispositions in terms of corresponding mental representations. But I will set that skepticism to the side here, to consider matters as they stand on the heavy-duty theorist's home turf. For the remainder of this chapter, I will, for the sake of argument, assume that having beliefs, desires, and intentions amounts to having language-like and/or picture-like mental representations with contents mirroring those of the that-clauses used in their appropriate ascriptions. Where relevant, I will note how issues differ from a light-duty perspective.

8.3 Quarantining: The Central Mistake

Most heavy-duty theorists who have theorized about pretense argue that, in order to explain how people come to have and act upon the kinds of dispositions evidenced during pretense, we should posit the use of mental representations that are not themselves beliefs, desires, or intentions. These mental representations are typically called "imaginings"—especially "propositional imaginings"—and are the kinds of *sui generis* imaginative states I claim we need not countenance. There are several reasons theorists have thought that these states of imagining that *p*—unlike suspecting that *p*, or being thankful that *p*—are irreducible to more basic folk psychological states. But the most obvious and influential traces to the simple thought that imaginings are mental representations with contents that, at least often, we disbelieve. As the psychologist Paul Harris puts it, pretense is thought to depend "on the ability to temporarily entertain a representation that is non-veridical, and known to be so" (2001, p. 252). Far from a cleaned-up bit of common sense, this is a controversial piece of empirical speculation—one that takes a heavy-duty folk psychological ontology for granted. It brings with it special puzzles that don't arise on a light-duty view. For once we are committed to pretenders harboring and being guided by representations they know to be non-veridical, we face the question of how they avoid confusing those representations with their beliefs—how, in Leslie's (1987) term, they avoid "representational abuse." The worry is that a person might end up representing one and the same banana as both a fruit and, say, a telephone. Such confusion would result in people trying to peel receivers and charge bananas. It seems we need a way to *quarantine* the representations guiding pretense from our beliefs, thereby preventing such confusion. Holding that we take a distinct cognitive *attitude* of imagination toward the relevant contents has been thought to answer the question of how this quarantining is accomplished (Nichols & Stich, 2000). It is observed that desire that *p* will not get mixed up with and contaminate a belief that not-*p*, due to the distinct attitudes taken toward the propositions. Just so, it is reasoned, if we take a distinct cognitive attitude of *imagination* toward the representations at work during pretense, this may serve to explain how a quarantine is maintained between what we imagine and what we believe.

This widespread view gets its canonical statement in Nichols & Stich (2000), who posit a "Possible Worlds Box" (subsequently dubbed the "Imagination Box") to sit alongside the more familiar "Belief Box" and "Desire Box" of heavy-duty cognitive architectures. The spatially suggestive metaphor of distinct "boxes" serves to strengthen the sense that a cognitive attitude is the right tool for the quarantining job (even if it is typically acknowledged that boxes only serve to symbolize functional similarities among representations—that they are "simply a way of picturing the fact that those states share an important cluster of causal properties that are not shared by other types of states in the system" (Nichols & Stich, 2000, p. 121)).

The problem with this general line of thought is that it just isn't clear why we should think that pretending requires a person to "entertain a representation that is non-veridical, and known to be so." If pretense does not require such, then there is no need to quarantine any representation that potentially conflicts with one's beliefs. The best way to think this through is to carefully consider which mental states a person needs to draw upon to carry out a pretense. Recall Sally, pretending to be a lion: she is crawling on all fours, saying "Rooooaaaarrrr!," swiping at the air with one arm, fingers bent in the shape of a claw. What, psychologically speaking, is required for her to carry this out? If this is a case of pretending to be a *lion*, she must be modelling herself after lions and not some other kind of creature. To do so, she needs to know something about lions. She doesn't need to know *much*. But if Sally has no idea what lions are, she cannot intend to make herself lion-like; perforce, she cannot pretend to be a lion (even if she might still inadvertently engage in behaviors that are lion-like).[1] Knowing some things about lions—that they walk on four legs, roar, and attack with their claws—she needs to draw on that knowledge to make herself *lion-like* in certain respects. Remembering that lions walk on all fours, she might decide that she will walk on all fours. Recalling that lions roar, she might decide to make a roaring type of sound. Being versed in games of pretense, she knows that her human roar needn't sound *very*

[1] This is compatible with our knowledge of *x*s only imposing loose constraints on our pretending to be an *x*. I agree with Doggett & Egan that, when you pretend to be a cat, "you're liable to act in accordance with the things that you know (or believe) about cats, but your beliefs needn't be rich enough to single out any particular sort of behavior that you think a cat would be liable to go in for in the imagined situation" (2007, p. 5).

much like a lion's roar. She knows that she only needs to go some distance toward making herself saliently lion-like. This might even involve her mirroring some actions that lions are only (stereotypically) *thought* to do, even if no lions actually take part in them. Such are the norms governing games of pretense, which she has learned through participating in such games with others.

On the face of it, her having and making use of the above intentions, beliefs, and desires suffices to explain her ability to pretend that she is a lion. Specifically, she exploits beliefs about the salient features of lions and the desire and intention to approximate some of those features in herself. To the extent that there are occurrent mental events responsible for the pretense, they can be events of *remembering* that lions are like such and such, and *deciding* to make oneself lion-like in this or that respect. All the while she retains a background belief that she is not, and will not become, a lion in the process of these actions. That belief ensures that she has not lost her mind.

Now, the orthodox view will likely agree that she has all these states—beliefs about what lions are like, and an intention to make herself lion-like—but will hold that something vital has been left out. The child, one might object, still needs to have an *imaginative state* with the content *I am a lion* (together with whatever other imaginative states might flow from it). This is the crucial mental representation that is "non-veridical, and known to be so." But it is hard to see what in Sally's actions requires us to say that she harbors such a representation. Why, in the process of remembering what lions are like and in making herself lion-like, would she need to mentally represent that *she* is a lion? She wants to *act like* a lion, not become one. Questions about what *she herself*—a five-year-old from Massapequa, Long Island—would do if, *per impossible*, she were a lion are not to the point. If she, herself, were a lion, then she would be a very odd-looking one, with remarkable, human-like cognitive capacities. If she herself were a lion, then her parents could not really be her parents at all—unless, somehow, they too were lions! Obviously, none of this comes to mind during her pretense. This is because, when we take part in such imitative pretenses, we are not making judgments about counterfactual situations where we ourselves are something else. We are just recalling the salient features of some type of thing—a lion, a hyena, a superhero—so as to mirror some of those features in our own actions and appearance.

Some have argued, to the contrary, that a child need not "consult" her beliefs in order to pretend (Doggett & Egan, 2007; Velleman, 2000, pp. 8–9). I do not know what it is to consult a belief—as one consults a tax professional?—but I agree that children don't do it when they pretend. Instead, they *make use of* their beliefs, in just the way we make use of our beliefs when we light the grill to make dinner, or when we drive to work. We don't pause to reflect on what our beliefs are about grill-lighting, or about the best route to work. Our beliefs guide our actions without our "consulting" them and (usually) without it crossing our minds that we have them. The same goes for pretending. Wanting to make herself lion-like, the child draws on her beliefs about lions and their salient features, without noticing that she is doing so.

8.4 Inner Speech as Imagining? A Digression

It might nevertheless seem just obvious that Sally enters a mental state with the content "I am a lion," because pretending children often *say* things—either overtly, or in inner speech—like "I am a lion!" Let's suppose that I say "I am a lion!" in inner speech while pretending to be a lion. Is that mental episode not a good candidate for a case of imaginatively representing the proposition: *I am a lion*?

First, it is not obvious which sorts of contents are represented by inner speech episodes. There is some reason to think that the contents of inner speech utterances only relate to the *sound* of the relevant spoken sentences and not to the meanings of the sentences themselves (Jackendoff, 1996; Langland-Hassan, 2014a). But let us grant, for the sake of argument, that the mental event we would intuitively describe as "saying 'I am a lion' in inner speech" represents the proposition *I am a lion*. Even so, it would not be a good candidate for a *sui generis* imaginative state. We have a general ability to mentally represent linguistic content—both heard and produced—without believing it. When listening to someone speak, for instance, we need to grasp *what is said* before any decision is made about which attitude to take toward the content of the utterance.[2] By the same token, we can utter arbitrary sentences aloud without believing, desiring, or imagining them, as when reading aloud a dubious political manifesto. Matters don't change when we move an utterance inside the head. In cases where we aim for our utterance—inner or outer—to be sincere, there is some reason (for heavy-duty theorists) to think there will be a corresponding mental representation—a belief—whose content matches that of the utterance. But all bets are off in cases, such as pretense, where the norm of truth-telling has been waived. In the context of pretense, saying "I am a lion," either aloud, or in one's head, can be part of a performance, or a bit of role-playing. It needn't be seen as expressing an internal state with the content *I am a lion*. It could, instead, be caused by a belief that, for instance, saying "I am a lion" will indicate to others (or reinforce for oneself) what one is up to. Further, Sally could easily pretend that she is a lion *without* saying anything aloud, or in inner speech; her actions, in such a case, would still be driven by her imaginings (whatever they are). Thus, for the heavy-duty theorist who is

[2] This phenomenon—of grasping what is said without believing it—is addressed in more detail in Chapter 9, on engaging with fictions. While I am happy to allow that there is a level of mental representation where we represent the content of another person's utterance without believing (or disbelieving) it, this is a basic aspect of language comprehension and not a plausible candidate for a *sui generis* imaginative state. After all, we exercise this sort of ability to represent-without-belief in innumerable contexts where imagination is never invoked, such as when reading a philosophy paper we don't believe or understand, or when listening to someone who we think is mistaken or lying.

committed to *sui generis* imaginings being a unified type of mental state relied upon to guide pretense, inner speech cannot be the relevant state type.

If inner speech has a cognitive role at all in pretense, it is most likely in spurring reasoning on a certain topic (Martinez-Manrique & Vicente, 2010). I might silently repeat to myself, "I am a lion…I am a lion…" as means to focusing my thoughts on features of lions and on how to make myself lion-like. Of course, I could have, to the same effect, said in inner speech: "Ok, what are some features of lions? How can I make myself lion-like?" Moreover, the same processing could have been triggered if someone else, exhorting me to pretend, exclaimed "You are a lion…you are a *lion*!" Understanding and being inspired to act saliently lion-like by that person's utterance does not require, or even suggest, the use of *sui generis* imaginative states in the guidance of the pretense. Matters are not changed when the utterance occurs within my own inner speech.

8.5 Leslie's Tea Party—a More Complex Pretense

Many simple pretenses are just like the lion example. A person draws on her existing beliefs in generalizations about some type of thing in order to make herself somewhat like that type of thing, while believing she is not, and will not in the process become, that type of thing. Consider Leslie's (1987) example where a child pretends that a banana is a telephone. How does she keep the representation "the banana is a telephone" quarantined from her belief that the banana is *not* a telephone? Simple. She does not *have* a thought with the content: "the banana is a telephone." Instead, she has a desire to make the banana telephone-like—to handle it in telephone-like ways—even though she knows it *isn't* one. She draws on her knowledge of telephones to satisfy that desire.

A likely complaint is that the lion and banana-telephone pretenses are overly simple and that it is only in explaining more cognitively demanding pretenses that *sui generis* imaginative states suggest themselves. In granting that there is nothing in the nature of ordinary pretense that demands *sui generis* imaginings, this objection cedes ground to the proposal that the A-imagining that guides pretense can be reduced to a collection of more basic folk psychological states. It maintains, instead, that only relatively complex pretenses present a clear need for *sui generis imaginings*.

What will qualify as a relevantly "complex" pretense? It is difficult to say, *a priori*. Perhaps the least question-begging examples to consider will be those others have relied upon in motivating their arguments for *sui generis* imaginings. The banana-telephone example is one. I will examine another now—the tea-party pretense from Leslie (1994) mentioned earlier—which both Leslie and Nichols & Stich (2000) use to motivate their theories.[3]

[3] The following discussion of Leslie's tea party draws on Langland-Hassan (2012).

Here Leslie describes several key moments in a tea-party pretense that N&S also highlight as calling for special explanation:

> The child is encouraged to "fill" two toy cups with "juice" or "tea" or whatever the child designated the pretend contents of the bottle to be. The experimenter then says, "Watch this!", picks up one of the cups, turns it upside down, shakes it for a second, then replaces it alongside the other cup. The child is then asked to point at the "full cup" and at the "empty cup" (both cups are, of course, really empty throughout).
>
> (Leslie, 1994, p. 223, quoted in Nichols & Stich, 2000, p. 117)

Ten out of ten two-year-olds in Leslie's experiment identified the cup that had been turned upside down as the "empty cup" and the one that had not been overturned as the "full cup." The question of quarantining, as applied to this example, is the following: how does the child, who really believes both cups to be empty, keep track of the fact that one of the cups is "full" in the pretense, without falling into a kind of representational "chaos" or "abuse" (Leslie, 1987), whereby the cup is simultaneously represented as both full and empty? What sort of cognitive mechanisms and representations make this possible?

N&S's answer will be familiar by now: while the child believes that both cups are empty, she simultaneously *imagines that* one of them is full. Imagining that one is full, on their account, amounts to entering into a *sui generis* imaginative state with the content: *that cup is full.* Her imagining that one of the cups is full guides her pretense behavior; at the same time, however, she never comes to believe that a cup is full—she never represents that the cup is full in *that* way—and so never commits representational "abuse."

Following our earlier strategy, we need to see how the child can take part in the pretense without ever having a thought with the content: *that cup is full.* Begin simply with the uncontested data: when asked, as part of the pretense, which cup is empty and which is full, the child (correctly) answers the experimenter's question by identifying the cup that was turned over as the one that is "empty," and the one that was not turned over as the one that is "full"—while believing all along that both are really empty. What sort of beliefs, desires, intentions, and perceptual experiences must the child have to accomplish this? I will map them out in some detail, as doing so will be helpful to answering questions about the psychology of pretense in addition to that concerning quarantining.

N&S correctly note that the child must have a desire to engage in the pretense—she must "want to behave more or less as [s]he would if *p*" (where *p* is "we are having a tea party"). I don't, however, think it's necessary to invoke a conditional ("if *p* then *q*") in describing this desire. It's enough that the child wishes to act like someone at a tea party. To act on this desire, she must have some beliefs about how people typically act at tea parties. These, too, N&S allow the child must have. N&S call such clusters of beliefs "scripts" or "paradigms" that detail "the way in which certain situations typically unfold" (2000, p. 126). And, of course, the child must be able to see (or otherwise perceive) what is actually going on. Is she being handed a cup, watching a kettle tip into a pouring position, being offered a cookie-sized object?

In my view, we can explain the child's behavior with these ingredients alone. Let's focus on the crucial step where the child correctly identifies the overturned cup as "empty," and the other as "full," even though both are believed to be empty. P will be used to indicate that a perceptual "attitude" is taken toward the content that follows, B for belief, and D for desire. (If one is suspicious of a genuine distinction between perceptual and belief attitudes, a B can be replaced for each P without affecting the account). I am continuing to work within the assumptions of a heavy-duty folk psychological ontology, where each that-clause within a mental state ascription implies a corresponding mental representation with much the same content.

P1: You say, "Let's have a tea party!" and start setting out dishes and cups. You do all of this with a familiar set of mannerisms [e.g., knowing looks and smiles, exaggerated movements and intonation, stopping actions short of normal goal points].

B1: *(inferred from P1)* You are starting a game where we act like people at a tea party, even if we're not at one.[4]

D1: I play this game, too.

P2: You are acting as if[5] you are pouring tea out of the teapot and into the cups.

B2: *(from D1 and P2)* I should act like you poured tea into the cups.

B3: *(from B2 and stored generalizations)* If you had poured tea into both cups, they would both now be full.

B4: *(D1 causes this to be inferred from B3)* I should act like both cups are full.

P3: You put down the bottle and say "watch this!"; you turn the green cup upside down and then put it back on the table, right side up.

B5: *(background beliefs)* When cups containing liquid are turned upside down, the liquid spills out. When full cups are not moved, they remain full.

B6: *(inferred from P3, B4, and B5)* If you had poured tea into both cups and overturned the green one, the green one would now be empty and the other one full.

B7: *(inferred from B6, due to D1)* I should act like the green cup is empty and the other one is full.

P3: You say, "Show me which cup is empty and which is full."

[4] This is the step where the child effectively recognizes that a pretense game is occurring—in line with my earlier discussion of pretense recognition, Chapter 7.

[5] "Acting as if" should from here forward be understood as equivalent to "acting in ways that would be appropriate if" and *not* as a mere synonym for "pretending that *p*."

D1—an abiding desire to play the game—then leads the child to use B7 in giving her answer: she points to the green cup to indicate that it is "empty," and then to the other to indicate it is "full."

Note that none of the beliefs appealed to here are "tagged" in any special way to indicate that they are not *real* beliefs (cf. Perner, 1991, pp. 53–67). Nor are these beliefs conceptually onerous—they do not, for instance, involve concepts of mental states. So, whether or not young children have well-developed concepts of folk psychological mental states, this account does not require it. In several places, the child desires to "act like" thus and such, and notes that the experimenter is "acting like" thus and such. This notion of "acting like" does not import or assume the notion of pretense; "acting like" here means the same as "acting as would be appropriate if," which we do when we are not pretending as well.[6]

The most distinctive aspect of the account I have sketched is that pretending that *the green cup is empty* does not involve the child's having a mental representation with the content: *the green cup is empty*. Nor does pretending that *the other cup is full* require a mental representation with the content: *the other cup is full*. Thus, at no time during the pretense does the child entertain a representation with a content that conflicts with—or even that "duplicates"[7]—that of any of her beliefs. This means that there is no mental state in need of quarantining. When the cups are initially "filled" during the pretense, the child does not need to infer (or believe) *that the cups are full*; rather, she needs to recognize that the experimenter is acting in salient tea-pouring ways, and to infer *that if tea had been poured into the cups, they would now be full*. And she needs to remember, going forward, that, as part of the game, they are acting like the cups are full. Instead of acting in lion-like ways—as in our earlier example—she needs to act in the-cups-are-full-like ways. Such beliefs and intentions pose no threat to any beliefs she has outside of the pretense. So it does not appear that a *sui generis* imaginative state must be exploited in order for a child to give correct reports about what is happening even in this relatively sophisticated group pretense.

8.6 Conditional Reasoning during Pretense

However, unlike the lion and banana-telephone pretenses, the tea party example involves the child inferring new counterfactual beliefs of the form: "if *x* had been the case, then *y* would be the case." Specifically, she infers that if a full cup had

[6] What makes these cases of "acting like" *x* is *y* cases of pretending that *x* is *y* is that they occur as part of a Pretense Episode, as defined in Chapter 7.

[7] Because the child *both* pretends that a certain cup is empty (after having been turned over) and believes it is empty, it might seem that an imaginative state is needed to capture the difference between *merely* believing it is empty and both imagining and believing that it is empty. But this is not so on the account I provide.

been turned over, it would now be empty. There is no reason to doubt that children have and make use of such beliefs. Harris (2001) details a variety of studies indicating that "young children [ages 3–4] have the competence for counterfactual thinking, spontaneously engage in such thinking, and deploy it in their causal judgments" (p. 252). And, of course, many who hold that imaginative states are relied upon in pretense do so because they think that such states are required for one to engage in the necessary hypothetical and counterfactual reasoning. For instance, on N&S's account, beliefs in conditionals of the form "if *p* then *q*" are in fact what guide one's pretending that *p* (2000, p. 128). N&S propose that, in order to *arrive at* such beliefs, one must first have a representation with the content of the conditional's antecedent (e.g., *p*) in the "Possible Worlds Box." On their view, when one wants to know what would happen *if p*, while not believing that *p*, one can safely store the proposition *p* in the "Possible Worlds Box" ("PWB") (or "Imagination Box" (Nichols (2004a)), and there carry out the inferences that rationally follow from it, given one's other beliefs. (Currie and Ravenscroft (2002, Ch. 2) espouse much the same view.) Thereafter, those inferences conducted "offline" can be imported into the consequent of a believed conditional with *p* as its antecedent. Indeed, according to N&S, it is the evolutionary function of the PWB to enable hypothetical reasoning (2003, p. 58). However, the PWB itself has no direct connections to action control systems (2000, p. 128).

I've already argued, in Chapters 5 and 6, that inferring new conditionals of this sort does not require one to represent the antecedent of the conditional "offline" (or in a PWB)—and, indeed, that doing so would be redundant. Anyone who would infer 'if *p* then *q*' after representing *p* via a *sui generis* imaginative state already has all the beliefs they need in order to infer the conditional without use of the imaginative state. Here I will offer a few additional remarks to bolster that account and indicate how it applies specifically to pretense.

Suppose that I want to reason hypothetically about what would happen if a wild boar entered the classroom during a college lecture. Call the proposition that a wild boar enters the classroom during a college lecture '*b*.' The desire to know what would happen if *b* will cause me to access whatever relevant generalizations I have stored about wild boars, college students, classrooms, professors, and so on. A few come to mind: wild boars are dangerous and excitable ('*w*'), wild boars getting loose in college classrooms is highly unusual ('*u*'), people are shocked and excited by highly unusual events ('*s*'), college students like to take pictures of exciting and unusual events on their phones ('*p*'), college students are frightened by dangerous animals ('*y*'), people scream when they are frightened ('*f*'), and so on. Having brought these generalizations to mind, I'm able to infer, *on their basis*, that if a wild boar enters a college lecture, then a dangerous, excitable animal will be loose in the room, shocking and causing fear in students, who will scream and try to take pictures of it with their phones. There is no need during all of this to put *b* (a representation with the content "a wild boar enters the classroom during a college lecture") itself in either the belief or desire "boxes"—or any box at all. Hence, there is no need to quarantine *b*. Turning back to the issue of pretense, if I want to *pretend* that a wild boar is running amok in a college classroom, the inferred (and now believed) conditionals just mentioned will be sufficient to guide a sequence of pretend behavior. I will have determined some likely results of it being the case that *b* and can rely on them in acting as would be appropriate if *b*.

On this picture, there is no need for quarantining during pretense *or* hypothetical reasoning, as neither require us to entertain contents we disbelieve. Nor is there any peculiarity in a person's ability to imagine or pretend that *p* while not believing that *p*—or indeed while believing that *p*. For the activity of imagining that *p*, *in these cases*, consists merely in retrieving one's beliefs in generalizations relevant to the proposition that *p* and using them to make judgments about what would likely happen if *p*, all of which may (or may not) guide a sequence of pretend behavior. There is no reason to think that one's ability to do any of this would be hampered or confused by a concomitant belief that not-*p*, or that *p*.

As for the pretender's ability to distinguish what is happening in the pretense from what is true outside of the pretense, the main difficulty is removed once we give up the idea that a cognitive system must sort through contradictory representations (e.g. 'the telephone is a banana' and 'the telephone is not a banana'), or through multiple copies of the same representation (e.g. 'the cup is empty' (as pretended) and 'the cup is empty' (as believed)), in distinguishing the actual from the pretend.

8.7 Inferential Disorderliness and the Outlandish Premise

Nichols & Stich note that when pretenders elaborate the details of a pretense, they often do so through a series of inferences that mirrors the beliefs they would form were the pretense real. Nichols (2006a) calls this phenomenon "inferential orderliness." In the tea party example, when one of the cups is overturned, the children infer that it has become "empty," just as they would have come to believe it was empty had it actually been filled and then overturned (or if they had simply learned through testimony that a full cup was overturned).[8] Currie & Ravenscroft highlight the same phenomenon, suggesting that the attitude underlying

[8] N&S also stress that such inferential orderliness is only a norm; in many cases things are inferred in an act of pretense that one would not normally come to believe or act out in reality. When told to imagine that Bob was in New York yesterday and London today, we will *typically* imaginatively infer that he traveled to London by plane (as we would likely come to believe were we simply told this information). But there will also be cases where, for whatever reason, we fill out the scenario by imagining that Bob made the journey via teleportation, or by flapping his arms. So, there is latitude in imaginative inference—a possibility of divergence from what we would believe were the situation real, a possibility for inferential *disorderliness*—that must also be accounted for.

propositional imagination is "belief-like" in that it "preserves the inferential patters of belief" (2002, p. 12).

Nichols & Stich account for inferential orderliness by positing that the same "inference mechanism" is applied to representations in the PWB as in the Belief Box—an identity of mechanism enabled by the representations in each box being "in the same code." To explain the occasional divergence from patters of inference characteristic of belief, N&S posit another cognitive mechanism they call the "Script Elaborator," whose job it is to "fill in those details of a pretense that can't be inferred from the pretense premise, the (altered) contents of the Belief Box, and the pretender's knowledge of what has happened earlier on in the pretense" (2000, p. 127). They admit they "know little about how [the Script Elaborator] works" (p. 144).

If we avoid positing *sui generis* imaginative states, simpler answers are available. On the view I am proposing, the beliefs in conditionals and generalizations that guide inferences and behavior in a pretense are generally *the very ones* that guide the corresponding inferences and behavior in real life. For example, if I am told, "pretend that Bob was in New York on Monday, and London on Tuesday," I will typically infer, as part of the pretense, that Bob got to London via airplane, just as I would infer that he'd gone by airplane if I believed, through testimony, that Bob was in New York on Monday and London on Tuesday. This "mirroring" is due to the fact that we tend to fill out pretend and actual scenarios by appeal to the same beliefs about how things normally go; in this case, the relevant belief is that people who travel that far that fast usually do so by airplane.

Why do we do it this way? Why does imagining that *p* (and pretending that *p*) feed off beliefs concerning what would be likely if *p*? Here I think we have a pseudo-question. Imagining that *p* during a pretense *just is* bringing to mind or generating beliefs concerning what would likely happen if *p*, or generalizations concerning *p*-like situations, based on background beliefs deemed relevant. The question of why the inferences drawn "in imagination" mirror those that would be drawn from "isomorphic" beliefs is puzzling only if one begins with the view that the representations involved in guiding a pretense are quarantined in their own "box." Only then will it seem attractive to attribute the mirroring to a mechanism that treats the representations in both boxes roughly the same way.

8.8 Cognitive Attention—Asking Ourselves Questions and Holding Propositions in Mind

On the account I have so far sketched, pretending requires us to draw on background knowledge of various sorts. It may seem that this process of recollection—of searching our own minds for information of a specific sort—would itself require us to enter into *sui generis* imaginative states (or something comparable). For instance, when pretending to be a lion, a child has to ask herself (though perhaps not consciously): what are lions like? When pretending to be at a tea party, I have to ask myself: what goes on at tea parties? Asking ourselves such questions allows us to focus on the pretense's subject matter, so as to retrieve what relevant knowledge we may have. While asking oneself a question is not the same thing as imagining a proposition, one might worry that I have just swapped the need to explain imagination for the need to explain the capacity to ask oneself a question. Further, it may seem that one of the important roles played by N&S's PWB—and *sui generis* imaginative states in general—is that it enables this sort of focusing of attention on a proposition.

In response, note first that such an attention-focusing role does not sit happily with the notion of a cognitive *attitude* of imagination. Psychological attitudes in general—such as belief, desire, and intention—do not, on anyone's account, have the function of focusing attention. We simply have too many beliefs, desires, and so on, for the attitudes themselves to account for how we attend to some (but not all) of them. If imagination really is "belief-like," or otherwise well characterized as a distinct cognitive attitude, imagining a proposition will not suffice for allowing one to cognitively focus on the proposition.

Second, the question of how attention is focused on a particular question or proposition, and relevant information subsequently retrieved, is entirely general, extending well beyond any questions to do with pretense or the consideration of hypotheticals. We ask ourselves questions as a means to retrieving relevant information all the time, without being tempted to describe ourselves as imagining. We might ask ourselves: "What's fifty-seven divided by ten?" "What kinds of things do they sell at Starbucks?" "Who is the governor of Ohio?" "How did I get here?" No one proposes to explain the mere raising of such internal queries in terms of a capacity for imagination. Matters are not changed if the self-initiated question has a hypothetical or counterfactual component. We can ask ourselves: What would happen if tea were poured into the cups? Or: How would physics have developed if Einstein were never born? Or: How would you feel if someone did that to you? The *mere* ability to turn our mind to a topic so as to retrieve information about it does not itself introduce the need for *sui generis* imaginative states. (And I have already argued that, once this information is retrieved, there is no need to token a *sui generis* imaginative state in making use of it.) Whatever mechanism or process enables attention to be focused on *non*-hypothetical questions and reasoning tasks will plausibly be the same one that allows focus on questions of the form: what would happen if *p*? So there is no motivation for thinking that it is only through entering a *sui generis* imaginative state that we are able to cognitively focus on a topic, question, or proposition.

Certainly, the process of asking oneself a question—so as to rustle memory or engage reasoning on a topic—is a cognitive ability that, like most, we would like to better understand. Yet, like the states of belief, desire, and intention, it is a folk psychological kind to which all sides are committed, independent of any debates surrounding pretense or imagination. For that reason, it is the right sort of piece with which to explain pretense and imagination.

8.9 Freedom and Pterodactyls

More troubling for my view may seem to be situations in which pretenses diverge from any beliefs we are able to generate about what would happen if the pretend situation really obtained—that is, where we pretend that p and our doing so involves our pretending things we think are very *unlikely* if p. For instance, we might pretend that we are at a tea party where, suddenly, a tornado strikes. Yet tea parties are rarely visited by tornados. This pretense cannot simply involve drawing on general knowledge about what happens at tea parties.

This is simply a standard case of the general freedom of imagination, however, which can be explained as a freedom to reason about topics of our own choosing (see Chapter 1). In the case of pretense, this "freedom" consists in our ability to insert a new premise into our imaginative projects whenever we wish and to draw out further inferences from there. "Inserting a new premise" n to an imaginative project that p amounts to asking oneself what would likely happen if p *and* n. Sometimes this involves reasoning about the likely consequences of scenarios that are themselves unlikely. For instance, you might pretend that a tea party is in full swing—drawing on background beliefs about tea parties to do so—when suddenly, because the pretense needs some spicing up, you decide to also pretend that a tornado strikes. Whereas before you were acting on some beliefs about what would likely happen if p, now you are generating some inferences about what would likely happen if p and n. You use stored generalizations about tornados to reason about how they would affect a tea party. We still needn't conceive of the freedom of imagination as a freedom to token representations we hold to be false.

Van Leeuwen (2011) describes a related case involving improvisational comedians, as a means to challenging what he calls "conditional belief" accounts of imagining.[9] These are accounts on which imaginings drive pretense indirectly by enabling the formation of conditional beliefs—where these beliefs are the actual guides of pretend actions (he includes N&S's theory among such views, and would presumably include mine as well). The actors begin their performance by pretending to be knights dueling. Yet, before long, the pretend knights have mounted pretend pterodactyls, continuing their duel aloft. Here the pretenders seem to proceed, in imagination, in ways that have nothing to do with what they

[9] My discussion of this case draws on Langland-Hassan (2016).

really believe would happen if the instigating premise of the imagining ("We are knights dueling") were true.

Focusing in on this case, suppose that Actor A starts the pretense by imagining that *I am a brave knight at a duel.* If imagining is just a matter of drawing out likely consequences from an initial premise *p*—or, in my terms, bringing to mind some generalizations about what happens in situations like *p*—then we should expect A's imaginings to unfold in accord with what A thinks would happen if *p*. On N&S's view, he might infer a conditional of the form: "If I were a dueling knight, I would be holding a sword…An opponent would be trying to stab me…I would speak in a formal cadence." And he will have arrived at this belief by a process of inference that took place via *sui generis* imaginative states in his Possible Worlds Box. For the consequents of the conditional are things he might come to infer if he believed the initial premise. On my view, it might be that the actor imagines that he is a knight by bringing to mind some generalizations, such as "knights engage in duels" and "knights hold their swords like so," using them to guide his knight-like behavior. And while he may infer related conditionals in the process, we need not assume that the beliefs that end up driving the pretense are always beliefs in conditionals (as emphasized in section 8.3, with respect to the child pretending to be a lion).

But how do we explain the sudden transition to imagining that they are jousting on pterodactyls? That is *not* something knights generally do. At this point, the ordinary process of thinking through the likely consequences of *p*, or of thinking about generalizations relevant to *p*, is interrupted by a desire for something more comedic to occur in the performance. (Their job is to entertain, after all.) Actor A decides that his riding a pterodactyl would be funny (more on this decision in a moment). This leads him to "intervene" on his prior imagining by asking himself: "What if I were doing all this *while riding a pterodactyl*?" This intervention may lead him to draw some further inferences concerning things that would happen if he were somehow riding a pterodactyl. He might not be too sure about what would happen in such a weird situation. But, for a pretense, he gives it a shot and doesn't worry if he's off base; it won't matter much for his purposes of entertaining. It occurs to him that pterodactyls *fly*. So he may draw some inferences about what would happen if he were dueling while *flying* on the back of a pterodactyl. Here he has to make use of whatever relevant background beliefs he has. He likely has some about *riding animals* (it's bumpy, they can be difficult to harness). He likely has some about *flying animals* (they go up and down). He likely has some about *people at great heights* (they get nervous). He might have some about *pterodactyls* (they are aggressive). All of these can now feed into his behavior, at his discretion. The general point is that, whenever an imagining diverges into something unusual or bizarre, this is because a new premise has been added to the initiating premise as a conjunct. This amounts to the agent's bringing to bear some other body of knowledge—e.g., about pterodactyls or riding animals—in order to enrich her pretense behaviors. In some cases a new conditional is inferred in the process; in others, we simply judge that we can make ourselves somewhat like some other sort of thing by doing thus and such.

Most of the pretend premises (e.g., I am swinging my sword) are discarded at some point during the pretense. This is why considering the conjunctive conditions and what would follow from them does not become unmanageable. Yet some premises remain as guiding themes (e.g., I am a knight). To add a new premise is just to bring to mind a new set of generalizations and use them in conjunction with the other background beliefs already being exploited. This allows the imaginative episode, as a whole, both to be constrained by one's existing beliefs and to freely diverge from anything one would infer from the initial premise alone.

Why did Actor A insert a premise having to do with *pterodactyls*, and not something else? Well, he wanted to shift the pretense to something more surprising, funny, and unusual—to something that would suit his goals, *qua* improvisational comedian. But why pterodactyls, in particular? Here the answer must trace to specifics of his psychology: what has he recently thought of or seen? What kinds of things does he generally find funny or surprising? Did someone mention dinosaurs earlier in the performance? The important point is that the answer will not involve positing a novel cognitive *mechanism*, process, or *sui generis* state. Coming to understand the work that N&S set aside for the Script Elaborator becomes part and parcel with understanding an agent's goals, intentions, and decisions more generally.

It is worth noting that the interesting question of why one premise ("I am a knight in a duel") is followed by another, outlandish one ("We are riding pterodactyls") is no better explained by appeal to *sui generis* imaginative states—be they propositional states or, as Van Leeuwen (2011) prefers, imagistic ones. We still face the question of *why* one *sui generis* state, and not some other, follows the previous one. The problem Van Leeuwen was after is that, in some cases, there seems to be no candidate *belief* that can play the relevant pretense-guiding role, because we simply don't believe conditionals of the right sort. That problem is solved by the allowance that we can insert new premises to our pretenses at will, via new conjuncts within the antecedent of the conditionals. We will do so whenever it serves our purposes. This answer, appealing to our intentions and desires, also provides a general account of why one outlandish premise might follow another—one that, it seems, most any theory must accept in broad outline.

8.10 Autism and Pretense

Before leaving the topic of pretense, I want to discuss one further argument that has been given for positing *sui generis* imaginative states—one that is quite different from others we have so far considered. Both Nichols and Stich (2003, p. 129) and Currie and Ravenscroft (2002) invoke a distinct cognitive attitude of imagination not only to explain pretense, but to explain third-person mindreading as well (where "third-person mindreading" is the ability to understand and predict others' behavior by inferring their mental states). Just as pretense, on their views, requires an ability to entertain and draw "belief-like" inferences from propositions one does not believe, so too does mindreading intuitively require the ability to take another's (potentially different) belief set into account and draw out implications from those beliefs "offline," so as to predict that person's behavior. If both mindreading and pretense capacities are sometimes simultaneously impaired while other higher cognitive capacities remain intact—as some argue is the case in autism spectrum disorder (ASD) (Baron-Cohen, 1989, 1995)—this would suggest that a single system underlies both. The idea that a single cognitive system, module, or attitude underlies both meshes well with the view that there are *sui generis* imaginative states, where such states are supported by this impaired system (though the support would be considerably stronger were a *double* dissociation available—such that other individuals are found capable of complex pretenses and mindreading, yet severely impaired in ordinary first-order reasoning). By contrast, on the view I have proposed, where imagining does not involve use of any *sui generis* type of mental state, there is no obvious reason to expect these two disabilities to co-occur.

There are two main problems with both N&S and C&R's appeal to these deficits in support of their theories. The first is that many people with ASD retain other abilities that N&S and C&R associate with imaginative states, while still showing the characteristic difficulties with mindreading and pretense. For, on both accounts, not only does the PWB (or "belief-like imaginings" for Currie and Ravenscroft) underlie our ability to engage in pretense and mindreading, it also allows for hypothetical and counterfactual reasoning. Yet hypothetical and counterfactual reasoning (and "supposing") *per se* are not impaired in children with autism. This removes any special support that the dissociations witnessed in ASD might lend to N&S and C&R's views.

Indeed, Scott et al. (1999) found that autistic children outperformed normal children of matched verbal age on some counterfactual reasoning tasks.[10] Interestingly, the performance of the autistic children declined only once they were prompted to form visual images while considering their answers to the questions.[11] Peterson and Bowler (1996) found that children with ASD responded appropriately to explicit counterfactual questions, such as "If Mummy hadn't

[10] Though see also Grant, Riggs, & Boucher (2004) for evidence of a link between counterfactual reasoning and mindreading abilities in children with autism.

[11] These results have been criticized (Leevers & Harris, 2000) as being due to a bias of autistic children to answer "Yes" to questions (the correct answer to each of the questions was in fact Yes). Yet, as Scott and colleagues point out, this fails to explain why their answers became considerably less

made the cake, where would the chocolate be?" and, in a later study (Peterson & Bowler, 2000) showed that autistic children have a facility with a kind of hypothetical reasoning they call "subtractive reasoning." Normal false-belief tasks can be rephrased using "subtractive" prompts such as "If the marble had not been moved, where would it be now?" in lieu of "Where does Sally believe the marble to be?" When the tasks were rephrased in this manner, autistic children were able to provide correct answers at levels comparable to those of their non-autistic peers. Further, children of all kinds they studied—normal, autistic, and with learning disabilities—who could not answer the subtractive questions could not answer the false-belief questions, either. This leads Peterson and Bowler to conclude that subtractive hypothetical reasoning, preserved in autism, is necessary but not sufficient for the kind of mindreading required in answering ordinary false-belief questions.

Hadwin and Bruins (1998) have also found that children with ASD can formulate counterfactual antecedents and consequences for various episodes. For instance, one child suggested that by wearing boots a story character could have prevented getting her socks muddy. And Jarrold et al. (1994) found that children with autism were able, when prompted, to engage in "object substitution" pretenses—pretending, e.g., that a pencil is a toothbrush—with equal facility to controls of equivalent verbal mental age (Jarrold, Boucher, & Smith, 1994). Further, we should remember that the mindreading deficits of autistic children are of special interest in the first place because their abilities to make hypothetical predictions using other commonsense theories—in particular, with "folk physics"—are comparably intact (Baron-Cohen, Leslie, & Frith, 1986).[12] On both N&S and C&R's theories, there is no reason that the PWB, or one's belief-like imaginings, should falter when put to the task of predicting another's behavior, but not the course of a billiard ball. Likewise, studies investigating awareness of the emotions in autism have shown that children and adolescents with autism perform comparably to controls on so-called "upward counterfactual reasoning" (i.e., reasoning about how things could have gone better) yet are impaired in "downward counterfactual reasoning" (i.e., reasoning about how things could have gone worse) (Begeer, De Rosnay, Lunenburg, Stegge, & Terwogt, 2014). Again, there is no reason to expect a general deficit with *sui generis* imaginative states to show this kind of content specificity. Thus, the data from ASD provides no special support to N&S or C&R's theories. However we are to understand the mindreading and pretense deficits in ASD, our explanations must be more nuanced than

accurate (involving many answers of No) once they were encouraged to form images while answering the questions (the correct answers were still all Yes).

[12] Some high-performing individuals with ASD (e.g., mathematical savants) even show a pronounced superiority in counterfactual reasoning tasks over the general population. See Baron-Cohen et al. (1999) for a discussion of several such cases.

that the individual has an impaired mental module, or difficulty generating a certain type of (imaginative) mental state.

This is not to deny an important link between the relative lack of pretense in ASD and the more general deficits in social cognition (or "mindreading") in ASD. The proper place to look for an explanation, however, is not theories of imagination, but, rather, theories of social cognition more generally. The two should not be run together. Research on social cognition has boomed since the mid-1990s, when the leading theories were monolithic in nature. The main debate at that time concerned whether our ability to understand other minds relied on something like a scientific theory, or, instead, something more like a process of simulation (Davies & Stone, 2001; Stich & Nichols, 1992). Today, much of the exciting research on social cognition in autism concerns far more basic "embodied" capacities—such as the ability to attend to and understand facial expressions (Dawson, Webb, & McPartland, 2005), to unconsciously coordinate one's bodily movements with those of another (Marsh et al., 2013), or to attend to relevant social stimuli, such as faces and directions of gaze (Dawson, Meltzoff, Osterling, Rinaldi, & Brown, 1998; Dawson et al., 2004). Far from having a simple inability to imagine, or to generate "offline" versions of "online" mental states, people with ASD have been shown to have a broad array of sensorimotor and cognitive abnormalities—including arrhythmic gaits (Calhoun, Longworth, & Chester, 2011; Shetreat-Klein, Shinnar, & Rapin, 2014), diminished linguistic abilities (Sahyoun, Belliveau, Soulières, Schwartz, & Mody, 2010), kinematic motor abnormalities (Forti et al., 2011; Fournier, Hass, Naik, Lodha, & Cauraugh, 2010), aberrant emotional responses to their own facial expressions (Stel, van den Heuvel, & Smeets, 2008), and broader attentional and executive functioning deficits (Just, Cherkassky, Keller, Kana, & Minshew, 2007). Understanding the nature of the impaired social cognition in ASD requires understanding the ways in which these attentional, sensorimotor, emotional, and linguistic differences both engender and reinforce "higher" mindreading deficits that are more typically the province of empirically-oriented philosophers of mind (Van Wagner, 2017). That important project is well beyond the scope of this book. The lesson, for present purposes, is that the constellation of social, cognitive, and motor deficits seen in ASD do not constitute the kind of clean dissociation in abilities that would provide special support for positing *sui generis* imaginative states.

8.11 Conclusion

We have now had a close look at the metaphysics, epistemology, and psychology of pretense. This chapter considered the question of whether we in fact make use of *sui generis* imaginative states in some, or even all, pretenses. That question is distinct, in ways I have explained, from the metaphysical question of what it is to pretend, and from the epistemological question of how we recognize pretense in others—both discussed in Chapter 7. A crucial step in undermining the claim that pretense draws on *sui generis* imaginative states, I have argued, is seeing that there is no need to "quarantine" certain mental representations during pretense. The supposed need for quarantining is often based on a groundless assumption concerning the cognitive-architectural requirements for hypothetical reasoning—namely, that to determine what would happen if *p*, one must token a mental representation with the content *p*. Nor does the tendency of pretense to gravitate toward the absurd give reason to posit *sui generis* imaginative states. When pretending, we are often motivated to reason about likely outcomes of scenarios that are themselves exceedingly unlikely. Our freedom to do so is one with the freedom of imagination (though not *all* cases of "the freedom of imagination" are to be explained in this way).

I also responded to the objection that my view tacitly posits something like a *sui generis* state of imagining in relying upon our ability to ask ourselves questions. This ability is something that occurs well outside of any contexts associated with imagination and is something all sides must provide an explanation of, independent of anything one wants to say about imagination. Finally, I argued that the pretense and other social deficits seen in ASD do not favor any particular views about the nature of imagination.

9
Consuming Fictions Part I
Recovering Fictional Truths

9.1 Imagination and the Many Puzzles of Fiction: Plan for the Next Three Chapters

The three chapters to come concern the role of imagination in our encounters with fiction. When we enjoy a fiction, our thought processes fulfill the criteria by which I defined A-imagining: we are engaging in rich, elaborated thought about the merely possible, fantastical, or unreal in an epistemically safe manner. As in earlier chapters, my question is not whether we really engage in A-imagining when we enjoy a fiction. I am sure that we do. My question is whether such imagining can be explained in more basic folk psychological terms.

Imagination commonly appears in the explanation of several distinct puzzles surrounding fiction. It's useful to split the puzzles into two classes. First, there are those having to do with the psychological states by which we *comprehend* what is going on in a fiction; second, there are those concerning how and why we become *immersed* in—or emotionally engaged by—fictions. The puzzles of comprehension are rooted in our need to maintain a mental registry of a fiction's events. When we take in a fiction, we typically don't *believe* the fictional events to be occurring, after all. How, then, do we keep in mind what is happening? A natural thought is that we imagine the events and that this imagining constitutes our mental registry of the fiction's events. A second, closely related, puzzle of comprehension concerns our ability to recover "implicit" or "implied" fictional truths. Grasping what is true in a fiction usually involves more than simply understanding what is explicitly stated in a text or shown in a film. We also need to extrapolate from those explicit fictional truths others that are merely implied—recognizing, for example, that the camera's lingering on a tombstone indicates that a certain character has died. It may be thought that imagination is the cognitive resource through which we do so. A third puzzle of comprehension, highlighted by the phenomenon of implicit fictional truths, is the question of what determines truth in a fiction. In virtue of what are some propositions true, and others false with respect to a fictional world? Here imagination has also been thought to provide an answer, with truths-in-fiction defined by some in terms of what an author prescribes her audience *to imagine* (Currie, 1990; Stock, 2017; Walton, 1990). A fourth puzzle of comprehension concerns the metaphysics of fictions themselves:

Explaining Imagination. Peter Langland-Hassan, Oxford University Press (2020). © Peter Langland-Hassan.
DOI: 10.1093/oso/9780198815068.001.0001

what makes one *text* a fiction and another a non-fiction, given that neither may correspond to what is true? Again it may be thought that imagination is part of the answer, with fictions being texts whose contents readers are prescribed to imagine, while non-fictions are (perhaps) texts whose contents we are prescribed to believe. To explain the A-imagining at work in fiction consumption in terms of a more basic collection of folk psychological states, we will need to show how these four puzzles of comprehension can been resolved without appealing to *sui generis* imaginative states.[1] That will be the project of this chapter.

The second set of puzzles—the puzzles of immersion—concern our tendency to become emotionally engaged by fictions. We may even, in some sense, "lose ourselves" in a fiction, being "imaginatively transported" (Kampa, 2018) to another (merely fictional) time and place. Naturally, we need to comprehend what is happening in a fiction in order to become immersed in it in these ways. But, on the face of it, comprehension of what is true in a fictional world does not entail immersion within it. We know this from our experience of fictions that we comprehend but don't enjoy. We might, for instance, have a quite comprehensive grasp of what is true in a fiction made for children, without being immersed in it at all. So, becoming immersed in a fiction involves something more than grasping what is true in the fiction. Some have thought this "something more" to be a *sui generis* form of imagination (Kind, 2011; Meskin & Weinberg, 2003; Nichols, 2006b; Spaulding, 2015; Van Leeuwen, 2016). Yet, even if one is convinced that imagination is somehow at work in immersion, it can be difficult to specify the precise nature of the involvement. Does imagination lead to immersion simply by causing relevant *emotions* to occur (Meskin & Weinberg, 2003)? Is it the imagistic aspect of imagination that generates emotion and, thus, immersion (Van Leeuwen, 2016)? Or does imagination generate immersion by somehow constituting a more direct cognitive acquaintance with fictional events than is otherwise available? A related, and very famous, puzzle—known as the "paradox of fiction"—concerns the *appropriateness* of such immersion: is it not irrational to become emotionally engaged in fiction, pitying or fearing characters we know to be unreal (C. Radford, 1975)? Reflection on the normative status of such emotional responses leads to questions about the nature of the responsible psychological states themselves. Are they belief-like imaginings, or ordinary beliefs, that generate these responses? Are they desires, or imaginative counterparts to desires (e.g., "i-desires") that are at work? Are the emotions themselves ordinary emotions, or

[1] It is important to appreciate that what makes something true in a fiction, and how we come to know about that truth, are distinct questions. For instance, it could be that facts about what is true in a fiction have nothing to do with imagination (as in Lewis (1978)), even if we must use imagination to become aware of those facts. Alternatively—as in both Walton (1990) and Stock (2017)—it could be that the notion of imagination must appear both in accounts of what make something true in a fiction (viz., one is prescribed to imagine it) and in an account of how we come to grasp what is true in a fiction. I will argue that it need not appear in either.

"quasi-emotions" (Walton, 1990)? The many puzzles surrounding immersion are tackled in Chapters 10 and 11. Each can be resolved, I argue, without the need to invoke *sui generis* imaginative states.

In describing the puzzles of immersion, I haven't distinguished between being emotionally engaged in a fiction and being immersed in it. Some may think that this misses a crucial distinction—that it is one thing to respond emotionally to a fiction, caring deeply about its characters, being moved by its events, and so on, and another to be *immersed* in it. The thought here is that immersion involves some deeper or more profound losing of oneself in the fiction, where one's grip on the distinction between what is real and what is pretend slackens... or something. I purposefully run together immersion and emotional engagement because I think that being immersed in a fiction is nothing over and above being deeply emotionally engaged by it. Emotional engagement comes in degrees; in high degrees we call it "immersion." To the extent that others insist on a deeper psychological distinction between being immersed in a fiction and being emotionally engaged by it, I think they are pointing to a bogus phenomenon. As Liao & Doggett (2014) observe, even method actors deeply immersed in their roles don't become confused at the presence of cameras filming them. Daniel Day Lewis, immersed in the character of Abraham Lincoln, isn't perplexed by the sophisticated lighting rigs hanging over his head. So, immersion is not simply believing—or almost believing—that some fiction is recording actual events. After all, we might believe some fiction to record actual events while not being the least bit immersed in it—as when watching a boring drama that we wrongly take for documentary. What matters for immersion is our emotional engagement; explain that, and we're done.

Finally, there is, in addition, a third set of puzzles surrounding fiction and imagination: the puzzles of *imaginative resistance* (Gendler, 2000; Liao, Strohminger, & Sripada, 2014; Miyazono & Liao, 2016; Weatherson, 2005). At the risk of leaving my discussion incomplete, I will not say much about these. Admittedly, the omission is with some prejudice. Many of the debates about imaginative resistance turn on the question of whether one does, or does not, imagine that *p* when consuming some fiction in which it is that case that *p*. (This is so, at least, with respect to the "imaginability" and "phenomenological" puzzles, sometimes distinguished from the "fictionality puzzle" or "alethic puzzle" (Gendler & Liao, 2016).) Making determinations of that kind requires that one is able to introspectively discriminate instances of imagining that *p* from instances of *very closely related* mental states—such as supposing, assuming, conceiving, or "merely entertaining the proposition" that *p*, which, it is said, do not similarly generate resistance. Because I don't think that the relation of imagining to these other states is at all obvious or well understood, I don't think that anyone is in a good position to make those introspective discriminations—especially not in the borderline cases concocted in attempts to defend one view concerning the cause of imaginative resistance over another (see, e.g., Gendler (2000) versus Weatherson (2005)). The legitimate puzzle I find interesting in this vicinity is what Liao and Gendler call the *ficitonality puzzle*: why we do we resist judging as true, in the fiction *F*, certain things the author apparently intends for us to judge true in *F*? To this I think Stock's (2005) response is along the right lines: we don't really *get* what the fictions are talking about in cases of such resistance—we don't know how to fill out the fictional world with additional, related truths; though more details or context might help us to do so. I hope to say more about this on another occasion.[2]

As noted, the balance of this chapter will focus on the puzzles of comprehension. Explaining our ability to grasp what is true in a fiction, I argue, does not call for *sui generis* imaginative states. Nor need we appeal to imagination in explaining what it is that makes something true in a fiction, or in what makes something qualify as a fiction in the first place. Chapter 10 begins discussion of the puzzles of immersion by going on the attack. I argue that *sui generis* imaginings are entirely redundant as explanations of fiction-directed affect and in fact offer no special leverage on the question of immersion. Chapter 11 then provides a positive account of how and why we become immersed in fictions—one that enables us to see how the related imaginings are explicable in more basic folk psychological terms. The bulk of that chapter develops a solution to the paradox of fiction, which, I argue, must be properly resolved if we are to understand the phenomenon of immersion.

I turn back now to the puzzles of comprehension, which will occupy us to the end of this chapter.

9.2 Understanding a Fiction—the First Puzzle

We don't believe everything we hear. We don't imagine it, either. Two cases in point:

[2] All right, I'll say more now. When we read a fiction, our "imaginings" in response consist, in large part, in inferences about what else is implicitly true in the fiction. (Such is my claim, defended later this chapter.) Suppose (as I believe) that Lewis's (1978) account of truth in fiction is essentially correct: *p* is true in fiction *F* if, at the nearest possible worlds where *F* is told as known fact, *p* is true. To apply this heuristic smoothly and efficiently, and so to enrich our understanding of a fictional world, we need to have an intuitive sense of how similar the nearest possible world where *F* is told as known fact is to our own. This lets us know how much of our own world can be imported to the fiction in the form of inferences about what else is implicitly true in the fiction. Imaginative resistance (of the "fictionality puzzle" sort) occurs when we come upon a proposition that suddenly suggests we were way off in our initial appraisal of how close that nearest possible world is. For instance, when, in the middle of an otherwise realistic fiction, we are told by a narrator that universal female infanticide is a good thing, we have to shift our thoughts to a possible world where such a thing could be said as known fact, before we can draw out any further inferences about what is true in the fiction. This isn't in itself a problem. Lots of fictions test the bounds of possibility. But when this shift occurs in the context of an otherwise ordinary fiction—one that has so far implied that the fictional world is very similar to our own—we become unsure of which sort of possible world to use as our model for filling in implicit truths: one nearby, or very far away? Further context may help to resolve this ambiguity and so to get our imaginings (in the form of judgments about what else is true in the fiction) flowing again.

> I am watching political pundits on TV. One of them says that *p*. But *p* is false! I understand what he is saying, but reject it out of hand. I don't pause to imagine the possibility of its being true.
>
> A philosopher has written a book on imagination. You understand the claims he is making, for the most part. But plenty of it you neither believe nor imagine.

Understanding what is being said while withholding belief is a part of everyday life. It is not something that requires imagination. Not intuitively, at least, and not on anyone's view that I am aware of. It could nevertheless be that, against appearances, simply understanding someone's speech, when we don't believe him, requires imagination. But we would need a special reason for thinking so. Of course, when we understand someone without believing him, it is not as though we form no related beliefs *at all*. Usually, we will form some beliefs about what the person has said—about what is true, *according to him*. But we might not form very many. At the end of a long, dubious lecture, we may only emerge with a few beliefs capturing the gist of what was said.

Taking in a fiction—a novel, a film, a play—is another context where we understand what is said while, for the most part, not believing it. And yet almost everyone in philosophy holds that understanding fiction centrally involves imagination (Currie, 1990, 1995; Kind, 2011; Meskin & Weinberg, 2003; Nichols, 2004a; Spaulding, 2015; Stock, 2017; Walton, 1990).[3] We might wonder why they do not, instead, hold that we understand a fictional text as we do the speech of someone we don't believe. After all, it won't be denied that we form beliefs about what is true in the fictions we enjoy, just as we form beliefs when listening to a known liar. We rely on such beliefs when we tell people about a fiction after the fact. Why, then, do *sui generis* imaginings *also* need to be involved in fiction comprehension—assuming, again, that they are not involved when listening to a known liar, or when comprehending a bad argument? It is unclear why the fact that the content we are comprehending is that of a fiction would introduce a special need for imagination.

One thought is that the difference traces to the comparable richness of fictional narratives. When we consume a fiction, we grasp *very many* propositions without believing them—perhaps more than when reading a philosophy paper, or when listening to a political debate. In the latter cases, we may believe *much* of what is said; whereas, when enjoying a fiction, we may believe none of it. It may seem, instead, that we make use of a "streaming mode" of our imagination, letting the fiction's entire content pass through our minds in the form of momentary

[3] Derek Matravers (2014) is a notable exception. Matravers' core argument is that the mental states and processes at work in consuming a fiction are essentially the same as those involved in consuming non-fictional narratives; it is therefore a mistake to associate a particular kind of mental state (imagining) exclusively with fiction. Whether he thinks that imagination is nevertheless involved in consuming *both* fictions and non-fictions is less clear, as discussed below.

imaginings. I take this idea of a streaming mode of imagination from Weinberg & Meskin (2006b) and Meskin & Weinberg (2003), who hold that fiction-appreciation involves use of the "Possible Worlds Box" (PWB) familiar from Nichols & Stich (2000). When we read a novel or watch a movie, they propose, "the representational contents of the fiction are placed into the PWB" (Meskin & Weinberg, 2003, p. 31). There are two "modes" in which the PWB can operate in this context, according to Weinberg & Meskin. First, there is "streaming mode," where we "simply open ourselves to a stream of content (as in ordinary experience)"; second, there is "punctate mode" where we put propositions into the PWB "one by one" (Weinberg & Meskin, 2006b, p. 196). "Both modes," they explain "are typical of imagining" (Weinberg & Meskin, 2006b, p. 196).[4] Kathleen Stock similarly proposes that the sort of imagining that occurs when we consume a fiction "can be largely passive" and may involve "little deliberate activity on the part of the reader other than reading and processing lines of text" (2017, p. 27). It seems that she also allows for something akin to a "streaming mode" of imagination.

It is worth considering this idea of a largely passive form of imagination. While imagining is typically seen as a kind of mental activity—as something we *do*—the need for a more passive form may seem acute when there is a rich amount of (unbelieved) content that needs registering—precisely as when consuming a fiction.

And yet, reality is very rich as well. Take a walk around town. An elementary school is letting out. Children are scattering onto buses, to the playground, to their parents. You form a few beliefs about these events—things you could later report—just as you will form a number of beliefs about any fiction you encounter. But most of it washes over you: their facial expressions, the snippets of conversation, the clothes they wore. You are perceptually aware of it all, just as you are perceptually aware of whatever play or film you may be watching. This awareness doesn't consist in your forming thousands of beliefs that last only a nanosecond; yet neither do you "stream" all of this reality though your imagination.[5] The same points apply to our engagement with fictions. Suppose that we are passively taking in a silent play. We watch the events unfold and form some beliefs about what is happening in the play. Setting issues of emotional immersion to the side, there is no reason to think that imagining is involved here, provided that it wasn't

[4] Recall, however, that on Nichols and Stich's view—which Weinberg & Meskin mean to adopt—ordinary pretense and hypothetical reasoning involve copying the entire contents of one's "Belief Box" into the PWB, aside from those contents that conflict with the "inserted" premise. So, strictly speaking, there are never just one or two propositions in the PWB—there must always be an extremely rich "stream" of content there. This somewhat blurs the distinction Weinberg & Meskin see between "streaming" and "punctate" modes.

[5] I am thus confused by the parenthetical remark—"(as in ordinary experience)"—that follows Weinberg & Meskin's description of the streaming mode, in the passage quoted above. Do they mean to suggest that simply perceiving the world, as we go about our ordinary lives, also involves streaming the world through our PWB? This would be a surprising view. Damage to one's PWB would, in that case, lead to severe deficits in ordinary perceptual awareness. I do not think that can be their view.

required when walking around town. Now add speech to the play; the characters are engaged in dialogue. Understanding the play now requires us to draw upon our capacity for language comprehension. But this changes nothing. We have already seen that comprehending language without believing what is said does not require imagination. So, no matter how rich the content of a fiction may be—and whether or not taking it in involves comprehending language—our passive perceptual awareness of it presents no clear need for *sui generis* imaginings. We can, if we like, call the passive reception of such content "A-imagining," on the grounds that it is a kind of epistemically safe metal-registering of rich, elaborated content concerning the fictional, unreal, and so on (though it is not a form of *thought*, if thought is assumed to be volitional). But it is easy to see that such instances of A-imagining are reducible to more basic folk psychological states of believing, perceiving, and understanding what is said. We have, then, an imagination-free solution to the first puzzle of comprehension.

Of course, consuming a fiction requires more active engagement with what is understood than simply listening to a liar or grasping the claims of a political opponent. Typically, we need to *fill out* our understanding of a fictional world by (actively) uncovering what is only implicitly true in the fiction from what is given by its explicit content.[6] This "filling in" of the fictional world in thought is perhaps a more obvious candidate for the "something more" in fiction comprehension that requires imagination. It forms the basis of the second puzzle of fiction-comprehension.

9.3 Imaginative Filling-in—the Second Puzzle

What we consider to be true in a fiction typically outstrips what the fiction explicitly states. In Lewis's (1978) example, it is true, in the Sherlock Holmes stories, that Holmes lives closer to Paddington Station than to Waterloo Station. Yet this is never explicitly stated in any of the stories; rather, it can be inferred from the fact that he is said to reside on Baker Street, which, in reality, is closer to Paddington than Waterloo. Or consider the famous "six word novel" attributed (perhaps apocryphally) to Hemmingway: "For sale: baby shoes, never worn." What we recover from the sentence, through a kind of inference, is more than what it explicitly states. This recovery requires an act of cognitive extrapolation beyond mere comprehension. If we form beliefs about things not explicitly stated, there is a legitimate question of how we arrived at those beliefs. Again it seems we may

[6] True, even "passively" understanding someone's speech requires a kind of active interpretation as well. Contextual cues are exploited in order to determine reference and resolve ambiguities. The point is simply that there is an additional interpretive aspect to fiction consumption over and above what is required for ordinary linguistic understanding.

have done so through a process that qualifies as A-imagining; we will have engaged in rich, elaborated thought about the unreal, fantastical, merely possible in an epistemically safe manner.

Arguably, the same sort of recovery-via-extrapolation occurs when we read non-fiction as well (Friend, 2008; Matravers, 2014). We need only suppose that Hemmingway's six word novel was an actual classified ad. In that case, too, we would arrive at an unfortunate inference—we would "fill out" our understanding of the actual world in ways we hadn't previously. Similarly, our appreciation of biographies and histories involves drawing inferences about the lives and times of their subjects, filling in details only implied by the text. In such cases, instead of adding to our beliefs about what is true in a fiction, we are adding to our beliefs about what occurred in the past. Both processes are equally "active" and inferential. If one invites imagining then so, it seems, does the other.

Here I am echoing points developed at length by Derek Matravers in his *Fiction and Narrative* (2014) (see also Friend (2008)). Matravers' conclusion—with which I concur—is that the psychology of fiction-consumption is not materially different from the psychology of *non-fiction* consumption. There is, as Matravers puts it "no mental state peculiar to our engagement with fiction."[7] We will need an account of how we recover implicit content from *both* fiction and non-fiction. Moreover, just as non-fictions lead us to engage in something like imagining in extracting their implicit content, fictions, at times, prescribe belief.[8,9] The still-pressing question, for our purposes, is whether imagining *in either context* will require *sui generis* imaginative states. Matravers appears to answer in the negative, arguing that "the most perspicuous account of our engaging with narratives [both fictions and non-fictions] available finds no role for the imagination" (2014, p. 3). His view deserves close scrutiny here. If he can make good on the claim that recovering implicit content from narratives (both fictional and non-fictional), and engaging with narratives generally, does not require *sui generis* imaginative

[7] Friend (2008) develops related arguments to the effect that a work of fiction cannot be defined *as such* by appeal to a distinctive psychological state involved in its reception.

[8] For instance, *The Great Gatsby* ends: "So we beat on, boats against the current, borne back ceaselessly into the past." Fitzgerald uses metaphor to prescribe belief in a deep fact about human existence. More mundane examples abound in historical fiction.

[9] It is true, as Stock (2017, pp. 168–9) objects, that we are more likely to form beliefs corresponding to the content of a non-fiction than we are corresponding to the content of a fiction. However, this is not, by itself, a difference that calls for the involvement of a *sui generis* imaginative state in one case, but not the other. So it is not a difference that suggests there is a mental state "peculiar to our engagement with fiction." Compare two people of radically different political views watching the right-leaning *Fox and Friends* newscast. One will assimilate content of the newscast to his beliefs (for the most part), while the other will not. There is a psychological difference between the dispositions of the individuals to form beliefs on the basis of what they understand from the different news sources. But it is not a difference that calls for an explanation in terms of imagination, or some other mental state peculiar to one, but not the other, partisan. Moreover, it is not as though consumers of fictions, or of rejected political narratives, do not form beliefs about what they are witnessing. They simply form beliefs about what is true *in a fiction*, or what is true *according to the hosts of Fox and Friends*.

states (or "the imagination," in his term), he will have accomplished a good deal of my work for me.

9.3.1 Sidebar on Matravers

First, a note on terminology: as noted above, I allow that consuming fictions involves A-imagining. My claim is that we can explain this A-imagining in more basic folk psychological terms. Matravers—at least at times—denies that consuming fictions involves imagining. We saw one place where he does so above. Elsewhere, he remarks: "the imagination is not needed as part of our account of engaging with representations," where "representations" include both fictions and non-fictions (2014, p. 5). By "the imagination" he seems to have in mind a *sui generis* mental state or faculty that cannot be reduced to other, more basic folk psychological kinds. We thus appear in agreement that consuming fictions does not involve use of *sui generis* imaginative states.

However, Matravers in fact wavers on whether imagination is at work in our comprehension of fictions. In other places he appears content to establish that engaging with both fictions and non-fictions requires imagination and that, therefore, the psychology of fiction and non-fiction consumption is materially the same. "What is needed is an account of *understanding* narrative," he writes. "*The extent to which such an account need make use of the imagination is an entirely open question*" (2014, p. 54, emphasis in original). The question of which of these quotations best represents Matravers' overall view deserves a close look; we make no progress in explaining imagination if our appreciation of both fictions *and* non-fictions requires *sui generis* imaginative states.

The key distinction Matravers advocates in place of the fiction/non-fiction distinction is that between confrontation situations and representation situations—this is what he calls "the real distinction" of interest (2014, pp. 45–58). Representation situations "are situations in which action is not possible because what is being represented to us is out of reach" (p. 47). These occur when we interact both with fictions—such as novels and films—and non-fictions, such as documentaries and histories. Confrontation situations, by contrast, are "situations in which action is possible" (p. 47). They occur where one is forced to navigate and interact with one's present (non-representational) environment, as when boarding the subway, cleaning up a glass of spilt milk, or facing a wolf in the woods. Here Matravers comments on the relation of confrontation situations and representation situations to imagination:

> Confrontations do not require the imagination; I do not need to imagine being confronted by a wolf if there is one before me. [However] Something is needed to explain my engagement with representations…If philosophy does need some notion of a DCA or 'make-believe', it applies to this category rather than only to fictions. (p. 53)

Matravers proposes that confrontation situations bear no essential relation to imagination, whereas representation situations plausibly do. In fact, he makes explicit appeal to the notion of a DCA (or "Distinct Cognitive Attitude") of imagination, of the kind posited by Nichols & Stich (2000) and Weinberg & Meskin (2006a, 2006b) in their discussions of pretense and fiction (and discussed in the earlier chapters of this book on pretense and conditional reasoning). The "Possible Worlds Box" of Nichols & Stich (2000) and the "Imagination Box" of Weinberg & Meskin seem to capture what Matravers sees as the distinctive psychological resource at work in representation situations, as opposed to confrontation situations.

In later chapters, Matravers fine-tunes this idea in drawing on the work of Philip Johnson-Laird (1983; Johnson-Laird & Byrne 2002) to propose, more concretely, that *mental models* are the cognitive states that play the mediating role in representation situations. He views mental models as neutral in their relation to both imagination (i.e., "make-belief") and belief:

> When reading a text, a reader is building a mental model of its content...the propositions take their place in this mental model whether they are beliefs or imaginings...The narrative could be either non-fiction or fiction. Some of these propositions we also believe, some we do not also believe. That is it; there is no need, on this account, for us to wander into the swamp consequent on postulating a mental state particularly linked to fiction.
>
> (Matravers, 2014, pp. 43, 78–9, 95)

We can think of mental models, on Matravers' view, as a kind of mental purgatory wherein the propositions relevant to engaging with a narrative—fictional or non-fictional—are represented and, potentially, elaborated before being incorporated into one's beliefs, or (in the case of fictions) simply cast aside.

Mental models are, in Matravers's term, the means by which we "engage" with a narrative, where engaging "includes...understanding it," but also involves making it "vivid to ourselves" (2014, pp. 76–7). Their having these roles meshes with the role that mental models play in Johnson-Laird & Byrne's (2002) influential account of conditional reasoning, discussed at the end of Chapter 5. For one way to make a narrative vivid for ourselves—to *engage* with it—is to fill in details about the situation it represents that are not part of its explicit content. And this can be done by representing other things that would be the case, were the explicit statements of the narrative true.

However, now that we have clarified the role that mental models might play within fiction appreciation—as enabling a kind of representation of what else would be true in the fictional world, given the fiction's explicit content—it is hard to see why they would not also be relied upon in confrontation situations. Suppose that a wolf appears before me on my path through the woods—a confrontation par excellence, and Matravers' own example. I quickly consider what to do. If I start to run away, the wolf will detect fear and start to chase. If I keep moving forward, it will feel threatened and may attack. If I slowly back away, it is more likely to stand its ground and let me return from whence I came. I decide to back away. My decision was arrived at through a quick bit of hypothetical reasoning, considering different possible courses of action and their likely outcomes. This involves thinking about merely possible wolves I cannot act upon, in other possible situations.

And so it is with many of the situations that confront us each day. Our success in navigating them requires us to consider and evaluate unrealized possibilities. If Johnson-Laird & Byrne (2002) are correct in their account of conditional reasoning, we make use of mental models in the processes. But, in that case, there is no deep *psychological* difference between being in a representation situation and being in a confrontation situation. Both kinds of situation will often involve the use of mental models (or, alternatively, a DCA of imagination). If there remains a "real distinction" between being in confrontation and representation situations, it is not clear what the distinction comes to.

On the other hand, there *may be* an important psychological difference between conditional reasoning and non-conditional reasoning—one that generates the many puzzles in philosophy and psychology discussed in Chapters 5 and 6. Likewise, it may be thought that daydreaming, remembering, and planning also draw upon the same resource as conditional reasoning—with that resource being none other than imagination itself. My argument in Chapters 5 and 6 was that we can explain the A-imaginings involved in conditional reasoning in more basic folk psychological terms. Inferences involving sequences of beliefs constitute the relevant episodes of hypothetical and conditional reasoning. Further, if my discussion at the end of Chapter 5 was correct, we can allow mental models into our ontology—and into our account of conditional reasoning—without committing to *sui generis* imaginative states. Mental models, I argued, can plausibly be seen as constituents of occurrent judgments, including judgments in favor of conditionals, disjunctions, and ordinary indicative propositions. Such occurrent beliefs, *qua* sets of mental models, include beliefs in the kinds of counterfactual conditionals essential to recovering implicit content from a fiction.

I will say more, momentarily, on the nature of the conditional reasoning that occurs during our engagement with fictions. The upshot, for Matravers, is that his sustained attack on the project of distinguishing fiction from non-fiction by appeal to imagination leaves us with the more difficult question of whether imagination—or something very much like it—is required for a wider array of stimulus-independent cognitive acts. Further, his distinction between confrontation and representation situations gains us no ground on understanding this resource, as it appears active in both. Instead of wandering "into the swamp consequent on postulating a mental state particularly linked to fiction" (2014, p. 95), we have entered the deeper, more treacherous waters of positing a special kind of mental state at work in representing and developing possibilities more generally. This leaves us, as well, with no clear psychological difference between representation situations and confrontation situations. Matravers has not kept us on dry land.

9.3.2 Recovering Fictional Content through Counterfactual Reasoning

When recovering implicit fictional content, we make inferences on the basis of what is explicitly true in the fiction. Often, this involves a kind of counterfactual reasoning about what else would be true in a world where the explicit content of a fiction is true. This insight forms the backbone of Lewis's (1978) influential theory of truth in fiction. But, as we will see, this is not *all* that recovering fictional content involves. Stock (2017) argues persuasively that other kinds of inferences concerning authorial intentions are relevant as well.[10] But let's focus first on the aspect of fictional content-recovery that does plausibly involve counterfactual reasoning. In developing his theory, Lewis offers two distinct, if related, analyses of what determines truth in a fiction. Both aim to account for implicit fictional truths; and both assign a central role to counterfactual reasoning. Focusing only on the first—"Analysis 1"—will suffice for our purposes here. According to Lewis, the explicit content of a fiction corresponds to those propositions that are true at every possible world where the fiction "is told as known fact rather than fiction" (Lewis, 1978, p. 41). This characterization of truth in a fiction does not, however, capture implicit truths, such as that Sherlock Holmes wears underwear and does not paint his toenails pink. For there will be *some* possible world where the Sherlock Holmes stories are told as known fact where Holmes *does* favor pink toenails and fewer sartorial restrictions. To include implicit fictional truths, Lewis invokes a similarity relation between the actual world and worlds where the fiction is told as known fact, as follows:

> A sentence of the form 'in the fiction f, φ' is non-vacuously true... [if and only if]... some world where f is told as known fact and φ is true differs less from our actual world, on balance, than does any world where f is told as known fact and φ is not true. (1978, p. 42)

Lewis's idea is that, when we opine on whether p is (perhaps implicitly) true in some fiction, we are asking ourselves the following: is some possible world where the fiction is told as known fact, and where p is true, more similar to the actual world than every possible world where the fiction is told as known fact and p is not true? Or, more simply, if the fiction were told as known fact, would it be that p? If the answer is yes, then p is true in the fiction; if the answer is no, then p is

[10] A similar line of argument for the relevance of authorial intentions has also been pursued by Lamarque (1990), Byrne (1993), Sainsbury (2014) and others.

false in the fiction.[11] Recovering fictional content—and thereby filling out one's understanding of the fictional world—is simply a matter of engaging in counterfactual reasoning of a certain sort. For instance, we might ask: is some possible world where the Sherlock Holmes stories are told as known fact and Sherlock Holmes paints his toenails pink more similar to the actual world than any where the stories are told as known fact and he does not paint his toenails that color? Here the answer appears to be no. In the actual world, men in late nineteenth century England were unlikely to paint their toenails pink. Thus, a possible world where the Holmes stories are told as known fact and where Holmes's toenails are pink is *not* more similar to our own than some where the stories are told as known fact and his toenails are unpainted. For this reason, it is false that, in the Sherlock Holmes stories, Holmes' toenails are pink.

The larger question we are after is whether recovering fictional content—and, in so doing, actively filling out our understanding of a fictional world—requires *sui generis* imaginative states. Supposing that one accepts a broadly Lewisian account of truth-in-fiction, answering this question turns on issues already discussed in Chapters 5 and 6, concerning the nature of counterfactual reasoning. If, as I argued there, reasoning our way to new beliefs in counterfactual conditionals does not require *sui generis* imaginative states, then neither does uncovering what is true in a fiction—at least, not insofar as the Lewisian view captures those truths. (I will consider the situation from the perspective of those who reject the Lewisian view momentarily.)

It is perhaps worth reemphasizing that, in proposing that we undertake this kind of conditional reasoning during fiction consumption, I am not suggesting that we utter the relevant "if-then" sentences in our heads, or that we are consciously aware of each step in each inference. Indeed, by itself, the claim that we engage in counterfactual reasoning while engaging with fictions has no phenomenological implications at all. Further, as we saw in Chapter 6, the nature of the mental states and processes underlying and giving rise to those judgments remains an open empirical question. I sketched a heavy-duty "how-possibly" story where the states are indeed all language-like mental representations tokened in one's "Belief Box." But we needn't commit to that view to hold that the relevant counterfactual reasoning can be explained (in light-duty terms) as involving inferences among beliefs about what would be true in the world most similar to our own where the fiction is told as known fact.

[11] Plausibly, the truth of some propositions—such as that Holmes wears brown shoes—is indeterminate in a fiction, in the sense that they are neither true nor false in that fiction. Lewis holds that a proposition *p* is neither true nor false in a fiction if, among the set of worlds most similar to the actual world where the story is told as known fact, *p* is true in some but false in others (Lewis, 1978, p. 43).

9.3.3 Imagery and the Development of Indeterminate Fictional Truths

Intuitively, our recovery and development of fictional content often involves the use of mental imagery. Some even find imagery central to our engagement with fiction (Van Leeuwen, 2016; Stokes, 2019). In Chapter 4, I argued that mental images can form proper parts of judgments, desires, and decisions. Thus, should we find that mental imagery plays an important role in the recovery of fictional content—and in our engagement with fiction more generally—this is consistent with the A-imaginings in which they are featured being judgments, desires, and decisions. Consider, for instance, the closing of Raymond Carver's story "Cathedral," when the narrator guides the hand of a blind visitor as they draw a cathedral. Registering the scene could involve making judgments such as:

JIG (In this story, the men's hands are: **a pair of hands holding a pencil together.**)

If the image in this JIG is vague or sketchy in its detail, the JIG can be seen as a true imagistic judgment about what is happening in the fiction. This judgment doesn't "say" anything about the character's hands that isn't true of them in the nearest possible worlds where the fiction is told as known fact. (Or, on an intentionalist conception of truth in fiction, it only "says" things about the character's hands that the author prescribes that we imagine.) However, it is also possible—particularly when imagery is involved—for an A-imagining to fill in the details of a story in ways that go beyond what is strictly true or false in the fiction, adding details such as a particular shade of brown to Sherlock Holmes's shoes that are left indeterminate by the fiction itself. Where the truth of a proposition (image-involving or not) is indeterminate in a fiction (see fn. 11), the JIGs that take such propositions as their contents will be of indeterminate truth as well.

However, in many cases where we imaginatively fill in details that are left indeterminate by a fiction, it is more accurate to view the imaginings as *decisions* than as judgments.[12] Suppose, for instance, that while reading "Cathedral" we are imagining the blind man to look rather like Jeff Bridges.[13] While some aspects of the man's appearance are made explicit by the text (such as that he has a beard), there is nothing in the text that suggests that he either must, or must not look much like Jeff Bridges. The man's facial appearance is indeterminate within a certain range of options, within which fall people who look like Jeff Bridges. In A-imagining the man as looking like Jeff Bridges, we have made a decision to develop the fiction in a certain way of our own; we have shifted out of the mode of

[12] This serves, *inter alia*, as a reply to Van Leeuwen (2020), who argues that the representation of propositions that one takes to be neither true nor false in a fiction requires *sui generis* attitudinal imaginings.

[13] I was spurred to consider this sort of case by a draft paper that Neil Van Leeuwen once shared with me—an ancestor to the now published Van Leeuwen (2020).

merely recovering what is true in the fiction to doing a bit of storytelling ourselves. The decision can be symbolized as:

DEC (I will experience the blind man in the fiction as being: **a Jeff Bridges-looking man**...)

Again, this just gives the *content* of the decision; there is no suggestion that this specific sentence runs through the head of a reader who generates what we would intuitively call an "image of Jeff Bridges" while reading the story. The point is simply that cases where we knowingly elaborate a fiction, for ourselves, in ways that go beyond what is true or false in the fiction can be seen as decisions to elaborate or experience the fiction in this or that way. Very often, these decisions have mental images as proper parts; this is why it feels right to describe the decision as a decision to *experience* the fiction in a certain way. The normal act of enjoying a fiction is a continual interplay of judgments about what is true in the fiction and decisions about how further to develop or experience the fiction for oneself. Thus, fiction *appreciation* is not a passive "streaming" of content from the page into the mind of the reader, but an ongoing collaboration between reader and author. This interactive element in the experience of fiction is obscured by standard accounts that assign to a single type of state—our *sui generis* "imaginings"—*both* the passive role of registering what is true in the fiction and the active role of developing the fiction for oneself. We get a clearer picture of what is going on, psychologically, when we don't try to assign all the interesting work to one kind of state.

9.4 Extracting Fictional Truths through Non-counterfactual Reasoning

So far, we have an account of how explicit and implied fictional content can be recovered from a fiction without the use of *sui generis* imaginative states—at least insofar as doing so simply requires counterfactual reasoning. However, as earlier noted, not all who think that imagination is essential to the appreciation of fictions agree with the Lewisian account of truth in fiction. (Not even Lewis himself thought that his Analysis 1 or 2 could explain *all* cases of truth in fiction.)[14] Recently, Kathleen Stock (2017) has mounted a counterargument on two fronts. First, she argues that truth in fiction is not, in general, to be understood in Lewisian terms, but instead by appeal to what the author intends one to imagine; and, second, she holds that the relevant imaginings at work in fiction appreciation are not, as a default, belief-like (nor, for that matter, are they beliefs). For an imaginative

[14] He describes the other relevant factors as instances of "carry-over from other truth in fiction" (Lewis, 1978, p. 45). These include genre-related inferences such as that a dragon-like creature breathes fire, even if it is not explicitly stated in the fiction that the creature breathes fire.

state to be "belief-like," in the relevant sense, is for it to inferentially interact with other imaginings in ways that beliefs with matching contents inferentially interact with each other—in the manner of the proposals of Nichols & Stich (2000), Currie & Ravenscroft (2002), Williamson (2016), and Weinberg & Meskin (2006a). Stock is willing to allow that counterfactual reasoning may be carried out through the use of imaginative states that are, at least in the moment, functioning in belief-like ways. Her core argument, however, is that "making inferences from fictional content as to what to imagine is not inevitably or even *often* like counterfactual thinking" (2017, p. 179). Thus, while she grants that "working out, relative to some background set of beliefs about the world, what would be the case given some initial imaginative premise, *may* be a defeasible route" to recovering fictional content, she emphasizes that:

> The process might [also] operate via a different route: for instance, working out what a given symbol was intended by the author to mean with respect to fictional content; or her use of a stock character, or some playful metafictional reference, or some innovative but meaningful use of language. (2017, p. 178)

Imagining in these cases, she observes, "is not exclusively aimed at what would be the case in the world, were some explicit sentences true" (p. 178). As support, Stock offers examples where background beliefs about fiction and language appear equally important to the content recovered from a fiction as the inferences we would be inclined to draw from the truth of a fiction's explicit content. For instance, genre conventions—as Lewis also noted (1978, p. 45)—are at times more relevant than the consideration of nearby possible worlds where the story is told as known fact. If a character has prominent incisors in a vampire book, Stock observes:

> she is often a vampire; yet a world in which a person is a vampire is much further away from the actual than one in which she merely has prominent incisors and is not a vampire. (Stock, 2017, pp. 52–3)

Other fictional truths Stock highlights are grounded in the use of symbolism, which "depends on seeing the fiction as a deliberate construct" (p. 54):

> Say that I read *Jane Eyre* and so imagine that (effectively) *Jane is locked in a red room*. In interpreting what else is made fictional in the light of this fact, I can permissibly draw upon a belief that *the use of a red room is intended by Brontë to symbolize a womb, and so imply, in conjunction with other content, that Jane is much affected by the loss of her mother*. I may then on the basis of these two thoughts derive the imagining that *Jane is much affected by the loss of her mother*.
> (p. 178, emphases in original)

Such examples serve Stock's larger project of defending "extreme intentionalism," the view that "the fictional content of a particular text is equivalent to exactly what the author of the text *intended the reader to imagine*" (2017, p. 1). Lewis's account of fictional truth is a direct competitor, as it aims to explain truth-in-fiction without any appeal to authorial intentions (or to imagination, for that matter). The different source of fictional truth, for Stock, puts different constraints on the imaginings used in our engagement with a fiction. Our imagining "is not exclusively aimed at what would be the case in the world, were some explicit sentences true," but rather

> Draws equally or even more heavily upon background beliefs about fiction and language: for instance, about the author and her characteristic technique; about conventions governing fictional reference, or genre, or symbolism, or words, and so on; and about how those might be adopted or playfully adapted. (p. 179)

I agree with Stock that, in many cases, recovering fictional content involves subtler reasoning than the kind of counterfactual extrapolation appealed to in a strict Lewisian account. The required interpretive tasks are more heterogeneous than that—as also noted by Walton (1990, pp. 184–7). This is so whether or not truth in fiction wholly depends on what the author intends us to imagine. Our question is whether admitting this heterogeneity create barriers to explaining the A-imagining that occurs during fiction appreciation in more basic terms.

Stock thinks that the answer is yes, arguing at length that fiction-related imagining can neither be understood as "belief-like" by default, nor *reduced to* belief. In fact, she takes explicit aim at a reductive view of imagination I've earlier defended in the context of explaining pretense (Langland-Hassan, 2012). Yet I see nothing in Stock's account that suggests fiction-directed imagining cannot be reduced to more basic kinds of folk psychological states, so long as we are prepared to grant that such imaginings can consist in one's using one's beliefs in a variety of different *kinds* of inferences. Indeed, the greater role we assign to the importance of background beliefs "about fiction and language" (including beliefs about genre, symbolism, and so on), the *easier* it is to see how fiction consumption can be explained without appeal to *sui generis* imaginings.

Consider Stock's example of vampire fiction: Hans, an experienced reader of vampire fiction, knows that characters with pronounced incisors typically turn out to be vampires. Grasping the fiction's explicit content, Hans judges that, in the fiction, Handsome James has pronounced incisors. Bringing to bear his background knowledge about the genre, he then judges that, in the fiction, Handsome James is a vampire. Nothing in the recovery of this fictional truth suggests a need for something other than belief and abductive inference. Hans needs to be a skilled reader. He needs to know when to let genre-norms trump other (Lewisian) principles for how to uncover fictional truths. But this sort of knowledge is not facilitated by imagination. For one could obviously have *sui generis* imaginative states (were there to be such) while lacking it.

What occurs in the reader's mind as she recognizes that Brontë is using the redness of Jane's room as a symbol? There are various possibilities, of course; but it is easy enough to characterize the recognition as an abductive inference along the lines of: *The redness of the room is highlighted in the text. It is probably not an accident that Brontë has highlighted the color of the room in this way. The color of the room likely serves to highlight something about Jane and her predicament. Jane lost her mother early in life. Perhaps, in resembling a womb, the color serves to emphasize that Jane is much affected by the loss of her mother.* This is not the easiest or most obvious inference one might arrive at. But it is the sort of thing that a skilled critic might uncover through a bit of reasoning. We can call this abductive reasoning "imagining," if we like. But it is another case of imagining that is given a more enlightening characterization when viewed as a straightforward abductive inference involving one's beliefs about the text and the use of symbolism by authors. It is again hard to see how this reasoning would be facilitated by the use of *sui generis* imaginative states; certainly, the use of such states (e.g., by the average undergraduate) would not be sufficient for uncovering this interesting bit of symbolism.

Stock effectively anticipates this sort of response:

> It is true, I suppose, that working out an author's intentions as to what is to be imagined in these latter ways may *loosely* be counted as a kind of 'inference' 'drawing upon' beliefs e.g. beliefs about authors, fiction, genre, history, language, etc. (2017, p. 178)

It is unclear why the inferences she mentions would count only "loosely" as inferences, but let's continue:

> But, crucially, the contents of these beliefs are not entering into inferences *directly* with imaginative content *as such*, as, allegedly, the contents of beliefs do according to the model I am criticizing. (p. 178)

Here Stock notes that, on the kind of model she is criticizing—where imaginings are "belief-like" and occur in their own cognitive "box"—there is no "direct" mixing of imagined and believed contents. For instance, on Weinberg & Meskin's view (Meskin & Weinberg, 2003; Weinberg & Meskin, 2006b), where the contents of a fiction are "streamed" through one's Imagination Box, any abductive inferences about symbolism must occur within a distinct Belief Box. For those judgments (e.g., "Brontë likely used red to symbolize a womb") concern the author's actions and do not, as it were, record facts about what is happening in the fictional world itself. Stock returns to the example of Jane's red room in developing this point:

> The imagining that *Jane is locked in a red room* concerns Jane *qua* orphan girl, former inhabitant of Lowood, future wife of Rochester... The belief that *the use of a red room is intended by Brontë...* (etc.) concerns the events of the book *qua* fictional constructs and elements of a novel composed by Brontë *as such*. There is little obvious sense in which these two kinds of thought, one imaginative and one a belief, come into *direct* inferential contact: for they take different scenarios as objects. (p. 179)

This passage suggests two distinct worries. The first is that there is a lack of "direct inferential contact" between imaginings and beliefs, even if both are involved in recovering fictional content. (The events of the fiction are imagined, we can suppose, and the facts about symbolism are believed.) The second is that the imaginings and the beliefs have "different scenarios as objects." There is the fiction *qua* artwork as one object. It is believed to contain symbolism. And there are *the events of the fiction* on the other. These involve Jane's room being red, but do not contain facts about Brontë's use of symbolism.

Taking the first worry first, the mere fact that a view (such as Weinberg & Meskin's) requires interaction between cognitive boxes does nothing to show that the resulting states fail to come into "direct inferential contact." Ordinary hypothetical inferences—judging that if p then q—require coordination between boxes on such views, as we saw in Chapters 5 and 6. Cross-box inferences can be as cognitively "direct" as an ordinary conditional inference. The second worry—concerning "different scenarios as objects"—is also easily explained away. Once we have deduced that the red color of the room is meant to highlight the significance to Jane of the loss of her mother, we are warranted in imagining—on that basis—that Jane is much affected by the loss of her mother. (NB This latter imagining may in turn simply be a judgment that, in the fiction, Jane is much affected by the loss of her mother.) A belief with the fiction as its object warrants an imagining with the events of the fiction as its object. There is nothing untoward or unusual in this. My judgments about what is true *in the particular soccer match I am watching* (e.g., that Luka Modrić has scored a brilliant goal) are typically influenced by my beliefs about what is true *of the game of soccer itself* (e.g., In soccer, goals are scored when the ball enters a goal). My thoughts simultaneously take two different objects: the events of a particular game, and the rules of all soccer games. There is nothing problematic in one thought, with one sort of object, motivating and justifying the other. Turning back to fiction, it is a distinct aesthetic pleasure to be at once intrigued by the events described and amazed at the author's ability in so describing them. There is no conflict in the idea that we shift between thinking about the fiction as such—appreciating its beauty and ingenuity—and what is true in the fiction itself, with each sequence of thought influencing the other. If this involves a kind of "split consciousness," it is nothing to regret.

9.5 Constraints on Fiction-related Imaginings?

Stock formulates a second attack on the idea that imagining is belief-like—or, indeed, a *species* of belief—by appeal to the different *constraints* operative on imaginings as opposed to beliefs. The trajectory of a propositional imagining, she tells us:

> can be significantly influenced by constraints other than those operative upon beliefs with the same contents: constraints connected to the particular goal of the imaginative episode, and the reasons of the thinker for undertaking it. *A fortiori*, the view that imagining is in fact a *species* of belief... is also impugned. (2017, p. 187)

According to Stock, the constraints in question:

> Depend on the particular instance and what the imaginative goal is, but might include: (in the case of writing fiction) beliefs or suspicions about what is funny, what is suspenseful, what is emotionally powerful, what is titillating (etc.); or (in the case of fantasizing) what causes the thinker pleasure. (p. 185)

Stock is right to emphasize the importance of constraints in any account of how imaginings develop. To hold that imaginings develop without *any* constraints leaves us with no positive account of why an author might bother to prescribe an imagining. Normally, when we speak of a sequence of thoughts being *constrained*, we have in mind they are constrained by a norm of truth or accuracy. What, exactly, would it be for a sequence of thoughts (imaginings) to be constrained by "beliefs or suspicions about what is funny, what is suspenseful, what is emotionally powerful," and so on? In the case where thoughts are constrained by a norm of truth, our arrival at thought that *p* is constrained by prior thoughts that *q*, *r*, and *s*, to the extent that the truth of *p* is guaranteed (or at least made likely) by the truth of *q*, *r*, and *s*—if, in other words, there is a *truth-preserving* principle of reasoning that warrants *p* on the basis of *q*, *r*, and *s*.

The "constraints" Stock has in mind would appear to be *humor-preserving*, or *suspense-preserving*, or *emotional-impact-preserving*. Doubtless, a *fiction* could end up being humorous, or suspenseful, or emotionally impactful—indeed it could be all three simultaneously. In such cases, we can, perhaps, say that the propositions comprising the fiction are humor-, suspense-, and emotional-impact-preserving.

But what could it mean to say that a sequence of discrete thoughts or propositions—or *imaginings*—develop in a humor-, or suspense-, or emotion-preserving way? In most cases, we will not be able to say whether an entire *page* of fiction is humor-, suspense-, or emotional-impact-preserving until we see how the fiction turns out on a larger scale. One and the same set of sentences can easily be humor-, suspense-, or emotional-impact-preserving in the context of one story, and not another. Unlike standard inference rules—such as *modus ponens*, or the statistical syllogism—which *can* be said to constrain thoughts or proposition-sequences one by one, *as they unfold*, there is no sense in which the norms governing humor or suspense-creation do so (supposing we could articulate such norms).

Of course, it remains true that an author may be *motivated* to write something funny, or suspenseful, or with emotional impact, and that these motivations will influence the fiction she creates. We can make sense of that easily enough: a goal to write a funny, or suspenseful, or emotionally impactful story will influence the sort of premises chosen as the basis for an imagining. One can then make a series of judgments about what else would likely happen, given such a premise. Those thought transitions will be constrained by normal *truth*-preserving inference rules. If one judges the development to hold promise for suspense, humor, or an emotional response, it continues forward. If it doesn't seem promising, one can change it by inserting new premises. In just the same way, the goal of a toothbrush manufacturer to minimize costs might constrain his imagining of new toothbrush designs. Beginning to develop a design using one polymer, he may shift to another if the chosen material presents engineering difficulties. But this involves no new (cost-preserving) constraint on his imaginings, different from the ordinary truth-preserving inferential constraints on belief. We have, instead, a very ordinary interaction between "top-down" input from one's intentions or goals—which determine the topic of one's reasoning—and the lateral, truth-preserving inferential constraints that move one forward from a given set of premises or decisions (Langland-Hassan, 2016). Quite generally, we are able to guide the subject-matter and course of our own reasoning without this guidance implying an ability to break free of the inferential constraints operative on beliefs. To have our inferences, as consumers of a fiction, appropriately "constrained," we simply need to have a good idea of the author's goals and interests in creating the fiction. And we have yet to see any reason why *sui generis* imaginative states would aid us in that endeavor.[15]

[15] Curiously, despite arguing that what is true in a fiction is whatever we are prescribed by the author to imagine (and despite her arguments that neither beliefs nor belief-like imaginings would suffice to recover fictional content), Stock does not think that any sort of imagining is *necessary* for determining what is true in a fiction. She compares grasping what is to be imagined in a fiction to grasping what is said during another's testimony (2017, p. 36). Typically, we will move immediately from understanding what a person says to believing what they say. But we need not do so; and we *do not* do so in cases where we mistrust the source, such as in the cases described at the outset of this chapter. Similarly, Stock proposes, "for fictional cognition, all the reader needs to do is understand

Now, I think that, for the skilled novelist, the psychology of fiction writing is considerably more complex than I have just described. I delve deeper into the psychology of fiction-*creation* in Chapter 12, on creativity. For now, this skeletal account suffices to show that Stock's appeal to authorial goals and interests can be made to cohere with a reductive view of imagination's role in fiction appreciation. Stock hasn't shown that our recovery of fictional content involves something other than reasoning with beliefs. She has just revealed some diversity and layers of complexity to that reasoning.

9.6 Reconciliation with Intentionalism—the Third and Fourth Puzzles of Comprehension

Up to this point, I have argued that we do not need *sui generis* imaginative states in order to recover explicit or implied fictional truths. As noted at the outset, it is a separate question whether a successful analysis of what it is to be true in a fiction must appeal to an irreducible notion of imagination; this was the third puzzle of comprehension. Likewise, there remains the fourth puzzle of whether imagination must be invoked in any plausible account of the difference between fictions and non-fictions.

We can view the third puzzle as asking whether any substantive analysis of the "in the fiction" operator must appeal in some way to a *sui generis* notion of imagination. We have already seen that, for Lewis, it does not. His means for filling the schema "'In the fiction *F*, *p*' is true iff _______" don't appeal to imagination. Of course, not everyone is convinced by Lewis's account. Kendall Walton, for instance, holds that "a fictional truth consists in there being a prescription or mandate to imagine something" (1990, p. 39). He has famously defended a schema along the lines of: "'In the fiction *F*, *p*' is true iff *F* is a prop in a game where there is a prescription to imagine that *p*" (though he backs away from this in more recent work (Walton, 2015)). Similarly, Stock defends a schema that is roughly: "'In the fiction *F*, *p*' is true iff the author of *F* intends the reader to imagine that *p*." Let's suppose, for the sake of argument, that Walton's and Stock's accounts of how to analyze the "in the fiction" operator are correct, insofar as we must appeal to an author's intentions (or a game's prescriptions) that we imagine

what she is intended to F-imagine, not F-imagine it" (p. 36). Thus, while "in most cases understanding what one is reflexively intended to F-imagine [and thus what is true in a fiction, according to Stock] and F-imagining that thing will co-occur," in other cases, "the reader merely understands what she is to imagine, but does not imagine it" (p. 36). So, clearly, even for Stock, there are ways of recovering fictional content that require no imagining. What does Stock think these ways might be? And why, given their availability, do we think that imagining is *ever* deployed in the process of recovering fictional content?

thus and such. What then? Must we resign ourselves to *sui generis* imaginings after all?

We needn't. Instead, we can agree (for the sake of argument) with either Walton or Stock's analysis and go on to ask: but *what is it* to imagine that *p* in response to a fiction? What is it that the author intends for us to do? Limiting ourselves to the context under discussion—that of recovering content from a fiction—a plausible reductive analysis suggests itself: imagining that *p* in recovering fictional content from a fiction *F* amounts to judging that, in the fiction *F*, *p*.[16] This analysis of what it is to imagine that *p* in response to a particular fiction enables an alternative intentionalist account of truth in fiction:

Doxastic Intentionalism: "In the fiction *F*, *p*" is true, iff *F* (or its author) prescribes or intends the reader to *judge that*, in the fiction *F*, *p*.

This criterion for truth in fiction will return all the same propositions as true in a certain fiction as the intentionalist account involving prescriptions to imagine—at least insofar as the latter is correct! After all, there are not going to be any propositions the author prescribes us to imagine that she doesn't also prescribe us to judge true in the fiction, if the intentionalist is correct.[17] And so we have an answer to the third puzzle of comprehension that is compatible both with the claim that imagination plays a key role in defining what it is to be true in a fiction and with the idea that the relevant imaginings are reducible to more basic folk psychological states (in this case, judgments about what the author prescribes us to judge true in the fiction). An important note, however: my claim is not that we can only imagine that *p*, in response to a fiction *F*, if we think it is true, in fiction *F*, that *p*. We might imagine the fiction to be going in ways we don't believe it to be going. The claim, instead, is that what it is for the author to intend the reader to imagine that *p*, in response to *F*—and so what it is for it to be true, in *F*, that *p*—is for the author to intend the reader to judge that, in the fiction *F*, *p*.

One might worry that this criterion is circular, however. After all, when we say that *p* is true in the fiction *F* just in case the author intends for us to judge

[16] In Chapter 10 I argue that what is normally referred to as "imagining that *p*" in response to a fiction *F* must be reconceived with an "in the fiction" operator—such that we don't simply imagine that *p* in response to *F* but, rather, imagine that, in the fiction *F*, *p*. I call this the "Operator Claim" and offer it as a kind of *reductio* of the orthodox view of imagination's role in fiction appreciation. I don't assume that view here, however. For now I simply claim that the phenomenon we colloquially call "imagining that *p*, in response to fiction *F*" is the same as judging that, in the fiction *F*, *p*.

[17] In some cases, authors purposefully lead readers to form a false belief about what is true in the fiction—only to render a surprise later. Those are also cases where readers are prescribed to imagine things that, it turns out, are not true in the fiction. Explanations of the imaginative phenomenon—as found, e.g., in Stock (2017, Ch. 2)—can be smoothly translated into the language of judgments.

that *p* is true in the fiction *F*, the "in the fiction" operator itself appears in the characterization of what it is for something to be true in the fiction. Yet, taken as an account of the truth conditions of the "in the fiction" operator (or of "what makes something true in a fiction"), it is not circular. Truth in a fiction is defined in terms of what an author prescribes (or intends) for us to judge true in the fiction. We can see that the account is not vacuous because it remains in competition with Lewis's view; for Lewis makes no appeal to an author's intentions or prescriptions at all when characterizing truth in fiction. Granted, the definition does not tell us what it is to be a *fiction* (I come to this below). But that is not what it aims to answer. It is, instead, an (intentionalist) answer to the question of what makes some propositions true in a fiction, and others not (the answer being: a proposition is true in a fiction only when an author intends the reader to judge that it is true in the fiction).

Though the account is not vacuous, it is open to two criticisms. First, one might ask how we go about determining what it is the author (or text) prescribes for us to judge true in the fiction. However, we can ask the same question with respect to the imagination-involving account: how do we figure out what it is that the author (or text) intends for us to imagine? Presumably not by imagining! Imagining, on an intentionalist view, is something we only do once we've determined what the author wants us to imagine. In any case, the two questions will likely get the same (messy) answer involving readerly know-how. It is know-how that we begin to acquire as soon as we learn to read and that sharpens as we become more sophisticated consumers of narrative, grasping how and when to attune to symbolism, when to apply or let slide genre-related assumptions, and so on. (Walton appears to agree about this messiness when contemplating the "disorderly behavior of the machinery of [fictional-truth] generation," noting that "fictional truths are generated in very different ways" (1990, pp. 184–6); Lewis's formal characterization of truth in fiction traces such know-how to three sources (1978, p. 45).)

A second objection one might raise is: what is it to be a fiction? This—the fourth puzzle of comprehension—is indeed a different question than: what is it to be true in a fiction? But if we cannot give an account of what it is to be a work of fiction without invoking imagination, it might seem that my imagination-free approach to explaining what it is to be true in a fiction is in trouble. One might press objection this by asking: *what is it* to judge that the author intends for us to judge that *p* is true in the fiction *F*—other than to judge that the author intends for us to imagine that *p*, in response to the fiction? The key to giving a satisfying answer to this question is to characterize what it is to be a work of fiction without appeal to imagination. I am not alone in thinking this can be done. Friend (2012) and Matravers (2014, pp. 98–101) each develop such accounts, motivated in part by the many difficulties inherent in trying to define fiction by appeal to imagination. The following rough-and-ready account is broadly in keeping with theirs and seems to me adequate for present purposes:

A Work of Fiction: a work of fiction is a set of sentences *S*, put forward by an author with the expectation that readers will believe that much, if not all, of what is said and implied by *S* is not true.

With this definition of "a work of fiction" in hand, we can give the following answer to the earlier question: to judge that the author intends for us to judge that *p* is true in the fiction *F* is to judge that the author of *F* intends for us to judge that *p* is stated or implied by a set of sentences *S* that the author has put forward with the expectation that readers will believe that much, if not all, of what is said and implied by *S* is not true. While the above characterization of fiction will admit of borderline cases—many of which are detailed in Matravers (2014) and Friend (2012)—the borders do not get any clearer when one introduces "imagination" into the mix. Nor, I think, are we left with the sense that there remains a deep puzzle, or loaded term, in the vicinity in need of further explanation.

9.7 Summary

Up to this point, I have sketched a view of how we recover fictional content that is consistent with the related imaginings being *judgments* and *decisions* of different kinds. We begin simply by taking in a fiction's explicit content, by whatever means we grasp linguistic content or perceive the world more generally. The examples of hearing political punditry and reading dubious philosophy showed that the mere phenomenon of understanding content without belief does not require, or even suggest, the use of *sui generis* imaginative states. To the extent that this content does not merely wash over us—to the extent that it is preserved in memory—this occurs in the form of beliefs about what has happened in the fiction. Of course, we don't form beliefs about *everything* we have been aware of in the fiction, just as we don't form beliefs about everything we are aware of when walking around town. The beliefs we do form enable us to reason conditionally about what else is likely true in the fiction, given its explicit content, and to thereby actively enrich our understanding of the fictional world. We recover more, or less, implicit content depending on how much work we put in to drawing out such inferences. Our appreciation of the fiction may be further enhanced by other kinds of inferences as well, concerning, for instance, particular genre conventions, or an author's apparent use of symbolism. Further, it is not only judgments about what is true in a fiction that constitute our mental registry of the fictional world. We also often make *decisions* about how to further develop or experience the fictional world for ourselves, in ways that add details that the fiction itself leaves indeterminate. This accounts for the active, collaborative aspect of fiction appreciation.

I concluded with an argument that the question of whether consuming fiction requires *sui generis* imagining is orthogonal to the question of whether fictional truths result from prescriptions to imagine. For we can grant, for the sake of argument, that fictional truths result from prescriptions to imagine while understanding the prescription to imagine that *p* (in response to fiction *F*) as the prescription to judge that, in the fiction *F*, *p*. Further, I argued, there is no vicious circularity in that proposal. The lack of circularity is evident in our ability to articulate what it is to be a fiction without appeal to imagination.

So much, then, for answering the four puzzles of fiction-comprehension in a way compatible with explaining the A-imagining at work in fiction consumption in more basic folk psychological terms. Now, so far I've said nothing about why it would be *fun* or *enjoyable*—or even upsetting—to engage with fictions. A sad omission, but necessary! Thus, still before us, in the two chapters to come, are the questions of why we become immersed in fictions, whether our doing so is rationally warranted, and what sort of mental states are responsible for that immersion.

10
Consuming Fictions Part II
The Operator Claim

10.1 Introduction

Last chapter I offered an account of how fictional content, both implied and explicit, is recovered without use of *sui generis* imaginative states. This and the next chapter shift focus to our immersion in fictions—to the fact that we become emotionally involved, concerned with, "lost in," moved by, and, well, *immersed* in compelling fictions. Explaining our immersion amounts, first and foremost, to explaining how and why we become emotionally involved in the fictions we enjoy. (At the beginning of Chapter 9, I considered the objection that immersion is something distinct from emotional involvement—that it involves "losing oneself" in the fiction in some other, more cognitive sense.) Many have thought that our being moved by fictions is due in part to our entering into *sui generis* imaginative states through which the fictional events are represented. Some then add to this picture that *sui generis* (belief-like) imaginative states combine with a second, desire-like form of imaginative state—what we can call "i-desires"—to generate fiction-related emotions. Over the next two chapters, I will argue that neither sort of imaginative state should form part of our account of immersion in fiction. We can better explain immersion by appeal to ordinary beliefs and desires about the fictions. Further, quite apart from its being *possible* that fiction consumption draws only on beliefs and desires, there are serious independent difficulties with the idea that *sui generis* imaginative states underwrite our immersion in fictions. These difficulties—which are the main topic of this chapter—disappear when we adopt a reductive approach to imagination, where the imaginings we experience in response to fiction amount to certain kinds of ordinary perceptions, judgements and desires.

10.2 The Operator Claim

In the Batman fictions, Gotham is a dangerous city, riddled with crime. Do I, myself, *believe* that Gotham is dangerous? Not exactly. Asked to name some dangerous cities, I don't list Gotham among them. What I believe is that, in the Batman fictions, Gotham is a dangerous city. If in casual conversation I leave out

Explaining Imagination. Peter Langland-Hassan, Oxford University Press (2020). © Peter Langland-Hassan.
DOI: 10.1093/oso/9780198815068.001.0001

the 'in the fiction' operator—asking, "What if Batman lived in Woodstock instead of Gotham?"—it is always there *sotto voce*. A formal account of my beliefs must make it explicit, in order to distinguish me from the person who truly believes that Gotham is a dangerous city and, for that reason, plans to avoid it on his next cross-country trip. Likewise David Lewis, in his influential account of truth in fiction, advises that we "not take our descriptions of fictional characters at face value," but instead "regard them as abbreviations for longer sentences beginning with an operator 'In such-and-such fiction…'" (1978, p. 37). In his example: "if I say that [Sherlock] Holmes liked to show off"—and thereby express my *belief* about Holmes—"you will take it that I have asserted an abbreviated version of the true sentence 'In the Sherlock Holmes stories, Holmes liked to show off'" (p. 38). It is the latter "true sentence" that is actually believed. I will be arguing that the same kind of disambiguation-by-operator is required in the case of fiction-directed imaginings as well. Call this the *Operator Claim* (OC):

OC: when recovering fictional content from a fiction *F* in which *p* is the case, we do not simply imagine that *p*; rather, we imagine that, in the fiction *F*, *p*.

Just as we need to include an 'in the fiction' operator within properly characterized beliefs about fictional entities, so too must we include such an operator when properly characterizing our imaginings concerning fictions. If correct, the Operator Claim undermines the main rationale for positing *sui generis* imaginative states in the explanation of immersion—and indeed in explaining our enjoyment of fiction more generally. Or so I will argue.

To appreciate the OC's importance, it will help to first map the landscape of popular positions on imaginative immersion as it now stands.

10.3 Mapping the Territory: Three Views

Not everyone who discovers that *q* is happy about it. Typically, only those who desired that *q* are glad at the discovery, and not those who desired that not-*q*, or who couldn't care less whether *q*. Likewise, judging that *p* will not usually, by itself, make someone anxious; negative affect only sets in if one also desires that not-*p*. So say the platitudes of folk psychology, and so I agree. A concrete case: Doggett & Egan are thrilled as the Red Sox batter circles the bases following his grand slam, while I watch the same events with sorrow. Why this difference in our emotions? Doggett & Egan desire that the Red Sox win, while I want their opponent, the Chicago Cubs, to prevail. Our desires themselves were not sufficient for the emotions we experienced; nor, for that matter, is belief that the Red Sox have hit a grand slam sufficient to arouse emotion in those who lack desires on the matter either way. The *pairing* of a cognitive with a suitably related conative state is essential.

True, not *all* emotional responses result from this recipe (Prinz, 2004; Robinson, 2005b). Some emotions are reflexive or "pre-cognitive" in nature. A door slammed shut by the wind may trigger fear and anxiety, without a belief/desire pair featuring in the explanation. But I don't think that is the case, in general, with respect to our emotional immersion in fiction. The best account of that immersion, I will argue, makes much the same appeal to suitable cognitive/conative state pairs as do explanations of our immersion in ordinary (non-fictional, non-pretend) events we enjoy, such as baseball games. I am joined in this thought by many others working on fiction and immersion, including Doggett & Egan (2012), Currie & Ravenscroft (2002), Kind (2011), and Spaulding (2015). A competitor to this approach holds that our (*sui generis*) imaginings generate emotional responses *directly*, irrespective of any conative states we may or may not have with respect to the fiction. Nichols (2004b, 2006b) and Van Leeuwen (2016) defend versions of that view. I have discussed Nichols' view elsewhere (Langland-Hassan, 2017) and will delay discussion of Van Leeuwen's until Chapter 11.

Provided that we are committed to the idea that cognitive and conative state pairs generate emotional response to fictions (in the normal case), there remain two controversial questions with respect to the nature of such pairs. The questions, and their most common answers, can be elucidated though an example. In the HBO mini-series *The Wire*, Wallace is a sixteen-year-old caregiver to his younger siblings and cousins, and occasional drug dealer. At the end of Season One, he is murdered by his peers on the off chance that he'll become a police informant. I felt anxiety and distress as the scene unfolded, having grown attached to Wallace. A first question we can ask about this case is: what are the specific cognitive and conative "attitudes" involved in generating the response? Are they imaginings, beliefs, desires, "i-desires" (Currie, 2010; Doggett & Egan, 2007, 2012), or something else? A second question is: what are the contents of those states? In particular, we will want to know whether the contents involve 'in the fiction' operators. Here are three popular approaches to answering these questions.

The Simple View: One set of responses, defended by both Kind (2011) and Spaulding (2015), is that the cognitive state is an *imagining* and the conative state is a *desire*, and that neither of those states involves an 'in the fiction' operator. So, in the example given, it might be an imagining that Wallace is dying that combines with a desire that Wallace survives that, together, serve to generate negative affect. I will call this the *Simple View*, following Currie (2010).[1] The Simple View is simple insofar as it meshes with our pre-theoretical tendency to describe ourselves as wanting Wallace to survive, and as imagining that he is dying.

[1] It bears noting that, on Currie's use of "the Simple View," the view is limited to making a claim about other conative states involved in fiction appreciation, and not on the nature of the cognitive state. Those who defend the Simple View will, however, typically agree that the cognitive state is an imagining of some sort, and not a belief.

The Change of Attitude View: A second style of view, defended by Currie (2010), Currie & Ravenscroft (2002), and Doggett & Egan (2007, 2012), gives a different answer concerning the nature of the conative state involved. Instead of holding that a desire that Wallace survives pairs with an imagining to generate negative affect, it proposes that we should posit an imaginative analog to desires—"i-desires"—to serve as the relevant conative state. It is my i-desiring that Wallace survives, while imagining that Wallace is being shot, that generates negative affect, with i-desires and imaginings combining to generate affect in roughly the same way that ordinary beliefs and desires do. I will—again following Currie (2010)—call this the *Change of Attitude View*. It is so named because it proposes a change to the conative attitude we might ascribe, pre-theoretically, when considering the case. It turns out we don't actually desire that Wallace survives; instead, we i-desire that he survives.

A motivation for the Change of Attitude View is that we are sometimes upset by what occurs in a fiction (as in a tragedy), even if we do not want to change the fiction to remove the upsetting feature (because we think the fiction is excellent as it is). Instead of describing us as somehow conflicted about how we want the fiction to be—both wanting Wallace to survive (because we like him) and wanting him to die (so that the fiction retains its dramatic integrity)—the Change of Attitude View proposes that we are in distinct states of desiring that the fiction remains as it is, while i-desiring that some event in the fiction does not occur. I will say more about this view and the argument just sketched in its favor below (section 10.5).

The Change of Content View: A third style of view—my own—is the *Change of Content View*. I again take the term from Currie.[2] The Change of Content view, as I will understand it, bears two important differences with both the Simple View and the Change of Attitude View. First, on the Change of Content View, the conative/cognitive state pair responsible for fiction-directed affect is a belief and a desire. This contrasts with the Simple View's claim that an imagining is (at least often) involved, and with the Change of Attitude's thesis that an imagining and an i-desire pair are (at least often) involved. Second, on the Change of Content View, both the belief and the desire include 'in the fiction' operators. This again contrasts with both the Simple View and the Change of Attitude View, insofar as neither hold that 'in the fiction' operators typically occur within the contents of the relevant emotion-generating states. Returning to the example from *The Wire*, on my view—the Change of Content View—it is my belief that, in the fiction, Wallace is being shot that combines with a desire that, in the fiction, Wallace survives, that generates negative affect. The Change of Content View is so named because,

[2] On Currie's version of the Change of Content View, the view only makes a claim about the conative state at work in generating fiction-directed affect (viz., that it is a desire with an 'in the fiction' operator within its content). On my version of the Change of Content View, I add that the relevant cognitive state is a belief (and not an imagining), where the belief *also* has an 'in the fiction' operator.

pre-theoretically, we may not include 'in the fiction' operators within the content of the attitudes we describe ourselves as taking toward fictions (even if they are always there *sotto voce*, as noted above). The Change of Content View is, however, consistent with a view where the states responsible for triggering our emotional responses to fiction are ordinary beliefs and desires.

I will now mount an argument for the Operator Claim that, if correct, favors the Change of Content View over both the Simple View and the Change of Attitude View. Like it or not, the operator-involving Change of Content View is the only coherent alternative for providing an explanation of fiction-directed affect, so long as we are committed to those explanations invoking suitable cognitive/conative state pairs.

10.4 To Which Fiction Do Your Desires Refer? Troubles for the Simple View

I begin by recounting an ingenious argument developed by Currie (2010)—with help from Tyler Doggett and Stacie Friend[3]—against the Simple View, as a means to promoting his own Change of Attitude (i.e., "i-desire") View. I will then argue that, with minor modifications, it poses an equally serious challenge to his own Change of Attitude View.

Currie imagines a fictional *BBC* drama—*Death of a Prime Minister*—the plot of which involves Margaret Thatcher being pursued by an assassin. While he does not, in reality, wish for Thatcher to be assassinated, he is, in the context of the fiction, hoping that she is assassinated. As he puts it, he is "on the side" of the film's clever villain. As he cheers for the assassin, the Simple View would characterize him as having the desire that Thatcher dies. But, if that were really his desire, Currie observes, "it should be satisfied by her [actual] death." And yet:

> It wouldn't be. Suppose that, while I am cheering for the play's assassin, Mrs. Thatcher runs in pursued by someone who proceeds to murder her. That would seem to me a wholly bad thing...this state, which we ignorantly call a desire, is not satisfied by the death of Mrs. Thatcher, but by her death *according to the fiction*. (2010, p. 635)

Currie concludes that the Simple View provides a wrong account of his fiction-directed conative state, insofar as it suggests that the state should be satisfied by events that would not satisfy it.

[3] Currie thanks both Doggett and Friend in the article for suggesting aspects of the argumentative strategy.

Currie's example exploits the fact that we sometimes desire events to occur in a fiction that we do not wish to occur in reality. He would be aghast if Thatcher were actually murdered; yet he wishes the assassin to succeed in the fiction. This helps us to see that Thatcher's actual assassination is not among the satisfaction conditions for the fiction-directed desire. This suggests that the Simple View has given the wrong account of the conative state at work. We can also create problems for the Simple View using examples where one's fiction and reality-directed desires appear to align. Suppose that I am watching a film where terrorists storm Buckingham Palace. The film's hero hatches a plan to drive the terrorists out. I feel anxiety as I follow along, imagining (let us suppose) that the terrorists haven't yet been driven out of the palace. Which desire of mine pairs with this imagining to generate anxiety? On the Simple View, it should be a desire that Buckingham Palace is free of terrorists. Yet if the desire that Buckingham Palace is free of terrorists were really contributing to my anxiety, I should be able to dispel that anxiety by turning on the news and confirming that there are not, in fact, any terrorists laying siege to Buckingham Palace. But, obviously, news reports about the peaceable state of Buckingham Palace are irrelevant to my concerns. For the unsatisfied desire in question does not concern the state of Buckingham Palace itself, but, rather, the events of the fiction I am watching. I desire that, *in the fiction*, Buckingham Palace is free of terrorists. This is why simply assuring myself that Buckingham Palace is in fact safe does nothing to ease my mind. And it is why my negative affect subsides the very moment I judge that, in the fiction, terrorists have been driven out of Buckingham Palace. At least, so says the Change of Content View.

This is not Currie's conclusion, however. He favors the Change of Attitude solution, which we will consider in a moment. First, a comment on the structure of these cases. One might find it suspicious that both examples make use of people and places that have counterparts in reality. It might give the appearance that the problem lies in characterizing desires when there is a real-world counterpart to some entity in a fiction, and not with the Simple View's general claim that we needn't include 'in the fiction' operators within fiction-related desires. However, the real-world counterparts merely serve to highlight a general need to disambiguate the object of one's desires when making claims about their ability to generate affect. The need to distinguish such desires at the level of content is thrown into relief by any situation where two entities—fictional *or* non-fictional—share the same name.[4]

For example, suppose that I want Mike Mulligan to win an election where the only other candidate is Mike Jones. You find me dejected after Mike Mulligan's

[4] By "share the same name" I mean the sense in which two people named 'John Smith' share the same name. More neutrally we could describe the situation as one where the names for two people or places are homonyms and homographs (i.e., the linguistic labels look and sound the same). This leaves open whether names, as such, are partly individuated by their referents.

loss. But why? I wanted Mike to win, and Mike *did* win. Well, the obvious answer is that the two instances of 'Mike' have different referents. A more thorough description of the desire and belief—that I wanted Mike *Mulligan* to win, and believe that Mike *Jones* won—instantly removes any appearance of a puzzle. What the Margaret Thatcher and Buckingham Palace examples highlight—though it is not obvious Currie himself recognizes it[5]—is that there are contexts where, in order to properly disambiguate the ascription of a desire that is elicited by a fiction, the fiction itself will need to be referenced in the content of the desire (as opposed to, say, a person's last name). But this reveals that we were only *abbreviating* our ascription of the state when we initially omitted mention of the fiction from its content. Where conversational context removes ambiguity in the intended object of reference—as it so often does, both within and outside of our engagement with fictions—we feel comfortable leaving out from our descriptions details like last names and titles of the fictions that feature the named characters. The resulting habitual omission of relevant 'in the fiction' operators, in the case of fiction-directed desires, can make them appear altogether unnecessary and even non-existent within the desires themselves; but that is *only* an appearance. Change the context—by highlighting fictional and real-life individuals with the same name, or (as we'll see below) fictional characters with the same name from different fictions—and the need for the operator is instantly felt.

I'll now build on these points to argue that 'in the fiction' operators are needed whether it is desires or i-desires that are active in fiction-appreciation, and so extend Currie's argument to the Change of Attitude View as well.

10.5 Troubles with I-desires

First, a few words on the nature of i-desires. I-desires are said to correspond to actual desires in roughly the way that *sui generis* "belief-like" imaginings are thought to correspond to ordinary beliefs. Currie & Ravenscroft (2002) and Doggett & Egan (2012) motivate i-desires—and their place within the Change of Attitude View—over both the Simple View and Change of Content View in part by appeal to their ability to solve a puzzle concerning the enjoyment of tragedies. Watching *Romeo and Juliet*, it seems we really want the couple to survive and are upset by their tragic suicides; on the other hand, most of us don't wish for *Romeo and Juliet* to be any different than it is—in particular, we don't wish for it to be rewritten so that it is no longer a tragedy. But this seems to suggest that we are

[5] Currie grants that his example is unusual in its appeal to characters based on actual people, but says, "I don't believe this affects the arguments' generality." "It would be odd to claim," he explains, "that, when fictions concern real things it is i-desires which are in play, but that in the case of fictions involving non-existents, real desires take over." However, my argument will be that the right conclusion is that it is *both* when fictions concern real things *and* when they involve non-existents that 'in the fiction' operators are needed—and that i-desires are not in play in either case.

somehow conflicted about how we want the fiction to be. Arguably, if we really want Romeo and Juliet to survive, then we should *also* want the fiction to be rewritten accordingly. And yet, few among us will advocate amending Shakespeare's work. (Much the same sort of example, keyed to *The Sopranos*, occurs in Doggett & Egan (2012).) Currie and Doggett & Egan's proposed exit from this impasse is to hold that we don't really desire that Romeo and Juliet survive; instead, we bear a desire-*like* imaginative attitude of *i-desire* to the proposition that they survive. And just as there is no conflict between imagining that *p* and believing that not-*p*, so too, they propose, is there no conflict between desiring that Romeo and Juliet perish (in line with the trajedy as it is) while i-desiring that they survive. We no longer have to say—implausibly, by their lights—that we have conflicting desires about how the fiction ought to unfold.[6]

What, exactly, is the difference between regular desires and *i*-desires, such that an i-desire that *p* and a desire that not-*p* will not conflict with each other? Currie gives us the following "test" for distinguishing the two:

(SC) A putative desire, A, is an i-desire and not really a desire if A has satisfaction conditions, a canonical statement of which makes reference to a fiction which is not also the object of A. (2010, p. 635)

The key idea here is that, while an i-desire has satisfaction conditions related to what happens in *Romeo and Juliet*, the fiction itself "is not also the object of" the i-desire. Essentially, Currie seeks to split the difference between the Simple View and the add-an-operator ("Change of Content") approach by stipulating that the

[6] Granting Currie & Ravenscroft and Doggett & Egan's points that we would not change the fictions in question even if we could, there is still a strong case to be made that we are nevertheless conflicted about how the fictions proceed. This is indeed the view I take on the matter. We want *Romeo and Juliet* to continue in existence as the excellent tragedy that it is, sure; but part of us also wants it to be different—we really do desire that, in the fiction, Romeo and Juliet live happily ever after. It is this conflict in desires that characterizes the experience of tragedy in fiction—as proposed by Nichols (2004b) and Weinberg & Meskin (2006a).

Obviously, this reply will be unsatisfactory to Doggett & Egan and Currie & Ravenscroft, who are adamant that we experience no such conflict about the course of tragedies. In light of this standoff, the best we can do, I suggest, is to reflect on how common it is to have desires that are at odds with one's strongest, most settled preferences. Amy Kind offers a vivid example:

> Consider a mother whose only child is a senior in high school. She wants her son to go away to university and she firmly believes that certain experiences can be achieved only if he does. Simultaneously, she fears having an empty nest, and thus she also wants her son to stay home and attend a local institution. Does this make her irrational? Surely not. Rather, it seems like a perfectly ordinary case of conflicting desires. (Kind, 2011, p. 429)

Questions of rationality aside, this mother quite plausibly has conflicting desires, despite being settled on the view that her son should go away to university. Given the opportunity to change his enrollment back to a local institution, she would not act on it any more than she would recommend rewriting *Romeo and Juliet*. And yet, as she looks around his room—at the old soccer trophies, the photos, the vacation souvenirs—she has a powerful desire that she knows she will not, and cannot act upon: to have him at home; to see him as a little boy again; to keep him from growing up. And why shouldn't she? Growing up is a kind of tragedy. She is conflicted, resigned as she may be to the proper course of events. A good fiction can generate much the same kind of conflict within our desires.

satisfaction conditions of i-desires pertain to what occurs in the fiction (in line with the operator approach), while holding that the content of the state makes no mention of the fiction (in accordance with the Simple View). So, for instance, the state that contributes to feelings of despair when Romeo dies is an *i-desire*, the content of which is that Romeo survives. This (putatively) makes "Romeo himself" the object of the desire, and not the fiction *Romeo and Juliet*. Just as regular desires pair with regular beliefs to generate affect, defenders of i-desires hold that i-desires pair with belief-like imaginings to generate fiction-directed affect. In the present case, the i-desire that *Romeo survives* combines with a (belief-like) imagining that *Romeo is committing suicide* to generate negative affect. While neither state includes reference to a specific fiction within its content, Currie proposes, a canonical statement of the i-desire's satisfaction conditions *will* make explicit reference to some fiction. The i-desire is satisfied if and only if, in the fiction, Romeo survives. (Similarly, the imagining that Romeo is committing suicide is "correct" or "appropriate" only if it is true, in the fiction, that Romeo is committing suicide.) Importantly, this picture avoids the problem that Currie's *Death of a Prime Minister* creates for the Simple View. The reason that Currie's fiction-directed desire that Margaret Thatcher is assassinated is not satisfied by an actual assassin's killing Thatcher in the theater is that Currie's (supposed) desire for her to be assassinated was really an *i-desire*. I-desires are satisfied by what is true in a particular fiction and not by what is true in reality.

Currie admits that this leaves i-desires with "odd satisfaction conditions" (p. 635). For such states can putatively be about an actual person (e.g., Margaret Thatcher)—in the sense of taking that person as their object—yet be satisfied (or not) according to how things turn out with respect to a mere fiction. Ordinarily, how things stand with the object of a conative state (viz., Margaret Thatcher herself) is the only matter relevant to judging whether that state is satisfied. We can reasonably ask: if my i-desire is really *about* Margaret Thatcher herself, why should what happens to a fictional character have any bearing on its satisfaction? The fate of the Thatcher character in *Death of a Prime Minister* has no causal influence over Margaret Thatcher *herself*, who, we are told, is the object of the desire. To simply say that this is how it is with i-desires—that they are about one thing, but satisfied by something causally unrelated to that thing—does little to diminish the puzzle.

A more decisive form of objection is available, however. For the same argument Currie runs against the Simple View can, with a few amendments, be applied to the i-desire view as well. Suppose that the BBC made multiple Margaret Thatcher-inspired fictions. *Death of a Prime Minister* is one, but there is also *A Dangerous Pearl*. Thatcher is pursued by an assassin in both. And let us suppose that I watch the first half of each film one afternoon, delaying their conclusions until the next day. When it comes to *Death of a Prime Minister*, I am rooting, with Currie, for the assassin. Yet, in *A Dangerous Pearl*, I want the Prime Minister to survive.

(In that film, the assassin's motivations are less compelling.) What is the proper characterization of these putative i-desires? Working with the tools Currie allows himself, neither i-desire can make reference to the particular fiction that elicited it. So it appears I am conflicted: I i-desire that Thatcher die; and I i-desire that Thatcher not die. Both i-desires take, as their object, Thatcher herself. But, of course, it seems wrong to say that I am conflicted. This is not a case of mixed emotions, after all. I am not "of two minds" in this sort of case. (Contrast my account of tragedy, in fn. 6.) I want one thing to happen to the Thatcher character in *Death of a Prime Minister*; and, as a separate matter, I want something different to happen to the Thatcher character in *A Dangerous Pearl.*[7] Something has gone wrong with the i-desire approach if it suggests I am in fact conflicted. For all my desires can be satisfied simultaneously, if things turn out the right way in each fiction.

We can further put pressure on the Change of Attitude View by showing how it wrongly predicts the situations in which an i-desire will be satisfied. Suppose that I have a single i-desire that Thatcher is assassinated, elicited by my viewing of *Death of a Prime Minister* (*DPM*). I have not yet viewed *A Dangerous Pearl* (*ADP*). Pausing *DPM* momentarily to make more popcorn, I stream, on my phone, the opening of *ADP*, in which she *is* assassinated—in the first minute, no less! (Here I mirror the feature of Currie's example where Thatcher herself is chased into the very theater where he is enjoying *DPM* and assassinated; one remains in the context where the initial i-desire is active, while being confronted by another Thatcher-iteration.) Yet I don't experience any sense of satisfaction, as I wasn't rooting for *that* assassin. But why shouldn't I be at least somewhat pleased, given that I (still) have an i-desire, elicited by *DPM*, that Thatcher is assassinated and, in watching the opening of ADM, imagine *that Thatcher is assassinated*?[8] The answer is plain: the content of the relevant desire (or i-desire) was more specific than that Thatcher is assassinated—or even that she is assassinated *in some fiction or other.* It was a quite specific desire (or i-desire) that, in *Death of a Prime Minister*, Thatcher is assassinated.

Currie might respond by reminding us that i-desires have satisfaction conditions relating to the different fictions that elicit them, which are not tracked by their contents. In that case, a person might i-desire that *p* while i-desiring that

[7] For reasons explained at the end of the previous section, this case does not require there to be a real-world counterpart to the fictional character(s). A similar example is easy to generate with different iterations of James Bond in different 007 films—as explained below.

[8] The dueling BBC dramas example can be levied against the Simple View as well. In that case, the problem is one's having a desire that Thatcher is assassinated (elicited by *Death of a Prime Minister*) and a desire that Thatcher is not assassinated (elicited by *A Dangerous Pearl*). Again one is wrongly characterized as being conflicted; and again one is left without explanation for why one's desire for Thatcher to be assassinated (elicted by *Death of a Prime* Minister) continues to generate negative affect, or feelings of suspense, even after one has imagined that Thatcher is assassinated (while watching *A Dangerous Pearl*). The clear solution to our problems here is to simply grant that the respective fictions make it into the content of our two desires. As they are desires about two different fictions, there is no cognitive conflict in having them.

not-*p* without being at all conflicted, just because the satisfaction conditions of each i-desire pertain to different fictions. However, one might wonder why the defender of the Simple View could not have made a similar move, appealing to differences in satisfaction conditions for regular desires with conflicting contents (e.g., the desire that Thatcher lives, and the desire that she is assassinated) to explain why Currie isn't thrilled when Thatcher is murdered before him in the theater. More troublingly, for both the Change of Attitude and Simple Views, such differences in satisfaction conditions could make no difference to the causes and effects of the states within a person's mind, which, we must assume, are determined entirely by a state's content and attitude. If we cast aside that assumption and claim, to the contrary, that different satisfaction conditions *can* make a psychological difference, even when the difference in satisfaction conditions is not reflected in a state's content or attitude, the explanatory value of the notions of attitude and content is undermined. A state's content and attitude would not suffice to determine its state's satisfaction conditions *or* its psychological role. A person could then potentially have two or more i-desires with the *same* content simultaneously, each of which played different cognitive roles. What theoretical role would the notions of content and attitude—the main explanatory posits in this debate—be playing on such a picture? Surely we will have taken a wrong turn.

A related response worth considering is that an i-desire will typically be cordoned off to, or "quarantined" within, just one imaginative project—occurring only "in the scope of" that project—while another i-desire with the same (or a conflicting) content may similarly interact only with cognitive states relating to the distinct fiction that elicited *it* (cf. Friend, 2003; see fn. 9). But this just leaves us with the question of how this quarantining-to-a-specific-project is accomplished. As we've seen in earlier chapters, the notion of a distinct cognitive (or conative) attitude is typically brought into play precisely to serve this kind of function. It is said that our imagining that *p* is quarantined from our belief that *p* precisely in virtue of the fact that we take a different attitude toward the propositions in each case (Nichols & Stich, 2000). The difference in attitude is supposed to account for the difference in functional role between the two states which nevertheless have the same content. This explanation of quarantining must be superfluous, or just mistaken, if it turns out that some i-desires are quarantined from imaginings that other i-desires are not quarantined from (The same point extends to regular desires as well, insofar as a defender of the Simple View may wish to appeal to distinct regular desires occurring only "in the scope of" different imaginative projects, in responding to the above objections.)

In any case, if one i-desire (or desire) is quarantined from a cognitive state while another i-desire (or desire) with the same content is not, the two conative states will *ipso facto* have different functional roles, despite having the same content. This will imply that we are indeed taking distinct attitudes toward the two propositions after all, insofar as attitudes are understood functionally. The price of maintaining an operator-free account of the content of the states is that we need to posit a distinct cognitive attitude for each new fiction we enjoy. Again something has clearly gone wrong.[9]

In a blog response to a short version of this criticism I raised elsewhere (Langland-Hassan, 2018b), Currie (2018) proposes that Bratman's (1992) notion of context-relative *acceptance* may help to dissolve the problem (where, again, the problem is our seeming to have conflicting i-desires elicited by distinct fictions in cases where, intuitively, we lack any conflicting conative states). While I don't want to pin the view on Currie—it was an informal blog post, after all—it is an interesting idea worth exploring, as others may find it attractive. He offers the example of a ship's captain who accepts that her ship is in a certain sort of danger with respect to one context, but not another. This person, he writes, "accepts P relative to one context and accepts not-P relative to another and that there is no contradiction in doing so." This is different than cases of "irrational acceptance" where "the captain becomes so confused that she accepts P and not-P in the same context." Currie's idea here is that i-desires (and perhaps "ordinary" imaginings as well) may be context-relative in the manner of acceptances, and that this would dissolve the apparent conflict in imagining that *p* (with respect to one fiction) while simultaneously imagining that not-*p* with respect to another.

However, the context-relativity of any acceptance (or imagining) must find its way into the agent's mind in some way or other. That is, there must be some psychological difference between the person who accepts P relative to context R and the person who only accepts P relative to context Q (where contexts R and Q are different)—even if both people otherwise have the same beliefs. That difference cannot be captured by appeal to the content or attitude of the state, as both accept that P. One might respond, "Well, the different contexts will reveal themselves in the different ways the acceptance that P functions in their broader cognitive economies." However, I take it as shared ground that such functional differences are to be understood in terms of different attitudes taken toward type-identical contents—that different attitudes essentially serve to mark different characteristic functions a certain type of contentful state may have. The proposal thus suggests that the same attitude is not taken toward the content P in each case, after all. So it

[9] Stacie Friend (2003) also discusses cases where a single character is portrayed in different ways in different fictions, giving rise to correspondingly different emotional responses. She explains away the apparent conflict in the responses by holding that they "occur within the scope of different imaginings." The question is: what determines the "scope" of an imagining, given that there can be dispositional imaginings, which Friend rightly allows ("We can say that my imaginings and feelings about Tess are dispositional: even if I am thinking about something else entirely, it would be accurate to say that I pity Tess"). Friend simply proposes that the contents of imaginings "remain attached to their sources and thus compartmentalized." But *how* do imaginings remain "attached" to a specific source, if not by their contents? It cannot be the mere fact that they are imagined. This is where we need an operator relativizing the contents to a specific fiction.

appears we either have to proliferate attitudes, or adjust the contents. Turning back to the case of consuming fictions, if we go the route of proliferating attitudes, we seem headed toward holding that we adopt a different attitude toward the propositions relevant to each different fiction we enjoy. If we adjust the content, then we are returning to the solution I initially proposed of invoking distinct "in the fiction *F*" operators.

Stepping back, all of these problems were lurking the moment Currie drew a distinction between the content and the satisfaction conditions of a conative state. When he first introduced the idea of i-desires having distinct satisfaction conditions from desires with the same content, the implicit suggestion was that this functional difference was to be accounted for by the nature of the distinct attitudes taken toward the content. It was in the nature of i-desire *as an attitude*, one might have supposed, that i-desires have fiction-related satisfaction conditions even when their contents make no mention of a fiction. Yet, as soon as there are multiple fictions afoot, it becomes clear that a single attitude of i-desire will be too blunt an instrument to determine *which* fiction's events are relevant to the satisfaction of any given i-desire.

10.6 The Life-expectancy of Fiction-directed Desires

There nevertheless remains a last response to consider on behalf of i-desires. With slight modifications, it can also be adopted by defenders of the Simple View. It could be argued that the i-desires (or, alternatively, ordinary desires) elicited by fictions are highly *condition-dependent*, in that we no longer harbor them when we are not actively attending to the fiction they concern. In that case, I would not retain i-desires (or desires) about the Thatcher of *DPM* when I am engaging with *ADP*, and so would not end up with conflicting i-desires (or desires) in the case I described above.

Currie himself considers and rejects this response when assessing whether a defender of the Simple View could use it in response to his own argument. The Simple View theorist, he notes, might say of the *Death of a Prime Minister* case that he has a long-term, stable desire that Thatcher lives, and a condition-dependent desire (while watching *DPM*) that she is assassinated. This could explain why his eagerness for Thatcher's assassination while watching *DPM* does not conflict with his general support of her outside of the fiction. Currie's example of the assassin running into the very theater where he is watching *DPM* and murdering her there aims to undermine this response. For in that case, he (arguably) remains in the very context where his condition-dependent desire (or i-desire) that she is assassinated (in *DPM*) is active; and yet, her actual assassination *still* does not satisfy any desire of his. This, Currie suggests, shows that *even if* the fiction-directed desire is condition-dependent, it is not a desire that Thatcher is assassinated. My response can piggyback on Currie's: instead of Thatcher being chased into the theater, suppose that we simply bring an iPad into the theater where Currie is enjoying *DPM* and show him a snippet of *ADP* where Thatcher is assassinated. No desire (or i-desire) of his is thereby satisfied; and yet he is imagining that Thatcher is assassinated (in response to *ADP*) and remains in the context where he (purportedly) i-desires that she is assassinated. Moreover, there is nothing to stand in the way of one's watching both films simultaneously, on two screens. It would be far-fetched to propose that one's i-desires (or regular desires) with respect to each fiction pop in and out of existence as one looks from screen to screen. Turning momentarily to *ADP*, I may still feel anxiety, or suspense, with respect to what is occurring in *DPM*. So the relevant desires persist. Yet neither could one say that I am in some sense conflicted about what I want, just in virtue of wanting the Thatcher character to perish in one, but not the other fiction.

In any case, I see no good reason to think that our fiction-directed conative states are, in general, highly condition-dependent. There are clear cases of stable, long-lasting fiction-directed desires. Whenever I return to a mini-series I've been watching, they are there at the ready, assuring that I'm instantly engaged. We can easily generate the same sort of puzzle we have been considering with respect to such stable desires. When James Bond is played by Sean Connery, for instance, I want him to succeed in saving the world; when he is played by Timothy Dalton, I am indifferent. These are stable dispositions. I retain them in my sleep. With my Connery-related desires in mind, we can say that, right now, I want James Bond to defeat the evil masterminds. But, then, why am I indifferent as I watch the Dalton-acted *License to Kill*? Well, the desire (or i-desire) in question was not directed at *that* James Bond. Properly characterized, my stable desire is that the James Bond of *Goldfinger*, and other Sean-Connery-acted-installments, saves the world. Again the notion of fictionality—and even of a particular fiction—must enter into the content of the state.

My arguments in favor of the Change of Content View have, up to this point, focused on fiction-directed conative states: desires and i-desires. I will now move toward a broader defense of the Operator Claim (OC), by arguing that the same points extend to our fiction-related ("belief-like") imaginings as well.

10.7 Imagining that, in the Fiction, *p*, and the Problem of Thatcher's Pearls

At the beginning of this chapter, I advertised a surprising conclusion I would endeavor to reach, dubbed the *Operator Claim*:

OC: when recovering fictional content from a fiction *F* in which *p* is the case, we do not simply imagine that *p*; rather, we imagine that, in the fiction *F*, *p*.

We will need to include 'in the fiction' operators within proper ascriptions of imaginings for much the same reason they are required within ascriptions of fiction-related desires (or i-desires).

First, we can find cases where doing without such operators commits one to ascribing contradictory imaginings where there are none. These mirror the dual BBC drama cases where the Simple View and Change of Attitude View wrongly ascribe conflicted desires (or i-desires) about Thatcher's assassination. Suppose again that I am watching the two Margaret Thatcher dramas on dual screens, shifting my attention from one to the other now and then. (It is not necessary to the example that I am watching the fictions at roughly the same time, provided, as earlier argued, that fiction-related desires and imaginings are not highly condition-dependent; the present version of the argument avoids depending upon that point, however.) In *A Dangerous Pearl*, Thatcher is always wearing a pearl necklace; in *Death of a Prime Minister*, she is never wearing one. On the ordinary account of things—making no use of 'in the fiction' operators—we have to say that I am simultaneously imagining that Margaret Thatcher is wearing a pearl necklace (as a result of taking in *ADP*) and imagining that Margaret Thatcher is not wearing a pearl necklace (as a result of taking in *DPM*). Is this a plausible account of things?

Set aside the BBC fictions for a moment. Can I, right now, imagine that Margaret Thatcher is wearing a pearl necklace *and* that Margaret Thatcher is not wearing a pearl necklace? I can certainly imagine one proposition *after* the other: I imagine that she is wearing a necklace; then I imagine that she takes it off. The question is: can I imagine one proposition while I am still imagining the other? This may be possible. Perhaps I can imagine a kind of macro-scale quantum non-locality, wherein Thatcher's necklace both is and is not around her neck. I will, in any case, place no barrier on imagining apparent contradictions of this sort. Yet this clearly isn't the imaginative project I am engaged in as I watch the two BBC drams. They are not forcing me to imagine a violation of folk physics. The more natural thing to say is that the imaginings take two different objects: *DPM*, with its events and characters; and *ADP*, with its own events and characters. I imagine that, in *A Dangerous Pearl*, Margaret Thatcher is wearing a pearl necklace; and I imagine that, in the *Death of a Prime Minister*, Margaret Thatcher is not wearing pearls. This instantly resolves the ambiguity and removes any suggestion that I am contemplating bizarre quantum phenomena. Yet this response is only possible if fiction-directed imaginings involve 'in the fiction' operators, just as fiction-directed beliefs and desires must.

Again one might respond that my simultaneous imaginative projects somehow remain quarantined from each other, as a means to omitting 'in the fiction' operators from our imaginings. One way to develop this response is to suggest that we have different imaginative dispositions with respect to each distinct fiction we enjoy. But this again recreates, within imagination itself, the need to quarantine contents from each other that the distinct cognitive attitude of imagination was originally introduced to explain (as in Nichols & Stich (2000), and Currie & Ravenscroft (2002)). In proposing distinct sets of dispositions relevant to each fiction we enjoy, we have, in effect, posited distinct *boxes* corresponding to each fiction. After all, the heavy-duty theorist's cognitive "box" is just a cognitive reification-cum-explanation of the fact that we ascribe different cognitive and behavioral dispositions with ascriptions of "imagines that *p*" than we do with ascriptions of "desires that *p*" or "believes that *p*." Now we are likewise forced into positing distinct boxes as an explanation for the different dispositions we ascribe with "imagining that *p* with respect to *Death of a Prime Minister*," as opposed to "imagining that *p* with respect to *A Dangerous Pearl*." We have simply multiplied the stock of primitive attitudes, each of which will have a somewhat different associated functional role. Where will it end? A person can be reading several different novels over the course of a week, keeping each well enough in mind to pick it up and follow along at a moment's notice. Such a reader has distinct "imaginative dispositions" relating to each novel. Is she exploiting a distinct cognitive box for each novel, each corresponding to a primitive, fiction-specific set of dispositions? Of course not. She simply has beliefs about what is happening in each novel that are accessed and *used* when engaging with each.

A second problem that results when we omit 'in the fiction' operators from our fiction-related imaginings is that we run into cases where we fail to experience the kind of affect we ought to, given our imaginings. Suppose that I am deeply engrossed in *Death of a Prime Minister* and form a strong desire that, in *DPM*, Thatcher is assassinated. (I am taking it as established, by earlier arguments, that such fiction-directed desires involve 'in the fiction' operators.) Pausing *DPM* momentarily, I watch the first few minutes of *A Dangerous Pearl*, where she is assassinated in the opening scene. On the standard view of fiction-consumption, I am now imagining that Thatcher is assassinated (in response to *ADP*). Yet this imagining does not generate positive affect in combination with my desire that, in *Death of a Prime Minister*, Thatcher is assassinated. Why not?

Well, intuitively, the imagining is not *about* the right fiction. What would it take for the imagining to *be* about the right fiction? The answer is clear: the specific fiction would need to feature in the content of the imagining. That is the only plausible way to render the imagining relevant to my desires about one, as opposed to the other, fiction—or, indeed, to any existing *fiction* at all. If I imagine that, in *DPM*, Thatcher is assassinated, this state can potentially combine with my desire that, in *DPM*, Thatcher is assassinated, to generate positive affect. But simply imagining that Thatcher is assassinated will not do the trick.[10]

[10] A last response to the OC worth considering mirrors the claim that our fiction-related desires are highly condition-dependent and therefore only temporary. Suppose that it is a general constraint on *sui generis* imaginings that we can only imagine *one proposition at a time*. In that case, there would

Conclusion: if our imaginings are to play a role in generating fiction-related affect, and if we are to avoid attributing contradictory imaginings where there are none, we need 'in the fiction' operators within our propositional, fiction-directed imaginings. Indeed, for our imaginings simply to *concern* one fiction, as opposed to another, relevant 'in the fiction' operators are required within the imaginings. This level of detail is always present in our mental states themselves, even if our ordinary verbal ascriptions of beliefs, desires, and imaginings often rely on context to provide it. Just as we might say, "The Dude hates the Eagles" in casually expressing our belief that, in *The Big Lebowski*, The Dude hates the Eagles, we may also say that we are imagining that The Dude hates the Eagles when, strictly speaking, we are imagining that, in *The Big Lebowski*, The Dude hates the Eagles. Focusing on the fact that emotional immersion requires appropriately matched cognitive and conative state pairs is simply a means for highlighting the fact that our ordinary, operator-less, ascriptions of imaginings are always elliptical for certain fuller, operator-involving contents that characterize our psychological states.

We shouldn't be *too* surprised by this. After all, why would things be any different for (supposedly) *belief-like* and *desire-like* imaginings than for beliefs and desires themselves? There is a difference between believing (falsely) that Gotham is a dangerous city and believing (correctly) that, in the Batman fictions, Gotham is a dangerous city. So too there is a difference between imagining that Gotham is a dangerous city and imagining that, in the Batman fictions, Gotham is a dangerous city.

be no threat of imagining contradictory propositions in the example involving Thatcher's pearls. For no two imaginings could remain on stage at the same time, as it were. In support of this view, it could be remarked that imaginings (unlike desires) are *occurrent states*, not dispositional or stored ones. When we think of other occurrent states—just as judgments, decisions, and *thinkings* more generally—the (roughly) one-proposition-at-a-time limit might seem to make sense. If we cannot *judge* or *decide* multiple propositions simultaneously, why think that we can imagine them?

The most significant problem with the "one-proposition-at-a-time" response is that it undermines the main rationale for invoking imagination in the primary contexts where it is thought to be required, including fiction appreciation, pretense, and conditional reasoning. Imagination is said to be the means by which we draw out inferences about what is true in a fictional world based on what is made explicit by the fiction itself. When, in *Pride and Prejudice*, Elizabeth reads that Lydia has gone to London with Wyckham, we imagine that she is devastated and concerned for her family's future. We imagine this just because we are *also* imagining that Elizabeth is in Victorian England, that Lydia is unmarried, that an unmarried woman eloping can undermine an entire family's reputation, that Elizabeth herself is unwed and hopes to find a husband, and so on. In general, what we imagine, based on our uptake of some new proposition expressed in a fiction, is determined by what else we are imagining *at the same time*, with respect to that fiction. Holding that we can only imagine one proposition at a time would prevent any inferential interaction among multiple imagined premises. This would render imaginings useless to the recovery of inexplicit fictional content. (Walton (1990, pp. 16–18) is one who, early on, saw clearly the need for dispositional imaginings that could account for the apparent inferential interplay among imagined propositions; see also Friend (2003)).

10.8 The OC's Implications

It is not due to a small oversight, or an easily corrected infelicity, that views positing i-desires and *sui generis* imaginings run into the problems discussed in this chapter. In separating the satisfaction conditions of i-desires from their content, Currie must rely on the attitude component of the state to account for why it has the specific satisfaction conditions it does, relating to what is true in one fiction and not another. Likewise, in omitting 'in the fiction' operators from "ordinary" imaginings, others implicitly push the burden of achieving reference to a specific fiction onto the notion of an *attitude*. Normally, the work of achieving reference to one entity, as opposed to another, is reserved for the notion of *content*. Content is the right tool for the job, as we are not limited to a single content in characterizing our dealings with all different entities. We are able to reorder and recombine our many concepts so as to generate thoughts with innumerable distinct complex contents—and correspondingly distinct satisfaction or correctness conditions. The notion of an attitude, by contrast, paints in broad strokes and, ordinarily, is used to account for quite general cognitive differences, such as the distinction between a state that *guides* and one that *motivates*. Relying on the notion of an attitude—be it an imagining or i-desiring—to direct our thoughts at one versus another fiction dissolves the distinction between content and attitude itself.

The curious upshot of all this is that we have rendered *sui generis* imaginings cognitively superfluous, to the extent that we expected them to do special work either in quarantining our cognitive representation of a fictional world from our beliefs, or in making our appreciation of a fiction somehow more cognitively direct than it would be if we had to rely upon beliefs about what is true in a fiction. We now see that *sui generis* imaginings (were there such) would serve their quarantining function in just the same way as ordinary beliefs—i.e., via operators. Further, if our immersion in a fiction really were threatened by the presence of 'in the fiction' operators within our beliefs, drawing on imagination would stand us no better. For the same operators must be present there as well. Given that all sides should, in any case, allow that we *have* beliefs of the form "In fiction *F*, *p*," for any fiction we can recall, we may as well let those beliefs—and the judgments in which they were formed—do the needed work in explaining our emotional responses to fiction (when paired with the relevant desires). There is no reason to call upon an additional state of imagining that, in fiction *F*, *p*, to do the same work in the same way. This point is bolstered by the fact that we already saw, in Chapter 9, that ordinary beliefs are sufficient to explain how we recover both implied and explicit content from fictions.

In the balance of this chapter I want to put this conclusion on firmer footing by addressing three independent worries one might have about the claim that beliefs and desires with 'in the fiction' operators serve to explain immersion. My full positive account of immersion won't be complete until Chapter 11, however, where I address the paradox of fiction.

10.9 Immersion in the Fiction as Such?

To be immersed in a fiction, as I have understood it, is to be deeply emotionally involved in the fiction and concerned for its characters. In earlier work, Currie (1990) finds fault with the sort of operator-laden view I propose, on the grounds that beliefs and desires with 'in the fiction' operators put us at too great a distance from the events of a fiction to render it compelling. He raises this objection in response to a view of Walton's:

> If we adopt Walton's proposal, we shall have to say that the reader does not take any attitude toward the propositions of the story, but instead takes the attitude of belief toward the propositions in which the propositions of the story are embedded. And if we do say this, it will remain a puzzle as to how our engagement with the story can generate strong feeling. We tend to distance ourselves from disturbing tales by reminding ourselves that they are only make-believe; if the content of the reader's thought is that it is make-believe that the governess is in danger, his feelings are likely to be inhibited. What makes me anxious is the thought that the governess is in danger: a thought I do not believe, but which I do make believe. (1990, p. 210)

Currie might extend this worry to my view in the following way. Returning to my earlier example from *The Wire*, in judging that, *in the fiction*, Wallace is murdered, I have reminded myself of the fictionality of the event. This judgment should cause emotional distance—not concern—as I am, in making it, reaffirming my awareness of the event's fictionality.

There is indeed a sense in which reminding ourselves that a fiction is a mere fiction can help to diminish its emotional impact. But reminding ourselves that a fiction is "only a fiction," in that sense, is not *simply* a matter of having a thought that the events it describes are fictional; it is a matter of putting the fiction into context with other, weightier matters. Suppose, by comparison, that I am immersed in a game of baseball: the Chicago Cubs are on the brink of a World Series victory. We can correctly characterize me as having thoughts involving an "in this baseball game" operator. I believe that, in this baseball game, the Cubs are only two outs away from winning; I believe that, in this baseball game, the Cubs are clinging to a one-run lead. These beliefs are partly responsible for my heightened affect. Should the Cubs end up blowing the lead and losing the series, I might try to console myself by meditating on the fact that it is "only a baseball game." I might, for instance, turn on the news, see evidence of real tragedy, and, putting the game in context, no longer feel so bad about the Cubs' latest misadventure. In one sense, I was always aware that the event was "only" a baseball game. The fact that it was a baseball game explains why I was interested in it in the first place; I *like* baseball. But, in another sense, I can remind myself that it is *only* a game—I can put the game in broader context—as a way of emotionally distancing myself from it.[11] This will involve more than simply judging that it is a game. It will involve actively comparing the significance of baseball games to other matters.

The same points apply to our appreciation of fictions. We generate beliefs about what is happening *in the fiction*, which combine with our desires about what is true in the fiction to generate affect. In the case of my watching Wallace being murdered in *The Wire*, my awareness that the fiction is indeed a fiction is essential to the emotions being bearable at all. As immersed as I was in *The Wire*, I had clearly in mind that it was only a fiction; this is why I was not *completely* horrified. (For a stark class of examples, consider dark comedy in the vein of *Dr. Strangelove*. Our awareness that the fiction is a fiction is obviously essential to explaining the resulting affect.) That said, if the affect becomes too intense or unpleasant during our engagement with a fiction, we may try to put it into broader context, comparing it to weightier matters, as a way of distancing ourselves from it, reminding ourselves that it is "only a fiction." Doing so will involve more than simply judging that such and such is a fiction (as though we had forgotten!). It will take an active attempt to compare the fiction's significance to other matters.

10.10 Does Immersion Involve an Imaginative "Spectrum"?

Susana Schellenberg makes a somewhat different appeal to *sui generis* imaginings in the explanation of immersion. She argues that when we become immersed in a pretense or fiction, it is because we are entering into mental states that are more belief-like than they are imagination-like (2013, pp. 508–11). For Schellenberg, these belief-like states do not involve 'in the fiction' operators; instead, they have the same content as the imaginings one has when not immersed in a fiction. As she sees it, we only become deeply immersed in a fiction when we move from imagining its content to doing something more like believing it:

> When a good actor plays a villain, she does not simply imagine that she is a villain. She immerses herself in her role. In doing so, she arguably adopts mental representations that are to some extent imagination-like and to some extent belief-like. (2013, p. 510)

[11] I owe this point to Maxwell Gatyas, who proposed it in conversation.

Schellenberg conceives of the situation in terms of a spectrum of cognitive boxes, with "pure" imagination on one end, pure belief on the other, and intermediate boxes between. "In nonimmersive cases of imagination," she explains, "propositions in the pure-imagination box are in play," whereas:

> In the case of imaginative immersion, propositions from the intermediate boxes are in play. Depending on how immersed one is, propositions from boxes closer to or farther from the pure-belief box are in play. (pp. 510–11)

So, according to Schellenberg—and in contrast to theorists such as Weinberg & Meskin (2006b) and Nichols (2006b)—"pure" imagination does not trigger emotion. However, there are many intermediate states between pure imagination and pure belief that do elicit related emotions. The difference between an adult who makes a lame show of pretending to be a lion and the child who gives full-throated performance is due to a difference in the types of mental states—almost-beliefs or pure imaginative states—underlying the acts. The existence of intermediate states also serves to explain the different *degrees* of emotional involvement one might have with a fiction or pretense: we become more emotionally involved the more we move from merely imagining a scenario to believing it is the case. On Schellenberg's view, these intermediate states will be *sui generis* semi-imaginings—cognitive states between pure imagination and pure belief. If we need intermediate cognitive states of this sort to explain immersion, we will have to give up on explaining A-imagining in more basic folk psychological terms. For not only does imagination remain *sui generis* on this view; there are a great many intermediate *sui generis* states besides.

However, the spectrum of emotional involvement and immersion that people experience when taking part in pretense and consuming fictions gives us no reason to think that ordinary beliefs and desires are not responsible at all times. The general phenomenon—being either more or less emotionally involved in a game or narrative—is common to contexts outside of pretense and fiction consumption and requires no special explanation. Consider a game of kickball. As with most sports, there is no *pretending* involved in playing kickball. It is just a game people play, with different levels of "immersion." Some people get *really into* kickball. Others, not so much. There is a psychological difference here. But it is not one that suggests that only one group is acting from beliefs about the game, while the other is simply imagining the game. The contrast between imagining and believing is not to the point. Those immersed in kickball, and those who couldn't care less, may indeed have more or less *the same* beliefs about the game. It is the nature and strength of their desires and interests with respect to kickball that makes for the difference. Similarly, Professor A and Professor B might experience quite different levels of immersion in the talk they are both attending, despite having much the same beliefs about what is being said. The reason is that the talk contradicts the published views of Professor A, while having nothing to do with Professor B's research program. Their different desires and interests explain their different levels of immersion.

The same points apply to games of pretense and our consumption of fictions. Some people really get into their pretense games and experience related emotions. Others are just going through the motions, perhaps at their children's behest. As with other kinds of games, it is a person's larger interests and motivations that will explain whether and to what degree they become immersed in the pretense (or fiction). Someone might become immersed in a pretense simply because they enjoy games of pretense, want to bring joy to their children, or (as in the case of professional actors) because they are being paid to do so. These explanations, which appeal to a person's more general interests and motivations, are the right *sort* of explanations for immersion within a pretense. Similarly, there are reasons that children will care more about the events in a fiction designed for children than adults; for the events—involving, say, an orphaned child forced to navigate the world alone—will speak more to the interests and desires of a child than an adult. There is no need to bring intermediate "boxes" into the picture.

10.11 Being Upset at the Fiction Itself, or Its Events?

An anonymous reviewer—the aptly-named "Reader Y"—raises an interesting objection. We can distinguish two ways of being upset by a fiction. The first is the ordinary way: something bad happens to a beloved character; we hold out hope that things will get better for him. The second is less common: we feel upset and betrayed by the fiction because something has happened that, aesthetically, is just *off*. We'd put our trust in the fiction—we'd invested hours of our lives in it—and now, either through bad judgment, or laziness, the writers have made the characters do something that is just, well, *out of character*; or they have inserted a hackneyed plot device where we thought none would occur. Again we are upset by the fiction, but it is different than the kind of upset we feel at a beloved character's unfortunate fate.

Granting the distinction in ways of being upset, it might seem that the latter cases are those where beliefs and desires about what happens *in the fiction* are especially relevant; they may seem more squarely directed at the fiction *qua* aesthetic product. This would suggest that ordinary cases of immersion—the ones I've taken as my explanandum—require some other treatment.

In response, we can make sense of the distinction here even if the negative emotions in each kind of case are triggered by beliefs and desires with 'in the fiction' operators. In each case, we have a desire that, in the fiction, *p*; and we are upset when we discover that, in the fiction, not-*p*. However, in the case where we are miffed by the narrative (or its writer's decisions), we also experience an erosion of trust in the narrative. *Not only* are we upset by what has happened in the fiction; we have now lost some of our faith that the authors of the fiction will meet aesthetic standards we thought were in place. This is disappointing and irksome in its own right, in proportion to how much time and energy we've already invested in the fiction. We wanted to continue investing in the fiction so as to enjoy its rewards; yet now we see that the desire to enjoy its rewards will never be satisfied. In addition to our trust being violated, something we found beautiful has been corrupted. We wanted the fiction to remain of high aesthetic quality and, now, it has not. In ordinary cases of immersion, where we are upset by fictional events, there are not these extra layers of discontent.

Compare the experience of tragedy (also discussed in fn. 6). There, too, we have desires that things go differently in the fiction; yet they are counter-balanced by stronger desires that the fiction remain as it is. Where the desires for the fiction to be different strongly outweigh our desires that the fiction remain as it is—where we really *do* want to rewrite the fiction—we start to lose faith in the fiction's value. We experience the added dimensions of resenting our prior attention to it, of being disappointed that future investment won't be worthwhile, and of being saddened that something beautiful has been dented or defiled.

10.12 Summary

It is a combination of our beliefs and desires about what is happening in a fiction that accounts for the emotions we experience in response to fictions. We need not bring a *sui generis* notion of imagination—or of i-desire—into the picture. It remains true, at a platitudinous level, that we imagine the events of the fictions we enjoy and that our doing so is in part responsible for our immersion in the fictions. However, there are ways of understanding what those A-imaginings consist in that are compatible with reducing them to a more basic collection of mental states—beliefs and desires, in particular.

These claims find support from the Operator Claim. Even if *sui generis* imaginative states and i-desires were deployed in fiction-appreciation, they, too, would need to feature 'in the fiction' operators. At that point, such states offer no explanatory benefit to explaining immersion that aren't also offered by beliefs and desires. Nor, as I argued in Chapter 9, need we posit *sui generis* imaginative states in order to explain how we recover implicit or explicit content from a fiction. If all this is correct, then beliefs and desires—and, at times, decisions—are sufficient to explain how we comprehend, cognitively develop, and emotionally respond to fiction.

There is, however, a last puzzle I still need to address. Even if you were convinced that beliefs and desires with 'in the fiction' operators were sufficient, in principle, to generate fiction-directed affect, you might still wonder where the desires come from. Why bother to have full-fledged desires about what is happening *in a fiction*? After all, it's only a fiction! The door seems to swing open again for imagination to provide an answer. It may seem that it is only in *vividly imagining* the events of a fiction that we come to have the desires that, in turn, pair with certain beliefs (or the imaginings themselves) to generate related affect.

It will require another chapter—the next—to untangle the many knots in this tempting line of thought.

11
Consuming Fictions Part III
Immersion, Emotion, and the Paradox of Fiction

11.1 Introduction

The previous two chapters argued that the best explanation of how we comprehend fictions, and of why we become immersed in them, will not appeal to *sui generis* imaginings. To summarize the positive picture I have so far proposed: recovering fictional content involves making a variety of different inferences, some of which require conditional reasoning, and none of which call for *sui generis* imaginings. Nor is there any obvious barrier to our immersion in fiction being explained by suitable pairs of beliefs and desires concerning the fictions themselves. The presence of 'in the fiction' operators within these beliefs and desires does not, I argued, put us at too great a cognitive distance from fictions to be immersed in them. Further, we've seen that such operators would in any case be required within *sui generis* imaginings, were they relied upon for fiction consumption instead.

There is still a missing piece, however. It can be summarized in the blunt question: why *care* about events you know to be fictional? To believe thus and such is true in a fiction is, after all, to believe that it is not *really* occurring. How could such beliefs be relevant to explaining our immersion in fictions? It might seem that these are precisely what must be "suspended" for us to become immersed in a fiction. A more intuitive picture, perhaps, is that we merely *imagine* the events of the fictions we enjoy. Then, it may seem, we are representing the events themselves and not dwelling on their fictionality—even if we still don't believe them to be occurring in reality.

Unsurprisingly, I lack sympathy for this picture. I sought to undermine it last chapter by arguing that 'in the fiction' operators would be required within *sui generis* imaginings as well. But I agree that more still needs to be said in defense of the positive proposal that beliefs and desires are the states responsible for our immersion in fiction. Facing up to the blunt question above—why *care* about events you believe to be fictional?—requires addressing a perennial puzzle in aesthetics: the (so-called) *paradox of fiction*. I will explain the paradox below and spend most of this chapter developing a novel response to it—one that supports my broader project of showing how the A-imagining that occurs during the consumption of fiction can be explained in more basic folk psychological terms. Before

Explaining Imagination. Peter Langland-Hassan, Oxford University Press (2020). © Peter Langland-Hassan.
DOI: 10.1093/oso/9780198815068.001.0001

turning directly to the paradox, however, I want to mount an independent argument against the competing view that *sui generis* imaginative states are involved in generating emotional responses to fiction—one that does not rely upon the arguments of last chapter. Its conclusion will serve to motivate the reductive account of A-imagining to come.

11.2 The Emotional Irrelevance of What We Merely Imagine

As earlier discussed, it is now widely agreed that *sui generis* imaginative states are involved in the generation of fiction-directed affect (Doggett & Egan, 2012; Gendler & Kovakovich, 2006; Kind, 2011; Meskin & Weinberg, 2003; Nichols, 2006b; Schellenberg, 2013; Schroeder & Matheson, 2006; Spaulding, 2015; Weinberg & Meskin, 2006b). The idea motivating these views is that imagining that *p* generates affective responses rather like believing that *p*. Friends of the view explain:

> According to the single-code hypothesis, then, the emotional systems will respond to pretense representations [viz., *sui generis* imaginings] much as they do to parallel beliefs. That is, if the pretense representation that *p* gets processed by an affective mechanism, the affective outputs should parallel those of the belief that *p*. (Nichols, 2004a, p. 131)

> There is no distinct anatomical region of the brain used for representing the merely imaginary... in spite of the fact that [fictional films] are all known simulacra, they are represented much as real things would be... once formed, these unimodal and multimodal representations have some of their characteristic effects including sending impulses to emotional centers.
> (Schroeder & Matheson, 2006, p. 28)

> When [in *Anna Karenina*] I read that some horrible misfortune has befallen Anna, that simulated belief [viz., *sui generis* imagining] can activate my affect systems just as it would if I had a real belief that an actual person has suffered such a misfortune. Thus my emotional response is appropriately robust.
> (Meskin & Weinberg, 2003, p. 24)

According to these views, if we imagine that lions are attacking the crowd at a circus, we will respond emotionally in much the same way we would if we believed lions were attacking the crowd at a circus. Some then offer cognitive-architectural explanations of this supposed mirroring. These theorists are not overly concerned with the fact that—by my lights, at least—our actual emotional responses to imagining are rarely *very* similar to what we would feel if we thought the imagined situation really obtained. I find that the emotions I experience in response to imagining that lions are attacking the crowd at a circus closely resemble those triggered by the realization that the dishwasher needs emptying, and not so much the shock I would experience at judging that lions are attacking a crowd. But neither am I sure how strong these theorists intend the parallel to be.

In any case, defenders of these views can modify and qualify their general claims to accommodate exceptions. Nichols (2006b, pp. 469–72) proposes that our emotional responses to what we imagine are often not as intense as what we experience in response to believing the same propositions simply because we do not develop the scenario as richly in imagination. For instance, when asked to consider our moral duties in a world where most of mankind has been wiped out by an asteroid, we do not, typically, draw out in imagination the devastating inferences concerning our loved ones that we would if we came to believe the premise. According to Nichols, this difference in how thoroughly the scenario is developed is itself grounded in our desires and interests, which may differ depending on whether a scenario is believed or imagined. He explains:

> I have strong and persistent desires for the health of my family, my friends, my colleagues. However, I often have no closely parallel desires about what happens in an imaginary scenario. Since what we desire affects recall and inference, this will have differential effects on what gets elaborated in the imagination. (2006, p. 471)

Differences in degree of "elaboration" between beliefs and imaginings, then, are called on to explain different degrees of emotional response.

I am not convinced by this response. For one, it isn't clear that we need to richly develop a scenario when reacting—strongly—to a newly believed proposition. Emotional shock can be immediate, as when we suddenly realize that we've neglected an important obligation. At the same time, we often take in (and, presumably, *imagine*) very elaborate fictions—such as alien-invasion films—without much emotional response at all. True, we may lack relevant desires in such cases; but, on Nichols's picture, desires are only relevant to explaining fiction-related affect insofar as they help to explain why our imaginings are richly developed, or not. (Otherwise, affect systems take input only from belief and imagination.) And, in the case of enjoying a fiction, we can assume the imaginings are richly developed simply as a function of our having to recover lots of fictional content. But there is another, broader problem with the idea that *sui generis* imaginings are the triggers for our immersion in a fiction.

The problem, roughtly stated, is this: we can choose what to imagine; but we cannot similarly choose the affect we experience in response to a fiction. And yet it seems we *should* be able to choose the affect we experience in response to fictions if that affect really is determined by our imaginings (and all else held equal).

More formally: If our affective responses to fictions are caused in part by what we are currently imagining (in the sense that certain imaginings are causally necessary form maintaining them), then we should be able to end such affective responses by stopping, or reversing, the relevant imaginings. But we cannot end such affective responses by stopping, or reversing, the relevant imaginings. Therefore, (by *modus tollens*) it's not the case that our affective responses to fictions are caused in part by what we are currently imagining (i.e., it is not the case that certain imaginings are causally necessary for maintaining our affective responses to fictions).[1]

An example: I am watching *Romeo and Juliet* and feel pity and shades of despair as the dual suicides unfold. To counteract these emotions, I should be able to imagine that Romeo and Juliet live happily ever after. For it is my imagining that they are committing suicide that, on the standard account, is essential to my experiencing negative affect.[2] Try as I might, though, I am unable to remove the pit in my stomach simply by imagining that Romeo and Juliet survive and live happily ever after. For I still believe that they die in the fiction! This belief easily overrides anything I might try to imagine.[3]

Examples are easily multiplied. We are engrossed in a heartwarming romantic comedy. Everything works out in the end and we are heart-warmed. But now, as the credits roll, we choose to imagine that the happy ending is upended—that the romantic relationship at the center of the narrative is permanently undermined by further (entirely avoidable!) misunderstandings.There is no difficulty in imagining such a thing. Yet it won't undermine our warm glow. By contrast, suppose that the film really contained the less satisfying ending in three additional minutes tacked on to the end. In that case, our emotional response really would be undermined. The reason is not that, in the second case, we are imagining that the relationship comes to a dismal end. We did that before, on our own, after the credits rolled. The reason is that we now *believe* that, in the fiction, the relationship flops.

It does not matter that when, of our own accord, we imagine the relationship ending, such an imagining would not be appropriate to the fiction, or that it is not what the fiction prescribes us to imagine. The fiction can *prescribe* whatever it

[1] Thanks to Shen-Yi Liao for spurring me to be more careful about the statement of this argument.

[2] Strictly speaking, this imagining should involve an 'in the fiction' operator, in line with last chapter's argument. I leave it off here, however, so as not to rely unnecessarily on that argument.

[3] One might object that, if I am right that "imagining that *p*, in response to fiction *F*" is just a matter of judging that, in the fiction *F*, *p*, then I *can't* imagine things that don't cohere with what I think is true in the fiction. The response here is that, when we imagine a fiction going in ways we believe it not to be going, this is not imagining "in response to fiction *F*" in the relevant sense. When I say that imagining that *p*, in response to fiction *F*, amounts to judging that, in *F*, *p*, this is offered as an account of the imagings used to recover fictional content—the imaginings that authors intend for readers to undertake in response to their fictions. This leaves open the possibility of other imaginings that conflict with what we judge to be true in the fiction. For instance, I might, while viewing *Romeo and Juliet*, judge that it would be a happier ending if they both survived and raised a family together. On my view, this would be an A-imagining that Romeo and Juliet survive and live happily ever after. It is clear, on my view, why such an imagining does not change the emotions I feel: what matters (and what is beyond my control) is what I judge to be happening in the actual *Romeo and Juliet*, not what I judge to be a happier ending.

wishes; it doesn't thereby force our hand. What we imagine is still up to us. Perhaps, one might suggest, engaging with a fiction poses a special barrier on our imaginative capabilities, or makes us extremely unwilling to imagine things that conflict with the imaginings prescribed by the fiction. Could it be that we experience a kind of *imaginative resistance* to imagining propositions that conflict with what a fiction asks us to imagine?

I don't think so. It does not *seem* difficult, while enjoying a play or a film, to imagine that things are going otherwise than as the fiction suggests. We don't get the classic feeling of blockage characteristic of other cases of imaginative resistance—as explored, e.g., by Gendler (2000). Moreover, the most common explanations of imaginative experience don't fit the case: we are not imagining an impossible proposition, or a violation of supervenience relations (Weatherson, 2005); we are not imagining propositions we find morally problematic (Gendler, 2000). To simply infer from our lack of emotional change during the imaginings that we in fact fail to bring about the contrary-to-fiction imaginings is question-begging.

Another response might be that, once we have imagined something and it has triggered a certain emotional response in us, it is too late to "turn around" the emotion with a subsequent contrary imagining.[4] This could be so even if the initial imagining was in some sense "up to us." By analogy: if I buy a lottery ticket and then win the lottery—the number choice having been "up to me"—I cannot undo the win by choosing to buy yet another ticket with a different number. Why, then, should I be able to undo an imagination-triggered emotion by generating new imaginings? However, the analogy is faulty. What's at issue is not whether we can change the fact that some past event occurred—be it a lottery win or the fact that an emotion was triggered. Of course we cannot. The question is what sort of causal intervention will be of the right sort to end an ongoing phenomenon. We know, for instance, that when anxiety is triggered at the recognition that the protagonist of a fiction is in serious danger, it will be relieved if we see that the protagonist is prevailing after all. Imaginings are supposed to have the power to effect that kind of reversal. And yet, from our examples, it seems clear that they do not.

We could consider other ways of preserving the idea that *sui generis* imaginings directly, or indirectly, generate fiction-related affect. But why do so when we have a promising alternative close at hand? What matters to my emotional state when enjoying a fiction is not what I am imagining, which can depart from anything the fiction prescribes, but what I am *judging* to be true in the fiction, combined with what I *desire* of the fiction. This offers a natural explanation for why I cannot adjust my emotional responses to fictions willy-nilly. For I can no more choose the judgments I make about what is true in a fiction than I can choose my judgments generally; *mutatis mutandis* for my desires about a fiction. It is my

[4] Thanks to Shen-Yi Liao for suggesting this worry.

beliefs (*qua* judgments) about what is true in the fiction that combine, in an unremarkable manner, with my desires about what is true in the fiction to generate fiction-related affect.

To bolster the plausibility of this answer, however, we need to understand why it is that we would ever have strong desires about what happens in a fiction, given that we never in fact enter into *sui generis* imaginative states when enjoying one. Answering requires that we confront and resolve the paradox of fiction. That is the project I turn to now. It will occupy me to the end of this chapter.

11.3 The Paradox of Fiction

The "paradox" of fiction concerns our emotional responses to fictions. That much, everyone agrees. Thereafter, things get murky. Some see the paradox as a puzzle about how (and if) our emotional responses to fiction can be *rational* or *warranted*. Others view it as a puzzle about how (and if) genuine emotional responses to fiction are *possible*.[5] Derek Matravers' formulation of the puzzle captures this ambiguity well:

> The problem is not primarily the fact that Anna [of *Anna Karenina*] does not exist but that...our regret that Anna was scorned *makes no sense* given that we believe that nobody was scorned. (Matravers, 2014, p. 112, emphasis added)

Does our regret make no sense as a matter of metaphysics—because one's regretting that p implies, necessarily, that one believes that p? Or does it make no sense as a normative matter, in the way it "makes no sense" to go fishing in the bathtub? These distinct questions can easily be confused or considered equivalent. My focus here will be on the *normative* question. When we are puzzled about why we would ever have strong desires about what happens in a fiction—and resulting emotions when the desires are satisfied or frustrated—our puzzlement concerns how it could be at all reasonable or appropriate to *care* about events we know to be fictional. Nevertheless, we will see that the two questions—normative and metaphysical—interact in complex ways. Putting the normative question to rest requires careful consideration of the metaphysical one as well. Theorists have invoked *sui generis* imaginings in their answers to both questions; in neither case, I will argue, is it helpful to do so.

The "paradox" is often expressed as an inconsistent triad, each claim of which has independent plausibility (Cova & Teroni, 2016; Currie, 1990, p. 187; Friend, 2016;

[5] Friend (2016) finds the same two questions at work in discussions of the paradox of fiction—labelling them the "descriptive" and "normative" puzzles, respectively.

Gendler & Kovakovich, 2006; Kim, 2010; Nichols, 2004a; Van Leeuwen, 2016). I will examine the triadic formulation shortly. For now, the heart of the paradox can be seen in the following contrast. Typically, the reasonableness of an emotional response to a situation depends on our believing the situation to obtain. We are alarmed when we hear shattering glass in the night, fearing that someone is breaking in; our fear dissipates when we realize that the cat has simply knocked a cookie jar off the counter. It would be unreasonable to continue fearing thieves, once we are convinced there are none present. Simply knowing that thieves are not, in fact, breaking in is sufficient to quell our fears.

Not so in our engagement with films, novels, and plays. Knowing that fictional characters and situations do not exist does little to undermine the emotions we feel toward them. To address the paradox of fiction, we need to come to terms with this discrepancy. Why are *some* of our emotions tightly constrained by beliefs about the reality of their objects, while others, apparently, are not? And what does this discrepancy tell us about the nature and rationality of our emotional responses to fiction?

Before answering, two prefatory remarks. Not everyone will find it proper to speak of the *rationality* of an emotion; it is, however, common to hold that emotions are accountable to standards of appropriateness, fittingness, or aptness of some kind. *Ceteris paribus*, it is proper to fear what poses a danger, improper to resent what caused you no insult, warranted to pity undeserved suffering, unwarranted to feel gratitude to those who betrayed you, and so on. In querying the appropriateness or fittingness of our fiction-elicited emotions, we are asking whether such emotions are appropriate, given that we do not believe in the existence of the characters and situations at which they appear directed. Adopting distinctions from D'Arms & Jacobson (2000), we can further specify that the puzzle concerns the *epistemic* rationality of our emotional responses to fictions, as opposed to their prudential or moral rationality. We want to know whether the emotions we direct at fictions are warranted in the situations in which they arise, irrespective of any idiosyncratic practical goals or moral views we may have.

A further distinction to note is that between an emotion's being *warranted* given one's epistemic situation and its being *apt* (or *fitting*) given the nature of its object. Compare: it is common to speak of a belief's being warranted whenever a person has good reasons for holding it. One's evidence might make one warranted in believing that *p*, even if *p* is false. In another sense, however, the belief that *p* is infelicitous when *p* is false; it is not "apt" or "fit," given the way things really are. Similarly, we might say that an emotion is warranted given one's epistemic situation, even if it is inapt, or unfitting, because the object of the emotion lacks any feature to which the emotion is an appropriate response. For instance, feelings of resentment toward a friend might be warranted by the mere fact that you have reason to think the friend has betrayed your trust. But, if the friend did not, in fact, betray your trust, then the resentment remains inapt and unfitting of its object. I will use the term "warrant" to capture the purely epistemic sense of appropriateness and the terms "fittingness" and "aptness" to capture the stronger sense of appropriateness that can apply to emotions, where the latter notions demand the object of the emotion to in fact have some feature that renders the emotion fitting or "correct."

11.4 Some Background on the Paradox

Radford (1975) sparked the modern literature on the paradox of fiction, concluding that our emotional responses to fictions are indeed irrational—or, in the terms above, both unwarranted and unfitting. Most others have sought to rationalize our responses to fiction in one way or another, revealing them to have a kind of epistemic warrant after all. In an early and influential answer to the paradox, Peter Lamarque (1981) proposed that we can respond emotionally to the mere "thought that *p*" without believing that *p*—and that this happens in many contexts outside of our engagements with fiction. More recent variations on this approach have emphasized the broader benefits of being cognitively "wired" in a way that allows for us to respond emotionally to non-actual situations (Gendler & Kovakovich, 2006; Van Leeuwen, 2016; Robinson, 2005; Weinberg & Meskin, 2006b; Nichols, 2004b). Related views hold that such responses are valuable precognitive reflexes of a kind (Carroll, 2003, p. 524; Matravers, 2014, p. 117). In each case, our emotional responses to fictions gain a kind of vindication through their participation in a general pattern of response that has benefits to our survival. On many of these views (excepting Matravers (2014)), our *imaginings* are responsible for the related emotions, not our beliefs about the fiction. It is the tendency of *sui generis* imaginative states to evoke emotions similar to those generated by beliefs with matching contents that is supposed to explain—or explain away—the apparent inappropriateness of responding emotionally to a fiction.

I will argue, to the contrary, that what rationalize—or fail to rationalize—our affective responses to fictions are features of the fictions themselves, in accordance with a set of norms specific to the appreciation of fiction. Evolutionary considerations are irrelevant, as are claims about *sui generis* imaginings and cognitive wiring. Others before me have also appealed to the importance of fiction-specific norms when theorizing about our emotional responses to fiction (Livingston & Mele, 1997; Currie, 1990, pp. 213–15; Friend, 2016). I will appropriate aspects of Livingston & Mele's (1997) and Gilmore's (2011) helpful discussions. However, the relevance of fiction-specific emotional norms to resolving the paradox of fiction has never, in my view, been properly articulated; nor have such norms been used, as I will use them, to show how irrelevant imagination is to the questions at the heart of the paradox. Currie (1990, pp. 213–15), for instance, makes note of the special norms relevant to fiction-appreciation while still maintaining that *sui generis* imaginings are nevertheless central to the paradox's resolution. More recently, Friend (2016, p. 226) observes that simply noting a difference in norms relevant to fiction consumption "does not resolve the problem" at the heart of the paradox and can look like "an *ad hoc* maneuver to avoid Radford's conclusion." At a minimum, we need some further explanation for why it is appropriate that the norms relevant to fiction-appreciation differ from those in place outside of fiction. My project here is to provide that further explanation, while dispelling the appearance that *sui generis* imaginings must play some role in it.

Carrying out this project requires first untangling the metaphysical and normative dimensions of the paradox (section 11.5). This will allow us to better appreciate what would, and what would not, undermine the reasonableness of our emotional responses to fictions. In the end, there is not a deep discrepancy between our everyday emotions and the emotions we direct at fictions. Both can be supported by reasons; and both can be shown unwarranted, and unfitting, when our reasons are overturned.

11.5 Distinguishing the Metaphysical and Normative Puzzles

We can begin at the first pages of Radford's (1975) article that sparked this debate. Radford asks us to consider how we would feel in two conditions: first, after reading an account of terrible suffering; and, second, after learning that the account is a fiction:

> Suppose then that you read an account of the terrible sufferings of a group of people. If you are at all humane, you are unlikely to be unmoved by what you read. The account is likely to awaken or reawaken feelings of anger, horror, dismay, or outrage and, if you are tender-hearted, you may well be moved to tears. You may even grieve.
>
> But now suppose you discover that the account is false. If the account had caused you to grieve, you could not continue to grieve. If as the account sank in, you were told and believed that it was false this would make tears impossible, unless they were tears of rage. If you learned later that the account was false, you would feel that in being moved to tears you had been fooled, duped. (1975, p. 68)

This thought experiment exploits what I will call a "rug-pull" structure: first, a person has an emotional response to a situation; and, second, revision of one of the person's beliefs pulls the rug out from under that response. The rug is pulled out in two senses: first, the emotional response itself dissipates; second, the response would no longer be warranted were it to continue, given one's newly revised beliefs. In Radford's example, we are asked to suppose that we've read (what we take to be) a genuine account of people who have suffered greatly. We are upset by the account.

Then we are told that it is only a fiction. At that point we are no longer saddened by the story. We are angry at being "fooled, duped." Sadness is unwarranted now that we know the events didn't actually occur. Learning that the events didn't occur pulls the rug out from the sadness itself, both bringing it to an end (at least typically) and rendering it unwarranted were it to continue.

Other rug-pull cases are easy to find. Above I gave the case of hearing glass shattering at night and fearing thieves. As soon as we conclude that thieves are not, in fact, breaking in, the rug is pulled out from under our fear in the two senses described: we are, in all likelihood, no longer afraid of thieves; and, should our fear continue, it is no longer warranted. Reflection on such cases makes it tempting to extract a general moral about emotions: reasonably maintaining an emotion concerning a situation requires us to believe the situation to have features that would make our response fitting or apt. The principle gains credence as a kind of inference to best explanation for the changes that occur in rug-pull cases. (Here I am in agreement with Cova & Teroni (2016).) Its truth would explain why our emotions dissipate when we make the relevant discoveries. This general principle indeed forms one of three claims in the inconsistent triad mentioned earlier, which many see as capturing the core puzzle generated by our emotional responses to fictions. Here is how Gregory Currie presents the triad:[6]

(1) We have emotions concerning the situations of fictional characters.

(2) To have an emotion concerning someone's situation we must believe the propositions that describe that situation.

(3) We do not believe the propositions that describe the situations of fictional characters. (Currie, 1990, p. 187)

The most common response to the inconsistent triad is to reject condition (2)—the condition that links emotions to beliefs in the reality of the objects of the emotions (though Walton (1990) famously rejects (1); and I will reject (3).)[7]

There is less consensus on *why* (2) should be rejected. This is where it becomes crucial to distinguish the metaphysical and normative versions of the paradox. To dispel the attraction of (2), one needs to be clear about which of its interpretations is in question: is the "must" in (2) the must of rational warrant, or of metaphysical necessity? As each reading has some plausibility,[8] both need to be

[6] Not everyone structures the triad in exactly this way, though Currie's formulation is frequently cited (e.g., by Matravers (2014, p. 105) and Nichols (2004a, p. 133)). It is also substantially the same as Gendler & Kovakovich's (2006, p. 241).

[7] In rejecting (3), I do not hold that we believe the explicit or implicit content of fictions. Rather, I hold that we believe the propositions that describe the situations of fictional characters (just as (3) denies). These are propositions such as: in *The Great Gatsby*, Carraway is Gatsby's neighbor; and, in *The Big Lewbowski*, The Dude drinks White Russians.

[8] I disagree with Matravers' view that "it is difficult to see that *C* [which is (2) in its metaphysical guise] has *any* intuitive appeal" (2014, p. 104, emphasis in original). Certain emotions fit the mold

addressed if one is to put the puzzle to rest. A few words about the metaphysical reading first.

If one comes to the table with a theory of the emotions on which central emotions such as fear, pity, and the like require an evaluative belief about the object of the emotions, then the metaphysical reading will of course seem correct. If, for instance, the emotion of pity contains, as a proper part, a belief that someone is suffering undeservedly, then there can be no pity without an attending belief in the object of the emotion. An attractive response to the resulting puzzle will then be to hold that the emotional states we experience when encountering fictions are similar to, but not strictly the same as, genuine emotions such as fear and pity. The responses may, instead, be "quasi-emotions" (Walton, 1990). It is no objection to this view to hold that our emotional reactions to fictions are too strong or phenomenologically rich to be "mere" quasi-emotions. Walton, the most prominent defender of the quasi-emotion view, allows that quasi-emotions can be both phenomenologically rich and physiologically acute. As he remarks with respect to the (imagined) theater-goer Charles, who appears frightened by the slime depicted in a horror film he is watching: "our question is whether [Charles's] experience, however intense, was one of fear of the slime." Walton clearly accepts that Charles has "a genuinely emotional experience," while insisting that "it was not fear of the slime" (1990, p. 197).

Waltonian quasi-emotions differ with genuine emotions in their associated behavioral dispositions. Part of what it is to fear something, for Walton, is to be disposed to flee from it. "Fear emasculated by subtracting its distinctive motivational force," he writes, "is not fear at all" (p. 202). Charles is not disposed to flee the slime by running out of the theater; so, however agitated he may be, what he is experiencing is not *precisely* fear of the slime—it is something else, something fear-like. To refute this view, by showing ordinary emotions like fear and pity to be wholly independent of such dispositions, one needs to mount arguments for a number of unobvious claims, such as that the behavioral dispositions that follow from believing that *p* are not essential to one's fearing that *p*, worrying that *p*, being happy that *p*, and so on. Simply pointing out the obvious—that we get really worked up about fictions and other imagined events—does not substantively engage the theorist who takes the metaphysical reading of (2) to record an important feature of "everyday" emotions. This is why the inference from Charles's agitated state when watching the slime to the conclusion that emotions are wholly independent of belief is "distressingly question-begging" (Walton, 1990, p. 200).

As it turns out, I will be one more who does not substantively engage the question of whether, for some emotions, (2) is correct in its metaphysical reading. Doing so would require me to defend a general theory of emotions, which is well

quite well. Regretting that *p*, or feeling ashamed that *p*, for instance, intuitively requires belief that *p*. At worst, the metaphysical version of (2) may be seen as an unwarranted overgeneralization from a few strong cases in its support.

beyond the scope of this chapter and indeed this book. But, in any case, I am not sure that Walton is wrong. Emotions are not *merely* beliefs and desires; but at least some emotions might well be complex states with beliefs and desires as essential *components* (Gordon, 1987). Such a view is a natural fit with the idea that our words for emotions gain a foothold in public discourse through their roles in folk psychological explanations—explanations that predict and explain behavior by ascribing beliefs and desires.

My interest remains in (2) considered as a *normative* principle. Yet, to ask if emotions can *reasonably* occur in the absence of relevant existence beliefs presupposes that they could *possibly* occur in the absence of such beliefs. Thus, simply moving on to ask the normative question, while leaving the metaphysical one unresolved, is risky on two counts. First, for those who think the metaphysical reading of (2) is correct, it may seem to leave the paradox of fiction unresolved; second, our answer to the normative question is left vulnerable to refutation by a theory of emotions that discovers deep connections between genuine emotions and beliefs about the objects of those emotions.

Fortunately, there is a way to table the metaphysical dispute to focus on the normative one, without begging any questions. For all sides agree that we have intense emotional reactions *of some sort* to fictions—raised heart-rates, sweaty palms, worry-like states, happiness-like states, anxiety-like states, and so on. We can then query together whether those responses to fiction are warranted and fitting, whether or not we agree that they are the very same *kind* of emotional states we experience outside of our engagement with fictions. Why, we can ask, should it be warranted and fitting to have intense worry-like, pity-like, and happiness-like states about fictional situations we *know never happened*?[9] After all, in the rug-pull cases that motivate (2), we don't normally retain worry-like, pity-like, or happiness-like states after learning that the objects of those states don't exist. (And, in the exceptional cases where we do, our doing so does not appear warranted.) So there remains a contrast in need of explanation, regardless of one's view on whether emotions require corresponding existence beliefs. In everyday rug-pull examples, judging that not-p tends to diminish, and render unwarranted, emotion-like states previously directed at the fact that p; not so in the case of our

[9] Walton thinks that once we conclude that Charles does not strictly *fear* the slime—because he is not disposed to flee it—there is no longer a need to rationalize any of his quasi-emotional responses. "One doesn't have reasons for things one doesn't *do*, like sweating, increasing one's pulse rate, involuntarily knotting one's stomach," he writes. "So there is no need to attribute beliefs (or desires) to Charles that will render these responses reasonable" (1990, p. 199). The plausibility of this respone hangs on describing Charles in purely physiological—and non-psychological—terms. Note that Charles has plenty of psychological reactions to the slime, whether or not we know how to describe them; and the warrant for these is certainly in question. Compare the case where one fears thieves breaking in, only to discover the cat having broken a cookie jar. If one remains agitated after learning that thieves are not breaking in, the agitation can no longer, on Walton's view, be called fear. Yet we can still query whether it is reasonable to remain emotionally agitated in one's new epistemic state.

engagement with fictions. Why, we can ask, is there this discrepancy? This is, I think, the key question behind the normative puzzle, and indeed behind the paradox of fiction.

The *other* puzzle still in play—which we leave unresolved—is a straightforward question about the nature of emotions. It is a question about which of the cognitive, sensory, and affective states that run together with an emotion in everyday contexts are essential to it. Our responses to fictions present dissociations among those features—e.g., we have the heart palpitations and anxiety of fear, without the tendency to run away. Fictions are, for that reason, enlightening test cases for a theory of emotions. But they are not the only such cases; similar dissociations and borderline cases can be found in the emotion-like states we experience when fantasizing, reasoning hypothetically, or reminiscing. So, to the extent that there is a non-normative puzzle afoot in the paradox of fiction—one we ignore by focusing on the normative question—it is simply the puzzle that borderline cases present for a theory of emotions. Having identified that puzzle for what it is, we can safely set it aside. Yes, something has been left unanswered, but it is nothing peculiar to our experience of fiction; nor will answering it alter our response to the normative puzzle. If our final theory of emotions tells us that the states we experience in response to fictions are not genuine emotions, we are still left with the normative question of why it is appropriate to have such strong emotion-like responses to fictions (when we generally don't in rug-pull cases). If, on the other hand, our final theory says that genuine emotions do not require beliefs in the reality of their objects, then we have rejected (2) as a metaphysical constraint on genuine emotions. But, in that case, we still have the normative puzzle before us: why are such emotions *warranted* (if they are), given what we know? In sum, no matter the formal theory of emotions we adopt, the normative puzzle needs answering independently.

11.6 Solving the Normative Puzzle: False Starts

Back, then, to our central question: the normative puzzle. To answer that puzzle, it obviously is not enough to point out that we *can* experience emotions (or emotion-like states) in response to fictions. This has been a recurring criticism of Lamarque's (1981) early solution. Lamarque famously rejects (2) on the grounds that: "I can be frightened by a thought or thought-cluster at a time when I am in no actual danger and do not believe myself to be in danger…I might find the thought of being stranded on a distant planet or being a monarch deposed in a military coup frightening *without supposing that this will, or even could, happen to me*" (p. 295, emphasis added). These claims are question-begging if offered as reasons for rejecting (2) as a metaphysical constraint, for the Waltonian reasons discussed above. Lamarque may only have intended them to undermine (2) in its normative guise, however. Even so, the argument still appears question-begging. Given

Lamarque's station in life—as a philosophy professor in a stable socio-political environment—it isn't at all obvious that his fear at the thought of being a monarch deposed in a military coup is reasonable. Certainly, there is nothing *prima facie* reasonable about fearing situations you think could not possibly befall you. If we were puzzled about how our emotional reactions to fictions could be warranted, reflection on Lamarque's cases will not leave us any less perplexed. This was, in effect, Radford's (1982) response: "Lamarque says...that I am frightened by my thoughts. But *they cannot hurt me*, and I know that of course...So the fear is irrational, absurd, incoherent, even though it is common place" (p. 262, emphasis in original).

On the other hand, it does seem reasonable—and not at all puzzling—to fear, or respond emotionally to, situations you think *might* befall you, even if you know they are not now the case. Gendler & Kovakovich (2006) pursue this thought as a means to overturning (2) as a general constraint on the rationality of an emotional response. Results in neuropsychology, they argue, support the claim that "without the tendency to feel something relevantly akin to real emotions in the case of merely imagined situations, we would be unable to engage in practical reasoning" (2006, p. 242). In support they cite work by Antonio Damasio and colleagues (Damasio, 1999; Damasio, Everitt, & Bishop, 1996) showing correlations between emotional deficits (in people with damage to prefrontal cortex) and impairments in practical reasoning. Damasio's findings suggest that our tendency to react emotionally when considering different possibilities is an integral part of our ability to plan our actions effectively. This has become known as the *somatic marker hypothesis*. Given these "facts about our cognitive architecture," Gendler & Kovakovich propose, "it *is* reasonable to employ the expression 'genuine, rational emotion' in describing both actual and fictional emotions" (2006, p. 243). ("Fictional emotions," for Gendler & Kovakovich, are emotions directed at fictions.) For "it is crucial to our ability to make rational decisions about various courses of action that we respond with genuine emotions to situations that we know to be non-actual" (p. 243). This point allows them to reject (2) in its normative guise.[10]

Yet, by tethering the reasonableness of our emotional responses to their usefulness in practical reasoning, they open the door to a reformulation of the inconsistent triad. Unlike the possibilities we consider during action-planning, fictions do not normally present us with different possible courses of action from among which we must choose. That is precisely why it seems odd to respond emotionally to them. Thus, such responses may still be an unwarranted (and impractical) over-extension of a tendency useful in action-planning to a context where it is

[10] It is worth noting that Gendler & Kovakovich's argument does nothing to undermine (2) as a metaphysical constraint, as all the data they discuss is consistent with Waltonian quasi-emotions being activated during hypothetical reasoning, in lieu of genuine emotions.

inappropriate, inapt, and even hazardous. In light of this, the defender of the paradox can simply reformulate condition (2) as:

(2′): To have an emotion concerning someone's situation we must (in the normative sense of 'must') believe the propositions that describe that situation, or believe the situation is of relevance to our future decision-making.

(2′) is no less plausible than (2) itself; it is, in effect, an elaboration of (2). After all, no one ever questioned the rationality of worrying that you'll get a ticket if you fail to pay the parking meter; here you were thinking about an unrealized possibility—getting a ticket—and feeling some anxiety. Yet (2′) remains inconsistent with our emotional reactions to fictions. Nor do Damasio's findings give us any reason to reject (2′) as a general constraint on the epistemic (or prudential) rationality of our emotional responses. (See Matravers (2006, pp. 260–2) for related criticisms.)

Perhaps what Gendler & Kovakovich really want to highlight in their appeal to the somatic marker hypothesis is that, due to our cognitive wiring, *we just can't avoid* responding emotionally to fictions and the imaginings they inspire. Further, they might continue, given that our being wired in that way is essential to our healthy functioning outside of our engagement with fictions, we are hardly to be faulted for our emotional responses to fictions. This is clearly Van Leeuwen's (2016) position; and it appears consonant with that of Meskin & Weinberg (2003) and Schroeder & Matheson (2006) as well. Van Leeuwen proposes that our responses to fictions are a natural byproduct of the fact that mental imagery "automatically" triggers affect, and that we typically form mental imagery when consuming fictions. He offers empirical evidence that imagery is processed in perceptual areas of the brain that have especially close ties to neural areas underlying affective responses. In virtue of this shared neural pathway, imagistic and perceptual states are able to automatically trigger affect, which, he argues, facilitates bodily preparedness for action, supports the evaluation of future actions (in the manner of Gendler & Kovakovich), and enables empathy-based moral appraisal (Van Leeuwen, 2016, pp. 95–101). Were we to somehow bring an end to our automatic affective responses to fictions, Van Leeuwen warns, "it would involve destroying something on which three important agential capacities depend" (p. 105). Thus, "anyone who scorns the human propensity to respond emotionally to fictions has just not understood the consequences of doing away with that propensity."

Similar points are made by a number of other theorists who see our responses to fictions as *affective reflexes*. By "manipulating such variables as speed, scale, lighting, and sound," Noël Carroll proposes, "the filmmaker often appears to have direct access to our nervous system, bypassing the cerebral cortex and triggering automatic affective reflexes" (Carroll, 2003, p. 524). Matravers agrees with this way of analyzing Charles's (apparent) fear of the green slime in Walton's example: "What Charles describes as 'being terrified' simply could be a vivid way of expressing the fact that he was shocked (an a-rational response therefore requiring no explanation in terms of objects) by a 'fast movement towards the camera.'" Charles is "involuntarily startled by a sudden and surprising turn of events on the screen" (Matravers, 2014, p. 117). Jenefer Robinson concurs, defending a general theory of emotions as "pre-cognitive" appraisals:

> Pre-cognitive affective appraisals do not discriminate between real and imagined scenarios...It does not matter to my emotion system (fear, anger, sadness, etc.) whether I am responding to the real, the merely imagined, the possible, or the impossible... (2005, pp. 145, 149)

Like Van Leeuwen and Gendler & Kovakovich, Robinson wants to vindicate such responses by appeal to their fitting a pattern that is advantageous to our survival. In reading *Anna Karenina*, she explains:

> It is adaptive to be able to sense one's wants and wishes, interests and goals to be at stake when reading and thinking about Anna Karenina...When I respond compassionately to Anna, I am sympathizing with her fate in a way that is socially adaptive. (2005, p. 148)

These responses to the paradox all miss the mark, in my view. Whether Gendler & Kovakovich and Van Leeuwen are correct in their interpretations of the empirical literature, or not, and whether Robinson is right that such responses are in some sense "adaptive," or not, these putative rationalizations *concede too much*. They offer sub-personal excuses for emotions that need no apology. Suppose—just as a thought experiment—that each of these theorists is wrong in his or her empirical claims. Suppose that Damasio's research assistant misread the data and that there is in fact no significant difference in the practical reasoning abilities of emotionally-impaired patients and controls. Suppose also that Van Leeuwen has misinterpreted the empirical evidence and that mental imagery has no special tendency to automatically trigger affective centers of the brain. And let us imagine that Robinson is simply wrong that it's "socially adaptive" to respond emotionally to non-existent entities; it turns out that doing so keeps us home Saturday nights watching movies, instead of out meeting new folks. Would we then be forced to conclude that our emotional responses to fictions are unreasonable and unwarranted after all?

Certainly not. What matters for their warrant is whether there are *good reasons* for our emotional responses to fictions. Whether one has good reasons, I will argue, is not a matter of one's neural wiring or evolutionary history.[11] The relevant

[11] To be clear, I don't deny that we *can* have reflex-like affective responses to fictions—a startle-response to an unexpected explosion, say. But this is, in general, the wrong way to think about our

factors—factors that can render a triggered emotion fitting or apt—are closer to the surface. The next section develops this point through meditation on the norms specific to fiction-appreciation. An important upshot will be that it is not (2) in the triad that needs rejecting. Whether or not (2) *is* correct, our emotional reactions to fictions give us no special reason to reject it. It can be granted that an emotion is unwarranted when we do not believe that its object has features that make it apt; for emotions we experience in response to fictions take as objects the fictions themselves. Such fictions exist and, typically, have features that render the responses apt (or so I will argue). We can instead reject (3), the proposition that we do not believe the propositions that describe the situations of fictional characters. For the propositions that describe the situations of fictional characters, it turns out, involve 'in the fiction' operators. In the process, further reasons will emerge for rejecting the approach taken by Gendler & Kovakovich, Van Leeuwen, Robinson, and "single code" theorists such as Meskin & Weinberg (2003) and Nichols (2004b).

11.7 Believing It Is a Fiction and the Norms of Immersion

What could be a good reason for responding as we do to characters and events we believe to be fictional? Ironically, the *first* reason one ought to give for such responses is that we believe the characters and situations to be fictional. We take a wrong step when we immediately go on the defensive, granting that our emotional reactions to fictions lack the kind of basis we would expect of an ideally warranted emotional response—conceding that they are, like reflexes or controlled hallucinations, in conflict with our beliefs about reality. Instead we should reply that our belief in the *unreality* of fictional characters and situations is part of what warrants the specific emotional reactions we have, and indeed coheres perfectly with them.

After all, taking in the latest alien-invasion film with only mild anxiety would be *insane* if we thought the film depicted actual events. Being amused during *The Big Lebowski* as "nihilists" urinate on The Dude's rug and dunk his head in the toilet would be cruel if we didn't take *The Big Lebowski* for fiction. Our disbelief in the reality of what we are reading or witnessing is an essential part of what renders the resulting emotions appropriate—not something that stands in the way of understanding them.

emotional reactions to fictions—even to glossy, megaplex, surround-sound movies, whose *modus operandi* is to shock the senses. Films that trade in razzle-dazzle can be as *boring* as any others. Whether we leap out of our seats when a character bursts out of a closet has little to do with the sound of the closet door swinging open or the shape of the knife being raised, and everything to do with whether the preceding story has engaged us. Reflexes don't care about that history, but people do.

Second, it is precisely because of this disbelief that there is no *mistake* underlying our emotional responses to fictions. When someone tells us what we already knew—that the fiction is indeed a mere fiction—no grounds have been removed for our reaction, no premise defeated. This marks the crucial difference with the rug-pull cases described above, where we do take the reality of the scenario to be a reason for our emotional reactions. In those cases, we have been caught in a mistake; a central reason for our reaction has been removed and the rug pulled out from under our response. By contrast, when we give the unreality of a fictional scenario as one of our reasons for reacting to a fiction as we do, our reasons cannot be undermined by pointing to that very feature.

This is not to say that there is no way of undermining our fiction-directed responses, however. This is a third important point. Indeed, were there no such way, this would itself suggest that the responses were not founded on or caused by any relevant beliefs—that they were reflexes of a kind. If, instead, we can find beliefs that, if revised, would render our responses to a fiction unwarranted (were they to continue), we have reason not to view those responses as automatic reflexes. To that end, suppose that, unwittingly, we are watching live news footage of an attack by extra-terrestrials, wrongly taking it to be a mere "mockumentary" in the style of *War of the Worlds*. We are experiencing mild anxiety, mixed with a bit of amusement, as we might be when watching an ordinary alien invasion film. If someone bursts into the room with the news that what we're watching is no fiction at all, our mild anxiety and amusement will immediately cease or—should it somehow continue!—become entirely unwarranted. We have an exact parallel to the ordinary rug-pull examples, with the only difference being that the belief overturned was in the fictionality of the events being witnessed. We believed that, in a certain fiction, Earth was being invaded. This belief provided (partial) warrant for the emotions we were experiencing. When the belief is removed—because the footage turns out *not* to be a fiction—our emotions are no longer warranted. Other, less pleasant emotions become warranted in their stead. The fact that warrant can potentially be removed in this way, however, shows that there *are* beliefs relevant to the response's appropriateness after all. Those who reject (2) wrongly suggest, to the contrary, that our responses "just happen" as a matter of cognitive wiring or pre-conscious, *a*-rational mechanisms—that we lack any beliefs and desires that could warrant them.

Our belief in the fictionality of what we are reading or watching is critical to explaining our affective responses for a second reason: it places us in an epistemic context where the factors relevant to explaining and justifying our emotions are different than when we are not engaging with a fiction. It opens the door to our having responses that are *aesthetically warranted*, insofar as such responses result from "the ability to recognize and respond to a work's aesthetically relevant features" (Livingston & Mele, 1997, p. 162; see also Gilmore, 2011). Developing and amending an earlier proposal from Currie (1990), Livingston & Mele (1997) spell out in detail a variety of norms relevant to assessing the appropriateness of a fiction-elicited emotion. More recently, Gilmore (2011) continues that project in an examination of the specific norms that apply to emotions generated in the context of fiction-appreciation, as contrasted to those that arise in everyday life. It will be useful to describe some of these norms here, as their appreciation helps to highlight the fact that our emotional engagement with fiction is typically grounded in reasons, and not reflexive, sub-personal mechanisms. (Note, however, that neither Livingston & Mele nor Gilmore offer their norms as part of a response to the paradox of fiction.)[12]

Livingston & Mele first articulate a norm of *emotional congruence* that is closely linked to truth in fiction:

> Some emotion, *e*, is a congruent response to some feature of a work just in case either (1) *e* is warranted by the work's fictional truths, or (2) *e* is intended by the author to be the appropriate response of the target audience. (1997, p. 171)

Livingston & Mele defend an intentionalist account of truth-in-fiction, allowing that what is true in a fiction depends crucially on the intentions of the author that thus and such be "imagined and accepted for the purposes of the fiction" (p. 170). Whether this is the correct account of truth-in-a-fiction needn't concern us here. The point is simply that our emotional responses to a fiction can be warranted, they argue, if the relationship between them and what is true in the fiction is "congruent with" the relationship between ordinary emotions and the things that elicit them outside of fictions:

> If anger is the appropriate response to a certain kind of unjustified aggression in reality, anger (though not necessarily of the same intensity) is also the congruent response to such events in fiction. (p. 171)

[12] Despite articulating a variety of distinctive norms relevant to assessing emotional responses to fictions, Gilmore does not appeal to such norms in resolving the paradox of fiction. Instead, he follows others, including Gendler & Kovakovich (2006) and Lamarque (1981), in advocating the "widely-defended" view that "our emotional response to what we take to be fictional instantiate a broadly exhibited disposition to respond behaviorally, cognitively, and affectively toward some kinds of stimuli in a way that is indifferent to their sources." Such responses are justified "as a class" by their general ability to "promote (or at least not conflict with) an individual's wellbeing or interests" (2011, p. 471). What, then, does he aim to accomplish in noting the distinctive norms relevant to fiction-appreciation? Gilmore explains: "even if the categorical rationality of such emotions is thereby secured [i.e., by 'source indifference'], we still need to ask under what conditions any particular emotional response fits its fictional or imagined object" (p. 471). Here appreciation of the relevant norms may help to answer those questions. However, if each *specific* emotional response is justified (or not) by appeal to a fiction-relevant norm, what need is there for some broader set of justifying criteria to provide warrant for the responses as a class? Moreover—as noted above—whether there are indeed "source indifferent" mental states, or not, and whether our general tendency to respond emotionally to what we imagine promotes our wellbeing, or not, are empirical matters. It could turn out that there are no such source-indifferent mental states, and that our imaginings do not increase our wellbeing. Even in that case, on Gilmore's own view, our *specific* emotional responses would nevertheless remain justified. Why, then, are they not the right place to look when asking for a solution to the paradox of fiction?

Their parenthetical remark—"though not necessarily of the same intensity"—is more important than they let on. The claim that they are making—or, in any case, that *should* be made—is that if anger is the appropriate response to a certain kind of unjustified aggression in reality, then a lesser degree of anger is normally the appropriate response to such events in a fiction. If it is appropriate to become extremely worried upon learning of an invasion by space aliens, then, according to the norm of congruence, it is appropriate to have a milder version of that emotion while attending to such events in a fiction.

This is not all there is to congruence, however. An emotion can also be congruent simply on the grounds of its being "intended by the author to be the appropriate response."[13] This is another norm distinctive to fictional engagement. When the Killer Rabbit mutilates individuals in Monty Python's *The Holy Grail*, laughter and amusement are appropriate responses—not because greater laughter and amusement would be appropriate if actual rabbits killed people in such a way, but because such a response was intended by the creators of the film. (I take the example from Friend (2016).) This allows for responses to "dark humor" to be appropriate—for us to appropriately laugh, or be amused by events in a fiction that we would never deem humorous if they really occurred.

A further norm of *artistic merit* also warrants mention, as it can trump considerations of congruence. Following Currie, Livingston & Mele note that "it is an aesthetic error to weep over the goings-on in sentimental trash, just as it is a mistake to howl in delight at the supposed ironies in what is in fact a botched melodrama" (1997, p. 173). Granting the inevitable difficulties in drawing bright lines in this territory—just *how bad* does a work have to be before it is inappropriate to be moved by it?—consideration of extreme cases makes clear the existence of such norms. We can easily imagine a terribly written and poorly acted tragedy—something concocted by a group of fifth graders over the course of a few hours. We ought not to be moved by it, even if it contains fictional truths to which a congruent response would be considerable sadness. Only if "the aspect of a work to which one responds is of at least moderate quality," Livingston & Mele conclude, is one "justified in responding congruently" (p. 173). When low degrees of artistic merit make congruent emotional responses inappropriate, they add, a *contrary* response may be appropriate instead: "artistic flaws warrant any item from a collection of responses that includes boredom, laughter, and whatever feelings accompany the winces and groans people manifest in response to fictional howlers" (p. 173). To groan and wince at a hackneyed punchline is a warranted response, just as feelings of outrage and sadness are appropriate in response to a brilliantly written scene where a sympathetic character is brutally murdered.

[13] Cf. Gilmore: "Something in a fiction can be fearsome…just because we are *caused* to feel fear toward it, if that is in accordance with the ends with which the work was designed" (2011, p. 483).

In each case, part of what warrants the response is the degree of artistic merit to which one is sensitive.[14]

In a similar vein, Jonathan Gilmore (2011) highlights distinctive ways that artworks elicit emotions "without supplying what would count as reasons for the emotions when they are held toward objects in real life" (p. 418). For instance:

> Fear toward events in the cinema or theater can be provoked by a menacing soundtrack, while a tendency to delight is triggered through cheerful music. We are often induced to see characters as morally contemptible or threatening by their being described or shown as physically ugly or deformed...or through their being accompanied by a character-specific leitmotif.
>
> (Gilmore, 2011, p. 481)

Gilmore goes on to detail a range of other aesthetic features (e.g., the thickness of a brushstroke, or the fragility of a sculptural material) that become relevant to explaining our emotional responses when we take an "external stance" to the work, "a stance that identifies elements of a fiction in terms of such artefactual aspects as character, plot, style, medium, meter tone...but not as the content that is represented" (p. 482). The use of such features to elicit emotions is possible, Gilmore proposes, due to the different *ends* to which fictions answer:

> Many fiction- and imagination-directed emotions...are generated in activities that are defined by ends—such as pleasure, entertainment, and absorption—that don't require that the emotions always be rationalized by the facts of the objects to which they respond. One may feel warmly disposed toward a figure in a painting only because the beauty of the work is designed to cause one to feel that way. (pp. 484–5)

The moral Gilmore draws—correctly, in my view—is that

> There are some kinds of reasons that justify an emotion felt toward a state of affairs represented in a fiction or imagining that would not justify that emotion when felt toward an analogous state of affairs in the real world. (p. 485)

The existence of emotional norms proprietary to fiction alerts us to the fact that we have at hand many different kinds of reasons we can appeal to when asked to justify our emotional reactions to fictions. We can talk about the events of the

[14] In addition to artistic merit, Livingston & Mele propose that *moral* norms are relevant and can trump considerations of congruence. If the content of a fiction is morally offensive—if, for instance, the author clearly intends the audience to share or adopt an offensive moral view—a contrary emotional response may be appropriate.

fiction itself as justification for why we have emotions that are milder versions of what we would experience in relation to such events were they actual. We can adduce the director's intent that the killer bunnies be seen as comedic. We can note the fiction's evocative language, its ingenious plot, the brilliance of the acting. We can observe that the characters are likeable and relatable, their predicament both familiar and compelling. We can appeal to the life-lessons the fiction teaches us by analogy and the light it sheds on people and events in our own lives. In short, we can give as *reasons for caring* the very things that film and literature critics highlight when they write a glowing review. Much of art criticism is simply this: the skillful rationalization of our emotional responses to art. When we point to such features of an artwork, we are offering evidence that our emotional reactions are apt and fitting of their objects, and therefore warranted.

11.8 But None of These Things Are Happening! Summary via Objection

One might fear that this response to the paradox is circular. We wanted to know how it could be reasonable (or warranted) to react emotionally to fictional characters and situations we know not to exist. And (to put it crudely) we are told that fictions have fiction-specific features that render our responses warranted. It may seem reasonable to stomp one's foot and repeat: but why are any of these emotional responses at all reasonable, given that we know the events are not occurring?

In response: they are reasonable because we can give good reasons for them—reasons that do not assume the events described by the fiction to have actually occurred. One reason we give for responding as we do is that we are engaging with a *fiction* and not, say, a documentary; another may be that the fiction is well crafted; a third may be that, in the fiction, tragic events occur to which our response is congruent. The kinds of reasons just given are the sort that people would ordinarily accept in explanation for why we responded as we did to a fiction. (See, e.g., Cova & Teroni (2016, pp. 933–4) for a survey confirming this claim.) If someone wishes to call the legitimacy of those reasons into question, they need to catch us in some kind of inconsistency, or reveal some other undermining factor.

Of course, that is precisely what Radford attempts to do with his rug-pull examples. Ordinarily, when we have an emotional response to some event, that response is undermined if we discover the event not to have occurred. Why doesn't this happen in the case of our engagement with fictions? Where is the important difference?

It is here: in the rug-pull cases Radford describes, the warrant one initially has for an emotional response is undermined when one discovers that what one *took to be* its object (e.g., a sick relative) does not exist. In the case of our response to fictions, we make no such undermining discovery. *All along*, we take the object of our emotions to be a certain fiction, together with its characters and events. Asked why we are responding as we do, we note that it is a fiction, that it has thus and such aesthetic features, that its story details events of thus and such kind (that render our response congruent), and so on. It is only if *those* reasons are undermined that the rug is pulled out from under our response. For instance, if we discover that the fiction itself does not exist—if, for example, the narrative turns out to be a *non*-fiction, or if it turns out we are unwittingly viewing an actual argument between actors—then our emotional reactions are indeed undermined and, potentially, become both unwarranted and unfitting. But we need not discover something so surprising as that there is no such fiction as we took there to be; it is often enough to discover that the fiction does not have a specific feature we adduced in our explanation for the emotion. If, for instance, our shock is revealed to have been based on our mishearing a bit of dialogue, then we will judge it to have been an unfitting response (but perhaps still a *warranted* one, due to what we *thought* we heard).

Far from being an exception to the rule, our emotional engagement with fiction is one more instance where specific features of some existing thing (viz., a fiction) elicit emotions, where specific features of the stimulus make certain emotions fitting or apt in response, and where our warrant for the emotions is undermined if we come to believe the object of the emotion lacks features that render the emotion an apt response. Provided that the fiction has the features we adduce, and provided that, in accordance with the specific norms governing fiction-consumption, those features are apt to elicit the kinds of emotions we experienced, the promulgator of the paradox has no credible means for undermining our reasons.

These points allow us to deepen the earlier criticism made of views that reject premise (2). For *even if* Damasio's somatic marker thesis is true (as adduced by Gendler & Kovakovich (2006)), and even if mental imagery shares neural processing pathways with perceptual experience (Van Leeuwen, 2016), and even if it is "adaptive" to respond emotionally to mere imaginings, our emotional reactions to fictions can *still* be unwarranted and unfitting. They will be unfitting when the fictions that evoke them lack features that render them apt; and they will be unwarranted when we do not believe the fictions that evoke them to have features that render them apt. The fact that our emotional responses to fictions *can* legitimately be undermined in these ways indicates that the solutions to the paradox that reject premise (2) prove too much, by excusing too much.

Gendler & Kovakovich and Van Leeuwen both show peripheral awareness of this problem. In the last paragraph of their paper, Gendler & Kovakovich note that, despite the cognitive architecture they posit, "there are plenty of circumstances where such emotional responses [to fictions] are very much out of place." This is because "our assessments of rationality and irrationality are, here [in engagements with fiction] as elsewhere, governed by conventional norms of appropriateness."

This is an odd last-minute concession. For understanding "conventional norms of appropriateness" and how they apply differently in our engagement with fictions than in other contexts would appear to be the entire question at issue when addressing the normative version of the paradox (which they take as their target). If the somatic marker hypothesis is not relevant to understanding these norms, how then is it relevant?

Van Leeuwen, on the other hand, qualifies his remarks by holding that the imagery that triggers emotional responses will only be generated if a fiction is "well crafted... in the relevant sense of 'well'" (2016, p. 103). Thus, a poorly crafted fiction, he can respond, will not elicit imagery and its attending emotions. This leaves us with the question of *why* we only generate imagery when enjoying a *well-crafted* fiction. Presumably the answer is that we only take an interest in such fictions; they are the only fictions that engage us. (It is not part of his account that we need imagery simply to recover fictional content—otherwise we would form imagery and experience related emotions when consuming poorly-crafted fictions as well.) But the whole question behind the normative puzzle is why it is reasonable to *care* about events we know never happened. Once our interest in a fiction (well-crafted or not) is made reasonable, our emotional reactions will come along as reasonable for free—whether or not anything Van Leeuwen says about the connection between imagery and emotion is true.

Finally, a last objection in this vicinity was put to me by Reader Y. Reader Y suggests that my discussion of fictional norms may leave open the main question at issue. To quote from Y's report:

> It's important to see that none of the material about whatever our warrant may be for our emotions can do any of the work that [Langland-Hassan] needs here. At best it gets him to, 'If you feel despairingly sad while engaged with *Romeo and Juliet*, here's why that's normatively appropriate.' But we lack from Langland-Hassan any sort of story about what should cause anyone who only has metafictional beliefs and desires to feel despairingly sad in the first place.

In referencing "metafictional beliefs and desires," Reader Y has in mind my appeal to beliefs and desires with 'in the fiction' operators—and specifically, my claim that these pair to generate fiction-directed affect. Why, asks Reader Y, should such states ever pair to generate sadness?

Well, why shouldn't they? I take it that Reader Y is normally satisfied when we explain someone's sadness by appeal to their strong desire that not-*p* and recent judgment that *p*. Why should it matter if the proposition *p* contains an 'in the fiction' operator? The form of explanation is the same. The beliefs and desires are the relevant causes.

What's really lurking behind Reader Y's objection, I think, is a Radfordian suspicion—still not exorcized—that there is something *inappropriate* or *unreasonable* about reacting emotionally to what one takes to be a mere fiction. If that were the case, then propositions that include 'in the fiction' operators would be exceptions to the general rule where a desire that not-*p* pairs with a judgment that *p* to generate negative affect. But why should we think propositions including 'in the fiction' operators are exceptions to the general rules governing how belief and desires cause affect? Reader Y does not say why. It is offered as obvious that someone who "only" has metafictional beliefs and desires won't experience significant affect. My hunch is that this apparent obviousness is grounded in Radfordian reasoning of the kind we've already dispelled in considering rug-pull cases. Appreciating the complex norms that govern our responses to fiction helps us to see what it would *really* take to pull the rug out from under those responses and render them unreasonable—and indeed unaccountable. When we see that no such rug is pulled out in the normal case of enjoying a fiction, we see that "metafictional" beliefs and desires generate no exception to the rule where a desire that not-*p* and a judgment that *p* will combine to generate negative affect.

11.9 Back to the Triad

My response to the paradox of fiction is now complete. But I haven't yet explained what to make of the inconsistent triad. That omission has been purposeful. There are subtly different ways to formulate the triad (and no *standard* way); I don't want my solution to appear hostage to one particular formulation. But it's nevertheless instructive to see how the points already made apply to the formulation we considered earlier. Here, again, is Currie's version of the triad:

(1) We have emotions concerning the situations of fictional characters.

(2) To have an emotion concerning someone's situation we must believe the propositions that describe that situation.

(3) We do not believe the propositions that describe the situations of fictional characters. (Currie, 1990, p. 187)

As earlier noted, the most common response is to reject (2), with the idea being that imagining that *p* generates emotional responses even when we do not believe that *p*. Now, I don't reject the platitude that imagining that *p* can, at least at times, generate emotional responses of roughly the sort that would be appropriate if one believed that *p*. But, in line with my broader project of explaining imagination, I give an account of what it is to imagine that *p* (in the context of appreciating a fiction) that appeals only to more basic states, such as beliefs and desires about what is true in the fiction. With that in mind, let's look more closely at condition

(3). It says that we do not believe the propositions that describe the situations of fictional characters. Just what *are* the propositions that describe the situations of fictional characters?

Consider an example: viewers of *The Big Lebowski* know that The Dude has strong musical preferences and, in particular, hates the Eagles. What proposition describes The Dude's situation? It is not: 'The Dude hates the Eagles.' That proposition is false. There is no actual Dude who, by hating the Eagles, could make it true. 'The Dude hates the Eagles,' is no truer than 'The Dude *loves* the Eagles.' Therefore, it cannot truly describe The Dude's situation. We will need a true proposition in order to give a true account of his or any situation. The relevant *true* proposition—the one that accurately describes the situation of this fictional character—is the proposition that, in *The Big Lebowski*, The Dude hates the Eagles. And, of course, if we have seen the movie, we *do* believe that proposition. The same points apply to other fictions we wittingly enjoy. So, contrary to proposition (3) of the triad, we *do* believe the propositions that describe the situations of fictional characters; for those propositions all involve 'in the fiction' operators. Rejecting (3), we can continue to accept (1) and (2) without conflict.

This way of defusing the triad may seem too cheap. It might seem to succeed (if it does) due to an infelicity in the way Currie formulates the triad. But, in fact, the reasons just given for rejecting (3) do not do any of the hard work in resolving the paradox. For even if one grants that the propositions that describe a fictional character's situation involve 'in the fiction' operators, this simply pushes the puzzle onto (2). For (2), in its normative reading, offers itself as a (partial) characterization of the appropriateness conditions for the emotions we have about "someone's situation." Namely, we must believe "the propositions that describe that situation," in order for the emotion to be warranted. In light of our new gloss on (3), accepting (2) requires us to accept that, when we have an emotion concerning a *fictional* character's situation, its warrant depends upon our believing that, in the fiction, thus and such. For propositions involving 'in the fiction' operators are the kinds of propositions that describe a fictional character's situation. But how could believing that a situation occurs *in a fiction* warrant an emotion like fear or anger about the situation? Now we are back to the main question that began this chapter. We can understand why the emotions are warranted if we can understand why it is warranted to have strong desires to the effect that, in the fiction, thus and such—desires which pair with beliefs that, in the fiction, thus and such to generate the emotions.

And why *shouldn't* we have such beliefs and desires? The traditional complaint against them is that it makes no sense to have strong desires about what happens in a *mere* fiction. But now we have seen that the plausibility of that complaint derives from a faulty analogy between Radfordian rug-pull cases and our engagement with fictions. As I argued last section, our emotional responses to fictions, and the desires that elicit them, are founded on reasons—reasons (and not mere reflexes) that can indeed be undermined if certain of our beliefs turn out to be false. Happily, our reasons are *not* undermined by the observation that we are responding to a fiction. The opposite is true. The responses are warranted, in part, by the belief that what we are responding to is a fiction. Thus, no reason is undermined—no rug pulled out from under us—when we are told that the characters we took for fictional are indeed fictional. It was in making this point, and in articulating the alternative norms that govern our engagement with fiction, where the heavy lifting in my account took place. Resolving the triad with those points in hand is then straightforward.

11.10 Summary

The last three chapters have considered the role of imagination in the consumption of fiction from a variety of angles. I have taken it as a platitude that we engage in A-imagining—rich, elaborated, epistemically safe thought about the possible, fantastical, unreal, and so on—in response to fictions. The key question has been whether this A-imagining can be characterized in more basic folk psychological terms. I have argued that it can. We began, in Chapter 9, with the question of whether recovering the implicit and explicit content of a fiction requires *sui generis* imagining. There my answer was no. Recovering fictional content may at times require counterfactual reasoning. Yet, as I argued earlier in Chapters 5 and 6, the A-imagining that takes place during conditional reasoning can itself be reduced to more basic folk psychological states. Further, we can agree with Stock that recovering fictional content is not *simply* a matter of reasoning counterfactually about what would be true were some other set of (fictional) propositions true. The other relevant bits of reasoning—concerning, e.g., what is true in the fiction given certain genre conventions, or given likely uses of symbolism by the author—can easily be seen as resulting from abductive inferences from one's existing beliefs about the particular fiction and the practice of fiction-making generally.

Chapters 10 and 11 moved on to consider whether it is the phenomenon of immersion within fiction that more definitively calls for *sui generis* imaginings. I began Chapter 10 with the Operator Claim, arguing that our *sui generis* imaginings (were there such) would require 'in the fiction' operators in order to be directed at the fictions we take them to concern. The truth of the Operator Claim undermines the main rationale for thinking that *sui generis* imaginings facilitate immersion. If the OC is correct, *sui generis* imaginings can put us in no more direct cognitive acquaintance with fictional events than beliefs with 'in the fiction' operators; further, the way in which the events of one fiction are "cognitively quarantined" from others "in imagination" will be the same way in which our beliefs about one fiction are quarantined from beliefs about another—viz., by the use of relevant 'in the fiction' operators.

To really understand immersion, I argued, we need to grasp why it is that we form strong desires concerning fictional events. Contrary to what many have supposed, appealing to imagination and "source indifferent" affective mechanisms does not help us here. Instead we need to confront and properly resolve the paradox of fiction. That was my primary aim in this chapter. The key is to understand why we are warranted in *caring* about fictional events. This requires, first, that we see clearly why there is a presumption against caring about fictional events in the first place. The answer lies in "rug-pull" cases of the kind Radford introduced into the literature. On reflection, we can see that the rug-pull structure does not apply to our engagement with fiction. In order to appreciate that fact, it helps to highlight the rational norms specific to fiction-appreciation. This clarifies why events that pull the rug out from under our emotional reactions in everyday life do not do so in our engagement with fiction. We become immersed in fictions *because* they are fictions, not in spite of their being fictions. Our emotional responses are not "indifferent" to whether something is a fiction; they are delicately calibrated in ways only appropriate if the stimulus is a fiction. It's not that our responses are only *truly* fitting if the fiction turns out to record actual events. Quite the opposite: only a discovery that what we took for fiction is non-fiction would reveal our responses to be unfitting.

12
Creativity

12.1 Introduction

Suppose that you are writing a book on imagination. Your next-door neighbor engages you on the topic: "So... it's about creativity?" If you're a philosopher of mind in the analytic tradition, you may be tempted to say no—to explain that being creative is one thing (a personality trait, say), while imagining is the use of a type of mental state or process that may, or may not, be closely linked to being creative. This is not an uncommon move.[1] But you can tell how it will sound before you say it: like a cop-out. People want a theory of imagination to shed some light on the nature of creativity. Even if there is a distinction to be made between "being creative," on the one hand, and the mental state of imagining, on the other, there is no margin in denying an important link between the two. If a theory of imagination leaves creativity a mystery, so much the worse for the theory. In this closing chapter, I will do my best to face up to the difficulties that creativity presents to a theory of imagination, even if much will remain unresolved.

Even on its face, creativity has an air mystery. As with imagination, it's tricky to specify the nature of the phenomenon we want explained when we ask for an explanation of creativity. It's easy to end up following the wrong scent, diverted by questions that don't get to the heart of the matter. It's also easy, as philosophers, to suffocate or oversimplify the topic in our efforts to say something precise. So, in the first half of this chapter, I want to focus on distinguishing the most interesting and difficult questions about creativity from others that might catch our eye. To that end I will discuss some recent work by philosophers of mind that, I think, misunderstands the nature of the explanatory task that creativity presents to us. Then I will move toward articulating and answering some of the most important questions about creativity, connecting those answers back to this book's broader project of explaining imagination.

[1] Currie & Ravenscroft (2002, pp. 8–10) make essentially this claim in explaining why they will not be discussing "creative imagination" in their book devoted to "recreative imagination." While they grant that some instances of creativity may rely upon recreative imagining, they do not see it as a limitation on their theory of recreative imagining that it shed no light on creativity. In their view, "getting things done by using recreative imagination is not definitive or even criterial for displaying creative imagination" (p. 11). While I agree that (in my terms) neither A-imagining nor I-imagining is sufficient for creativity, it is still, I think, a strong desideratum on any theory of A-imagining (or "recreative imagining") that it meaningfully connect imagination to our capacity for creativity.

Explaining Imagination. Peter Langland-Hassan, Oxford University Press (2020). © Peter Langland-Hassan.
DOI: 10.1093/oso/9780198815068.001.0001

12.2 Creativity and A-imagining

Creativity, as a feature of persons, is nothing other than the ability to make creative products. To understand our own creativity, then, we need to know what it is that makes a product—be it a work of art, a marketing plan, or a car design—creative. Happily, there is a general consensus on two features being necessary and jointly sufficient for a product's being creative: novelty and value (Boden, 2004; Carruthers, 2018; Gaut, 2003; Paul & Kaufman, 2014).[2] The novelty condition, intuitively, is that there be something original, uncopied, or distinctive about the work.[3] The value condition holds that there is something *good* or *useful* about the product's novelty. Here the notion of value is to be taken as entirely general, extending from monetary, to practical, to aesthetic value; to be valuable is simply to be valued by people. Thus, *merely* novel creations—extemporaneous scribbles and babbles—do not clear the bar as creative; nor do hundred dollar bills, sapphire rings, and other merely valuable objects. (Whether there could be an *aesthetically* valuable product that was not novel is less clear; supposing that Warhol painted 100,000 Campbell's Soup cans, would each one be aesthetically valuable? Each one creative?)

Bones can be picked with this characterization of a creative work, certainly. There may be some creative works with little value and some with little novelty. But value and novelty at least serve as characteristic features of creative works. If we can explain how it is that people are able to produce works that are highly valuable in their novelty, we will have gone a good way toward explaining creativity.

Imagination enters the picture when we consider the grounds for a person's creativity. To be creative you need a good imagination—you need to be *imaginative*. This might be a controversial psychological claim if it assumed a specific theory about the kinds of mental states, processes, or representations involved in being "imaginative." But here I only mean to voice a platitude. There are no creative geniuses lacking in imagination; and there are no creative acts in which the creator's imaginativeness played no role. This is just because being creative and being imaginative come to the same thing, as a matter of platitudes. What about the different *senses* of imagining—A-imagining and I-imagining—distinguished

[2] "Creativity is the ability to come up with ideas or artefacts that are *new, surprising, and valuable*" (Boden, 2004, p. 1).

[3] Following Boden (2004), we can distinguish products that are novel with relation to the creator's personal history—in that they are not a matter of the person simply repeating something she has seen someone else do, or that she has done before—from products that are *historically* novel, in that they are significantly unlike anything the culture has previously witnessed. Boden calls the former "Psychological Novelty," and notes that psychologically novel products can be valuable and praiseworthy even when they are not historically novel. As historically novel products are a sub-set of the psychologically novel products, we can confine our investigation to psychologically novel products without loss. (Boden follows the same procedure.)

in earlier chapters? How do they relate to "being imaginative" in the sense (trivially) equivalent to being creative?

There appears no very tight connection between I-imagining—i.e., the having of (seemingly) image-like mental states—and being imaginative. Mental images likely feature in the thoughts of imaginative people, sure. But they're also present in the thoughts of the least imaginative and least creative among us. This must be true if, as is generally thought, imagery is an essential feature of much episodic memory (Schacter, Addis, & Buckner, 2007; Michaelian, 2016b). Some creative products will certainly rely, for their conception, on the use of mental imagery. But some will also rely, for their conception, on non-imagistic mental representations as well, supposing there are such. There is no obvious reason to think that having thoughts in a particular (imagistic) *format* is closely linked to the general capacity for creativity.

On the other hand, imaginativeness does seem closely tied to the notion of A-imagining. Imagining, in the A-imagining sense, is the having of rich, elaborated sequences of thought about the possible, fantastical, or unreal, in an epistemically blameless way. The notion of an imaginative, creative person is of someone who is good at thinking of unobvious possibilities and new ways of doing things that result in valuable products. It seems clear that the former would support the latter. How else are we to think of unobvious possibilities than by thinking—in rich, elaborated ways—about the merely possible? And how else are we to arrive at new ways of doing things than by considering many different possible actions and scenarios and selecting from among them? Having a basic capacity for A-imagining may not be sufficient for being imaginative in the sense that is equivalent to being creative. But it appears at least necessary.

This link between A-imagining and being imaginative is still a superficial one, however, as it doesn't commit us to any substantive thesis about the nature of the mental states and processes involved in A-imagining. In earlier chapters, I've argued that the A-imagining that occurs during pretense, conditional reasoning, and fiction-appreciation can be explained in more basic folk psychological terms—as drawing exclusively on beliefs, desires, intentions, and so on. To the extent that creativity requires conditional reasoning—as it surely does, at times—those prior arguments can be applied to the problem of creativity in showing how (some of) the A-imagining required for creativity is explicable in more basic folk psychological terms. Indeed, I think there is much to be said for the view that creativity draws on quite general reasoning and problem-solving skills (Weisberg, 2006) including, especially, abilities for conditional reasoning.

But there is much more to the story than that. There are mental processes relied upon in the generation of the most valuable creative works that, I will argue, are not well characterized as inductive or deductive *inferences* of any sort. This puts pressure on the idea that they could be characterized as bouts of conditional reasoning—or, indeed, as any kind of *reasoning* at all. Creative cognition, and the

A-imagining it involves, is less rule-governed and more associative—less proof-like and more dreamlike—than inferential trains of thought. My aim in what follows is to shed some explanatory light on these cases of A-imagining, some of which are unlike anything else so far discussed in this book.

12.3 The Easy versus the Hard Problems of Creativity

We first need to recognize that creativity comes in degrees. Creativity is in that way like intelligence. No healthy human has literally *none*. We are all capable of being *somewhat* creative. This leaves us with a choice in what to take as our target when trying to explain creativity. One option is to focus on the question of how creativity is at all possible in human beings. Here the goal would be to reveal some cognitive abilities, states, or processes shared by everyone, without which creativity would be impossible—perhaps contrasting humans to some species of animal (goldfish?) that lacks creativity altogether, precisely because it lacks this kind of state, faculty, or cognitive ability. Alternatively, we could ask, more narrowly, what it is that separates the exceptionally creative from the rest of us. My focus will be on this second question. I want to know what it is about Dylan, Dickinson, Bjork, and Nabokov that sets them apart. If this cannot precisely be known, then I at least want to brush against the answer and feel its outlines. This will require comment on the kinds of abilities and mental processes exploited in more modest creative efforts. Keeping one eye on the masters, however, will ensure that we don't undersell the problem.

Philosophers and psychologists often focus instead on the first question, addressing the issue of how creativity is at all possible in creatures like us (Carruthers, 2002, 2011, 2018; Stokes, 2014). This is due in part to the *prima facie* clash between the kinds of computational theories of cognition featured in many naturalistic accounts of mentality, on the one hand, and the *novelty* and *freedom from constraint* associated with creativity, on the other. It seems odd, to many, to suppose that a computer program following fixed algorithms could be capable of generating the sort of novelty required in a creative product.[4] If we are indeed sophisticated computers of a kind, the question extends equally to ourselves. The puzzle grows more acute in a context—such as contemporary philosophy of mind—where inductive and deductive inference are the primary psychological transitions formally modelled and discussed. On the face of it, creativity requires a capacity for a-rational trains of thought—an ability to transcend or sidestep anything so pre-determined as a rational inference.[5]

[4] Boden (1998, 2004) has done much to challenge this assumption, however.

[5] See Carruthers (2018) for a recent attempt to deal with this problem by inserting quasi-random associative processes within an otherwise deterministic, mechanistic cognitive architecture to achieve "constrained stochasticity."

But once we take account of the fact that creativity comes in degrees—granting that every child's stick-figure portrait is *a bit* creative—the nature of the puzzle can begin to elude us. For there are already computer programs capable of generating novel musical pieces (Cope, 1991), abstract visual art (Cohen, 2009), poems (Vandegrift, 2016), and even "co-authored" novels (Olewitz, 2016). Visual artworks created by Cohen's AARON algorithm have been displayed in major museums; free-verse written by Scholl's poetry-generating algorithm has been selected (unwittingly!) for publication in literary magazines (Merchant, 2015). Existing programs are capable of generating, from a photograph, an impressionistic image in the style of Monet, and—more impressively, in my view—of flipping the processing so as to create a realistic photograph-like image from an existing Monet (Zhu et al., 2017). The elegance and sophistication of such products will continue to increase. Google recently initiated the Magenta project, aimed at using machine learning to "generate compelling art and music" (https://magenta.tensorflow.org/). Its researchers have already moved well beyond the problem of generating novel musical works to focusing on how to create AI capable of composing artistic products with valuable aesthetic characteristics. For instance, one project aims to create AI that can compose and perform music with expressive *feel* (https://magenta.tensorflow.org/performance-rnn). Thus, it is the creation of works of considerable aesthetic *value*—and not mere novelty—that currently poses the most significant challenge to researchers in artificial intelligence.

A response to consider at this point, however, is that it is the *writer* of such programs who is the creator of the resulting artworks and not the programs themselves. If that were the case, then even the capacity for "mere" artistic novelty might remain beyond the grasp of such programs. This would leave the door open to holding that minimal creativity is, for all we know, something we cannot model on a contemporary computer. But there is little basis for such skepticism. A human being is no more responsible for his or her own creation than is a computer program. And yet we manage to be creative. We would be no less creative were it revealed that, like computer programs, we are the products of an intelligent designer. Unless one is going to take issue with the entire project of explaining human cognition in computational terms, there is no reason to deny that some current programs display *a degree of* creativity in generating the products that they do. After all, we wouldn't dream of calling our children uncreative if they presented us with the same.

My point here is not to suggest that computer scientists already understand and can perfectly model creative cognition. It is to focus attention on what most needs explaining. Notwithstanding current AI, there is much about creativity we do not yet understand. Distinctions from Margaret Boden (2004) help to pinpoint what that is. (NB I will put these distinctions to my own ends and do not mean to hold Boden to my understanding of them—only to credit her where due.) Boden distinguishes three forms of creativity: combinatorial, explorative, and transformational (pp. 3–7).[6] *Combinatorial* creativity consists in "making unfamiliar combinations of familiar ideas," typically by means of an interesting analogy. "Think of a physicist comparing an atom to the solar system," she writes, "or a journalist comparing a politician with a decidedly non-cuddly animal" (p. 3). Ideas are "combined" in the sense that two things not normally associated are shown to have an interesting, even enlightening connection. The combination need not be by analogy; it can simply involve putting two things together—two ingredients, say—in a new and valuable way.

Explorative creativity, on the other hand, occurs in the context of a discipline or practice with a codified set of rules or principles—such as chess, or landscape art. It is possible to work entirely "within the rules" of chess to arrive at a creative move—a novel means of attack—just as it is possible to work entirely within the rules of deductive logic to arrive at a creative proof, or to use one's understanding of visual perspective to make a creative painting of a new landscape. In each case, Boden proposes, we do so by exploring the possibilities available within a particular "conceptual space." In the arts, the "rules" or "principles" explored can be understood as the basis for a particular *style*—be it the style employed by a caricature artist in the park, by John Coltrane in his rendering of jazz standards, or in the impressionisms of Monet. Once there is a recognizable style in play, we can—at least potentially—extract a set of principles or heuristics that can be used to generate additional works in that style. When a work manages to be creative through the artist's exploration and exploitation of these principles and heuristics, we can say it has explorative creativity. Boden analogizes *explorative* creativity to the driving of new routes on roads that are already created. I will understand it, somewhat less metaphorically, as a kind of creativity grounded in one's ability to draw out inferences from a set of premises, in accord with a fixed set of rules. So defined, it remains an open question whether there are indeed such a set of principles or rules underlying, say, Coltrane's improvisatory stylings, or Monet's impressionism. The point is simply that explorative creativity is the kind of creativity that occurs through the exploration and application of such rules and heuristics, where available.

It is only through *transformational* creativity that the limits of a particular style are transcended, the governing rules rewritten, and something occurs that cannot comfortably be characterized as an inference. This may consist in depicting objects in an entirely new way (think of the *first* cubist painting), deciding to ignore the requirement of rhyme (as in free verse), or using a formerly non-musical element as music (such as Jimi Hendrix's musical use of guitar-amplifier feedback)—something akin to the construction of new roads on which to drive. In Boden's

[6] These are in fact my terms for her three notions, which she does not explicitly name as such.

evocative terms, the creator changes the rules or style such that "thoughts are now possible which previously (within the untransformed space) where literally inconceivable" (2004, p. 6). These acts constitute what Boden sees as "the deepest cases of creativity." While I agree with Boden about the relative value of this kind of creativity, I want to suggest an amendment (or perhaps just a clarification) to how it is understood. Transformative creativity does not only occur when some new *style* of work is generated. It can occur *within* a style as well. A particular lyric or melody within a song of a recognizable genre may be so surprising, insightful, and inspired that it cannot be seen as an extrapolation of the style, but, rather, a tiny revolution within it. One doesn't have to be the first abstract expressionist for one's abstract expressionism to be transformative in its specific gestures; and a jazz musician needn't play something no longer recognizable as jazz in order for his performance to be transformative. For creativity to emerge in its transformative guise, the valuable novelty in a product simply needs to result from something other than the following of an explicit formula, or the teasing out of implications. It needs to result from something *non*-inferential. In what follows I will aim to provide a more positive characterization of what that is.

Despite emphasizing these three "kinds" of creativity, I doubt clear distinctions can be drawn in every case. We can expect borderline instances of each and creative products containing elements of all three. I have introduced them for their heuristic value in helping us to separate and more clearly articulate different questions about creativity and its relationship to imagination. We can begin to see how they help in that endeavor by considering a fairly ordinary case of creative cognition: the Build Challenge.

12.4 The Build Challenge

My son's fifth grade science teacher gives the class a Build Challenge at the end of each week. The students are split into groups, with each group receiving the same set of materials and a particular challenge to complete with those materials. For one challenge, each group was given six sheets of notebook paper, 10 inches of tape, and five paper clips with which to create the tallest free-standing structure they could. Completing the task required creativity. The students had never before faced the task of building a tall structure with precisely those materials; and they arrived at products unlike any they had made before, with varying degrees of value. (Groups caught copying the designs of other groups—i.e., *not* being creative—were disqualified.)

The winning group taped the top of a notebook page to its bottom, so as to make a cylinder. Then they stood the cylinder vertically on one end and set a second piece of paper across the top of the cylinder. That piece of paper served as the floor upon which a second cylinder was placed, its base secured with a second piece of tape. The process was continued up to three floors. This was, without question, a creative solution to the problem. It required combinatorial creativity, insofar as students needed to find new ways of combining objects not normally combined. And it required explorative creativity, as students needed to explore the many possibilities for exploiting the known properties of the objects given. The important realization was that tape could be applied to a piece of paper, so as to make a cylinder, and that such a cylinder would have both height and sufficient stability for the process to be iterated. It did not, however, require transformational creativity—at least, not obviously. There was no new architectural concept or construction paradigm exploited. The paper was folded into a familiar shape; tape was used as tape. The winning design was something many of the students likely would have come to with a bit of prompting. The key was to focus on the right properties of the materials so as to infer their most effective combinations.

Despite the evident need for creativity in winning a Build Challenge, it is not hard to see the exercise as a reasoning task—as a bit of complex problem-solving. The desired end result was clear: the tallest structure in the class. The properties of the materials were well known. The problem was how to combine those materials to achieve the end result. (I faced a similar "build challenge" moments ago, trying to determine what sort of sandwich could be made from the items in the fridge.) There is nothing inherent in such problem-solving that cries out for a *sui generis* mental state that stands apart from one's beliefs, desires, and intentions. In exhibiting explorative creativity, the students needed to reason hypothetically about what would happen if the materials were arranged in a variety of different ways. And we have already seen that hypothetical reasoning does not, by its nature, require *sui generis* imaginative states (Chapters 5 and 6). It may have been that arriving at the best answer required students to generate mental imagery of the paper in different configurations—that mental imagery figured in the hypothetical reasoning itself. But we have also seen (Chapters 3 and 4) that the presence of imagery within a mental state is consistent with the state's being a judgment, such as: JIG (the paper taped end to end and turned on its side would be: **a vertical column**...). The combinatorial creativity displayed involved students' making the paper function like a column; the the notions of a sheet of paper and of a column were in that sense "combined." This can even be viewed as a case of object pretense: pretending that the paper is a column. Such pretenses, I argued in Chapter 8, do not require anything other than ordinary belief and desire.

All of this stepwise reasoning will be facilitated by the depth of one's knowledge of the materials in question and general experience with making structures of different kinds. But none of it calls out for states irreducible to beliefs, desires, and intentions. We can instead appeal to sequences of judgments and decisions that build on each other: the judgment that the paper can be made into a column leading to a decision to see what can be done with the paper in the shape of a column, for instance; this decision may then elicit a judgment that the paper can be secured to the desk with tape; then one may judge that another piece of paper could rest horizontally on top of the secured column, and so on; these judgments lead to decisions to carry out the plan. If the plan doesn't work—if it turns out that the column is too narrow to support a piece of paper laying horizontally across its top—one has to go back to the drawing board, to act on, and develop, another hunch.

Return now to the platitude that creativity requires A-imagining. It looks like the A-imagining relied upon for *this* bit of creative cognition is explicable in more basic folk psychological terms. This will be possible, as a rule, whenever the relevant cognition can be characterized as a series of inferences—provided, again, that neither conditional reasoning nor pretense require *sui generis* imaginative states, as argued in previous chapters.

12.5 Losing the Scent—Recent Missteps in Linking (*Sui Generis*) Imaginings to Creativity

Nevertheless, most contemporary philosophers who have considered the matter seem confident that creativity draws on imagination as a central resource and that such imaginings are irreducible to other, more basic kinds of folk psychological states. One might think they were driven to this view by cases of creativity *unlike* the Build Challenge—cases not comfortably seen as problem-solving. But, in fact, to my knowledge, none of the considerations they offer introduce phenomena not already seen in the Build Challenge. I will survey a few of these views now, as a means to clarifying the real challenge that creativity presents to theories of imagination.

Some put forward *a priori* arguments of the kind dismissed in Chapter 1, which overlook the possibility of imagining being a complex folk psychological state. Here is Berys Gaut:

> Imagination is peculiarly suited...to be the vehicle of active creativity—to be that faculty we employ in being actively creative. For one can imagine various states of affairs without being committed to their truth or to carrying them out, so one can try out various options. In contrast, to believe some proposition is to be committed to its truth, and to intend something is to be committed to carrying it out if one can. (2010, p. 1043)

As evidence for this analysis, Gaut—in earlier work—offers the following Moorean contrasts. There is awkwardness on the order of incoherence in saying: "*p*, but I don't believe that *p*," or "I will *x* if given the opportunity, but I don't intend to *x*." Yet there is no awkwardness in saying, "I am imagining that *p*, but I don't believe that *p*," or "I am imagining that I am *x*-ing, but I don't intend to *x*" (Gaut, 2003, pp. 279–80). This, he concludes, is because imaginings "lack the intrinsic ends of belief and intention," and, indeed, "seem to lack any intrinsic end at all... imagination thus exhibits a kind of freedom" needed for creative cognition (pp. 279–80).

Now, the question of interest here is not whether imagining is in some sense "free" and used in acts of creativity—both are platitudes we should accept. What matters is whether such imaginings can be understood in more basic folk psychological terms. Gaut offers the Moorean contrasts as evidence that they cannot, as they show imaginings to have different (or non-existent) "intrinsic ends." Yet, like other superficial arguments for imagination's irreducibility considered in Chapter 1, the Moorean contrasts only serve to establish that imagining that *p* is not the same thing as believing or intending that *p*. It leaves open the possibility that imagining that *p*—like suspecting that *p*—is a complex mental state that can be broken into simpler, more general parts of some other (folk psychological) kind. After all, we can quite sensibly say: "If *p*, then *q*, *r*, *s*, *t*, *u*, and *v*... but I don't believe that *p*." And I have made the case that at least some episodes of imagining that *p* amount to making judgments in favor of rich conditionals with *p* as their antecedent. In that case, imagining that *p* is indeed consistent with one's not believing that *p* *and* with the imagining's consisting in the use of *other* beliefs. Gaut, and a chorus of others, may object that not all cases of imagining that *p* can receive such treatment. There I agree. The question, however, is not whether there is one specific kind of belief, desire, or decision that can be equated with each case of imagining that *p*, but whether there is always *some* more basic state or other that any arbitrary instance of imagining that *p* might be. To establish that there is not requires subtler arguments than an appeal to general Moorean contrasts. For there is no *prima facie* reason to think that all the mental activities that satisfy the commonsense criteria for being A-imaginings must receive the same analysis; as earlier discussed, imagination appears heterogeneous to many *even on its face*.

Peter Carruthers, in a series of papers, links creativity to imagination by very different means, describing a developmental pathway from pretend play to creativity, with imagination at the root of each. Both creativity and pretense, he tells us, "can be seen as sharing essentially the same cognitive basis, in so far as both involve exercises of imagination" (2002, pp. 228–9). Carruthers does not explicitly argue that "exercises of imagination" cannot be viewed as the exploitation of more basic propositional attitude states. However, in elaborating his position, he approvingly cites theorists who explicitly endorse such a view—including Nichols & Stich (2000). And, in other work, Carruthers finds it "very plausible" that imagining, conceived of as a distinct cognitive attitude by Nichols & Stich (2000), "can't be reduced to believing, or to desiring, or to any combination thereof (nor can it be reduced to any sort of planning or intending)" (Carruthers, 2006, p. 89).

In explaining the connection he sees between pretense and creativity, Carruthers notes:

> Each involves essentially the same cognitive underpinnings—namely, a capacity to generate, and to reason with, novel suppositions or *imaginary scenarios*. When pretending, what a child has to do is suppose that something is the case...and then think and act within the scope of that supposition...Similarly, when adults are engaged in the construction of a new theory, or are seeking a novel solution to a practical problem, or are composing a tune, they have to think: 'Suppose it were the case that P', or 'Suppose I did it like *this*' or 'Suppose it sounded like *so*'. (2002, pp. 229–30)

In later, co-authored work, Carruthers places imagination within the context of the "GENPLORE" model of creativity developed by Finke and colleagues (1992), according to which creative action involves both a generative phase, where a new idea emerges, and an exploratory phase, where the idea is developed and expanded. Carruthers and Picciuto propose that imagination, *qua* supposition, is involved in both phases:

> Perhaps what pretense does, then, is provide practice in making suppositions and reasoning within their scope, thus supporting both the 'generate' and 'explore' components of GENEPLORE creativity.
>
> (Picciuto & Carruthers, 2014, p. 215)

On the one hand, it can certainly be granted, on a platitudinous level, that both pretense and creative action require us to generate suppositions and, further, that childhood pretense allows us valuable practice in doing so. This leaves open the question of whether such "supposings" or "imaginings" are basic cognitive states or, instead, reducible to others. As Carruthers (2006, p. 89) appears to maintain that the relevant supposings make use of a *sui generis* type of state or cognitive module, we are brought back to the earlier debates (of Chapters 5–8) concerning whether the imaginings at work in pretense and conditional reasoning must be viewed as *sui generis*, irreducible states. Like Nichols & Stich (2003), Picciuto & Carruthers cite the difficulties people with autism show with both pretense and (certain forms of) suppositional reasoning as evidence that there is a single type of state or module relied upon by both (2014, pp. 211–12). But, as noted earlier (Chapter 8), little can be inferred from the co-presence of any two deficits in autism; ASD is a multi-faceted developmental disorder affecting many aspects of cognitive, emotional, perceptual, and sensorimotor functioning. The fact that people with autism show a characteristically abnormal gait (Rineheart et al., 2006; Calhoun et al., 2011), for instance, does not warrant the inference that a single cognitive module underlies both pretense and ambulation.

In any case, the debate to be had with Carruthers over the nature of the imaginative states exploited in pretense, conditional reasoning, and—by extension—creativity, has in large part already occurred in earlier chapters. I will not revisit it here. The important point for present purposes is that, in emphasizing the importance to creativity of thinking "within the scope of a supposition," Carruthers does not introduce or aim to explain any phenomenon that is not itself a kind of drawing-out-of-inferences (albeit "offline," through the use of *sui generis* imaginative/suppositional states). Nor has he introduced or explained any aspect of creativity that we didn't already face in addressing the Build Challenge, which also plausibly required hypothetical reasoning. If transformative creativity really is non-inferential in nature, as suggested earlier, then it is no easier explained by appeal to inferences drawn "in imagination" than it is by appeal to inferences drawn within one's beliefs.[7]

Dustin Stokes—also the author of several articles on imagination and creativity—takes an approach closer in spirit to Gaut's in arguing that creativity relies upon *sui generis* imaginative states. Stokes (2014) develops, to my knowledge, the most detailed philosophical argument for *sui generis* imaginings' being necessary to creativity. Stokes begins by distinguishing "truth-bound" mental states, such as beliefs, whose function it is to "faithfully represent the information of some conceptual space," from non-truth-bound states, which lack that function. He then proposes that creativity makes essential use of non-truth-bound states. This is because:

> Any cognitive state that functions to faithfully represent the information of some conceptual space—be that cognitive state a true belief, propositional or procedural knowledge, or a memory—can at best play a necessary but insufficient role in the thinking required for an accomplishment like [Bach's] *The Well-Tempered Clavier*. *Truth-bound cognitive states*... are rarely sufficient for creative thought. (Stokes, 2014, p. 160, emphasis in original)

Stokes goes on to conclude that "imaginings" are the best candidates for being the relevant non-truth-bound states at work in creativity. Why, exactly, does creativity require the use of non-truth-bound states? In explanation, Stokes offers a thought experiment reminiscent of Frank Jackson's (1982) Mary, the brilliant neuroscientist who knows all the physical facts about visual perception but still doesn't know what it's like to see red. Stokes asks us to consider "Super-Bach," who:

[7] It is worth again mentioning Carruthers' more recent work (2018), in which he takes a very different (and I think promising) approach to explaining creativity, positing quasi-random associative processes that generate thoughts or ideas semantically related to a task at hand. I do not have space to discuss this newer view here. It bears noting, however, that he is silent, in that work, on the relation of imagination to these associative processes.

> Knew *everything* there was to know—both in terms of all the facts and all of the relevant skills—about the clavier, tempered tuning, and the 12-tone scale. This would not have been sufficient for the creation of *The Well-Tempered Clavier*... Super-Bach's knowledge (just like actual Bach's knowledge) of the space would indeed constrain his composition, but this knowledge alone would not amount to, afford, or even imply the musical work in question. This is for the simple reason that there is nothing in this conceptual domain, or cluster of domains, that includes or entails (by itself) *The Well-Tempered Clavier*. (2014, p. 157)

Certainly, it would be odd to propose that a piece like *The Well-Tempered Clavier* arrived to Bach as a kind of deductive or inductive inference from his standing knowledge—irrespective of any goals, desires, values, or intentions he may have had. But as soon as we give Super-Bach some desires and intentions—to write a new piece using the clavier, to incorporate the 12-tone scale in an innovative way—it is not *obvious* that any more exotic non-truth-bound state is required. As we saw above, Carruthers would envision Bach as reasoning: "Suppose it sounded like *so*." Granted, Super-Bach needs to have a reason for exploiting his existing knowledge and skills as he does. He needs goals, interests, and aesthetic values—all of which are non-truth bound states—that lead him to draw particular connections and try out new combinations. In that sense, non-truth-bound *motivational* states are indeed necessary, as they are for the creation of any artifact. But we don't yet have a clear role for *sui generis* imaginings.

What Stokes still finds missing is an ability for Super-Bach to engage in "cognitive manipulation." Unlike Super-Bach, actual Bach:

> Presumably imagined, working from within the constraints that he imposed for himself, how certain musical combinations and structures would achieve certain goals. He did not, as it were, simply read off or abstract from the relevant music-theoretic information. He had to manipulate, by use of the imagination, that information (or perhaps add to it) in ways unbound to accurately representing it. (2014, pp. 162–3)

Stokes's argument here is still difficult to follow. We can agree that no new music will arrive as an inductive or deductive inference from what one knows, without relevant goals and desires intervening. But what is it to use information "in ways unbound to accurately representing it"? When we *use* information we do not, in general, *represent* that very information in any way at all. What Stokes seems to have in mind is that, in cognitive manipulation, we often start with representations whose contents we believe and then move on to make use of related representations whose contents we do not believe—at which point the information ceases to be "truth-bound." But once we've seen that hypothetical reasoning, and "considering new possibilities" does not in general demand *sui generis* imaginative states

(Chapters 5 and 6), we need some other reason to think that the kind of cognitive manipulation at work in creativity does.

The issues get a bit clearer when we move away from a complex piece like *The Well-Tempered Clavier* to consider less exalted creative works. For according to Stokes, "even minimally creative thought and behavior require cognitive manipulation" (2014, p. 165). He offers the example of children who are asked, as part of experiments on creativity and cognitive flexibility, to draw "nonexistent houses, people, and animals." A typical work produced in response is a simple figure that combines elements of two categories—a house with eyes as windows, for example. On the one hand, such drawings were in general "quite predictable—largely generated in line with the relevant conceptual schemes" (p. 165). However, Stokes asks:

> Are any of these drawings possibly enabled *merely* by the relevant conceptual knowledge? We know that the subjects consistently deployed their concepts of HOUSE, PERSON, etc., to make their drawings; was this knowledge sufficient? No. The concepts of HOUSE and PERSON, no matter how rich, will not (by themselves) enable a child to draw a house with eyes for windows, a mouth for a front door, and arms and legs. These cross-category changes require the child to cognitively manipulate, rather than faithfully mirror, the conceptual space in particular, albeit minimal, ways. These drawings require non-truth-bound cognitive states. (p. 165)

The key claim here is that drawing a house with eyes requires the child to "cognitively manipulate, rather than faithfully mirror, the conceptual space." What does this mean? Suppose that I am simply *told* to draw a house with eyes for windows. Does this require me to cognitively manipulate my conceptual space? I don't see why it would. I know how to draw a house. I know how to draw eyes. I follow the task instructions by drawing a house with eyes. This requires no adjustment to my concept of a house, or to my concept of eyes. Does doing this require that I enter into states whose contents I disbelieve? I don't think so. There's a perfect parallel here to the most simple cases of pretense discussed earlier (Chapters 7 and 8). To pretend to be a lion, I need to recall what lions are like and use that knowledge to make myself somewhat lion-like. But I do not need to represent that *I am a lion*; there is no need, either, to readjust or modify my concepts of lions or of myself. There is no need, then, to enter into any cognitive state that is in some sense "non-truth-bound." The same goes for making a drawing of a lion-like house: I draw a house and, recalling a lion's salient features, aim to mirror some of those features in the drawing. As Boden notes, this sort of novel category-combination is:

> easy to model on a computer. For nothing is simpler than picking out two ideas (two data structures) and putting them alongside each other...a computer could merrily produce novel combinations till kingdom come. (2004, p. 7)

Would Stokes hold that, in achieving such combinations, the computer must exploit its own functional analog of non-truth-bound states? Presumably he must. But there is no clear reason why we should.

12.6 Back to the Deep Waters

Despite these criticisms, I think that Stokes is on the right track in observing that there is nothing in Bach's knowledge that "includes or entails" the various pieces he composes. The problem is that we don't get from Stokes a clear picture of why his knowledge, *together with* his goals and interests, is not a sufficient mental resource for the piece's creation. To move in that direction, let's consider a more complex creative activity: writing a story. Just as the science teacher assigns a "build challenge" with limited materials, we can imagine a creative writing teacher assigning the following *story challenge*: confining yourself to thus and such characters (a wife, husband, identical twin boys), thus and such setting (Los Angeles in the mid-1970s), and thus and such problems (a contaminated swimming pool; a heart attack), write the best story that you can. Writing the story will require, *inter alia*, reasoning hypothetically about how such individuals might interact, and what would happen if they did this, that, and the other. So far we have a close analogy to the build challenge. A difference is that the "materials" provided by the fiction writing assignment are more open-ended. Decisions will need to be made about their finer features. Do the twins get along, or are they rivals? We can decide that they are rivals and see how that affects the equation. If the story progresses well, we can stick with that decision about what is true in the story; if it does not, we can revise it. Was the pool contaminated by accident, or by design? Again a decision needs to be made about what is true in the story. Once it is made, the story can be developed with that element as one of the "materials." The process of making a decision about what is true in the story and extrapolating about what might happen in such a situation builds on itself cyclically until one arrives at a satisfactory product—a finished story. Writing the story, then, requires an ability to make decisions about the materials to use, to reason hypothetically about likely results of combining them, and to make aesthetic judgments about the value of those results. We can see plenty of *combinatorial* and *explorative* creativity in such work. But none of this creates any obvious need to draw upon states other than beliefs, judgements, decisions, and desires—not lest we re-litigate the debates of earlier chapters. The same points apply to many daydreams, which can be seen as a set of decisions about what is happening in a story we are telling ourselves. (See Chapter 4 for more on daydreams.)

I do think that a story could be written in the way just described—as a kind of interplay between one's goals, values, inferential capacities, and the constraints that have been set. Simply writing a story, then, does not require any *sui generis* imaginative states. However, I don't think that a very *good* story could be written in this way! Or, to put a finer point on it: such an explanation of the psychology of story-writing does not give us any insight into how one should go about writing a good story. We will do well to focus on this gap in the explanation. For as we saw at the outset, the notion of a creative product is inherently value-laden—there has got to be something valuable about the novelty in the product. That value, like creativity itself, comes in degrees. And if we confine ourselves to explaining creative products at the low end of the value spectrum, we are likely to miss the most interesting puzzles creativity presents to us. We may come to see creativity as little more than the dogged application of reasoning heuristics and aesthetic rules of thumb in the service of one's goals and desires. This is nothing that is not already well simulated by current artificial intelligence. To move forward, we need to think more about the difference between a generic fiction and a great fiction, a passable song and a classic, a stick figure and a masterpiece. That is the project I turn to now.

12.7 Songwriters on Songwriting

Paul Zollo's (1997) interviews in *Songwriters on Songwriting* are a valuable resource for anyone interested in the nature of songwriting, and in artistic creation more generally. Zollo is able to draw accomplished songwriters into exceptionally deep, careful, and often hilarious reflection on their craft. I will quote a number of their responses at length to reveal a common theme. They all gesture at something less accountable, less conscious, less reasonable, and more dreamlike in the process of artistic creation than we have so far considered.

Paul Simon: "I don't consciously think about what a song should say. In fact, I consciously try *not* to think about what a song should say...As soon as your mind knows that it's on and it's supposed to produce some lines, either it *doesn't* or it produces things that are very predictable. And that's why I say I'm not interested in writing something that I thought about. I'm interested in *discovering* where my mind wants to go, or what object it wants to pick up...If it doesn't come to me in that surprising way, I don't tend to believe it or get excited about it...I mean, it may be that that's what is slowing me down to such a slow pace, you know, that I keep waiting for this stuff instead of just writing. But just writing what? How do I know what I'm going to write if I don't discover it? If I make up what I'm going to write, all I'm going to write is what I saw on television or what I read in the paper or what I saw...it's not going to be from the underground river of your subconscious. Because that just comes to the surface occasionally and you have to capture it when it happens."

(Zollo, 1997, pp. 95, 98, 120)

Bob Dylan: "It's nice to be able to put yourself in an environment where you can completely accept all the unconscious stuff that comes to you from your inner workings of your mind. And block yourself off to where you can control it all, take it down... There's no rhyme or reason to it, there's no rule... Still staying in the unconscious frame of mind, you can pull yourself out and throw up two rhymes first and work it back. You get the rhymes first and work it back and then see if you can make it make sense in another kind of way. You can stay in the unconscious frame of mind to pull it off, which is the state of mind you have to be in anyway... It's a magical thing, popular song. Trying to press it down into everyday numbers doesn't quite work. It's not a puzzle. There aren't pieces that fit. It doesn't make a complete picture that's ever been seen." (Zollo, 1997, pp. 72, 81–2)

Leonard Cohen: "If I knew where the good songs came from, I'd go there more often. It's a mysterious condition. It's much like the life of a Catholic nun. You're married to a mystery... Things come so damn slow. Things come and they come and it's a tollgate, and they're particularly asking for something that you can't manage. They say, 'We got the goods here. What do you got to pay?' Well, I've got my intelligence, I've got a mind. 'No, we don't want that.' I've got my whole training as a poet. 'No, we don't want that.' I've got some licks, I've got some skills with my fingers on the guitar. 'No, we don't want that either.' Well, I've got a broken heart. 'No, we don't want that.' I've got a pretty girlfriend. 'No, we don't want that.' I've got sexual desire. 'No, we don't want that.' I've got a whole lot of things and the tollgate keeper says, 'That's not going to get it. We want you in a condition that you are not accustomed to. And that you yourself cannot name. We want you in a condition of receptivity that you cannot produce by yourself.' How are you going to come up with that?" (Zollo, 1997, p. 335)

With respect to writing the song "Anthem," Cohen remarks:

"I didn't start with a philosophical position that human activity is not perfectible. And that all human activity is flawed. And it is by intimacy with the flaw that we discern our real humanity and our real connection with divine inspiration. I didn't come up with it that way. I *saw* something broken. It's a different form of cognition."

Neil Young: "Usually I sit down and I go until I'm trying to think. As soon as I start thinking, I quit... then when I have an idea out of nowhere, I start up again. When that idea stops, I stop. I don't force it. If it's not there, it's not there, and there's nothing you can do about it... There's the conscious mind and the subconscious mind and the spirit. And I can only guess as to what is really going on there." (Zollo, 1997, pp. 354–5)

On the one hand, each of these songwriters has a mass of articulable knowledge about songwriting—theories, strategies, influences, and goals they *can* put into words and consciously exploit. To give a small sampling from elsewhere in the interviews: Dylan recommends changing the key of a song when stuck on where to go with it, or working backwards to a lyric with a particular rhyme in mind. Simon bounces a rubber ball to achieve the right focus and emphasizes finding a first line for a song that "has a lot of options"; Cohen works in the morning but recommends trying everything: "thought, meditation, drinking, disillusion, insomnia, vacations..." We can include among these the strategy of *trying not to consciously think* about what the song should be like. In addition to these little "tricks," each has mastered the (fungible) "rules" of different musical genres and knows a great deal of music theory—concerning keys, song structures, harmony, and so on. They know what roads there are to drive on and have paved many of them themselves. Without question, prior practice and expertise are essential components to the kind of creativity we most value.

And yet, for all their practice and expertise, and all their tricks and heuristics for facilitating creativity in themselves, these songwriters are still *waiting*... they are waiting on something else. Their practical skill, theoretical knowledge, goals, values, and desires only take them so far—far enough, I think, to write a passable song, a creative song. But not far enough to write a *great* song. For the latter, something else is required. This "something else" is not an active examination of logical space through the use of non-truth-bound mental states. In trying to explain what it is, they each appeal instead to "the subconscious"—or, for Cohen, to "a condition of receptivity that you cannot produce by yourself." It is from within this condition that *transformative* creativity may emerge—creativity that they are at a loss to explain in terms of *reasons* and that, therefore, is not happily analyzed as kind of means-to-ends *reasoning*. Insights from across the arts and sciences no doubt often spring from the same obscure source. In drawing on it, one appears no longer simply to be combining elements in predictable ways, or exploring the possibilities within a fixed logical space. I want to investigate this condition in the balance of this chapter, to see what more can be said of it and its relation to imagination.

It must first be granted, however, that these songwriter reflections don't constitute an explicit argument that transformative creativity draws on some mental resource "not happily analyzed as a kind of hypothetical reasoning." I think their comments are, instead, *strongly suggestive* of the need for some other account—one that doesn't see artistic creation as a stepwise inferential process. Should that hunch prove incorrect and transformative creativity simply a rarefied form of deductive, inductive, or abductive reasoning, this would only render our work in explaining creativity easier, as I've already shown how a good deal of A-imagining can be understood as the making of inductive and deductive inferences of different kinds (including in favor of conditionals). The problem I saw with Stokes' and

Carruthers' examples was that they didn't highlight the need for anything *other than* ordinary hypothetical reasoning in creativity. The songwriter reflections give us a better sense of where we need to go if we are to face up to the full challenge that creativity presents.

12.8 Creativity and the Subconscious

Let's suppose that transformative creativity very often, or even always, draws upon the subconscious, as these songwriters propose. What would this tell us about the role of imagination in transformative creativity? On the one hand, it is natural to say, as a kind of platitude, that songwriters are relying upon their imaginations in their moments of transformative creativity. And it seems reasonable to add that they are (at least often) engaging in rich thought about the possible and the fantastical, in an epistemically blameless way. To that extent, they are engaged in A-imagining. On the other hand, two platitudinous features of imagination appear at odds with its being involved in such cases. First, imagining—in both the I-imagining and A-imagining senses—is a paradigmatically *conscious* phenomenon, familiar to our mental lives. Yet the songwriters emphasize the need to draw upon the subconscious, and the importance of quieting the conscious mind. This is one reason to think that the imagining they undergo—subconsciously—is not the same sort of process we are familiar with from everyday imaginative acts. Second, one of the key characteristics that, for many, distinguishes A-imagining from believing or judging is its being subject to the will. We can imagine whatever we *choose* to imagine, it is said, and this is the source of its freedom. Yet being subject to the will in this way cuts directly against everything the songwriters have to say about the resource needed for transformative creativity. Whatever it is that lies in the subconscious, it cannot be forced or willfully controlled. Songwriting is instead "a waiting game," a "mystery," with no "rhyme or reason" to it. Try as one might to purposefully bring it about, "nothing works," Cohen laments. To the contrary, when he feels himself *trying* to think of the next line, Neil Young knows he needs to stop.

In earlier chapters I proposed reductive accounts of A-imaginings, such as occur during ordinary pretense or hypothetical reasoning. It is possible—*just* possible—that the kind of (putatively) subconscious cognitions relied upon for transformative creativity are subconscious versions of these same processes. In that case, were we to shine a light on the subconscious during transformative creativity, we'd simply see more of what we are already familiar with from our conscious episodes of action planning and conditional reasoning (whatever that might be!). But I doubt that is the case. Why, after all, would it be so important for the process to occur subconsciously, and without being subject to the will, if the very same resource were available consciously? We should instead consider other possibilities for the kind of mental process that might realize A-imaginings in this context. While *some* A-imaginings relied upon for creative cognition may be much the same as those underlying pretense, conditional reasoning, and the appreciation of fictions, others—including especially those required for transformational creativity—may be quite different. To understand them, I will argue we need to consider a role for *associative* thought processes—ways of transitioning from one mental state to the next that are not determined by principles of reasoning (be they inductive, deductive, or probabilistic), but that are also not at all *random*. (The difference between an associative transition in thought and a deductive or inductive one will be clarified momentarily.)

Before doing so, a word on the relation of transformative creativity to some competing accounts of A-imagining. As we have seen in earlier chapters, the most fully-developed theories of A-imagining focus on its role in guiding pretense, facilitating conditional reasoning, and explaining our engagement with fiction. A key feature of many such accounts is their proposal that the dynamics holding among *sui generis* imaginative states mirror those that hold among beliefs with the same contents (Currie & Ravenscroft, 2002; Doggett & Egan, 2012; Nichols & Stich, 2000; Weinberg & Meskin, 2006b; Williamson, 2016). Such imaginative states are said to be "belief-like" in this respect. The fact that they develop in ways that mirror belief-like inductive and deductive inferences is supposed to explain why they can be relied upon when reasoning our way to conditionals, recovering inexplicit fictional content, and generating pretenses that follow realistic scripts. Yet this cuts against their suitability for explaining transformative creativity, which, it appears, requires something other than drawing out implications from a set of premises. These theorists may respond that it is only a norm or regularity of the poisted *sui generis* states that they have belief-like inferential characteristics—that this "default mode" can be suspended in acts of transformative creativity. Would that open the door to such states serving in explanations of transformative creativity as well?

Perhaps, but only at the cost of turning one's theory into mush. These *sui generis* imaginings would then, at times, be paradigmatically conscious mental states, under volitional control, with tight belief-like inferential characteristics and, at other times, unconscious states unbounded by any inferential constraints and beyond control of the will. It is not flatly impossible for there to be a mental Jekyll-and-Hyde of this sort, with one set of causes and effects in one case, and quite the opposite in another. But we might then wonder: is there anything imagination *can't* do? Could it then be that some of what we *thought* were ordinary beliefs and desires are in fact *sui generis* imaginings that have ditched their default mode and are now behaving *exactly* like beliefs and desires? It's an unhappy possibility to consider, bordering on incoherent. At a minimum, it would require a way of identifying and typing states other than by their causes and effects. If there is any default position in this area, it should be that the states exploited in transformative creativity (alluded to by the songwriters, above) and hypothetical reasoning are different in kind. This is compatible with their still being A-imaginings, however, so long as we allow A-imaginings themselves to be heterogeneous.

In any case, I don't think this criticism would come as an unwelcome surprise to the philosophers in question. Currie & Ravenscroft are explicit in distinguishing "creative imagination" from "recreative imagination," holding they are only theorizing about the latter (2002, pp. 9–11), while Nichols & Stich (2000) and Williamson (2016) never make any effort to extend their views to creativity, nor to other subconscious processes beyond control of the will. The point is worth emphasizing, however, that *whether or not* one posits *sui generis* imaginative states to explain pretense and hypothetical reasoning, there remain *further* challenges in characterizing transformative creativity. We cannot "buy" explanations of both by positing a single *sui generis* type of imaginative state without, in effect, positing a state with quite distinct functional roles in different contexts. And that just raises the question of whether we indeed have just a single type of state at work in each context. In short: we all need to say something *new* about transformative creativity.

12.9 Creativity and Associationism

The songwriter reflections are intriguing in the way they highlight the need for mental transitions beyond conscious control—transitions that are difficult to characterize as *inferences*. As mysterious as this may seem in the context of creative cognition, it is not so unusual that our thoughts unfold in non-inferential patterns beyond conscious control. Suppose that you are asked to name as many animals as you can in thirty seconds. Will you be able to explain why you thought of the specific animals you did, and not others? Perhaps you will think of a farm and use that setting to generate ideas. This will still leave open the question of why some farm animals came to mind, and not others—and why a farm itself came to mind, and not some other place where animals are found, such as a zoo, a forest, or an African savannah. In answer to such questions, we can of course *speculate*. ("It's probably because I saw a copy of *Animal Farm* on the table this morning.") But, in most cases, we will just be making an educated guess as to why a specific setting or animal sprang to mind. It will not be that we made a choice to think of animals in that order, or desired to think of a farm more than a zoo. Folk psychological explanation comes up empty-handed in such cases, insofar as there are no beliefs, desires, or intentions available to explain why we first settled on the farm as a prompt, or why a chicken was the third, instead of the fourth, animal that came to mind.

In this sense, there are quite unremarkable aspects of ordinary cognition that are no more *rationalizable* than Paul Simon's spontaneous arrival at the lyric,

"There's a girl in New York City who calls herself the human trampoline."[8] This is not to say there is no explanation *at all* for these things. It is instead to say that the explanation will not appeal to a sequence of folk psychological states deployed in an act of practical reasoning. And where there are no steps of reasoning to be adduced, the transition in thought cannot be considered an inference. For inferences, traditionally understood, are simply transitions in thought that follow a reason scheme (such as *modus ponens*, or statistical induction), whereby one thought provides the reason for the next.[9]

Yet, despite our inability to explain the order of animals uttered as the result of an inference, there may be associative explanations available, whether or not we are in a position to articulate them. The same may be true for Simon's lyric, even if the associations are more obscure. So we will do well to consider the nature of associative explanation in more depth, as a means for broadening the tools we have for thinking about creative cognition in cases where it outruns anything we can comfortably characterize as an inferential processes.

We can begin with some background on associationism as a general approach to understanding transitions in thought. Associationist theories of thought have had adherents from the British empiricists (most notably Hume), through Skinnerian behaviorists, to present-day connectionists. Associationist principles are also alive and well within contemporary empirical psychology—particularly evident in work on so-called "semantic networks" (Collins & Loftus, 1975; Goñi et al., 2011; Sowa, 1991). While these approaches all differ in important ways, each is committed to what Eric Mandelbaum (2017) calls, somewhat pejoratively, "a certain arationality of thought." On any associationist approach, Mandelbaum explains:

> A creature's mental states are associated because of some facts about its causal history, and having these mental states associated entails that bringing one of a pair of associates to mind will, *ceteris paribus*, ensure that the other also becomes activated.

What leads one thought to follow another, on an associationist picture, is not adherence to a deductive or inductive reason scheme, but rather "facts about [one's] causal history." Unlike the inductive or deductively warranted thought

[8] In Simon's telling: "That line came to me when I was walking past the Museum of Natural History. *For no reason* I can think of. It's not related to anybody or anything. It just struck me as funny" (Zollo, 1997, p. 110).

[9] John Pollock connects the dots between inferences, reasons, and reasoning as follows: "Reasoning proceeds by constructing arguments for conclusions, and the individual inferences making up the arguments are licensed by what we might call reason schemes" (Pollock, 2008, p. 451). Reason schemes, for Pollock, are equivalent to inference rules—such as *modus ponens*, in deductive reasoning, or the statistical syllogism of probabilistic reasoning (viz., "This is an A and the probability of an A being a B is high. Therefore, defeasibly, this is a B."). The individual inferences of an argument collectively make up the reasons for the conclusion.

transitions that are the centerpiece of heavy-duty conceptions of folk psychology (discussed in Chapter 2), associative thought transitions "are not predicated on a prior logical relationship between the elements of the thoughts," and are "not based on the logico-syntactic properties of thoughts" (Mandelbaum, 2017). They are based instead on associative relations among the thoughts, which consist in two thoughts having been causally contiguous in the past (e.g., "The bell is ringing. Food is being dispensed."), or bearing some other non-logical, causal relation (such as contiguity in a neural semantic network (Collins & Loftus, 1975)). The causal facts responsible for two thoughts being associated may at times contrive to elicit thought transitions mirroring those of someone following a particular reason scheme. But they need not by nature. Associative transitions in thought, Mandelbaum notes, can be:

> Just a stream of ideas that needn't have any formal, or even rational, relation between them, such as the transition from THIS COFFEE SHOP IS COLD to RUSSIA SHOULD ANNEX IDAHO, without there being any intervening thoughts. This transition could be subserved merely by one's association of IDAHO and COLD, or it could happen because the two thoughts have tended to co-occur in the past, and their close temporal proximity caused an association between the two thoughts to arise (or for many other reasons).
>
> (Mandelbaum, 2017)

Taken as a claim about the nature of *all* thought processes, associationism is controversial and at direct odds with the "heavy-duty" computational theory of mind defended by Fodor and others (see Chapter 2). Less contentious is the claim that at least some thought processes are associationist in nature. Consider, for instance, *free association*. In naming things we associate with, say, Isaac Newton (apples, gravity, wigs, Fig Newtons...), different ideas or concepts trigger each other, due to their being associated with the initial concept. We are not drawing inferences but simply associating one thing with another. Associative transitions can also plausibly occur among propositional thoughts, and not merely concepts.[10] Many ordinary cases of propositional memory—remembering that *p*, because one has just judged that *q*—are plausible examples. Judging that you will need to drive to work today (= *q*), may, for instance, remind you that the car could use an oil change (= *p*). It is not surprising that thinking of driving would prompt you to

[10] Associationism comes in both "pure" and "impure" variants, where impurity amounts to thoughts having structure (such as predicative structure) over and above anything that can be accounted for in purely associative terms. A common challenge to pure associationist theories is that they cannot account—in purely associationist terms—for the difference between thinking about *x* and then about *F* (because being *F* is associated with *x*), from thinking that *x is F* (Fodor, 2003; Mandelbaum, 2017). I consider an impure associationist account here—where not all thought must be explained in associationist terms—as it is likely to have wider appeal.

remember that you should change the oil. But neither is this case of remembering well viewed as an *inference*, made in accordance with an abstract reasoning scheme. Thinking about driving to work simply reminded you that the car could use an oil change.

Less obvious, and more controversial, is whether we acquire *new* beliefs through associative processes. Mandelbaum's example of moving from the thought that "this coffee shop is cold," to "Russia should annex Idaho," would be an example of this, supposing the second thought were a newly acquired belief. Let us suppose, for the sake of argument, that we do at times arrive at new beliefs through associative processes. As Mandelbaum notes, calling such a process an *inference* would be something of an oxymoron, insofar as the notion of an inference carries with it the implication of a rule or principle relating the relevant propositions, in virtue of which one provides rational warrant for the other. A dog's associative thought transition from "The bell is ringing" to "Food is being dispensed" may have the air of an inference, but the principle that links the two is brute causal contiguity. Any thought at all, on any topic, that comes to follow "The bell is ringing" due to constant causal contiguity would qualify as the same kind of "inference."

Where a proper inference occurs, there is the possibility of providing a folk psychological description of the states it involved. For to give a folk psychological explanation for why one has inferred what one has is simply to attribute a collection of thoughts that *rationally warrant* those that follow them. And a thought rationally warrants another insofar as the transition from one to the next is explained by the following of a reason scheme. Accordingly, when we find ourselves at a loss to explain—even to ourselves—a certain sequence of ideas or thoughts we have had, it is often because there is no way of seeing the sequence as a set of reasonable *inferences*, and hence no available folk psychological explanation for why we should have thought what we did. In such cases, it will be tempting to attribute their genesis to something beyond conscious control—to something, perhaps, "in the subconscious." In some cases, the appeal to the subconscious may be quite correct. But another possibility is that the entire process occurred consciously, and that we are unable to *explain* it just because it was not an inference—and, hence, not something to be rationalized via the attribution of beliefs, desires and a reason scheme governing their relations.

Consider again the case of generating animal names as quickly as you can: it could be that there is unconscious reasoning taking place that explains why we come up with the specific animals we do, and that this is why we are unable to give any clear account of why we named just those animals in that order. Alternatively, it could be that the animals that were chosen each followed each other in the order they did due to associative factors we are simply unable to articulate. In that case, the relevant processing was only unconscious in the sense that we do not have conscious awareness of the associative principles that move us from one thought to the next. But the thoughts themselves were, perhaps, conscious. There need not have been some further acts of picking and choosing from among possible names that occurred subconsciously, and which we would apprehend were we to shine a light on the subconscious.

The point I am after here is that the mental processing that songwriters and other artists often attribute to the subconscious may be associative in nature, and, *ipso facto*, not the sort of thing to be viewed as an inference. In that case, we should expect the relevant thought transitions to be inexplicable to the people having them—insofar as they are not subsumable under patterns of practical reasoning involving beliefs and desires—even if they were in fact entirely conscious. With this idea in mind, I will look in some detail at an actual associative process carried out in a recently developed artificial neural network. My claim will not be that it gives an accurate model of what in fact goes on during creative cognition—only that it *might*. Importantly, its mere possibility throws light on a whole range of strategies for explaining transformative creativity, and for relating such creativity to A-imagining.

12.10 Generative Adversarial Networks

Connectionist networks—otherwise known as "artificial neural networks" or "neural nets"—are schematic models of neural activity, representing sets of neurons connected to each other by varying degrees of strength. Different sets (or "layers") of "nodes" in a neural network serve as analogs for different sets of neurons, with input nodes standing for sensory-perceptual neurons, output notes corresponding to motor output neurons, and hidden layer nodes corresponding to all the relevant neural activation in between.[11] During a lengthy training process, during which the strength of the connections among the many different nodes in each layer are adjusted in response to its errors and successes, networks can be trained to accomplish complex tasks mirroring human perceptual discriminative capacities, such as face recognition, object identification, and phonology to text translation. Adjusting the strength of a connection within an artificial neural network is meant to serve as an analog to the strengthening and weakening of synaptic connections between neurons that occur during learning and development. As earlier remarked (Chapter 2), much of connectionism's appeal lies in the clear picture it provides of how specific cognitive abilities could be realized in a physical object with the structure and causal dynamics of the human brain.

While the general ideas behind connectionism have been widely discussed in philosophy and psychology since the 1980s, the last ten years have seen an exponential increase in the complexity of the tasks such networks are able to carry out.

[11] See Garson (2018) for a helpful primer on the basics of connectionist networks.

This is due in large part to substantial new investments by companies like Google, Facebook, Apple, and Amazon in developing the necessary theoretical and technological tools. As these models, and the algorithms that implement them, have grown in complexity, adding substantially more "hidden layers" of nodes between input and output, they have become known as "deep" neural networks. In 2020, Google Translate, Amazon's voice-to-text assistant Alexa, and Facebook's face-recognition software are some of the most visible applications of this technology.

In a "supervised" deep neural network, the network gains its discriminative abilities by being "trained" on a preexisting set of stimuli that have already been appropriately labelled. For instance, to create a network that can discriminate turtle images from images other animals, we might start with a large collection of photos of animals serving as input. The person training the network already knows which pictures are of turtles and which are not. The activation of each individual input node in the network, we can suppose, is determined by a single pixel's level of illumination in each image. Yet there will be just two output nodes corresponding to the answers: turtle/not-turtle. At the beginning of training, the weights among nodes in the hidden layers between inputs and outputs are randomly distributed. When the network's input nodes register the first picture, *some* of the connections among nodes in the hidden layer will have been "correct" in the sense that, due to their weighing, they favored activation of the output node corresponding to the correct response ("turtle" if indeed it was a picture of a turtle). The network's learning is then *supervised* in the sense that, after each new input is registered and a verdict given, the weights of the connections that favored the correct response are slightly strengthened, while those of the connections favoring the wrong response are decreased (using the same fixed "backpropagation" algorithm). Over the course of many, many trials and subsequent re-weightings, the network gradually becomes more reliable at activating the "turtle" output node when and only when the input image is of a turtle.

Importantly, this learning process does not involve giving the network a set of explicit rules and reason schemes by which to identify turtles. For instance, the network is never given a rule to follow such as: "If X has a round shell, and four legs, and a reptilian head, THEN X is a turtle." Its discriminations may well *conform* to such a rule, insofar as it only identifies things with round shells, four legs, and reptilian heads as turtles. The point, however, is that its training never involved its receiving such a rule but, rather, the gradual adjustment of the strength of connections between hundreds of nodes in hidden layers. Partly because of this, a well-trained network will be less "brittle" than a rule-governed classification system, with the system less likely to rule out a stimulus on the basis of its missing a particular salient trait. Moreover, programmers themselves do not need to know any such a rule in order to set up and supervise the network. Someone just needs to tell the trainer of the algorithm which pictures are of turtles and which are not, so they can adjust weights accordingly. (And, as we will see in a moment, even this degree of "supervision" is not always necessary.) Because the network is not using any explicit rules or reason schemes in making its judgments, the sequence of states within the network leading up to its judgment are not *inferences* in our earlier-defined sense. The algorithm is not manipulating symbols in a stepwise, serial manner to compute anything akin to *modus ponens*, or the statistical syllogism. Its computations are instead distributed and parallel. The weightings of many different nodes simultaneously influence the network's output. And these weightings themselves are simply established through trial and error. If the network is trained on a sufficiently broad set of stimuli, including turtles of exotic appearance, it can come to classify turtles correctly without anyone's being able to articulate the rule that it is following to do so. Indeed, researchers typically have to conduct a separate experiment, with carefully constructed stimuli, to determine which features a network is in fact favoring when making its discriminations.

Now, when we think about creativity, we are interested in how creative products are *generated*, not in how they are discriminated from each other. But a neural network initially set up to discriminate a type of thing can, in effect, reverse its processing to generate plausible new instances of that type. These are called *generative neural networks*. Taking input from what would be considered the output node of a discriminative network, a generative network exploits the same set of weightings in the opposite direction to generate an instance of something likely to fall within the class of things the network was initially set up to discriminate. An ingenious method was recently developed for fine-tuning these generative networks, by pitting two networks—a generator and a discriminator—against each other (Goodfellow et al., 2014). Taken as a pair, these are known as *generative adversarial networks* (GANs) (Goodfellow et al., 2014; Radford, Metz, & Chintala, 2015). The generator has the role of producing outputs likely to fall within a certain class of things (turtle images, say), while the discriminator has the role of detecting whether the output of the generative network is indeed a member of the class of objects the discriminator has been trained to detect. When the discriminator is able to detect that the output of the generator does not fall within the class of things the discriminator was set up to detect (e.g., images of turtles), the hidden nodes within the generator are adjusted to decrease weightings that favored the "not a turtle" response in the discriminator. Likewise, whenever the discriminator is "fooled" by the generator, classifying something as a turtle image that was really just a creation of the generative network, the discrimator's weights are adjusted accordingly to deemphasize weightings that led it to give a false positive. This "double feedback loop" allows each network to continually fine tune itself against the other. The generator gets successively better at generating convincing members of the class to be discriminated, while the discriminator grows increasingly adept at discriminating real members from phonies.

In one striking deployment of GANs, researchers at Nvidia created a generative network capable of producing photorealistic images of (non-existent) celebrities

(Karras, Aila, Laine, & Lehtinen, 2017). The network was originally trained on thousands of photographs of celebrities gleaned from the internet. This was an instance of "unsupervised" training, however, in the sense that the images were not contrasted to another set of, say, non-celebrity images. Rather, taking only the celebrity images as input, the network was able to extract regularities within the set to calibrate itself for later discriminating celebrity images from images of other things (e.g., non-celebrities). The network's fine-grained discriminative capacity was subsequently used in reverse to generate images of (nonexistent) people who sort of look like celebrities—i.e., possible members of the set of things it was trained to discriminate. (It is an oversimplification to say the discriminative network is simply "run in reverse" when in generative mode; but the idealization is harmless for our purposes). This generative network was fine-tuned by being placed in a double feedback loop with a mirror-image discriminator network that received the same unsupervised training. After thousands of iterations, and resulting adjustments to each network, a generative network emerged capable of creating photorealistic images people who have a "celebrityish" look to them; human observers cannot reliably discriminate them from photos of actual celebrities they do not know (Metz & Collins, 2018).

Now to the philosophical relevance of GANs. As noted, my claim will not be that human creative cognition in fact relies upon processes akin to GANs—only that it *might*, and that the very possibility of its doing so opens up a range of promising strategies for answering the puzzles we have confronted about transformative creativity. With this in mind, suppose that we could ask a system deploying such a GAN how it came up with the image it generated of a possible celebrity. What would it say? There would be no set of deductive or inductive rules it could mention—not if it was speaking truthfully—and, thus, no sequence of states that constituted the following of such rules. The image was not arrived at by drawing inferences, or by following an explicit procedure whose inference schema could be stated in English. And yet we can understand its generation as resulting from a complex, distributed computation arrived at though an unsupervised learning process, during which it latched on to regularities it could not itself name.

Suppose now that the thought-transitions that occur during transformative creativity are rather like the GAN processing just described. We should not, in that case, be surprised to find that songwriters, novelists, painters, and the like are not able to fully explain why or how they arrived at their products, or to characterize their insights in inferential terms.[12] For while there are no doubt *some* processes involved in creativity that can be seen as inferential, our most finely

[12] Boden (2004, pp. 134–8) also discusses connectionism as a means to explaining the associative processes apparently at work in creative cognition, highlighting "the ability of neural networks to learn to associate (combine) patterns without being explicitly programmed in respect of *those* patterns" (p. 137).

tuned generative capacities may in fact be associative in nature. Artists receive "unsupervised training" through years of exposure to works they find aesthetically interesting and inspiring. They are, in effect, extracting regularities from the raw data to which they are exposed, in a way that cannot be linguistically expressed or formulated into a maxim. Eventually, they become sufficiently adept as critics to reverse their discriminative capacities in generating novel works of their own—possible members of the set of works on which they were trained. Being skilled discriminators of aesthetic value (and the features on which it depends), they are able to serve as their own adversarial networks, setting off alarms and changing their approach when their works do not meet the standards of those they admire.[13] Through an iterative process of revision and criticism, they eventually arrive at their goal. They are unable to distinguish their own work from a "fake"—i.e., from something lacking in the kind aesthetic features they have trained themselves to discriminate. Yet their abilities will in a sense remain a mystery to themselves, as there will never be clear *reasons* they can provide for how or why they made what they did—for the process was not inferential. They may as well chalk it up to "the subconscious."

It may, however, seem that the analogy to GANs leaves no room for genuine originality to emerge—at least, not orginality of the sort we expect of *transformative* creativity, which was our explanandum. The GAN that generates celebrity*ish* photos is, after all, highly imitative in nature. It succeeds precisely by making images indistinguishable from those in a preexisting set. How would something like a GAN create room for a new *style* to emerge? How do we get from fine-grained imitation to creative generation?

Two points in response. First, most art—even great art—*is* highly imitative in nature. Consider Dylan's debt to Woody Guthrie, or Amy Winehouse's to Billie Holliday. An artist's work is understood, in the first instance, in relation to her influences. Second, and more important, we have to consider the diversity within each person's "training set." A GAN trained only on images of celebrities is like a poet who only ever read the work of William Carlos Williams. Such a poet would likely write poems too highly derivative of Williams to be considered creative in any transformative sense. But now add to her training set thousands of poems from the middle ages to present day—an idiosyncratic cluster weighted by her tastes and interests. In understanding and enjoying the works within that set, she is implicitly tuning her generative capacities to a singular frequency—one that distills her individual training and that emerges with an identity of its own. The same capacities—the same network—may one day be exploited in the generation of new poems in an original, transformative style.

[13] Here again is Paul Simon: "So I let the songs go this way and that way and this way and whatever way it is and basically what I do is be the *editor*: 'Oh, that's interesting. Never mind *that*, that's not so interesting. That's good, *that's a good line*'" (Zollo, 1997, p. 95).

Where could *imagination* fit in to all this? Because GANs make use of connectionist "deep" neural networks that rely upon parallel distributed processing, it is not proper to describe them as exploiting language-like representations in a stepwise, serial fashion. This means we cannot accurately describe them in heavy-duty folk psychological terms (see Chapter 2); there is no fit to be made between notion of a GAN and, say, a Belief Box or Imagination Box. Yet we can still give light-duty folk psychological descriptions of the GAN processing, insofar as the processing gives rise to certain dispositions in the system that can be described and tracked in folk psychological terms. Supposing that the celebrity-photo-generating GAN were embedded within a system we were otherwise comfortable describing in (light-duty) folk psychological terms, it seems reasonable to describe its generative processing as "imagining possible celebrities," insofar as it results in images of celebrity-like faces. Likewise, the poet who was just described as using GAN-like processing can be seen as imagining possible poems and possible next lines. Yet we could alternatively, and equally accurately, describe the celebrity photo GAN-system as *judging* that certain images look like celebrities, and the poet as *judging* that thus and such would be a good poem, or as *deciding* that thus and such would be a good next line. In short, the dispositions we ascribe—invoking imagining in one case, and judging and deciding in the other—are essentially the same. It is, then, possible to explain this sort of (transformative) imagining in more basic (light-duty) folk psychological terms.

12.11 The Importance of Being Earnest

The account I have sketched of transformative creativity, and of the imaginings it involves, aims to show how creativity can rely upon years of training, even if experts are unable to articulate the principles behind their work, or to generate new works by following an explicit procedure. We can see why trying *intentionally* to come up with a creative new song might backfire—why Neil Young is right to stop when he senses himself trying to think up the next line of a song, or why Paul Simon tries not to think about what a song will be about. For in trying to think our way to an answer, we will be tempted to reason our way there through a set of inferences. ("If I have lyrics x, y, and z, then I ought to follow them with…what??") This is not the way works are created on the model of a GAN. Trying to arrive at the next line as an inference will leave us spinning our wheels. A better analogy is that we must learn to play our minds like an instrument, letting the strings ring out in their natural tuning.

But this last analogy—and indeed the entire appeal to GANs above—may seem to paint too simple a picture. To generate great art, could it really be that we just need to reverse our discriminative capacities and let 'er rip? No. We have to recall Leonard Cohen's dismal assessment that, when it comes to eliciting the state of mind needed for writing a good song, "nothing works." This much is evident from the fact that many a refined critic, with carefully tuned discriminative capacities, cannot *create* compelling work. What are they missing?

We first must take account of the basic teachable skills necessary to any particular field. It doesn't matter how refined your taste in piano concertos may be. If you haven't learned to play the piano, and don't grasp the basics of music theory, you won't be able to write a concerto yourself. The same goes for painting, fiction-writing, philosophizing, songwriting, and any other creative endeavor: there are essential skills and techniques—the sort of things imparted in MFA and PhD programs—whose mastery requires practice. These are necessary to convert one's discriminative capacities into productive ones. The interesting question is what *more* transformative creativity still requires. To move closer to an answer—to really understand the bait on Bob Dylan's line[14]—we need to pan out from neural networks and teachable skills to consider matters of character and motivation. Here Matthew Kieran's writings on creativity are particularly illuminating, in ways I'll describe in the next section. We will not arrive at a guide for how we ourselves can take our place among the great artists, of course. But, with luck, we will gain a better understanding of their process.

12.12 Character, Creativity, and Conscious Dreams

Matthew Kieran (2014) analyzes creativity as a virtue of character, prioritizing traits like courage, patience, and honesty over intellectual capacity. Whether one is working in art, philosophy, or science, he notes:

> It takes honesty to evaluate the nature and value of what one is doing properly; it takes courage to be prepared to fail; it takes humility and open-mindedness to recognize when one has gone wrong; and it takes perseverance and fortitude to continue to work at something for its own sake or in seeking to do justice to an idea. (2014, pp. 132–3)

Kieren's claim isn't that you need to be a *saint* to generate transformative creative works. It's rather that there are specific virtues—diligence, open-mindedness, courage, fortitude—that tend to promote one's ability in that direction. Such character

[14] From Zollo's (1997) interview with Dylan:

ZOLLO: "Arlo Guthrie recently said 'Songwriting is like fishing in a stream; you put in your line and hope you catch something. And I don't think anyone downstream from Bob Dylan ever caught anything.'" [Much laughter].

ZOLLO: Any idea how you've been able to catch so many?"

BOB DYLAN: "It's probably the bait."

virtues are as much a requirement for transformative creativity as are training in the basic skills of an art, or the development of an ability to tell the aesthetically good from the bad. They affect one's ability to gain the required skills in the first place, of course; but, equally important, they raise the odds that one will overcome the drives that "tend to pull us toward compromise, self-deception, and over-inflated estimations of the nature and value of what we do" (p. 133).

Kieran rightly draws links between these virtues and the having of "intrinsic motivations," where these are motivations grounded in "values internal to the relevant domain." Compared to the person with extrinsic motivations, someone with intrinsic motivations will be "more sensitive to and motivated by reasons bound up with the goods internal to the activity in question" (p. 129). For instance, if one's motivation is intrinsic,

> a subject is more likely to take risks, more likely to attend in an open-minded way to what she's done, envisage different possibilities, and be directed by thought in action toward realizing the inherent values in a given domain. (p. 129)

By contrast, when the motivation is extrinsic, we'll be inclined to take shortcuts and apply formulaic strategies, using the product as means to some other end. Work done in the service of extrinsic goals, Kieren adds, "often only coincidentally tracks and typically pulls away from the intrinsic values of the given domain" (p. 131). "The extrinsically motivated agent is keying into certain social dynamics and goods," he adds, "where the aesthetic quality and value is coincidental to such" (p. 130).

There are two kinds of social courage Kieran identifies that facilitate transformative creativity. First, there is a kind of courage-through-modesty required in honestly assessing one's own efforts and abilities; second, and perhaps more importantly, there is the courage required to maintain an intrinsic motivation—for this requires dismissing, as irrelevant, the approval of others; and, more troublingly, it may expose oneself to ridicule. I am reminded again of a comment from Zollo's interview with Paul Simon, where Simon describes the self-imposed barriers that lead to "writer's block":

> When I have writer's block (though I don't think of it as writer's block anymore), what it is is that you have something to say but you don't want to say it. So your mind says, 'I have nothing to say. I've just nothing more to say. I can't write anything. I have no thoughts.' Closer to the truth is that you have a thought that you really would prefer not to have. And you're not going to say that thought. Your mind is protected. Once you discover what that thought is, if you can find another way of approaching it that isn't negative to you, then you can deal with that subject matter. (Zollo, 1997, p. 98)

Simon is pointing to a kind of courage—in front of oneself and others—needed to overcome the natural self-censors that shield us from our more unpleasant, offensive, vulnerable, or embarrassing thoughts. The word "courage" doesn't quite capture this virtue, as it seems equal parts humility and patience. But we at least have an inkling for why the virtue is not easily acquired—and why "freely" generating thoughts worth recording is not as easy as it might seem. Each of us has an armada of self-protective rationalizations aimed at stopping it.

Earlier, in connection to GANs, I spoke, metaphorically, of transformative creativity resulting from learning to play one's own mind like an instrument, letting its strings ring out in their natural tuning. To be more precise about what that might involve, the idea is this: self-conscious, self-protective, reason-concerned thought may perhaps interfere with the production of the kinds of new thoughts and connections that would result from running our discriminative capacities in reverse (as on the GAN model). For the latter sort of associative thoughts will reflect the actual shape of our minds—as weathered by experience—as opposed to what we might wish that shape might be. The artist's mantra of "try not to try" can be heard as a directive not to interfere, through self-editing and self-censorship, with such associative thought production. This is much easier said than done, of course, because obeying the self-censoring, self-rationalizing inner voice is so fundamental to being a socially engaged human being. It is not only a matter of skill, but also of character that one is able to obey the artist's directive to ignore it. It takes a certain kind of courage, perhaps to the point of recklessness, to lower your defenses in order to, in effect, dream while awake. The comparison to dreaming is intended literally: for in dreams, too, our self-supervisory, reason-giving systems fall away to let our more interesting fears, wishes, desires, and quirks reveal themselves. Dreams are indeed evidence that we all *have* the basic ability to generate rich, creative scenarios without *feeling like* we are doing so. The person skilled in transformative creativity has gained the special ability to summon, shape, and explore those states while awake. That skill is inseparable from his or her character.

We can, then, explain a person's creativity *in part* by appeal to their interest in the intrinsic features of the form itself, together with their more general character virtues: their patience in developing and revising their work, their humility in accepting critique, their courage to risk looking like a fool, their confidence in their own abilities. If we want to understand why one person with a highly developed aesthetic sense and finely tuned discriminative skills shows transformative creativity, while another does not, their respective characters and motivations are good places to look. These traits will feed back into the development of their aesthetic skills and discriminative abilities: the deeper a person's concern for the intrinsic values of a discipline, and the greater their diligence, the more time and effort will be expended in sharpening their aesthetic sense and productive skills.

Through it all, a certain foolhardy courageousness will be essential to quieting the self-conscious, self-rationalizing mind, so as to let its proper tuning ring out.

12.13 Concluding Thoughts

There are many things we might wish to explain about creativity. I have tried to focus on those most pressing from the perspective of contemporary philosophy of mind, with an eye toward shedding some light on the nature of the "imaginings" required for creative cognition. I drew distinctions among kinds of creativity—combinatorial, explorative, and transformative—in order to highlight a more basic distinction between *inferential* and *non-inferential* (associative) thought processes. While I suggested that transformative creativity most obviously requires the latter, that link is itself a bit artificial. Some acts of transformative creativity may well result from complex inferential processes, while some explorative and combinatorial creativity may draw upon non-inferential associative processes. Ultimately, the distinction between an inferential and a non-inferential thought process cuts deeper than the heuristic distinctions I have made among "kinds" of creativity. It also cuts differently (if not deeper) than the distinction between imagining and judging. Just as imaginings can be seen as in some sense inferential in nature (as it is by those who see it as a kind of "offline" inference (e.g., Nichols & Stich, 2000; Currie & Ravenscroft, 2002; Williams, 2017), judgments can be seen as associative—as they were by early associationists, such as Hume, and as they are within theories of judgment modelled on contemporary neural networks. So if the reflections of songwriters and other artists convince us that not all creative cognition can be inferential in nature, they don't yet tell us whether such cognition requires *sui generis* imaginative states, or judgments instead.

In any case, the fact that artists lack any sense of control over their most important generative cognitions suggests that such states are not well analyzed as the kind of (conscious, controllable) cognitions that *sui generis* imaginings are normally thought to be. Instead I offered recently developed generative adversarial neural networks as possible models for how we should think about creative cognition that is not inferential in nature. Such computational structures—like all artificial neural networks—have the advantage of being modelled on the structure of the brain, and of showing how both pattern-recognition *and* the generation of novel products that fit a certain pattern can occur in an "unsupervised" manner, without need for specific inferential principles to be programmed in at the start. While we do not yet know the extent to which human creativity draws on similar processes, there are promising and rapidly developing research programs in place.

Finally, there are questions about creativity that aren't well answered by appeal to a cognitive architecture shared (presumably) by all humans. After all, the ability for transformative creativity is not evenly dispersed. This is why I concluded with some thoughts on character and motivation, which contribute essentially to the development and refinement of our basic capacities for creative cognition. There is a sense in which we all have the cognitive tools needed for transformative creativity; whether we are able to cultivate, refine, and exploit them is a matter of character.

References

Ackermann, W., & Hilbert, D. (1928). *Grundzüge der theoretischen Logik*. Berlin: Springer.

Adams, Ernest W. (1970). Subjunctive and Indicative Conditionals. *Foundations of Language*, *6*(1), 89–94.

Addis, D. R., Pan, L., Vu, M., Laiser, N., & Schacter, D. L. (2009). Constructive Episodic Simulation of the Future and the Past: Distinct Subsystems of a Core Brain Network Mediate Imagining and Remembering. *Neuropsychologia*, *47*, 2222–38.

Arcangeli, M. (2014). Against Cognitivism about Supposition. *Philosophia*, *42*(3), 607–24.

Arcangeli, M. (2018). *Supposition and the Imaginative Realm: A Philosophical Inquiry*. New York: Routledge.

Arcangeli, M. (2019). The Two Faces of Mental Imagery. *Philosophy and Phenomenological Research*. doi:10.1111/phpr.12589

Arp, R. (2008). *Scenario Visualization*. Cambridge, MA: MIT Press.

Austin, J. L. (1958). Pretending. *Proceedings of the Aristotelian Society, Supplementary Volumes*, *32*, 261–78.

Austin, J. L. (1975). *How to Do Things with Words* (Vol. 75). Oxford: Clarendon Press.

Austin, J. L. (1979). Pretending. In J. O. Urmson & G. J. Warnock (Eds.), *Philosophical Papers* (pp. 253–71). Oxford: Oxford University Press.

Aydede, M. (2015). The Language of Thought Hypothesis. In E. N. Zalta (Ed.), *The Stanford Encyclopedia of Philosophy* (Fall 2015 ed.). Stanford, CA: Stanford University Press.

Balcerak Jackson, M. (2016). On the Epistemic Value of Imagining, Supposing, and Conceiving. In A. Kind & P. Kung (Eds.), *Knowledge through Imagination* (pp. 41–60). Oxford: Oxford University Press.

Baron-Cohen, S. (1989). The Autistic Child's Theory of Mind: A Case of Specific Developmental Delay. *Journal of Child Psychology and Psychiatry, and Allied Disciplines*, *30*(2), 285–97.

Baron-Cohen, S. (1995). *Mindblindness*. Cambridge, MA: MIT Press.

Baron-Cohen, S., Leslie, A., & Frith, U. (1986). Mechanical, Behavioral and Intentional Understanding of Picture Stories in Autistic Children. *British Journal of Developmental Psychology*, *4*, 113–25.

Baron-Cohen, S., Wheelwright, S., Stone, V., & Rutherford, M. (1999). A Mathematician, a Physicist and a Computer Scientist with Asperger's Syndrome: Performance on Folk Psychology and Folk Physics Tests. *Neurocase*, *5*, 475–83.

Barrouillet, P., Gauffroy, C., & Lecas, J.-F. (2008). Mental Models and the Suppositional Account of Conditionals. *Psychological Review*, *115*(3), 760.

Bartlett, G. (2018). Occurrent States. *Canadian Journal of Philosophy*, *48*(1), 1–17.

Bechtel, W., & Richardson, R. C. (2010). *Discovering Complexity: Decomposition and Localization as Strategies in Scientific Research*. Cambridge, MA: MIT Press.

Beck, J. (2018). Marking the Perception–Cognition Boundary: The Criterion of Stimulus-Dependence. *Australasian Journal of Philosophy*, *96*(2), 319–34. doi:10.1080/00048402.2017.1329329

Begeer, S., De Rosnay, M., Lunenburg, P., Stegge, H., & Terwogt, M. M. (2014). Understanding of Emotions Based on Counterfactual Reasoning in Children with Autism Spectrum Disorders. *Autism*, *18*(3), 301–10. doi:10.1177/1362361312468798

Bennett, J. (2003). *A Philosophical Guide to Conditionals*. Oxford: Clarendon Press.

Block, N. (1981). *Imagery*. Cambridge, MA: MIT Press.

Boden, M. A. (1998). Creativity and Artificial Intelligence. *Artificial Intelligence, 103*(1), 347–56. doi:https://doi.org/10.1016/S0004-3702(98)00055-1

Boden, M. A. (2004). *The Creative Mind: Myths and Mechanisms*. Hove: Psychology Press.

Bratman, M. E. (1992). Practical Reasoning and Acceptance in a Context. *Mind, 101*(401), 1–16.

Brogaard, B., & Gatzia, D. E. (2017). Unconscious Imagination and the Mental Imagery Debate. *Frontiers in Psychology, 8*(799). doi:10.3389/fpsyg.2017.00799

Buttelmann, D., Carpenter, M., & Tomasello, M. (2009). Eighteen-month-old Infants Show False Belief Understanding in an Active Helping Paradigm. *Cognition, 112*(2), 337–42.

Byrne, A. (1993). Truth in Fiction: The Story Continued. *Australasian Journal of Philosophy, 71*(1), 24–35.

Byrne, A. (2007). Possibility and Imagination. *Philosophical Perspectives, 21*(1), 125–44.

Byrne, R. (2005). *The Rational Imagination: How People Create Alternatives to Reality*. Cambridge, MA: MIT Press.

Calhoun, M., Longworth, M., & Chester, V. L. (2011). Gait Patterns in Children with Autism. *Clinical Biomechanics, 26*(2), 200–6. doi:http://dx.doi.org/10.1016/j.clinbiomech.2010.09.013

Carroll, N. (2003). Art and Mood: Preliminary Notes and Conjectures. *The Monist, 86*(4), 521–55.

Carruthers, P. (2002). Human Creativity: Its Cognitive Basis, Its Evolution, and Its Connections with Childhood Pretence. *British Journal for the Philosophy of Science, 53*(2), 225–49.

Carruthers, P. (2006). Why Pretend? In S. Nichols (Ed.), *The Architecture of Imagination* (pp. 89–110). Oxford: Oxford University Press.

Carruthers, P. (2011). Creative Action in Mind. *Philosophical Psychology, 24*(4), 437–61.

Carruthers, P. (2018). Mechanisms for Constrained Stochasticity. *Synthese*. doi:10.1007/s11229-018-01933-9

Chalmers, D. (1996). *The Conscious Mind: In Search of a Fundamental Theory*. Oxford: Oxford University Press.

Chalmers, D. (2002). Does Conceivability Entail Possibility? In T. Gendler & J. Hawthorne (Eds.), *Conceivability and Possibility* (pp. 145–200). Oxford: Oxford University Press.

Chasid, A. (2017). Imaginative Content, Design-Assumptions and Immersion. *Review of Philosophy and Psychology, 8*(2), 259–72.

Chemero, A. (2011). *Radical Embodied Cognitive Science*. Cambridge, MA: MIT Press.

Chihara, C. S., & Fodor, J. A. (1965). Operationalism and Ordinary Language: A Critique of Wittgenstein. *American Philosophical Quarterly, 2*(4), 281–95.

Churchland, P. M. (1981). Eliminative Materialism and the Propositional Attitudes. *Journal of Philosophy, 78*, 67–90.

Churchland, P. S., & Sejnowski, T. J. (1989). Neural Representation and Neural Computation. In L. Nadel, L. Cooper, P. W. Culicover, & R. N. Harnish (Eds.), *Neural Connections, Mental Computations* (pp. 15–480). Cambridge, MA: MIT Press.

Clark, A. (2013). Whatever Next? Predictive Brains, Situated Agents, and the Future of Cognitive Science. *Behavioral and Brain Sciences, 36*(3), 181–204.

Clark, A. (2015). *Surfing Uncertainty: Prediction, Action, and the Embodied Mind*. Oxford: Oxford University Press.

Cohen, H. (2009). The Art of Self-Assembly: The Self-Assembly of Art. Paper presented at the Dagstuhl Seminar on Computational Creativity.

Collins, A. M., & Loftus, E. F. (1975). A Spreading-activation Theory of Semantic Processing. *Psychological Review, 82*(6), 407.

Cope, D. (1991). *Computers and Musical Style.* Oxford: Oxford University Press.

Cova, F., & Teroni, F. (2016). Is the Paradox of Fiction Soluble in Psychology? *Philosophical Psychology, 29*(6), 930–42. doi:10.1080/09515089.2016.1164306

Currie, G. (1990). *The Nature of Fiction.* Cambridge: Cambridge University Press.

Currie, G. (1995). Imagination and Simulation: Aesthetics Meets Cognitive Science. In M. Davies & T. Stone (Eds.), *Mental Simulation: Evaluations and Applications* (pp. 151–69). Oxford: Basil Blackwell.

Currie, G. (2002). Desire in Imagination. In T. S. Gendler & J. Hawthorne (Eds.), *Conceivability and Possibility* (pp. 201–21). Oxford: Oxford University Press.

Currie, G. (2010). Tragedy. *Analysis, 70*(4), 632–8.

Currie, G. (2018). Reply to Peter Langland-Hassan. Retrieved from https://junkyardofthemind.com/blog/2018/7/17/reply-to-peter-langland-hassan

Currie, G., & Ravenscroft, I. (2002). *Recreative Minds: Imagination in Philosophy and Psychology.* Oxford: Clarendon Press.

D'Arms, J., & Jacobson, D. (2000). Sentiment and Value. *Ethics, 110*(4), 722–48. doi:10.1086/233371

Damasio, A. R. (1999). *The Feeling of What Happens.* New York: Houghton Mifflin Harcourt.

Damasio, A. R., Everitt, B. J., & Bishop, D. (1996). The Somatic Marker Hypothesis and the Possible Functions of the Prefrontal Cortex. *Philosophical Transactions of the Royal Society B: Biological Sciences, 351*(1346), 1413–20.

Davies, M., & Stone, T. (2001). Mental Simulation, Tacit Theory, and the Threat of Collapse. *Philosophical Topics, 29,* 127–73.

Dawson, G., Meltzoff, A. N., Osterling, J., Rinaldi, J., & Brown, E. (1998). Children with Autism Fail to Orient to Naturally Occurring Social Stimuli. *Journal of Autism and Developmental Disorders, 28*(6), 479–85. doi:10.1023/a:1026043926488

Dawson, G., Toth, K., Abbott, R., Osterling, J., Munson, J., Estes, A., & Liaw, J. (2004). Early Social Attention Impairments in Autism: Social Orienting, Joint Attention, and Attention to Distress. *Developmental Psychology, 40*(2), 271.

Dawson, G., Webb, S. J., & McPartland, J. (2005). Understanding the Nature of Face Processing Impairment in Autism: Insights From Behavioral and Electrophysiological Studies. *Developmental Neuropsychology, 27*(3), 403–24. doi:10.1207/s15326942dn2703_6

Debus, D. (2014). 'Mental time travel': Remembering the past, imagining the future, and the particularity of events. *Review of Philosophy and Psychology, 5*(3), 333–350.

Dennett, D. C. (1989). *The Intentional Stance.* Cambridge, MA: MIT Press.

Dennett, D. C. (1991). Real Patterns. *Journal of Philosophy, 88*(1), 27–51.

Denton, E. L., Chintala, S., & Fergus, R. (2015). Deep Generative Image Models Using a Laplacian Pyramid of Adversarial Networks. Paper presented at the Advances in Neural Information Processing Systems Conference.

Doggett, T., & Egan, A. (2007). Wanting Things You Don't Want: The Case for an Imaginative Analogue of Desire. *Philosophers' Imprint, 7*(9), 1–17.

Doggett, T., & Egan, A. (2012). How We Feel about Terrible, Non-existent Mafiosi. *Philosophy and Phenomenological Research, 84*(2), 277–306.

Dretske, F. (1991). *Explaining Behavior: Reasons in a World of Causes.* Cambridge, MA: MIT Press.

Dretske, F. (2002). A Recipe for Thought. In D. Chalmers (Ed.), *Philosophy of Mind: Classical and Contemporary Readings* (pp. 491–9). Oxford: Oxford University Press.

Edgington, D. (1995). On Conditionals. *Mind, 104*, 235–329.
Edgington, D. (2008). I—Counterfactuals. Paper presented at the Proceedings of the Aristotelian Society (Hardback).
Egan, F. (1995). Folk Psychology and Cognitive Architecture. *Philosophy of Science, 62*(2), 179–96. doi:10.1086/289851
Evans, J. S. B., Newstead, S. E., & Byrne, R. M. (1993). *Human Reasoning: The Psychology of Deduction*. Hove: Psychology Press.
Evans, J. S. B. T. (2002). Logic and Human Reasoning: An Assessment of the Deduction Paradigm. *Psychological Bulletin, 128*(6), 978–96. doi:10.1037/0033-2909.128.6.978
Evans, J. S. B. T., & Over, D. E. (2004). *If: Supposition, Pragmatics, and Dual Processes*. Oxford: Oxford University Press.
Evans, J. S. B. T., Clibbens, J., & Rood, B. (1995). Bias in Conditional Inference: Implications for Mental Models and Mental Logic. *Quarterly Journal of Experimental Psychology, 48*(3), 644–70.
Finke, R. A., Ward, T. B., & Smith, S. M. (1992). *Creative Cognition: Theory, Research, and Applications*. Cambridge, MA: MIT Press.
Fodor, J. A. (1974). Special Sciences (Or: The Disunity of Science as a Working Hypothesis). *Synthese, 28*(2), 97–115.
Fodor, J. A. (1975). *The Language of Thought*. New York: Crowell.
Fodor, J. A. (1987). *Psychosemantics: The Problem of Meaning in the Philosophy of Mind*. Cambridge, MA: MIT Press.
Fodor, J. A. (2003). *Hume Variations*. Oxford: Oxford University Press.
Forti, S., Valli, A., Perego, P., Nobile, M., Crippa, A., & Molteni, M. (2011). Motor Planning and Control in Autism: A Kinematic Analysis of Preschool Children. *Research in Autism Spectrum Disorders, 5*(2), 834–42. doi:10.1016/j.rasd.2010.09.013
Fournier, K. A., Hass, C. J., Naik, S. K., Lodha, N., & Cauraugh, J. H. (2010). Motor Coordination in Autism Spectrum Disorders: A Synthesis and Meta-Analysis. *Journal of Autism and Developmental Disorders, 40*(10), 1227–40. doi:10.1007/s10803-010-0981-3
Frege, G. (1879). *Begriffsschrift, a Formula Language, Modeled upon that of Arithmetic, for Pure Thought*. Reprinted in *From Frege to Gödel: A Source Book in Mathematical Logic, 1879–1931* (pp. 1–82). Cambridge, MA: Harvard University Press, 1999.
Friedman, O., & Leslie, A. (2007). The Conceptual Underpinnings of Pretense: Pretending Is Not "Behaving-as-if." *Cognition, 105*, 103–24.
Friedman, O., Neary, K. R., Burnstein, C. L., & Leslie, A. (2010). Is Young Children's Recognition of Pretense Metarepresentational or Merely Behavioral? Evidence from 2- and 3-year-olds' Understanding of Pretend Sounds and Speech. *Cognition, 115*, 314–19.
Friend, S. (2003). How I Really Feel about JFK. In M. Kieran & D. M. Lopes (Eds.), *Imagination, Philosophy, and the Arts* (pp. 43–62). London: Routledge.
Friend, S. (2008). Imagining Fact and Fiction. In K. Stock & K. Thomson-Jones (Eds.), *New Waves in Aesthetics* (pp. 150–69). New York: Palgrave Macmillan.
Friend, S. (2012). Fiction and Genre. *Proceedings of the Aristotelian Society, 62*(2), 179–209.
Friend, S. (2016). Fiction and Emotion. In A. Kind (Ed.), *The Routledge Handbook of the Philosophy of Imagination* (pp. 217–30). London: Routledge.
Garson, J. (2018). Connectionism. In E. N. Zalta (Ed.), *The Stanford Encyclopedia of Philosophy* (Fall 2018 ed.). Stanford, CA: Stanford University Press.
Gaut, B. (2003). Creativity and Imagination. In B. Gaut & P. N. Livingston (Eds.), *The Creation of Art: New Essays in Philosophical Aesthetics* (pp. 268–93). Cambridge: Cambridge University Press.
Gaut, B. (2010). The Philosophy of Creativity. *Philosophy Compass, 5*(12), 1034–46.

Gendler, T. (2000). The Puzzle of Imaginative Resistance. *Journal of Philosophy*, *97*(2), 55.

Gendler, T. (2006). Imaginative Contagion. *Metaphilosophy*, *37*(2), 183–203.

Gendler, T., & Liao, S.-y. (2016). The Problem of Imaginative Resistance. In J. Gibson & N. Carroll (Eds.), *The Routledge Companion to Philosophy of Literature* (Vol. 97, pp. 405–18). London: Routledge.

Gendler, T. S., & Kovakovich, K. (2006). Genuine Rational Fictional Emotions. In M. Kieren (Ed.), *Contemporary Debates in Aesthetics* (pp. 241–53). New York: Blackwell.

Gentzen, G. (1934). Untersuchugen über das Logische Schliessen, *Mathematische Zeitschrift*, 39, 176-210, 405-431.

Gettier, E. (1963). Is Justified True Belief Knowledge? *Analysis*, *23*(6), 121–3.

Gilmore, J. (2011). Aptness of Emotions for Fictions and Imaginings. *Pacific Philosophical Quarterly*, *92*(4), 468–89.

Goldman, A. (2006a). Imagination and Simulation in Audience Responses to Fiction. In S. Nichols (Ed.), *The Architecture of Imagination* (pp. 41–56). Oxford: Oxford University Press.

Goldman, A. (2006b). *Simulating Minds*. Oxford: Oxford University Press.

Goñi, J., Arrondo, G., Sepulcre, J., Martincorena, I., Vélez de Mendizábal, N., Corominas-Murtra, B., . . . Villoslada, P. (2011). The Semantic Organization of the Animal Category: Evidence from Semantic Verbal Fluency and Network Theory. *Cognitive Processing*, *12*(2), 183–96. doi:10.1007/s10339-010-0372-x

Goodfellow, I., Pouget-Abadie, J., Mirza, M., Xu, B., Warde-Farley, D., Ozair, S., . . . Bengio, Y. (2014). Generative Adversarial Nets. Paper presented at the Advances in Neural Information Processing Systems Conference.

Goodman, N. (1983). *Fact, Fiction, and Forecast*. Cambridge, MA: Harvard University Press.

Gopnik, A., & Astington, J. W. (1988). Children's Understanding of Representational Change and Its Relation to the Understanding of False Belief and the Appearance–Reality Distinction. *Child Development*, *59*(1), 26–37.

Gordon, R. M. (1987). *The Structure of Emotions*. New York: Cambridge University Press.

Graham, G., & Horgan, T. (1988). How to Be Realistic about Folk Psychology. *Philosophical Psychology*, *1*(1), 69–81. doi:10.1080/09515088808572926

Grant, C. M., Riggs, K. J., & Boucher, J. (2004). Counterfactual and Mental State Reasoning in Children with Autism. *Journal of Autism and Developmental Disorders*, *34*(2), 177–88. doi:10.1023/b:jadd.0000022608.57470.29

Greenberg, D. L., Eacott, M. J., Brechin, D., & Rubin, D. C. (2005). Visual Memory Loss and Autobiographical Amnesia: A Case Study. *Neuropsychologia*, *43*(10), 1493–502. doi:S0028-3932(05)00015-1 [pii]10.1016/j.neuropsychologia.2004.12.009

Grice, H. P. (1989). *Studies in the Way of Words*. Cambridge, MA: Harvard University Press.

Grill-Spector, K., & Malach, R. (2004). The Human Visual Cortex. *Annual Review of Neuroscience*, *27*(1), 649–77. doi:10.1146/annurev.neuro.27.070203.144220

Grush, R. (2004). The Emulation Theory of Representation: Motor Control, Imagery, and Perception. *Behavioral and Brain Sciences*, *27*, 377–442.

Hadwin, J., & Bruins, J. (1998). *The Role of Counterfactual Thought in Children's Judgements of Sadness*. Paper presented at the XVth Biennial Meeting of the International Society for the Study of Behavioral Development, Berne, Switzerland.

Harris, P., & Kavanaugh, R. D. (1993). Young Children's Understanding of Pretense. *Monographs of the Society for Research in Child Development*, *58*(1), i–107.

Harris, P. L. (2000). *The Work of the Imagination*. Oxford: Blackwell.

Harris, P. L. (2001). The Veridicality Assumption. *Mind and Language*, *16*(3), 247–62.

Hinton, G., Deng, L., Yu, D., Dahl, G. E., Mohamed, A. r., Jaitly, N., ... Kingsbury, B. (2012). Deep Neural Networks for Acoustic Modeling in Speech Recognition: The Shared Views of Four Research Groups. *IEEE Signal Processing Magazine, 29*(6), 82–97. doi:10.1109/MSP.2012.2205597

Hogrefe, G.-J., Wimmer, H., & Perner, J. (1986). Ignorance versus False Belief: A Developmental Lag in Attribution of Epistemic States. *Child Development, 57*(3), 567–82.

Hohwy, J. (2013). *The Predictive Mind*. Oxford: Oxford University Press.

Hume, D. (1738/2012). *A Treatise of Human Nature*. Chelmsford, MA: Courier Corporation.

Jackendoff, R. (1996). How Language Helps Us Think. *Pragmatics and Cognition, 4*(1), 1–34.

Jackson, F. (1982). Epiphenomenal Qualia. *The Philosophical Quarterly (1950-), 32*(127), 127–36.

Jackson, F. (1987). *Conditionals*. Oxford: Blackwell.

Jarrold, C., Boucher, J., & Smith, P. K. (1994). Executive Function Deficits and the Pretend Play of Children with Autism: A Research Note. *Journal of Child Psychology and Psychiatry, 35*(8), 1473–82. doi:doi:10.1111/j.1469-7610.1994.tb01288.x

Jaśkowski, S. (1934). *On the Rules of Suppositions in Formal Logic*. Oxford: Clarendon Press.

Johnson-Laird, P. N. (1983). *Mental Models: Towards a Cognitive Science of Language, Inference, and Consciousness*. Cambridge, MA: Harvard University Press.

Johnson-Laird, P. N. (1996). Images, Models, and Propositional Representations. In M. de Vega, M. Intons-Peterson, P. N. Johnson-Laird, M. Denis, & M. Marschark (Eds.), *Models of Visuospatial Cognition* (pp. 90–127). Oxford: Oxford University Press.

Johnson-Laird, P. N., & Byrne, R. M. J. (2002). Conditionals: A Theory of Meaning, Prgamatics, and Inference. *Psychological Review, 109*(4), 646–78.

Johnson-Laird, P. N., Byrne, R. M., & Schaeken, W. (1992). Propositional Reasoning by Model. *Psychological Review, 99*(3), 418–39.

Just, M. A., Cherkassky, V. L., Keller, T. A., Kana, R. K., & Minshew, N. J. (2007). Functional and Anatomical Cortical Underconnectivity in Autism: Evidence from an fMRI Study of an Executive Function Task and Corpus Callosum Morphometry. *Cerebral Cortex, 17*(4), 951–61. doi:10.1093/cercor/bhl006

Kampa, S. (2018). Imaginative Transportation. *Australasian Journal of Philosophy, 96*(4), 683–96.

Kaplan, D. (1968). Quantifying in. *Synthese, 19*(1–2), 178–214.

Karras, T., Aila, T., Laine, S., & Lehtinen, J. (2017). Progressive Growing of GANs for Improved Quality, Stability, and Variation. *arXiv preprint arXiv:1710.10196*.

Kieran, M. (2014). Creativity as a Virtue of Character. In E. Paul & S. B. Kaufman (Eds.), *The Philosophy of Creativity* (pp. 125–46). Oxford: Oxford University Press.

Kim, S. (2010). The Rationality of Emotion toward Fiction. *Midwest Studies in Philosophy, 34*(1), 106–19.

Kind, A. (2001). Putting the Image Back in Imagination. *Philosophy and Phenomenological Research, 62*(1), 85–109.

Kind, A. (2011). The Puzzle of Imaginative Desire. *Australasian Journal of Philosophy, 89*(3), 421–39.

Kind, A. (2013). The Heterogeneity of the Imagination. *Erkenntnis, 78*(1), 141–59. doi:10.1007/s10670-011-9313-z

Kind, A. (2016a). Imagining under Constraints. In A. Kind & P. Kung (Eds.), *Knowledge through Imagination* (pp. 145–59). Oxford: Oxford University Press.

Kind, A. (2016b). Introduction: Exploring Imagination. In A. Kind (Ed.), *The Routledge Handbook of Philosophy of Imagination* (pp. 1–11). New York: Routledge.

Kind, A., & Kung, P. (2016). Introduction: The Puzzle of Imaginative Use. In A. Kind & P. Kung (Eds.), *Knowledge through Imagination* (pp. 1–37). Oxford: Oxford University Press.

Kitcher, P. (1981). Explanatory Unification. *Philosophy of Science*, *48*(4), 507–31.

Kosslyn, S. (1994). *Image and Brain: The Resolution of the Imagery Debate*. Cambridge, MA: MIT Press.

Kosslyn, S., Pascual-Leone, A., Felician, O., Camposano, S., Keenan, J. P., Thompson, W. L., . . . Alpert, N. M. (1999). The Role of Area 17 in Visual Imagery: Convergent Evidence from PET and rTMS. *Science*, *2*(5411), 167–70.

Kosslyn, S., Thompson, W. L., & Alpert, N. M. (1997). Neural Systems Shared by Visual Imagery and Visual Perception: A Positron Emission Tomography Study. *Neuro-Image*, *6*, 320–34.

Kosslyn, S., Thompson, W. L., & Ganis, G. (2006). *The Case of Mental Imagery*. New York: Oxford University Press.

Kosslyn, S. M., Behrmann, M., & Jeannerod, M. (1995). The Cognitive Neuroscience of Mental Imagery. *Neuropsychologia*, *33*(11), 1335–44. doi:https://doi.org/10.1016/0028-3932(95)00067-D

Kripke, S. A. (1980). *Naming and Necessity*. Cambridge, MA: Harvard University Press.

Kung, P. (2010). Imagining as a Guide to Possibility. *Philosophy and Phenomenological Research*, *81*(3), 620–33.

Lamarque, P. (1981). How Can We Fear and Pity Fictions? *British Journal of Aesthetics*, *21*(4), 291–304.

Lamarque, P. (1990). Reasoning to What Is True in Fiction. *Argumentation*, *4*(3), 333–46.

Langland-Hassan, P. (2012). Pretense, Imagination, and Belief: The Single Attitude Theory. *Philosophical Studies*, *159*, 155–79.

Langland-Hassan, P. (2014a). Inner Speech and Metacognition: In Search of a Connection. *Mind and Language*, *29*(5), 511–33.

Langland-Hassan, P. (2014b). What It Is to Pretend. *Pacific Philosophical Quarterly*, *95*, 397–420.

Langland-Hassan, P. (2015). Imaginative Attitudes. *Philosophy and Phenomenological Research*, *90*(3), 664–86. doi:10.1111/phpr.12115

Langland-Hassan, P. (2016). On Choosing What to Imagine. In A. Kind & P. Kung (Eds.), *Knowledge through Imagination* (pp. 61–84). Oxford: Oxford University Press.

Langland-Hassan, P. (2017). Imagination, Emotion, and Desire. Retrieved from https://junkyardofthemind.com/blog/2017/8/5/imagination-emotion-and-desire?rq=Langland-Hassan

Langland-Hassan, P. (2018a). Imagining Experiences. *Nous*, *52*(3), 561–86. doi:doi:10.1111/nous.12167

Langland-Hassan, P. (2018b). To Which Fiction Do Your Imaginings Refer? Retrieved from https://junkyardofthemind.com/blog/2018/6/24/to-which-fiction-do-your-imaginings-refer

Lassiter, D. (2017). Probabilistic Language in Indicative and Counterfactual Conditionals. *Proceedings of SALT*, *27*, 525–46.

Lawrence, S., Giles, C. L., Tsoi, A. C., & Back, A. D. (1997). Face Recognition: A Convolutional Neural-network Approach. *IEEE Transactions on Neural Networks*, *8*(1), 98–113.

Ledig, C., Theis, L., Huszár, F., Caballero, J., Cunningham, A., Acosta, A., . . . Wang, Z. (2017). Photo-realistic Single Image Super-resolution Using a Generative Adversarial Network. Paper presented at the Proceedings of the IEEE Conference on Computer Vision and Pattern Recognition.

Leevers, H. J., & Harris, P. L. (2000). Counterfactual Syllogistic Reasoning in Normal 4-year-olds, Children with Learning Disabilities, and Children with Autism. *Journal of Experimental Child Psychology, 76*, 64–87.

Leslie, A. M. (1987). Pretense and Representation: The Origins of "Theory of Mind." *Psychological Review, 94*, 412–26.

Leslie, A. M. (1994). Pretending and Believing: Issues in the Theory of ToMM. *Cognition, 50*, 211–38.

Lewis, D. (1972). Psychophysical and Theoretical Identifications. *Australasian Journal of Philosophy, 50*, 249–58.

Lewis, D. (1973). *Counterfactuals*. Oxford: Basil Blackwell.

Lewis, D. (1978). Truth in Fiction. *American Philosophical Quarterly, 15*(1), 37–46.

Liao, S.-y., & Doggett, T. (2014). The Imagination Box. *Journal of Philosophy, 111*(5), 259–75.

Liao, S.-y., & Gendler, T. (2011). Pretense and Imagination. *Wiley Interdisciplinary Reviews: Cognitive Science, 2*(1), 79–94. doi:10.1002/wcs.91

Liao, S.-y., Strohminger, N., & Sripada, C. S. (2014). Empirically Investigating Imaginative Resistance. *British Journal of Aesthetics, 54*(3), 339–55.

Lillard, A. (1993). Young Children's Conceptualization of Pretense: Action or Mental Representation State? *Child Development, 64*(2), 372–86.

Livingston, P., & Mele, A. (1997). Evaluating Emotional Responses to Fiction. In M. Hjort & S. Laver (Eds.), *Emotion and the Arts* (pp. 157–76). Oxford: Oxford University Press.

Lormand, E. (2007). Phenomenal Impressions. In T. Gendler & J. Hawthorne (Eds.), *Perceptual Experience* (pp. 317–53). Oxford: Oxford University Press.

Lycan, W. G. (2001). *Real Conditionals*. Oxford: Oxford University Press.

Mandelbaum, E. (2017). Associationist Theories of Thought. In E. N. Zalta (Ed.), *Stanford Encyclopedia of Philosophy* (Summer 2017 ed.). Stanford, CA: Stanford University Press.

Manktelow, K. I. (1999). *Reasoning and Thinking*. Hove: Psychology Press.

Marr, D. (1982). *Vision: A Computational Investigation into the Human Representation and Processing of Visual Information*. New York: Henry Holt.

Marsh, K. L., Isenhower, R. W., Richardson, M. J., Helt, M., Verbalis, A. D., Schmidt, R. C., & Fein, D. (2013). Autism and Social Disconnection in Interpersonal Rocking. *Frontiers in Integrative Neuroscience, 7*(4). doi:10.3389/fnint.2013.00004

Martin, M. G. F. (2002). The Transparency of Experience. *Mind and Language, 17*(4), 376–425.

Martinez-Manrique, F., & Vicente, A. (2010). "What the…!" The Role of Inner Speech in Conscious Thought. *Journal of Consciousness Studies, 17*(9–10), 141–67.

Matravers, D. (2006). The Challenge of Irrationalism, and How Not to Meet It. In M. Kieran (Ed.), *Contemporary Debates in Aesthetics and the Philosophy of Art* (pp. 254–66). Oxford: Blackwell.

Matravers, D. (2014). *Fiction and Narrative*. Oxford: Oxford University Press.

McGinn, C. (2004). *Mindsight: Image, Dream, Meaning*. Cambridge, MA: Harvard University Press.

Merchant, B. (2015). The Poem that Passed the Turing Test. *Motherboard*, February 5.

Meskin, A., & Weinberg, J. M. (2003). Emotions, Fiction, and Cognitive Architecture. *British Journal of Aesthetics, 43*(1), 18–34. doi:10.1093/bjaesthetics/43.1.18

Metz, C., & Collins, K. (2018). How an A.I. "Cat-and-Mouse Game" Generates Believable Fake Photos. *The New York Times*. Retrieved from https://www.nytimes.com/interactive/2018/01/02/technology/ai-generated-photos.html

Michaelian, K. (2016a). Against Discontinuism: Mental Time Travel and Our Knowledge of Past and Future Events. In K. Michaelian, S. B. Klein, & K. K. Szpunar (Eds.), *Seeing the Future: Theoretical Perspectives on Future-Oriented Mental Time Travel* (pp. 62–92). Oxford: Oxford University Press.

Michaelian, K. (2016b). *Mental Time Travel: Episodic Memory and Our Knowledge of the Personal Past*. Cambridge, MA: MIT Press.

Miyazono, K., & Liao, S.-y. (2016). The Cognitive Architecture of Imaginative Resistance. In A. Kind (Ed.), *The Routledge Handbook of Philosophy of Imagination* (pp. 233–46). New York: Routledge.

Moran, R. (1994). The Expression of Feeling in Imagination, *The Philosophical Review, 103*(1), 75–106.

Murphy, D. (2017). Brains and Beliefs: On the Scientific Integration of Folk Psychology. In D. Kaplan (Ed.), *Explanation and Integration in Mind and Brain Science* (pp. 119–45). Oxford: Oxford University Press.

Nagel, T. (1974). What Is It Like to Be a Bat? *Philosophical Review, 83*(4), 435–50.

Nanay, B. (2010). Perception and Imagination: Amodal Perception as Mental Imagery. *Philosophical Studies, 150*(239–54).

Nanay, B. (2016). Imagination and Perception. In A. Kind (Ed.), *The Routledge Handbook of Philosophy of Imagination* (pp. 124–34). New York: Routledge.

Nanay, B. (2018a). The Importance of Amodal Completion in Everyday Perception. *i-Perception, 9*(4), 2041669518788887. doi:10.1177/2041669518788887

Nanay, B. (2018b). Multimodal Mental Imagery. *Cortex, 105*, 125–34. doi:https://doi.org/10.1016/j.cortex.2017.07.006

Nichols, S. (2004a). Imagining and Believing: The Promise of a Single Code. *Journal of Aesthetics and Art Criticism, 62*, 129–39.

Nichols, S. (2004b). Review: Recreative Minds. *Mind, 113*(450), 329–34. doi:10.1093/mind/113.450.329

Nichols, S. (2006a). Introduction. In S. Nichols (Ed.), *The Architecture of the Imagination* (pp. 1–18). Oxford: Oxford University Press.

Nichols, S. (2006b). Just the Imagination: Why Imagining Doesn't Behave Like Believing. *Mind and Language, 21*, 459–74.

Nichols, S. (Ed.) (2006c). *The Architecture of Imagination*. Oxford: Oxford University Press.

Nichols, S. (2008). Imagination and the I. *Mind and Language, 23*(5), 518–35.

Nichols, S., & Stich, S. (2000). A Cognitive Theory of Pretense. *Cognition, 74*, 115–47.

Nichols, S., & Stich, S. (2003). *Mindreading: An Integrated Account of Pretence, Self-Awareness, and Understanding of Other Minds*. Oxford: Oxford University Press.

Noordhof, P. (2002). Imagining Objects and Imagining Experiences. *Mind and Language, 17*(4), 426–55.

Oaksford, M., & Chater, N. (2003). Conditional Probability and the Cognitive Science of Conditional Reasoning. *Mind and Language, 18*(4), 359–79. doi:10.1111/1468-0017.00232

Olewitz, C. (2016). A Japanese AI Program Just Wrote a Short Novel, and It Almost Won a Literary Prize. *Digital Trends*, March 23.

Onishi, K. H., & Baillargeon, R. (2005). Do 15-month-old Infants Understand False Beliefs? *Science, 308*(5719), 255–8. doi:10.1126/science.1107621

Onishi, K. H., Baillargeon, R., & Leslie, A. (2007). 15-month-old Infants Detect Violations in Pretend Scenarios. *Acta Pscychologica, 124*, 106–28.

Oxford English Dictionary (2009). "imagine, v." Oxford: Oxford University Press.

Parkhi, O. M., Vedaldi, A., & Zisserman, A. (2015). Deep Face Recognition. Paper presented at the British Machine Vision Conference.

Paul, E., & Kaufman, S. B. (2014). Introducing the Philosophy of Creativity. In E. Paul & S. B. Kaufman (Eds.), *The Philosophy of Creativity* (pp. 3–14). Oxford: Oxford University Press.

Peacocke, C. (1985). Imagination, Possibility and Experience. In J. Foster & H. Robinson (Eds.), *Essays on Berkeley: A Tercentennial Celebration* (pp. 19–35). Oxford: Clarendon Press.

Pearson, J., & Kosslyn, S. M. (2015). The Heterogeneity of Mental Representation: Ending the Imagery Debate. *Proceedings of the National Academy of Sciences, 112*(33), 10089–92. doi:10.1073/pnas.1504933112

Pearson, J., & Westbrook, F. (2015). Phantom Perception: Voluntary and Involuntary Nonretinal Vision. *Trends in Cognitive Sciences, 19*(5), 278–84. doi:https://doi.org/10.1016/j.tics.2015.03.004

Pelletier, F. J. (2000). A History of Natural Deduction and Elementary Logic Textbooks. *Logical Consequence: Rival Approaches, 1*, 105–38.

Perner, J. (1991). *Understanding the Representational Mind*. Cambridge, MA: MIT Press.

Perrin, D. (2016). Asymmetries in Subjective Time. In K. Michaelian, S. B. Klein, & K. K. Szpunar (Eds.), *Seeing the Future: Theoretical Perspectives on Future-oriented Mental Time Travel* (pp. 39–61). Oxford: Oxford University Press.

Peterson, D. M., & Bowler, D. M. (1996). Subtractive Reasoning and False Belief Understanding in Autistic, SLD and Non-handicapped Children. Paper presented at the British Psychological Society, Developmental Psychology Section Annual Conference, Oxford, UK.

Peterson, D. M., & Bowler, D. M. (2000). Counterfactual Reasoning and False Belief Understanding in Children with Autism. *Autism, 4*(4), 391–405.

Picciuto, E., & Carruthers, P. (2014). The Origins of Creativity. In E. Paul & S. B. Kaufman (Eds.), *The Philosophy of Creativity: New Essays* (pp. 199–223). Oxford: Oxford University Press.

Picciuto, E., & Carruthers, P. (2016). Imagination and Pretense. In A. Kind (Ed.), *The Routledge Handbook of Philosophy of Imagination* (pp. 314–25). New York: Routledge.

Pitt, D. (2020). Mental Representation. In E. N. Zalta (Ed.), *The Stanford Encyclopedia of Philosophy* (Spring 2020 ed.). Stanford, CA: Stanford University Press.

Pollock, J. (2008). Defeasible Reasoning. In J. E. Adler & L. J. Rips (Eds.), *Reasoning: Studies of Human Inference and Its Foundations* (pp. 451–70). Cambridge: Cambridge University Press.

Prinz, J. J. (2004). *Gut Reactions: A Perceptual Theory of Emotion*. Oxford: Oxford University Press.

Putnam, H. (1975). The Meaning of "Meaning." *Minnesota Studies in the Philosophy of Science, 7*, 131–93.

Pylyshyn, Z. (2002). Mental Imagery: In Search of a Theory. *Behavioral and Brain Sciences, 25*(2), 157–237.

Quilty-Dunn, J., & Mandelbaum, E. (2018). Against Dispositionalism: Belief in Cognitive Science. *Philosophical Studies*, 175(9), 2353–72. doi:10.1007/s11098-017-0962-x

Radford, A., Metz, L., & Chintala, S. (2015). Unsupervised Representation Learning with Deep Convolutional Generative Adversarial Networks. *arXiv preprint arXiv:1511.06434*.

Radford, C. (1975). How Can We Be Moved by the Fate of Anna Karenina? *Proceedings of the Aristotelian Society*, Supplementary Volumes, *49*, 67–80.

Radford, C. (1982). Philosophers and Their Monstrous Thoughts. *British Journal of Aesthetics, 22*(3), 261–3.

Reisberg, D. (1996). The Nonambiguity of Mental Images. In C. Cornoldi, R. Logie, M. A. Brandimonte, G. Kaufman, & D. Resisberg (Eds.), *Stretching the Imagination: Representation and Transformation in Mental Imagery* (pp. 119–72). Oxford: Oxford University Press.

Rescher, N. (2018). Reductio ad Absurdum. *Internet Encyclopedia of Philosophy.* Retrieved from https://www.iep.utm.edu/reductio/

Richert, R. A., & Lillard, A. S. (2004). Observers' Proficiency at Identifying Pretense Acts Based on Behavioral Cues. *Cognitive Development, 19*(2), 223–40. doi:https://doi.org/10.1016/j.cogdev.2004.01.001

Rinehart, N. J., Tonge, B. J., Iansek, R., McGinley, J., Brereton, A. V., Enticott, P. G., & Bradshaw, J. L. (2006). Gait Function in Newly Diagnosed Children with Autism: Cerebellar and Basal Ganglia Related Motor Disorder. *Developmental Medicine and Child Neurology*, 48(10), 819–24.

Robins, S. (2020). Defending Discontinuism, Naturally. *Review of Philosophy and Psychology*. https://doi.org/10.1007/s13164-020-00462-0.

Robinson, J. (2005). *Deeper than Reason: Emotion and Its Role in Literature, Music and Art.* Oxford: Oxford University Press.

Rubin, D. C., & Greenberg, D. L. (1998). Visual Memory-deficit Amnesia: A Distinct Amnesiac Presentation and Etiology. *Proceedings of the National Academy of Sciences of the USA*, *95*, 5413–16.

Ryle, G. (1949/2009). *The Concept of Mind.* New York: Routledge.

Sahyoun, C. P., Belliveau, J. W., Soulières, I., Schwartz, S., & Mody, M. (2010). Neuroimaging of the Functional and Structural Networks Underlying Visuospatial vs. Linguistic Reasoning in High-functioning Autism. *Neuropsychologia, 48*(1), 86–95. doi:http://dx.doi.org/10.1016/j.neuropsychologia.2009.08.013

Sainsbury, M. (2014). Fictional Worlds and Fiction Operators. In Manuel García-Carpintero and Martí Genoveva (Eds.), *Empty Representations: Reference and Non-existence* (pp. 277–89). Oxford: Oxford University Press.

Schacter, D. L., & Addis, D. R. (2007). Constructive Memory: The Ghosts of Past and Future. *Nature*, *445*(7123), 27. doi:445027a [pii]10.1038/445027a

Schacter, D. L., Addis, D. R., & Buckner, R. L. (2007). Remembering the Past to Imagine the Future: The Prospective Brain. *Nature Reviews Neurosciences*, *8*(9), 657–61.

Schellenberg, S. (2013). Belief and Desire in Imagination and Immersion. *Journal of Philosophy*, *110*, 497–517.

Schiffer, S. (1981). Truth and the Theory of Content. In H. Parret & J. Bouveresse (Eds.), *Meaning and Understanding*. Berlin: Walter de Gruyter.

Schmidhuber, J. (2015). Deep Learning in Neural Networks: An Overview. *Neural Networks*, *61*, 85–117. doi:https://doi.org/10.1016/j.neunet.2014.09.003

Schroeder, T. (2006). Propositional Attitudes. *Philosophy Compass*, *1*(1), 65–73.

Schroeder, T., & Matheson, C. (2006). Imagination and Emotion. In S. Nichols (Ed.), *The Architecture of the Imagination* (pp. 19–40). Oxford: Oxford University Press.

Schwitzgebel, E. (2002). A Phenomenal, Dispositional Account of Belief. *Nous*, *36*(2), 249–75. doi:10.1111/1468-0068.00370

Schwitzgebel, E. (2013). A Dispositional Approach to Attitudes: Thinking Outside of the Belief Box. In N. Nottelmann (Ed.), *New Essays on Belief* (pp. 75–99). London: Macmillan.

Scott, F. J., Baron-Cohen, S., & Leslie, A. (1999). 'If Pigs Could Fly': A Test of Counterfactual Reasoning and Pretence in Children with Autism. *British Journal of Developmental Psychology*, *17*(3), 349–62.

Scott, R. M., & Baillargeon, R. (2009). Which Penguin Is This? Attributing False Beliefs about Object Identity at 18 Months. *Child Development, 80*(4), 1172–96.

Searle, J. (1983). *Intentionality: An Essay in the Philosophy of Mind.* Cambridge: Cambridge University Press.

Searle, J. R. (1980). Minds, Brains, and Programs. *Behavioral and Brain Sciences, 3*(3), 417–24.

Sellars, W. (1956). Empiricism and the Philosophy of Mind. *Minnesota Studies in the Philosophy of Science, 1*(19), 253–329.

Shepard, R. N., & Metzler, J. (1971). Mental Rotation of Three-dimensional Objects. *Science, 171*(3972), 701–3.

Shetreat-Klein, M., Shinnar, S., & Rapin, I. (2014). Abnormalities of Joint Mobility and Gait in Children with Autism Spectrum Disorders. *Brain and Development, 36*(2), 91–6. doi:http://dx.doi.org/10.1016/j.braindev.2012.02.005

Shoemaker, S. (1968). Self-knowledge and Self-awareness. *Journal of Philosophy, 19*, 555–67.

Silver, D., Huang, A., Maddison, C. J., Guez, A., Sifre, L., Van Den Driessche, G.,... Lanctot, M. (2016). Mastering the Game of Go with Deep Neural Networks and Tree Search. *Nature, 529*(7587), 484–9.

Sinhababu, N. (2016). Imagination and Belief. In A. Kind (Ed.), *The Routledge Handbook of the Philosophy of Imagination* (pp. 111–23). New York: Routledge.

Slotnick, S., Thompson, W., & Kosslyn, S. (2005). Visual Mental Imagery Induces Retinotopically Organized Activation of Early Visual Areas. *Cerebral Cortex, 15*, 1570–83.

Sowa, J. F. (1991). *Principles of Semantic Networks: Explorations in the Representation of Knowledge*. Burlington, MA: Morgan Kaufmann.

Spaulding, S. (2015). Imagination, Desire, and Rationality. *Journal of Philosophy, 112*(9), 457–76.

Stalnaker, R. C. (1968). A Theory of Conditionals. In W. L. Harper, R. Stalnaker, & G. Pearce (Eds.), *Ifs* (pp. 41–55): Dordrecht: Springer.

Stel, M., van den Heuvel, C., & Smeets, R. C. (2008). Facial Feedback Mechanisms in Autistic Spectrum Disorders. *Journal of Autism and Developmental Disorders, 38*, 1250–8.

Stevenson, L. (2003). Twelve Conceptions of Imagination. *British Journal of Aesthetics, 43*(3), 238–59.

Stich, S. P. (1983). *From Folk Psychology to Cognitive Science: The Case against Belief.* Cambridge, MA: MIT Press.

Stich, S., & Nichols, S. (1992). Folk Psychology: Simulation or Tacit Theory? *Mind and Language, 7*, 35–71.

Stich, S., & Tarzia, J. (2015). The Pretense Debate. *Cognition, 143*, 1–12.

Stock, K. (2005). Resisting Imaginative Resistance. *Philosophical Quarterly, 55*(221), 607–24. doi:10.1111/j.0031-8094.2005.00419.x

Stock, K. (2017). *Only Imagine: Fiction, Interpretation, and Imagination*. Oxford: Oxford University Press.

Stokes, D. (2014). The Role of Imagination in Creativity. In E. Paul & S. B. Kaufman (Eds.), *The Philosophy of Creativity* (pp. 157–84). Oxford: Oxford University Press.

Stokes, D. (2019). Mental Imagery and Fiction. *Canadian Journal of Philosophy, 49*(6), 731–54.

Strawson, P. F. (1970). Imagination and Perception. In L. Foster & J. W. Swanson (Eds.), *Experience and Theory* (pp. 31–54). Amherst, MA: University of Massachusetts Press.

Strawson, P. F. (1986). "If" and "⊃." In R. Grandy & R. Warner (Eds.), *Philosophical Grounds of Rationality: Intentions, Categories, Ends*. Oxford: Oxford University Press.

Strohminger, M., & Yli-Vakkuri, J. (2017). The Epistemology of Modality. *Analysis*, *77*(4), 825–38. doi:10.1093/analys/anx058

Tenenbaum, J. B., Kemp, C., Griffiths, T. L., & Goodman, N. D. (2011). How to Grow a Mind: Statistics, Structure, and Abstraction. *Science*, *331*(6022), 1279–85.

Tye, M. (1991). *The Imagery Debate*. Cambridge, MA: MIT Press.

Van Fraassen, B. C. (1980). A Temporal Framework for Conditionals and Chance. In W. L. Harper, R. Stalnaker, & G. Pearce (Eds.), *Ifs: Conditionals, Belief, Decision, Chance and Time* (pp. 323–40). Dordrecht: Springer.

Van Gelder, T. (1990). Compositionality: A Connectionist Variation on a Classical Theme. *Cognitive Science*, *14*(3), 355–84.

Van Gelder, T. (1998). The Dynamical Hypothesis in Cognitive Science. *Behavioral and Brain Sciences*, *21*(5), 615–28.

Van Leeuwen, N. (2011). Imagination Is Where the Action Is. *Journal of Philosophy*, *108*(2), 55–77.

Van Leeuwen, N. (2013). The Meanings of "Imagine" Part I: Constructive Imagination. *Philosophy Compass*, *8*(3), 220–30.

Van Leeuwen, N. (2014). The Meanings of "Imagine" Part II: Attitude and Action. *Philosophy Compass*, *9*(11), 791–802.

Van Leeuwen, N. (2016). The Imaginative Agent. In A. Kind & P. Kung (Eds.), *Knowledge through Imagination* (pp. 85–109). Oxford: Oxford University Press.

Van Leeuwen, N. (2020). Imagining stories: attitudes and operators. *Philosophical Studies*. doi:10.1007/s11098-020-01449-4

Van Wagner, T. (2017). *A Pluralistic Account of Social Cognition in Autism Spectrum Disorder*. University of Cincinnati (dissertation).

Vandegrift, D. (2016). Can Artificial Intelligence be Creative? *Medium*, June 9.

Velleman, J. D. (2000). *The Possibility of Practical Reasoning*. Oxford: Oxford University Press.

Walton, K. (1990). *Mimesis as Make-Believe: On the Foundations of the Representational Arts*. Cambridge, MA: Harvard University Press.

Walton, K. (2015). Fictionality and Imagination: Mind the Gap. In K. Walton, *In Other Shoes: Music, Metaphor, Empathy, Existence* (pp. 17–35). Oxford: Oxford University Press.

Wason, P. C. (1968). Reasoning about a Rule. *Quarterly Journal of Experimental Psychology*, *20*(3), 273–81.

Weatherson, B. (2005). Morality, Fiction, and Possibility. *Philosophers' Imprint*, *4*(3), 1–27.

Weinberg, J., & Meskin, A. (2006a). Imagine That! In M. Kieran (Ed.), *Contemporary Debates in Aesthetics and the Philosophy of Art* (pp. 222–35). Oxford: Blackwell.

Weinberg, J., & Meskin, A. (2006b). Puzzling over the Imagination: Philosophical Problems, Architectural Solutions. In S. Nichols (Ed.), *The Architecture of Imagination* (pp. 175–204). Oxford: Oxford University Press.

Weisberg, R. W. (2006). *Creativity: Understanding Innovation in Problem Solving, Science, Invention, and the Arts*. Hoboken, NJ: John Wiley & Sons.

Wellman, H. M., Cross, D., & Watson, J. K. (2001). A Meta-analysis of Theory of Mind: The Truth about False Belief. *Child Development*, *72*, 655–84.

Williamson, T. (2005). I—Armchair Philosophy, Metaphysical Modality and Counterfactual Thinking. Paper presented at the Proceedings of the Aristotelian Society (Hardback).

Williamson, T. (2007). *The Philosophy of Philosophy*. New York: Blackwell.

Williamson, T. (2016). Knowing by Imagining. In A. Kind & P. Kung (Eds.), *Knowledge through Imagination* (pp. 113–23). Oxford: Oxford University Press.

Wiltsher, N. (2016). Against the Additive View of Imagination. *Australasian Journal of Philosophy*, *94*(2), 266–82.

Wimmer, H., & Perner, J. (1983). Beliefs about Beliefs: Representation and Constraining Function of Wrong Beliefs in Young Children's Understanding of Deception. *Cognition*, *13*(1), 103–28.

Wittgenstein, L. (1953). *Philosophical Investigations.* Oxford: Blackwell.

Yablo, S. (1993). Is Conceivability a Guide to Possibility? *Philosophy and Phenomenological Research*, *53*(1), 1–42.

Zeman, A., Dewar, M., & Della Sala, S. (2016). Reflections on Aphantasia. *Cortex*, *74*, 336–7.

Zhu, J. Y., Park, T., Isola, P., & Efros, A. A. (2017). Unpaired Image-to-image Translation Using Cycle-consistent Adversarial Networks. *Proceedings of the IEEE International Conference on Computer Vision* (pp. 2223–32).

Zollo, P. (1997). *Songwriters on Songwriting.* New York: Da Capo Press.

Index

For the benefit of digital users, indexed terms that span two pages (e.g., 52–53) may, on occasion, appear on only one of those pages.